Design, Gestaltung, Formatività

Philosophies of Making

Design, Gestaltung, Formatività
Philosophies of Making

Patricia Ribault (Ed.)

Birkhäuser

Basel

Contents

Giving Form

Form Given

Design, Gestaltung, Formatività
An Introduction

Patricia Ribault

We do because we exist. All the same. Our existences are by themselves, even if imperceptibly, disturbances, margins, cracks in the global functioning. Through these interstices, these gaps, possibilities for disorder are continuously at hand.[1]

September 2, 2020, Gui de Chauliac University Hospital, Montpellier: for the first time in my life, I assist at an awake brain operation performed by the French neurosurgeon Hugues Duffau. Renowned all over the world for his outstanding results, he is also known as the "*enfant terrible* of neurosurgery," thanks to an at once exploratory, interdisciplinary and eminently personal way of operating that is atypical. This extraordinary mix of skills and attitudes interests me. My aim is to try to understand what makes him the prodigy described by my colleague Thomas Picht (also a neurosurgeon), that is, what constitutes his "individual talent"[2]—that which, in a tradition with such clear rules, makes him unique among his peers

There, I discover a world—neurosurgery—previously unknown to me, and yet everything he says or does reminds me of a world familiar to me—the world of art, design or craft practices. When we meet, Duffau explains at length how he sees his trade, how he puts it into practice and transmits it. He describes the extraordinary process of waking his patients up and getting them to participate in the operation by talking through it with them.[3] Above all, though, he chats to me about the piano and jazz, about technique and improvisation, composition and interpretation. I am struck by how he searches tirelessly, not for the perfect gesture or for maximum efficiency (he brushes aside my initial hypothesis that compared his role to that of the master, to one who knows and who, therefore, masters), but for something more sinuous, less clear-cut, something to do with demiurgy and curiosity, with intuition and, dare one say it, with creation.

1 Jean-Luc Nancy, *Que faire ?* (Paris, Galilée, 2016), 57.

2 To allude to the title of T. S. Eliot's essay "Tradition and the Individual Talent" [1919], in T. S. Eliot, *The Sacred Wood and Major Early Essays* (New York: Dover, 1998).

3 Duffau explains his operating procedure in detail in *L'erreur de Broca. Exploration d'un cerveau éveillé* (Paris: Éditions Michel Lafon, 2016).

Creation, Intuition, Improvisation

Inseparable from knowledge, creation is for Duffau as much a "phenomenon," the driving force of human activity, as well as a useful, and far from "wasteful," function of the brain—"a way of combating the tyrannical hierarchy of our self-taught brain, which prefers to repeat engrained gestures rather than to abandon itself to improvisation, which is, however, vital so as to explore new worlds."[4] In his practice, creativeness manifests itself in two ways: in the exploration and representation of the plasticity of the brain, notably using real-time functional mapping[5] in the operating theater; then, more abstractly, through a kind of letting go at the moment of operation (the "abandonment to improvisation"), a sort of to-and-fro between what he calls "top-flight automatisms" and decisions dictated by his intuition, which allow him to "push the limits"—his own, as well as those of science. The paradox is that, if Duffau's designs require a total grasp of the procedure, they are just as dependent on loosening that grasp.[6] Duffau does not equate his task to the execution of a program in which every parameter is regulated; it's more like a jazz piece, virtuosic, certainly, but based as much on his every gesture's being fine-tuned by a talent for improvisation as on his prodigious technical mastery. A surgeon claiming that part of his action cannot be reduced to calculation or premeditation risks going out on a limb. It amounts to upsetting a separation of powers, which, according to philosopher Christian Béthune, has remained unchallenged in the Western philosophical tradition and which "seeks first and foremost to divorce expression from action and differentiates theory from practice, what drives from what is driven, and the intelligible from the sensory."[7] In this light, improvisation is an alien intruder—a sign of unwanted expressiveness, since it implies that "gesture and action can coexist simultaneously without it being possible to pull them apart."[8] Like a pragmatist philosopher, Duffau thus envisages his action as a "moment of collective individuation,"[9] comparable to a jam session during which the performative aspect of operations is expressed. Improvisation is not only meaningful; it can be shared so as to actualize knowledge.

We could add a third, more fundamental creative dimension to this practice, which consists in its shaking up the established order, elaborating new protocols, creating new knowledge, developing "that aptitude for thought that constitutes our chief asset."[10] For Duffau, this undoubtedly takes the form of a "meta-network of cognition" connected, in a broader way, to a certain state of knowledge, establishing new norms and new ways of being. "Making," in this sense, is what Jean-Luc Nancy calls "a matter of being and not of producing,"[11] a form of engagement that goes beyond individual gestures and implies an openness that can lead to a way out: "'doing' is inseparable from 'existing': being exposed also entails leaving oneself open to being able to invent or appropriate goals or tools, relationships or effects."[12] In the end, such ways of "doing" constitute a living process for considering tradition—and therefore transmission—not as the unthinking respect for preestablished rules but as an ongoing dialogue with what has been learned, at once absorbed and questioned, reproduced and transformed, and perhaps abandoned, even. For philosopher Olivier Morin, this is "flexible transmission, something that has always entailed the reconstruction of what is transmitted."[13]

According to art historian Horst Bredekamp, Duffau's dialogue with brain matter might be compared to Michelangelo's with marble while carving. "He does not

4 Duffau, *L'erreur de Broca*, 218.
5 Duffau defines himself as a surveyor, who places a set of numbered scraps of paper at key points of the brain and white fibers he has identified by testing them with electrical stimulation, thereby allowing him to delimit a perimeter beyond which he may no longer act at the risk of deteriorating essential cognitive or motor functions. See "Exploration d'un cerveau éveillé," in Duffau, *L'erreur de Broca*, 149–68.
6 On the operating table, a neurosurgeon obviously cannot rely solely on intuition and each area of the brain is rigorously monitored by electrical stimulation as part of the operating protocol.
7 Christian Béthune, "De l'improvisation," in *Nouvelle revue d'esthétique* 1, no. 5 (2010): 153–60, https://www.cairn.info/revue-nouvelle-revue-d-esthetique-2010-1-page-153.htm (retrieved August 25, 2021).
8 Ibid.
9 Ibid.
10 See Didier Semin, "Buckminster Fuller: In Praise of the Imperfect," in the present volume, 169.
11 Nancy, *Que faire ?*, 57.
12 Ibid., 56.
13 Olivier Morin, *Comment les traditions naissent et meurent* (Paris: Odile Jacob, 2011), 13.
14 In a lecture given on June 22, 2021, part of the online lecture series "On Gestaltung" (May 11–June 22, 2021), initiated by Jörg Petruschat and myself, and organized and moderated by Babette Wiezorek and Susanne Stauch at the Department of Theory and History, weißensee kunsthochschule berlin, https://www.matters-of-activity.de/en/activities/5048/on-gestaltung (accessed August 8, 2021).

project an ideal model into the material, but starts with a general idea, observing, questioning the marble block, from which he removes pieces gradually, constantly adapting his initial idea to its reactions."[14] As Bredekamp underlines, this is a process and not the linear application of an ideal form embedded in the material long before.[15] "Each stroke of the chisel marks a response to the internal activity of the marble, rather than the imposition of a form on passive, inert matter." Likewise, Duffau checks on his patients while they are awake using cerebral function tests, stimulating the neuronal networks and subnetworks constituting their cerebral activity in real time, scrutinizing every response, hesitation, and silence, and reacting by removing or leaving in situ part of the cerebral tissue infiltrated by the tumor.

That morning, before my very eyes, I watch as he prepares himself mentally, sitting in a corner of the operating theater, as concentrated as a tightrope walker before stepping onto the wire or as an actor before the curtain rises, picturing each scene, inwardly rehearsing every gesture, anticipating what he's going to do, what he *knows* he's going to do, and what he's going to discover and touch with his finger. In the course of every operation, he strives to gain, to enlarge knowledge; it is something anchored in everything he has learned, and yet it stretches out toward the unknown. Then Duffau enters the scene, calm and precise, methodical, "as if he knows exactly where the tumor is located and how to remove it," his assistant tells me. Playing the score like a virtuoso, he proceeds step by step, each one made clear to him by twenty-five years spent getting to grips with and exploring the central nervous system in what is a ceaseless dialogue with that sometimes unpredictable and always both active and reactive matter we call the brain of a conscious human.

Seeing Right

When "getting his hands dirty," Hugues Duffau works as much like a motorcycle repairman—who knows every bolt and drive belt of the machine he's peering into—as a pianist such as Glenn Gould, who would search tirelessly for the correct form, for the music, in the infinite variations permitted by the eighty-eight keys of the piano, by the score and by his own interpretation.[16] In a now famous book, "philosopher and mechanic" Matthew B. Crawford compares his practice to that of a surgeon, whose judgment is "simultaneously technical and deliberative":[17] "You come up with an imagined train of causes for manifest symptoms and judge their likelihood before tearing anything down. This imagining relies on a stock mental library, not of natural kinds or structures, like that of the surgeon, but rather the functional kind of an internal combustion engine, their various interpretations by different manufacturers, and their proclivities for failure. You also develop a library of sounds and smells and feels."[18]

When materialized in practice through decisions, this *imaginary of repair* common to both professions combines an abstract mode of projective thinking with a concrete form of practical judgment, effectively erasing the traditional dichotomy between the "liberal" and the "mechanical." Crawford ventures further in a discussion of the capacity to see things and internalize that representation: "Seeing things is not always a simple matter. Even on the relatively primitive vintage bikes that were our specialty, some diagnostic situations contain so many

15 In the Renaissance, there was a widespread belief that the form was already latent in the marble and that the sculptor's task was simply to uncover and release it. See Rudolf Wittkower, *Sculpture: Processes and Principles* (Harmondsworth: Penguin Books, 1998).

16 In connection with this idea, readers might like to listen to the "re-performance" of Johann Sebastian Bach's *Goldberg Variations* as recorded by Glenn Gould in 1955. Designed and realized by the software company Zenph, this re-performance does not consist in remastering an aging recording but in rerecording it on an acoustic piano equipped with a computer and a piece of innovative software capable of playing it again without the loss of the slightest inflection in tempo and touch. Such technology raises intriguing questions about the technical reproducibility of a work of art, both in terms of composition and interpretation. See https://www.youtube.com/watch?v=Ah392InFHxM (accessed August 19, 2021).

17 Matthew B. Crawford, *Shop Class as Soulcraft: An Inquiry into the Value of Work* (New York: Penguin Books, 2010), 25.

18 Ibid.

19 Ibid., 27.

20 The concept that Bachelard explores in the five studies devoted to the "imaginative forces of our mind" are: *The Psychoanalysis of Fire* (1938; 1964), *Water and Dreams* (1942; 1983), *Air and Dreams* (1943; 1988), *Earth and Reveries of Repose* (1948; 2011), and *Earth and Reveries of Will* (1948; 2002).

variables, and symptoms can be so under-determining of causes, that explicit analytical reasoning comes up short. What is required then is the kind of judgment that arises only from experience; hunches rather than rules."[19]

Once again, we encounter Duffau's idea of intuition taking up where rational judgment leaves off, not as a decision-making process superimposed over reasoning, but as a consequence of experience—an extra quality added to technical mastery to round it off. *Intueri* in Latin means "to look carefully."

For the neurosurgeon, the ability to "see right" consists in two things: firstly, in being able to identify and then mentally picture the structures and networks of the brain and their connectivity, something Duffau manages to do with the minimal use of neurofunctional imaging techniques. Secondly, his ability to "see right" also resides in delegating some of his decisions to a less rational mode of relating to the various ingredients of a complex situation, through a kind of enlightened improvisation (paradoxical though this may sound), an intuitive knack developed by many years of practice. This is surely the source of his "individual talent" and also what makes his practice so tricky to model. How does he represent (that is, picture) this knowledge, encode it in his own central nervous system, and then translate it into just the right delicate gestures when operating on his patients? Is it possible to transpose this manner of undertaking a project based on cutting-edge expertise and on an eminently personal way of embodying and expressing it? In this regard, philosophers Gaston Bachelard and Gilbert Simondon offer avenues for reflection, the former with his concept of material imagination,[20] the latter with that of technical imagination, which he sees as indissoluble from invention.

Performativity of the Imagination

Bachelard distinguishes two forms of imagination: one consists in associating images with forms (formal imagination) and the other, more fundamental, deals in direct images of matter, those which do not yet make sense or possess order or form, and which arise from direct contact with matter (the material imagination). "The eye assigns them names, but only the hand truly knows them"[21]: a kind of technological memory that records corporally and psychologically the impressions matter lays down in it, initiating a process of interpretation and transformation. Matter resonates, echoes (literally), worms its way in; and this double reflection gives rise to primal, primordial images. This is the "creative imagination"[22] Bachelard opposes to the "reproductive imagination," defining it concisely: "The counsel to see well at the base of the culture of realism easily outweighs my own paradoxical advice to *dream well*, to remain faithful to the oneiric archetypes deeply rooted in the human unconscious."[23] Dreaming, then, means allowing "imagined images" to form, images capable of becoming ideas; dreaming is the opposite of combining or reproducing previously seen fragments of a reality. It is the foundation, perhaps, of that "library of sounds and smells and feels" Crawford refers to; or of that long, preparatory phase during which Duffau pores over magnetic resonance images (MRIs) of his patients' brains. Alloyed to the surgeon's visual and tactile knowledge of functional anatomy, this preliminary task of observation allows him to record the information necessary for the smooth progress of the operation and dispense with all visualization equipment in the operating theater other than a camera to film the operation and a real-time ultrasound system.[24]

21 Gaston Bachelard, *Water and Dreams: An Essay on the Imagination of Matter*, trans. E. R. Farrell (Dallas: Dallas Institute of Humanities and Culture, 1982), 1.

22 A concept created in 1900 by the philosopher Théodule Ribot, author of *L'imagination créatrice* (reprinted by Éditions L'Harmattan, 2007). My thanks go to Didier Semin for this valuable reference.

23 Gaston Bachelard, *The Earth and Reveries of Will: An Essay on the Imagination of Matter*, trans. Kenneth Haltmann (Dallas: Dallas Institute of Humanities and Culture, 2002), 2.

24 In the operating room, Duffau even works without a microscope and seems to be one of the only neurosurgeons (if not the only one) known to perform operations in this manner.

25 We employ the term *performativity* here in the (broad) sense which Richard Schechner, one of the founders of performance studies, employed it, that is, as "the result of the awareness of the performative *potential* of an action, event or object." See Josette Féral, "De la performance à la performativité," *Communications*, 92, no. 1 (2013): 205–18, here 208.

26 Bachelard, *Water and Dreams*, 2.

27 Gilbert Simondon, *Imagination et invention* (1965–1966) (Paris: puf, 2014), 150.

28 Gilbert Simondon, *On the Mode of Existence of Technical Objects*, trans. C. Malespina and R. Rogrove (Minneapolis: Univocal Publishing, 2017), 74.

29 This expression—the most accurate one to describe the approaches in this book—I've borrowed from Gilles A. Tiberghien, whose text in the present volume is entitled "Formativity: A Philosophy of Making," 41.

This *imagining* performativity[25] operating upstream of any attempt to give form appears as a fundamental ontological mechanism for explaining the expressive or technical gestures that constitute the core subject of the present volume. And if, as Bachelard maintains, "matter is the very principle that can dissociate itself from form,"[26] it is its individualizing power that constitutes the cynosure of our thinking here—an infinite reservoir of possible becomings, which can take the shape of objects, gestures, images, systems, or ideas. For the philosopher Gilbert Simondon too, imagination and invention are inextricably linked, invention supposing a problem that needs to be solved by detours thanks to a faculty for thinking up representations and perceiving intermediate levels of compatibility for the elements: "Human and animal life alike constantly require confronting the partial novelty of situations with an activity that organizes its operating modes."[27] This activity presupposes a kind of "technical imagination as being defined by a particular sensitivity to [the] technicity of elements."[28]

Philosophies of Making, Philosophies of Doing

The example of Hugues Duffau stands for me at the heart of the issues rehearsed in each text and project in this book: philosophies of making,[29] which are above all ways of being when working that operate as much through their modes of mental representation—projections—as through acts that continually probe into and dialogue with matter, the body, and technical equipment generally. Constantly evolving and increasingly hybridized, these practices are also the crux of widespread and timeless fundamental questions concerning our species' propensities for demiurgy. To be convinced of this concern, it is enough to glance at the contents page of this book, full of references to processes of formation, experimentation, invention, creativity, of perfection and imperfection, of tinkering and *bricolage*, of materiality and dematerialization, of making and of the urge to make. The authors—each in their own way and each within their discipline—question the notions of design, *Gestaltung*, and formativity,[30] as much on the theoretical or conceptual level as with respect to the gestures of those who make them. For those who handle materials, the task is not simply to present their work; it is also to describe their singular relationship to technology and invention, as well as their processes of implementation. What are the salient links between the gestures of a neurosurgeon and those of an artist, designer, typographer, craftsman, do-it-yourselfer, choreographer, engineer, or biologist? What are the common features of their practices, in the way practitioners understand them and implement them, in their approaches to the materials (with which) they work and in the processes of shaping they embark on and that embark them? What is the *spunto*, the spark? What are the values and principles governing their research? What is it that puts up such a resistance, to the point sometimes of jeopardizing the whole project? The three concepts in our book title each shed light on these questions in turn.

Gestatio

When I joined the Cluster of Excellence »Image Knowledge Gestaltung« at Humboldt University in 2015, the German concept of *Gestaltung* felt both familiar and alien to me. Although they do not share the same etymology,[31] I had noted a certain proximity between the French notion of *geste*[32] and that of *Gestaltung*: as

30 I have opted to keep the three terms *Design*, *Gestaltung* and *Formatività* in their original languages for the title of the volume, because it has proved extremely difficult, if not impossible, to convey every semantic facet by some English equivalent. In a pinch, the term *formatività* can be anglicized as "formativity." It is of course this polysemy that gives rise to the richness of the dialogues and questionings contained in the book.

31 In the word *gesture*, there is the idea of the body moving, arms and hands especially (from Latin *gestus*: "attitude," "movement of the body," "mimic," "play"), as well as that of doing, behaving, acting, from *gerere*: "to accomplish," "perform," "bear" (as in *gestatio*: "to carry within oneself"). While *gesture* is more concerned with bodily attitude, the French *geste* refers to the physical and the technical (often highly complex in nature: ballet, craft, surgery) with a wider range of acts of moral import. As for the term *Gestaltung*, which can be translated as "shaping" or "formation of form(s)," it is of German origin (sixteenth century), from the noun *Gestalt* ("shape," "figure," "appearance") and the verb *gestalten* (past participle of *stellen*: "to set," "place," "arrange"), literally "that which is placed," therefore "to form," "conceive," "configure," "organize." As a process, *Gestaltung* is indissociable from the concept of *Gestalt*, particularly in the twentieth century, with the study of human sensations and perception as undertaken by Gestalt psychology. I thank Jörg Petruschat for his valuable remarks on the notion of *Gestaltung*, which he discusses at length in his writings,

conducts, as figures of work, and exploratory modes of thought, *geste* ("gesture") and *Gestaltung* imply a particular relationship to time and duration, a latency, if you will, between the idea, the dream, or the image (the point of departure), and the realization of a more or less clearly envisaged plan. Between these two moments exist every possible way of building, combining, and making, which the concept of *Gestaltung* as well as the theory of formativity embraces. It is precisely in this interval—we might call it *room for maneuver*—or in this space of indetermination (the interstices and gaps Jean-Luc Nancy mentions in the epigraph to this introduction) that the theoretical premise of the book is situated.

It then remained for me to clarify the relationship between *Gestaltung* and design,[33] which remained unclear in my eyes. In 2018 my colleague Tiago da Costa e Silva and I organized a workshop at the Humboldt University in Berlin, and at the Max Planck Institute for Colloids and Interfaces (MPIKG) in Potsdam, which was informed by three landmark texts: Italian philosopher Luigi Pareyson's theory of *formatività*,[34] defined as the "inseparable union of production and invention"; German psychiatrist and art historian Hans Prinzhorn's interpretation of the notion of *Gestaltung*, understood as an "impulse" pertaining to a "expressive need";[35] and French philosopher Pierre-Damien Huyghe's consideration of the relationship between form and design "as one element in a tension that underpins the industrial world."[36] Desirous of relating these theoretical points of view to real objects, artworks, and technical, scientific, and artistic processes, we invited art and design researchers from the École Nationale Supérieure des Arts Décoratifs (Ensad) and the École Nationale Supérieure de Création Industrielle (ENSCI) in Paris to present their research, together with biologists and material science engineers from the MPIKG.[37]

The three founding texts of this line of thinking have allowed me to place the terms *design*, *Gestaltung*, and *formatività* on a new philosophical footing that from the start interweaves discipline, process, and theory. In this, I believe, lies the latent efficacity of this bold if inescapable interrelation. It is bold, because, in throwing three "big" words like these into one pot, there is always the risk they become diluted in some vast, somewhat flaccid whole where each cancels the other out—yet it is inescapable, since their scope allows them to be treated as a single productive, conceptual unit. Of course, I have chosen to take this approach, and the risk has proved worthwhile, since the discussion has been enriched by such important contributions that I felt it necessary to compile them. Hence the present book, which questions processes of shaping by comparing and extending the field of *Gestaltung* to the field of design and to the concept of formativity.

In the first part of the book—"Giving Form"—philosophers, historians, psychologists, and researchers in cultural history and theory investigate processes of conceiving and producing forms; while in the second—"Form Given"—artists, designers, engineers, and scientists discuss forms they have made in the course of their work. Their thoughts build into a mosaic of ways of doing and thinking about creative activity—philosophies of making marked by contemporary techniques and the issues in aesthetics, production, and society that inform them. I requested each to choose five to eight images from their work and to reflect on the types of forms they encounter in their practice, to describe them and to advance elements of analysis to explain how they devise and implement them: these forms range from objects, images, and performances to typography, scientific proto-

e.g., Jörg Petruschat, "'Wicked Problems': A Few Remarks on Design as Research," in *Integrative Design: Essays and Projects on Design Research*, ed. Ralf Michel (Berlin, Boston: Birkhäuser, 2019), 11-31.

32 A notion to which my PhD dissertation is devoted: "Pour une ontologie du geste. À notre corps défaillant" (2009).

33 See Patricia Ribault, "Form as a Given / Giving Form," in *+ultra: knowledge & gestaltung*, ed. Nikola Doll et al. (Leipzig: E. A. Seemann, 2017), 117–20. In more than one way, the present volume takes up where that article left off, that is to say at the work of forms: "Thus, giving form consists in working on the world of possibilities, starting from what is already potentially there—matter, technique, knowledge—and what remains at the margin, between inside and outside, between the given of life and what can still be taken, within reach of hand and mind, always concurrently offering and equivocating," 120.

34 Luigi Pareyson, *Estetica. Teoria della formatività* (Milan: Bompiani, 1988).

35 Hans Prinzhorn, *Artistry of the Mentally Ill* [eds. 1922, 1923, 1968], trans. E. von Brockdorff from 2nd ed. (Berlin: Springer, 1972), 42. The French edition, *Expressions de la folie : dessins, peintures, sculptures d'asile*, trans. A. Brousse and M. Weber (Paris: Gallimard, 1984), contains additional material.

36 See Pierre-Damien Huyghe, "Form in the Sphere of Design," in the present volume, 69.

cols, and technical systems. The authors retrace the genesis and evolution of their project(s), discussing the issues at stake and charting a course to the heart of their discipline, in conjunction with or independently of other fields.

Though it is almost impossible to summarize such a diversity of approaches, this heterogeneity constitutes a line of force: the performativity of materials and how they are formed always depends on the relations between certain capacities (of a body, a piece of equipment, a technique, a form of behavior) and the variants of conduct which, if they set limits to them, likewise strive to exceed them through processes of formation and transformation which are anything except linear. It is the etymological meaning of the word *performance* that we employ here. It comes from the Old French *parformer*: "to shape," "to finish," always inseparable from the idea of work (*travail*), which consists in constantly navigating between project and outcome, between the expected and the unexpected, attempt and (often fruitful) failure, cobbling together (*bricolage*), and deconstruction/construction, all knitted together and leaving that opening that seems necessary for every form of transfer—or for what French psychoanalyst Daniel Sibony has eloquently termed *trans-faire* ("trans-making").[38] The possibilities for disorder Jean-Luc Nancy refers to in the epigraph to this introduction also lay down conditions for the possibility of making; they concern less the production of new objects or new results than creating new modes of transformation and the modelization of this making. It answers at the same time an eminently contemporary question that consists less in making, still, than in making (or unmaking) differently. "How to do?" takes the place of "what is there to be done?"[39]

The format of the second part differs substantially from the first: the image becomes the focus of attention, while the texts, all shorter, aim mainly at briefly introducing the research and commenting on each figure in a "super caption." While the first section reads as a critical analysis of ways of making (art, design, forms), in the second, it is materials, concepts, and techniques that are manipulated and made to resonate with the questions raised in the first. The second part does not, however, present a list of demonstrations; it proposes instead a series of echoes, some obvious, some oblique, to the theoretical approaches in the first. The opening texts in the volume treat of the three terms of the work, enriched by critical approaches to form and function, asymmetry, *bricologie*,[40] to invention and imperfection, to engineering for the living and to the futures of design. If some of these texts refer more to individual works while others deal with entire processes, all question the definitions, limits, and possible perimeters of the processes of forming.

Formatività

Of the three terms in our equation, *formatività* (formativity)[41] is probably the least familiar. Published for the first time in 1954 under the title *Estetica. Teoria della formatività*, Luigi Pareyson's study does not try to deploy a theory of forms, which the author warns from the outset would only be ambiguous, but a theory of the *process* of forming—form being understood "as an organism, driven by its own vital energy and endowed with its own internal lawfulness."[42] This aspect proves of fundamental importance for the present volume, which considers not only human modes of production, but also the modes of organization and development

37 An institutional and conceptual forum, this inaugural encounter was also an immersion into its potential exploration through visual art. It was followed by several interdisciplinary performative events in both Paris and Berlin, including an unforgettable workshop in the Pompidou Center in Paris, "Behavioral Matter," featuring a good hundred researchers in the human sciences, the natural sciences, engineering, and art and design, centered on the agency of materials (March 15–17, 2019; see https://www.matters-of-activity.de/de/activities/3629/behavioral-matter).

38 "This machine is called *Transfer*, it motors away in the heart of language, it pushes us to do, but it exceeds all that we can do, it drives us, propels us to other ways of doing and thinking; it is our *trans-faire* machine." Daniel Sibony, *Entre dire et faire* (Paris: Éditions Grasset et Fasquelle, 1989), 8.

39 Nancy, *Que faire ?*, 58.

40 A neologism coined by Thomas Golsenne from *bricolage* and *technology*. See Golsenne, "Bricology: An Anthropology of Making Art," in the present volume, 109.

41 Since *Estetica. Teoria della formatività* has not yet been published in English, I have asked for the preface to the 1988 edition and the beginning of the first part ("Specifications of Art") to be translated here. It opens the present volume. See Luigi Pareyson, "*Estetica. Teoria della formatività*: Preface to the 1988 edition, followed by 'The Specification of Art,'" in the present volume, 23.

42 Pareyson, "Preface to the 1988 edition" in the present volume, 23.

of matter in general and of living forms in particular. By insisting on the idea of an internal law of form and on its dynamic character, Pareyson's theory parallels the concept of *Gestaltung* and its concern with process. As an aesthetic, the theory of formativity applies to art, which the philosopher considers as the supreme achievement of any operation of formation ("art is pure formativity"[43]), but, even in the preface, he invites the reader to consider it in the broader perspective of general philosophy, "also applicable to other fields of experience."[44] This is precisely what we propose to do: to consider formativity as an operative principle of the experience of doing and making, in the historic sense of *operare* ("to act," "to work"): "This activity, which is generically inherent to all experience, and which—if appropriately specified—constitutes that which we rightfully call art, is 'formativity,' that is, a sort of *making* which, as it makes, also devises the 'way of making': production which is at the same time and indivisibly invention. All aspects of human industriousness [*operosità*], from the simplest to the most complex, have this irremovable and fundamental aspect of formativity."[45]

It is ways of making that are observed, explored, and analyzed in this book, more than the resulting works. Or rather, these productions, artistic or no, are here considered as formative—that is to say, as thought and made in one and the same movement that simultaneously executes and invents. In other words, all human activity can and must find its own way of being done. The art of making is doing an art of doing; doing with art, and not the opposite: "It takes art to do anything: in all fields it's a matter of 'making *with* art,' that is, of fueling with inventiveness and ensuring the success of any *making* present in a given operation. In other words, from the most humble of techniques right up to the greatest of inventions, there is the deployment of formativity, and therefore the need for art."[46]

Any experience can be formative, a workman, artist or philosopher's gestures, as much as a surgeon's. Formativity transpires in everyday acts as well as those that produce great works, be they objects or concepts, practical or speculative accomplishments. "Whatever the activity is that one intends to practice, it is always a matter of posing problems, constituting them originally from the formless data of experience, and finding, discovering, or rather inventing their solutions."[47]

The formative dimension of every operation can also be related to Hugues Duffau's definition of brain plasticity, as a function or capacity to organize and reorganize information networks—adapting, for instance, to the emergence of a tumor. "Nothing," writes Duffau, "is fixed once and for all in the brain: permutations, oscillations, interchangeability, reciprocity ... these are the keywords of this model."[48] As Gilles A. Tiberghien points out, "[f]ormativity relates to knowledge derived from the senses, since to form is to know and one cannot know without forming."[49]

There remains though the question of the *spunto*, the starting point of any form and thus of any process of formation. For Pareyson, one has to look for the origin of form in the activity of the artist, or rather in his latent ability to see these *spunti* springing up around her—a kind of active and reactive expectation the Italian philosopher calls "formative intentionality": "This is a will to art, which absorbs all spiritual life in an intentional formativity and becomes an energy charge, a way of seeing while forming and of looking while building, which, triggered by the most fleeting opportunity, converts the least accident into a point of departure."[50]

43 Pareyson, "The Specification of Art," in the present volume, 35.
44 Pareyson, "Preface to the 1988 edition," 25.
45 Pareyson, "The Specification of Art," 31.
46 Ibid., 32.
47 Ibid.
48 Duffau, *L'erreur de Broca*, 136.
49 Tiberghien, "Formativity: A Philosophy of Making," 45.
50 Pareyson, *Esthétique. Théorie de la formativité*, trans. Gilles A. Tiberghien (Paris: ULM, 2007), 96 (trans. David Radzinowicz).

Tiberghien makes a parallel between this notion and the "power of formation" Paul Klee sees as common to art and nature; and to the "operation of forces" that lead to form in the thought of John Dewey—a kind of organic thrust that is invariably sparked by an "impulsion."[51] Here again the theory of formativity overlaps with the concept of *Gestaltung* as adumbrated by Prinzhorn—that is to say as an "expressive need" manifested by "impulses for configuration."[52]

Gestaltung

The German term *Gestaltung* may be translated into English as "organization," "presentation," or "animation," as well as by "design," "layout," or "decoration," depending on whether the stress is laid on its role in structuring space, thought, or matter, or on its capacity to make visible or "receptive." Up to a point, *Gestaltung* incorporates the demiurgic movement of the act of creation, here thought of as an act of production. Although the term dates back to the sixteenth century,[53] two almost contemporary manifestations of the concept interest us particularly. In 1919 Walter Gropius published the *Bauhaus Manifesto*, in which he associated the ideas of form and forming with those of construction, creation, and inspiration. He employs the terms *Gestalt* and *Gestalten* three times: first to designate the complex forming of construction ("die vielgliedrige Gestalt des Baues"), then the ultimate source of creative inspiration ("Dort ist der Urquell des schöpferischen Gestaltens"), and finally as a unifying principle of the architecture of the future ("den neuen Bau der Zukunft, der alles in einer Gestalt sein wird").[54] What interests us here is the attention to the *dynamics* of form—"the paths to form" as mentioned by Paul Klee in his notebooks[55]—and how this dynamic still means something to us, a century later, because it situates art, architecture, and design not on the level of finished forms but on that of what *animates* them.

Then, three years after the publication of the *Manifesto*, in 1922, Hans Prinzhorn published in German his *Artistry of the Mentally Ill*. In this incisive treatise on the limits between psychiatric pathology and creative expression, he designates the "impulse to *Gestaltung*" as a universal principle and develops an account of the drive for expression based on works of art produced by patients (mainly schizophrenics) in the psychiatric clinic at Heidelberg where he worked. His study led him to generalize this concept as a primordial need or urge for individual expression: "That basic process would be essentially the same in the most sovereign drawing by Rembrandt as in the most miserable daubing by a paralytic: both would be expressions of the psyche."[56] We hear in this statement an echo of Pareyson's idea that in all human activity "there is deployment of formativity, and therefore the need for art." What Prinzhorn designates in turn as the "tendency," "impulse," or "urge" to *Gestaltung*,[57] corresponds, according to him, to a fundamental need of expression. This idea, inherited from the architect Gottfried Semper, who considered artistic creation as a need or urge (*Bedürfnis*),[58] is at once key to his theory and problematic. It is problematic because the idea of expressive urge sounds like an oxymoron, since expression stands on a line at the polar opposite of need. But it is precisely for this reason that Prinzhorn's theory hinges on the urge for *Gestaltung*: because it defines his idea of man—an irreducible articulation between what is a priori necessary and what is a priori superfluous. The sole finality of this upsurge is the very urge to put into form: "The expressive urge can be understood only as an ever-present atmosphere, like the erotic."[59] In this

51 See Tiberghien, "Formativity: A Philosophy of Making," 50.
52 Prinzhorn, *Artistry of the Mentally Ill*, 6.
53 See note 31.
54 W. Gropius, *Bauhaus-Manifest* (Weimar, 1919).
55 "The study of creation deals with the ways that lead to form. It is the study of form, but emphasises the paths to form rather than the form itself. The word *Gestaltung* suggests as much." Paul Klee, *Notebooks*, vol. 1: *The Thinking Eye*, trans. Ralph Manheim, ed. Jürg Spiller, (London: Lund Humphries, 1961), 17.
56 Prinzhorn, *Artistry of the Mentally Ill*, xviii.
57 He goes so far as to state that the exact term does not matter, ibid., 15.
58 "Art acknowledges but one master, need," in Gottfried Semper, *Kleine Schriften*, gen. ed. H. and M. Semper (Mittenwald: Mäander, 1979), 217, quoted by Roland Recht in "Viollet-le-Duc et Gottfried Semper: leurs conceptions du patrimoine monumental," *Revue germanique internationale*, no. 13 (2000), http://journals.openedition.org/rgi/780 (accessed September 17, 2021). I thank Didier Semin for the information that Prinzhorn's doctorate was on Semper.
59 Prinzhorn, *Artistry of the Mentally Ill*, 14.

sense, Prinzhorn's theory appears as rather radical, because it places *Gestaltung* in the metaphysical rather than the psychological realm. If a human being cannot satisfy this fundamental urge for expression, then they cannot be considered as authentically human.

This "primitive force, [this] creative power that sees and forms"[60] can likewise be compared to John Dewey's *impulsion* and Pareyson's *spunto*—impulses that unfold into forms (*Gestalten*), be they things, artworks, operations, etc. The act of forming should not be considered as the slavish execution of orders sent down by some all-powerful decision-making authority, intellectual or inspired, but as a living process that makes do with the contingencies inherent in every act of giving form. One might also speak about resistances—by the material, the body, or the environment—to an intention, desire, and drive; or even of "explementation,"[61] to counter a certain programmatory tendency, "by listening to what matter says to us—or, rather, what it 'makes us say'."[62] Since it covers conception, operation, and invention as much as drawing, modeling, and representation, the notion of *Gestaltung* can be considered as "holistic force,"[63] a powerful, timeless structuring principle acting under the dual aegis of the activities of both expression and making.

Design

In contrast to the concept of *Gestaltung* and to the theory of formativity, design is on the face of it a field of activity that is clearly delimited, both historically and conceptually. But, in conjunction with terms such as *disegno*, *dessein* ("intention") and drawing, its polysemy transpires through many factors. This is the subject of the interview between Emanuele Quinz and Giovanni Anceschi transcribed here.[64] As the means of production are increasingly rationalized, the act of giving form has been divided into two: the craftsmanship of the past has split into engineering and design for the conception and, for manufacture, industry. Design has thus emerged in parallel with the extinction of a certain notion of work, based on the oral and manual transmission of an experience formed and transformed by individuals who have shaped and adapted it over generations. Through their skill and their understanding of the diverse elements that make up the whole, it was these "tool bearers"[65] who ensured humanity's technological ascent, thanks to their capacity to oversee and regulate the production environment and the task of transforming matter. The advent of technical entities of a wholly new kind subsequently deprived them of these functions. In the nineteenth century, "technical individuals" able not only to transform matter but also to mediate between various elements in the operating chain appeared: machines. More or less self-regulating, they progressively constituted the industrial productive body, to a large extent replacing production units such as artisan workshops and manufactories during the eighteenth century.

As a *practice of conception*, design thus arose from a rift in the act of production, something that at the outset created a tension in its mode of existence. The mechanization of the means of production coincided with such a leap forward in technology that the arrival of machines generated new registers of forms and communication within the industrial apparatus. One does not produce the same bowl or plate if it is thrown by hand by a potter, automatically stamped out by

60 Hans Prinzhorn, "À propos de l'art des aliénés," in *Expressions de la folie*, 373. This passage is translated from the French edition of the book, which includes this text that Prinzhorn wrote in French, probably following a lecture.
61 A term coined by Samuel Bianchini in "Attempts at Explementation: Combining Material and Symbolic Operations in Art and Design Research," in the present volume, 355.
62 Ibid, 356.
63 To adopt the expression used by Claudia Mareis in *Theorien des Designs zur Einführung* (Hamburg: Junius, 2016), 56.
64 See Emanuele Quinz, "From *Gestalt* to *Gestaltung*. A Conversation with Giovanni Anceschi," in the present volume, 133.
65 Simondon's term in *On the Mode of Existence of Technical Objects*, 119.

metal gauge, cast in a plaster mold, or turned out by an isostatic press from a steel and polyurethane mold. The design of a model requires acquaintance with the production tool in dialogue with its capacities and limits, as well as a certain free space in which the designer can operate. This margin may be technological or cultural; it implies *give*—the space necessary between two pieces so they have room to play with.

In the text reproduced here, philosopher Pierre-Damien Huyghe questions the position of design in the light of this relativity, which he detects in three founding tenets in the history of the discipline.[66] As he puts it, the notion of form is "an element under tension."[67] Following the precepts of the architect Frank Lloyd Wright, he takes up the idea that, since machines have replaced craftsmen, industry is faced with "[finding] the 'cadences of form'."[68] This task has fallen to the designer. In other words, form must not be dictated by technicality or function, but by an aesthetic, even rhythmic imperative lying outside the register of function. "The task for design is surely rather to devise and to create designs for seating and shapes inherent in the potential and dynamic properties of the materials and textures of our era."[69]

The quest for formal rhythm thus implies questioning not only the apparatus of production, but also (and perhaps more essentially) the material qualities specific to a given age. Hence, whatever works *through* and *on* a period can be brought to light and made to resonate in the exercise of design. For the designer, the aim ought to be, *through* forms, to show the dialectic between a given technical unit, its functions, and the environment in which it finds itself. In this, the field of design lies at the junction between a program (that of industry) and a way of making, a "touch" which belongs rather to art. By coupling form and function ("Form and Function are One"), Wright does not subordinate form to an assigned function; he opens up a space for what is not in advance written or fixed by some potential predetermined use. "For Wright form is of a different nature. It operates on the level of the actual conditions of its presence, of its coming into being. It is an approach that has at least two consequences. On the one hand, since the connection between form and function is reciprocal, it is not enough for the design materializing this connection (this was the horizon of Sullivan's diktat) to make (the) form 'follow' (the) function: it will in some way affect the thrust of these functions. In addition, once the concept of functionality is no longer regarded as neutral, or as sufficiently defined by and of itself, design forestalls the unlimited deployment of functions."[70]

To follow the reasoning of Jörg Petruschat, another severe critic of the idea according to which design is subject to the supposedly indisputable authority of function, form does not *follow* function; it accompanies and might even precede it: "The deepest reason for *Gestaltung* is to be found in the form, not the purpose."[71]

The prevailing vision of design in this book is thus of a dialectical process of *configuration*,[72] that is to say of disposition (in the etymological sense of "positioning side by side") of what can be formed, always in relation to various contextual realities: a given technical device, an eco-socio-political context, a function or set of functions, space, time, etc. In this sense, the field of definition proposed by Vincent Beaubois in his PhD dissertation is enlightening: rejecting a unilateral definition of design, he prefers to speak of "design practices" (in the plural), so as

66 László Moholy-Nagy's "Design for Life"; Raymond Loewy's "Ugliness doesn't sell"; and Frank Lloyd Wright's "Form and Function," in correlation and opposition to Louis Sullivan's contention that "form follows function" (or "form *ever* follows function").
67 Huyghe, "Form in the Sphere of Design," 70.
68 Ibid., 71; Wright's terms are found in *The Essential Frank Lloyd Wright: Writings on Architecture*, ed. B. Brooks Pfeiffer (Princeton: Princeton University Press, 2008), 338.
69 Ibid., 72.
70 Ibid., 75.
71 Jörg Petruschat, "First There Is Form: Some Critical Remarks About the Belief That Form Follows Function," in the present volume, 88.
72 Using the term, "which translates the German word *Gestaltung*," employed by Giovanni Anceschi in Quinz, "From *Gestalt* to *Gestaltung*," 144.

"to place the emphasis on the inseparably mental and material set of operations that lead to the genesis of a thing."[73] Conception is made practice, field of action, inventive gesture, and is not confined to problem-solving, the execution of a plan, or the production of an object. It is a mode of doing/making and thinking that is expressed by image-objects, models, diagrams, analog or digital modeling, all of which are formal interventions. Thus, "design is defined less by its products than by its power: its powers of anticipation, of projection, of construction of the material environment of life; and its ability to transform our gestures, our habits, and our way of relating to this environment."[74] Therein lies its evident modernity, but also its potentially double-edged quality, referred to by both Martin Müller (talking about the control of the living by bio-design[75]) and Wolfgang Schäffner, contrasting the "destructive design strategy" that entails the depletion of natural and cultural resources with "a form of design,"[76] a design 2.0 characterized by both "fundamental openness" and an attention to biological materials and natural processes.[77] This is the vision in which design and *Gestaltung* meet, as modes of formation and in-formation whose future is uncertain—in other words, as formativity.

In fine, we become aware that the latent power of design as a mode of relation and not as a hylomorphic principle of control and domination of matter, stems from a capacity to seize the things of the world, in the literal as well as metaphorical sense, to turn them over and over, to articulate them with other practices, other disciplines, and eventually bring into being "open" forms in the sense Umberto Eco understands them—that is to say as forms which leave us, "when faced with the provocation of chaos and its possibilities, receptive, responsible."[78] These *philosophies of making* help us think about what we make, what we can make, and perhaps even how to do it. But, at a time of "the inexorable degradation of what is produced,"[79] they also spur us into action. Jean-Luc Nancy's "*que faire?*" finds an echo in Enzo Mari's "*che fare*" for both authors, the question is above all one of making sense so as to be able to face up. Facing up to the "flow of 'producing'"[80] or to the "weakness of thought"[81] means committing oneself above all to what one does. Making as a mode of doing implies a mode of thinking; if we don't want to lose the pilot's handbook for "Spaceship Earth" for good, we are going to need, more than ever, all the rationality and ingenuity in worldmaking we are capable of. "Knowledge, power and duty leave intact something of 'doing': that effectivity which is not that of an object, nor that of an active or passive power, nor even that of an effect coming from a cause, but that which resides in the fact of an existence."[82] This overwhelming "response-ability"[83] is ours and it will, let us hope, lead us as much to make as to undo, the better to redo.

Translated from the French by David Radzinowicz

73 Vincent Beaubois, "La zone obscure du design : Une pensée des pratiques de conception (d')après Gilbert Simondon" (PhD diss., Université Paris Nanterre, 2019), 138.
74 Ibid., 33.
75 See Martin Müller, "The Will to Engineer: Synthetic Biology and the Escalation of Zoëpolitics," in the present volume, 159.
76 In the German version of his text, the wording is even plainer: "Essentiell dabei ist die Form einer Gestaltung." See Wolfgang Schäffner, "The Design Turn 2.0," in the present volume, 188.
77 Ibid.
78 Umberto Eco, *L'œuvre ouverte* [1962], trans. Chantal Roux de Bézieux (Paris: Seuil, 1965), 293; in an addition to this edition.
79 Enzo Mari, "Che fare," manifesto for the exhibition *Che fare*, Galerie Alain Gutharc, Paris, 2009.
80 Nancy, *Que faire ?*, 96.
81 Mari, "Che fare."
82 Nancy, *Que faire ?*, 96.
83 To employ a term coined by Donna Haraway in 1992 and popularized more recently by other philosophers, feminists, and new materialists, such as Karen Barad and Vinciane Despret.

Giving Form

Giving Form

Estetica. Teoria della formatività Preface to the 1988 edition followed by "The Specification of Art"

Luigi Pareyson

Preface[1]

Aesthetics is the field in which Benedetto Croce's predominance went unchallenged for an inordinate length of time. Even until the early postwar years, Croce's aesthetics was the only model in Italy ever to be cited. But by then, new needs were pushing to the fore: first of all, it was more urgent than ever to discuss those themes that Croce's censorship had so detrimentally excluded from Italy; furthermore, it was necessary to elaborate categories that could satisfy the needs of the new context. This was the starting point and the ambitious premise of this book, which was published in installments in a philosophy magazine between 1950 and 1954.

Instead of beating around the bush with the umpteenth critique of Croce's aesthetics, the book went straight to the heart of the matter, and in place of the Crocian principles of intuition and expression, it proposed an aesthetic of production and formativity. In art, it was time to stress the doing rather than the contemplating. And if—despite the clumsiness of the term—it was decided for this theory to be known as "the aesthetics of formativity" rather than "the aesthetics of form," that was most of all down to two reasons. First of all because the term *form*, given its multitude of meanings, cannot but end up sounding ambiguous, and risks being passed off as the mere opposite of *matter* or *content*, thereby conjuring up the *vexata quaestio* of formalism and contentism. Instead here, form is viewed as an organism, driven by its own vital energy and endowed with its own internal lawfulness: a totality unrepeatable in its singularity, independent in its autonomy, exemplary in its value, both resolved and open at the same time in its definiteness

1 This text is the translation of the preface from: Luigi Pareyson, *Estetica. Teoria della formatività* (Milan: Tascabili Bompiani, 1988), 7–12.

that embraces an infinity, perfect in the harmony and unity of its law of coherence, and complete in the reciprocal adjustment between the parts and the whole. Secondly, the decision was made so as to immediately clarify the dynamic character of form, of which it is essential to produce a result; indeed, the success of a formation "process," given that form cannot be seen as such unless it is viewed in the act of concluding—and at the same time including—lies in the moment of production that places an end to it and draws its success from it.

Here, two great traditions proved helpful. First of all, the ancient concept of art as *poieîn*, as *making*, in which nevertheless there remained on the sidelines the distinction between art in the true sense and as mere technique; and second, the no-less-ancient concept of the organism, which had been so admirably defined and entrusted to debate throughout the history of philosophy by Plato and most of all by Aristotle. But these two traditions had to be considered in terms of their modern elaboration. On the one hand, there was the need in art to shed light on the technical and craft aspect, all too overlooked by Croce, while still maintaining all the specific characteristics of artistry; here the observations of Poe, Flaubert, Valéry, Stravinsky, and many other similar figures served as a stimulus to study the compositional and constructive aspects of artistic activity, in its both calculated and adventurous nature. And on the other hand, the need to study the life of forms by one who most painstakingly analyzed—in artistic activity as well as in nature—its birth, growth, maturity, and fertility: that is, by Goethe, and in those who, in the field of philosophy, were on a par with him, such as Schelling. Not to mention the need to follow the developments of this perspective through critics such as Focillon, as well as in contemporary philosophers such as Bergson and Guzzo, or Whitehead and Dewey. Artistic activity as it is presented in art thus appeared as that which brings together within itself the attempt and the organization, from where we find the attempt to explain how such different and antithetic terms may converge (and not just awareness and spontaneity, as in Romantic aesthetics, which does not contemplate the tentative nature of the artistic operation and organization as being intrinsic to its own success); in the manner adopted to resolve this difficulty perhaps also lies the newest side of the theory proposed, as well as constituting the heart of the research itself.

The theory of aesthetics put forward by this book intended to be thoroughly philosophical, but for that very reason, excluded the need or the possibility to start out from a preestablished philosophical system, almost as if it were a matter of deducing its consequences or applying its principles to the field of aesthetics. Philosophy as such has a nature which is at the same time concrete and speculative; its statements are of value only if they are the result of a reflection on experience, and only if—insofar as they emerge no less from their contact with experience—they manage to provide schemas with which to interpret it and criteria by which to judge it. Philosophy and experience are inextricably linked, and the circle established between them is not vicious but extremely fertile, an essential requisite for the validity of philosophical thought. The aesthetic theory proposed in this publication both draws on and returns to the aesthetic experience, in keeping with the abovementioned notion of philosophy as based on the inseparability of experience and reflection, and thus paves the way to ever-new input and ever-new developments. It is rooted in a living contact with aesthetic experience as may be deduced from both the industriousness of artists, studied as much in terms of their actual production as in their precious reflections and statements on it, and from the activity of art readers, performers, and critics, as well as from the attitude of producers and contemplators of beauty wherever it may be found, be it in the natural or the practical and intellectual spheres.

And just as the starting point for this approach to aesthetics was not a preestablished philosophical system but firsthand and direct experience, likewise its point of arrival could not but be a general concept of art, presented as concluded and definitive but, as it were, a concept deemed *operative*: one far removed from any claim to envelop and sum up the *essence* of art once and for all, but one that might be used as a *regulative* and orientating principle within the artistic experience. In other words, a concept that—being the result of an investigation of aesthetic experience, aimed at qualifying its sense and potential—was therefore capable of providing valid criteria for it to be penetrated and assessed. The aesthetic theory proposed in this book is thus not a metaphysics of art, but rather an analysis of the aesthetic experience: not a definition of art considered in abstract terms as an end in itself, but a study of man making art and in the act of making art. In other words, a philosophical reflection carried out on aesthetic experience with a view to problematizing it as a whole, to highlighting its potential, to marking out its territory and confines, to clarifying its human significance and developing its scope for universality.

Herein we find both the systematic and open nature of this theory, along with its capacity to resist being bogged down in supervenient theories, but rather to draw inspiration from them for its further consolidation. In the face of contrasting theories, it was instead able to offer a conceptual framework in which to place them, avoiding their preconceived rejection, and providing a field of thought within which to embark on a discussion of ideas with a view to their reciprocal enhancement and exploration. This explains how it managed to maintain its relevance even after several decades, holding out against the onset of the vehement waves of various Marxist, psychoanalytical, sociological, and structuralist art theories. It must be said that this theory puts forward a theory of art which is classical enough to absorb the inherent requirements of those currents, yet also precise enough to be used to offset their reductionist tendencies: in art, they intensely and almost exclusively accentuate historical, material, social, anthropological, and cultural conditioning, to the point that the works are often considered no more than mere documents, stripped of that truly artistic quality which instead the present theory never ceases to demand and to point out, just as it is always ready to reaffirm the profoundly human nature of art compared to formalistic theories which at times seem to regain favor in certain circles.

Just a word to recall the twofold nature of this book, which is strictly philosophical yet at the same time open to everyone. It is a philosophical text, yet despite dealing with aesthetics and issues of art, it could be entirely retranscribed in terms of general philosophy, also applicable to other fields of experience, and so readers versed in philosophy are invited to approach it from this point of view. Nevertheless—in keeping with the idea that, even to deal with his own issues, the philosopher must and can make use of a common language—it does not draw on technical or specialist terminology, and thus may be read by one and all, even by those who do not have a strictly philosophical training, especially if they have a mind to focus on the less general parts and those closest to their own experiences.

Of course, the book is very systematic and demands consideration in this systematicity by those who wish to have a strictly philosophical understanding of it. But it is written in such a way that it might be read partially or by dipping into it here and there, for every point constitutes an independent and complete treatment, in such a way that each single section may be considered whole in its own right.

In this preface, it may be useful to provide an outline that serves as a guide to the reading of the book. The central concept is that of formativity, understood as the inseparable coupling of production and invention: "to form" means "to make" by inventing both the "way of making," that is, "to create," proceeding only by repeated attempts toward its achievement and thereby producing works that are "forms." It studies formativity in human activity as a whole, picking out that formative nature in every operation of mankind in which it is both production and invention together in the abovementioned sense. But it then stops to ponder most of all what characteristics this formativity takes on once it is specified in art itself.

In art, formativity is specified by endowing itself with contents, matter, and law. The *contents* are the entire life of the artist, that is, his personality in the act of constituting himself not only as the formative energy but even the "way of forming," or rather "style," and of being present in the work only in terms of style. This invites us to go beyond the age-old quarrel between contentism and formalism, for in art the spirit is style and the style is spirit, allowing us to avoid any disquisition on the concept of "expression": in art there is nothing more to be said than the making, or rather the making itself is a way of saying. *Matter* is, perforce, physical matter; once we become aware of this necessity, we may cut out any dispute on technique and manifestation, for in art, *to form* means forming matter, and the work is nothing but formed matter. In the artistic process, the definition of the formative intention and the adoption, interpretation, and formation of matter are one and the same thing, meaning that in the work, body and soul become identified in one another: spirituality and physicality are thus the same thing. Lastly, the *law* of art is its own achievement: the artist has no other law than the individual rule of the work being made, nor any other guide than the foretaste of its successful completion. Hence the work is, at the same time, the law and result of a formation process; only in this way may it be understood how in art, not only are attempt and organization in accordance, but they even refer to one another and join forces, since the work acts as a formant even prior to its existence as a formed entity.

In order to grasp the artistic value of the work, we therefore need to consider it as a formed form and a forming form at the same time, that is, as a law of the process of which it is also the result: making it the object of not so much a genetic as rather a dynamic consideration, since art is both a *facere* and a *perficere*, and the work unveils its own irreplaceable perfection only to those capable of grasping it in the process by which it adapts to itself. Only then does the work appear unmodifiable in its "completeness," fertile in its "exemplarity," and we may see just how absurd it is to imprison it within a supposed insularity without a trace of the stages of the process that it concludes and continues to include, unaware of that fabric which unites the various works as a continuation of styles, schools, and traditions. And it is only then that we may truly "interpret" and "judge" the work, because on the one hand to interpret means to execute, and to execute means to render and bring the work to life as it itself desires; on the other hand, to judge means to compare the work as it is with what it itself wished to be. And both are only possible if we approach the work as a law unto itself.

As all human activities are formative, herein lies the potential for beauty in every work, be it speculative, practical, or utilitarian, without that leading to aestheticism. Knowledge too is formative, just as knowledge is sensitive, capable of grasping the "thing," producing or rather "forming" its image, in such a way that this may be "successful," that is, that it may reveal and grasp, and indeed is the thing. The "process" of knowing is therefore the "interpretation" in which we attempt to produce the image that makes the thing, and the "success" of this knowing lies in "contemplation," where image and thing identify with one another in a single form; from here we have the possibility of natural beauty—for things are beautiful insofar as they are seen as forms—and to reach so far, we need to know how to interpret them, penetrate them, and devise a revelatory image. This also gives rise to a doctrine of interpretation, viewed as "knowledge of forms by a person," that is, at the same time personal and revelatory, which is as it were infinite. This on the one hand opens up a path toward a general theory of interpretation, considered originary and therefore intrinsic to every human operation and relation; and on the other, it explains the manifold interpretability of artworks and how the execution of a work may be neither unique nor arbitrary, for it is always a person in flesh and blood who, from his point of view, tries to render and bring to life the work as *it itself* wishes.

This is the general outline of the book, which nevertheless also deals with a great number of issues specific to aesthetics. We might at least cite the following by way of example. First of all, the problems presented by the complex and adventurous process by which the artist, by attempting and correcting and redoing, produces the work: inspiration, practice, and improvisation; the dialogue with matter and the dominion achieved over it through the obedience it demands; the technique and language of art, and the inherited, transmittable aspect of it: the artistic process as it progresses from the "outline" to the "sketch" right through to the finished work. Furthermore, the work's relationship with its forerunners and with the figure of the artist and his biography; the relationship between technical problems and spiritual contents; the correspondence between the style and the historical/personal humanity that comes into artistic existence here; the "world" of the artist as it is revealed through the *form*. Issues are dealt with posed by the very reality and life history of the artwork: the division and distinction between the arts; the possibility for translations, transcriptions, reductions, and reproductions; alterations to the physical consistency of the work, such as mutilations, the wearing down of the materials, human negligence, the sheen of time; the training of the artist through the teaching of technique, instruction in rules and the imitation of models, the very possibility for learning, of precepts and imitation, along with their positive and negative outcomes; the schools, styles, genres, tradition, and the potential of the history of art. And further still: the communicative and social nature of art; its relationship with nature and with the various activities of man, such as the relationships between art and morals and between art and philosophy; the issue of aestheticism in its various forms; the profoundly human interest aroused by art. Lastly, the distinction between aesthetics and poetics, and the multitude of the poetics and programs of art; not to mention the issues relative to access to artworks: taste in its universality and personality; the scope for the interpretation of the work; the "faithfulness" or "freedom" of its execution; the relationship between personal interpretation and judgment on the artistic value; the public execution of the artwork; the issue of criticism and the equal admissibility of all critical methods; and the both historical and speculative nature of aesthetics.

This book was partly preempted and partly followed by other books by the author; *I problemi dell'estetica*, *Teoria dell'arte*, *L'esperienza artistica* (Milan: Marzorati, 1966, 1965, and 1974), and *Conversazioni di estetica* (Milan: Mursia, 1966), which may be viewed as useful supplements to this book.

The Specification of Art[2]

1. What is Aesthetics

Aesthetics would appear to occupy one of those outlying or marginal areas of philosophy in which it is unclear just where the philosophical discourse starts and ends, and where one may wonder whether its own technicians and experts might not in fact have more right than philosophers to speak of it, or in this case the creators, contemplators, and judges of beauty and of art.

This position of aesthetics is undoubtedly interesting and thought-provoking, if not indeed privileged, given that philosophical thought makes its appearance, tackling concrete and clearly defined issues in such a way as to demonstrate its utility and efficacy even to the layman: one by one, problems arise from the boundless experience of the production and contemplation of beauty. Philosophical reflection, having brought them into focus, then resolves them by drawing on universal and systematic insights, while at the same time constantly renewing itself. There is no fear that this might disperse the unity and systematicity of philosophical thought, or that it might drag them down to the level of trivial or secondary issues. First of all, aesthetics is not a part of philosophy, but rather philosophy as a whole focused on the issues of beauty and art; secondly, the specific issues of aesthetics, by dint of being particular, do not cease to be philosophical at all, and by no means give way—in terms of difficulty—to more general issues, committed as they are to a more immediate and peremptory verifiability of the solutions offered. It may rather be said that aesthetics is a fortuitous example of the meeting point between two paths of philosophical reflection: the path leading up, which draws universal results from meditation on concrete experience, and the path leading down, which draws on these results in order to interpret experience and resolve the problems it presents. Indeed, aesthetics clearly shows that the two paths cannot be separated from one another, for in philosophy, experience is at the same time the object of reflection and verification of thought, while thought is the result and guide of the interpretation of experience.

But this position of aesthetics, if it is not outlined with clarity and unequivocally subtracted from all ambiguity, may give rise to dangerous misunderstandings. It's clear that the result first of all is the impossibility of artificially deducing an aesthetic from a predefined philosophical system, independently of the artistic experience, as if the philosopher could frame the phenomena of art in a procrustean bed of a philosophy all ready to go. But this understandable reaction to philosophy as vacuous abstractness often degenerates into diffidence with regard to pure speculation, and the comprehensible recall to the enlivening contact with experience often looks like abandonment to the coarsest form of empiricism. On the pretext of concreteness and experience, the last word is given to critics and artists at the expense of philosophers: being an artist or a critic thus becomes the only merit on which to discuss matters of aesthetics. Aesthetics ends up losing its philosophical nature, and therefore also its confines and autonomy, coming to be identified with the practice of criticism itself, or with poetics, that is, with the specific programs of art, or even worse, running the risk—as often occurs—of becoming the stage of inconclusive and amateurish divagations.

2 This text is the translation of the chapter "Specificazione dell'arte" from Luigi Pareyson, *Estetica. Teoria della formatività* (Milan: Tascabili Bompiani, 1954), 15–27.

The fact is that the vacuous verbalism is not corrected by turning it into brute empiricism: setting aside aesthetics for artists and critics as such is an error symmetrical to that of allowing philosophers to construct aesthetics independently of the artistic experience, merely deducing it from a presupposed philosophy. It's entirely true that the philosopher, alone, is not capable of formulating an aesthetic: he must draw on aesthetic experience, and the most direct testimonies of it are provided—apart from by the contemplators and lovers of beauty, both natural and intellectual—by none less than artists and critics, whose declarations are not only extremely useful (I might even say essential and indispensable), given that the philosopher cannot speak of art except by expanding the discourse of the artist and the critic onto a speculative level. But it is also true that the discourses artists and critics make on art as such are not yet philosophical, and so bringing them into aesthetics as such means inverting terms and confusing levels, which does not sound at all like a limitation of the artist or critic, occupied as they are in the immense undertaking of making and judging art: one would remain in the field of notation, highly concrete and perhaps extremely acute, yet detached and rhapsodic, unaware of universality and systematicity: extremely useful to the philosopher, yet in need of investigation, clarification, verification as well as of both speculative and systematic elaboration.

We thus need to recognize that aesthetics is philosophy, and it is only its status as philosophy that may justify its research and maintain its autonomy; however, we also need to acknowledge that this does not mean at all that it must be lost in the clouds of sterile abstraction and abandon any familiarity with experience. Aesthetics, just like the whole of philosophy after all, has both a speculative and a concrete nature: concrete insofar as it draws on experience and keeps to it, resolutely forbidding itself from failing to take it into account in its deductions, speculative insofar as it rises above experience in order to reflect on it, viewing it as its own object, carefully preventing itself from sinking down to its level or identifying with it; concrete insofar as only its own problems are drawn exclusively from the firsthand context of aptly interrogated experience, speculative insofar as it sets out to define the value, meaning, foundation, and possibility of experience itself. And what's most important is that these two characteristics are indivisible, so once artificially separated, they degenerate and lose their nature: it's not real speculation but empty abstractness, that which is not focused on experience, drawing its problems from it and verifying its own solutions within it. It is not concreteness but confused empiricism, that which does not maintain a due distance from experience in order to reflect on it and to theorize its possibility. Aesthetics is constituted by this twofold reference to the speculative nature of philosophical reflection and to its vital contact with experience: that reflection which is not aesthetics, not being fueled by the experience of art and beauty, is boiled down to no more than a word game; nor is it that experience of art or of beauty which, not having been elaborated on a speculative level, ventures no further than description.

Aesthetics thus lies at the meeting point between philosophy and experience, carefully avoiding any confusion and any illegitimate intrusion. Only on the basis of this explicit clarification may its position become a fertile meeting point, in which on the one hand the philosophers and, on the other, the artists, historians, and critics, not to mention psychologists, sociologists, pedagogues, technicians, engineers, and so on may intervene on a level footing, each bringing their own sensi-

3 Editor's note. The notion of *operosità* is extremely difficult to convey in English and unfortunately the translator of the text is at present unable to pursue their thoughts on this problematic term. Over the course of intense discussion, the terms *endeavour*, *activity*, *operativity*, *laboriousness*, and even *being-at-work* were proposed, with *industriousness* being the final choice. This word, like all the others, only partially captures the special nuances of meaning with which Pareyson endows *operosità*, but it does at least refer both to a doing and to the result of this doing. Gilles Tiberghien encountered similar difficulties for the French edition, his note—which is both that of a translator and a connoisseur of Pareyson's œuvre—proving particularly enlightening: "The notion of *operosità* is very important in Pareyson's discourse and he refers to it throughout the book. It designates the whole of human activity, both real and virtual, the entirety of human working [*l'œuvrer*], as well as the ability to (make a/do) work [*œuvrer*]; it is a doing that involves both the desire and the drive to do—both of which are intrinsic to humanity—together with the doing itself and its results." Tiberghien chose to translate it into French as *pouvoir opéral* ("operal power"). Luigi Pareyson, *Esthétique. Théorie de la formativité*, trans. Gilles A. Tiberghien (Paris: ULM, 2007), 32 (trans. David Radzinowicz).

tivity and competence from their field, yet all remembering they have to produce philosophy, which as such must be in contact with art, that is, that they have to draw on that extremely fertile point in which philosophy and experience, by virtue of being indissolubly joined, are also clearly distinct and not interchangeable.

2. The Issue of the Specification of Art

Saying that aesthetics is a philosophical reflection on the aesthetic experience does not mean being trapped in a circle, given that aesthetics draws on the entirety of experience, and if duly examined, will be sure to show and point out—within its vast field—the aspects or the areas that have an aesthetic or artistic nature. After all, art—like any other activity—would never come to define itself as a specific operation if the entire spiritual sphere did not contain and prepare it in some way, or if the entirety of experience did not already have its own aesthetic and artistic nature: as an operation inherent to artists, art cannot but emerge from the intentional and programmatic accentuation to be found throughout human experience, and which accompanies—indeed, constitutes—every display of human industriousness (*operosità*).

This activity, which is generically inherent to all experience, and which—if appropriately specified—constitutes that which we rightfully call art, is "formativity," that is, a sort of *making* which, as it makes, also devises the "way of making": production which is at the same time and indivisibly invention. All aspects of human industriousness, from the simplest to the most complex, have this irremovable and fundamental aspect of formativity. Human activities cannot be performed if not in the concrete form of operations, that is, in movements destined to culminate in works. However, it is only by taking on form that the work may become such, in its individual and unrepeatable reality, now detached from its creator and living a life of its own, brought together in the indivisible unity of its coherence, open to the acknowledgment of its value and capable of demanding and obtaining it: no activity is productive if it is not also formative, and no successful work is not also form.

Every operation implies first of all a *making*: there is no operation if not through completing, performing, producing, and building (*realizzando*). There are operations in which this executionary and constructive (*realizzativo*) aspect is visible, if not indeed on full view, as in the production of objects; less evident, yet not for this reason less effective, is its presence in other operations, such as in those for example which are only concerned with thinking or acting: even the exercise of thought and moral activity call for a *making*, without which they would not be expressed in concrete practices or thoughts. We cannot think if not by carrying out movements of thought with which we pass from judgment to judgment, from reasoning to reasoning, connecting and sorting here and there; in other words, putting together a complete totality, and above all explicitly formulating thoughts, that is, articulating them as propositions. Likewise, everyday life unfolds through movements that define and outline—or rather depict—ideals, goals, tasks, and intentions, and through movements that execute and implement actions, habits, and natures. Thus, both thought and moral life require the exercise of that constructive and productive activity without which no operation is possible.

Furthermore, as works are always single, it may be said that it is impossible to make them without thereby also inventing the way in which they are to be made. Whatever the activity is that one intends to practice, it is always a matter of posing problems, constituting them originally from the formless data of experience, and finding, discovering, or rather inventing their solutions; it is always a matter of concluding operations, bringing them to completion, that is, of producing by implementing, completing, and executing, and capturing that movement of invention in a work that is sketched out and put together on the basis of an internal law of organization; it's always a question of making and inventing the way of making at the same time, so that the execution is the application of the individual rule of the work in the very act which is its discovery, and so that the work is "successful" insofar as, through its making, the way in which it must be made is found.

In brief, whatever the specific nature of the activity may be, operating always entails that process of production and invention which forming consists of, for all successful works are forms endowed with independence and exemplarity.

3. The Aesthetic Nature of the Entirety of Experience

The fact that art in the strict sense needs to emerge from this generic and common formativity appears clear first of all from the fact that it is indeed on the basis of the latter that we may say there's an essentially "artistic" aspect to the whole of the spiritual sphere. By virtue of the fact that in the whole of human industriousness there is an inventive and innovatory side as a primary condition for any form of realization, and it is for this very reason that there may be art in every human activity, indeed there is the art *of* every human activity. It takes art to do anything: in all fields it's a matter of "making *with* art," that is, of fueling with inventiveness and ensuring the success of any *making* present in a given operation. In other words, from the most humble of techniques right up to the greatest of inventions, there is the deployment of formativity, and therefore the need for art.

Furthermore, it's the very formative nature of the entire sense of human industriousness that explains how we can speak of beauty with regard to any work: since there is no work which is not also form, we may understand how every successful work is always also beautiful. Just as the creation of any value is impossible without the creation of artistic value, likewise the evaluation of any work is impossible without an aesthetic appreciation. When we say, for example, that a moral action, a virtue, a characteristic, a reasoning, a demonstration, or an essay are "beautiful" or "fine," we may think that in these cases, the predication of beauty or fineness might have an exclusively metaphorical nature and thus be stripped of its proper meaning. Of an action that has a clear moral value, we often speak of it as a fine act, and speaking of good souls, we often say that they are embellished with virtues, and of a person with a benevolent disposition, cordial and jovial, we may say he has a fine character, and often we speak of fine reasoning, or in the case of a particularly successful demonstration, carried out with a linear development and a faithful exposition of the theme that reconciles simplicity and completeness in pondered equilibrium, we might attribute the quality of elegance, while in an essay, we might admire the harmony of the construction on which, with skilled suppleness, the thought revolves, penetrating and exploring the topic while holding it all together with solid and indivisible cohesion.

In these cases, we are certainly proceeding toward an aesthetic judgment, and thus we are quite right to make use of such language, for we are speaking here of successful works, and the work—whatever the activity carried out in its creation may be—cannot succeed except by becoming a form, defined and coherent, for no activity, be it moral or speculative, may be expressed in works unless it deploys that process of invention and production that forming consists of. Now, the nature of the form is none other than its contemplability, that is, its beauty, and so the very process of interpretation with which we come to make a moral or speculative appreciation of a practical work or one of thought also gives rise to the emergence of the nature of the form which it inevitably possesses, and therefore to an aesthetic appreciation.

While there is no work that, albeit not explicitly artistic, is not form, the very act by which it is appreciated and evaluated as a work ensures that it is appreciated and evaluated in terms of form: the aesthetic evaluation coincides with the specific appreciation—without, however, becoming identical to it. Considering the practical and speculative value of a moral work or one of thought also entails considering its aesthetic value, as it means acknowledging that only with an effort of invention and production was it possible to achieve the creation of the work, that is, it is only as a form that it is and can be a work, and more precisely, a moral work or one of thought. That's why, just as one grasps the singular moral or speculative value produced by such works, one often sits in contemplation before them: the theoretical or practical value of those works does not appear before me without its aesthetic value also and at the same time doing so; seeing them as works means also seeing them as forms, and so contemplating their beauty means enjoying such contemplation. Here is a case in which the beautiful coincides each time with the good and the true without its meaning's being absorbed by them, and in which goodness and truth appear as beauty without being reduced to it. There is no confusion of values, and we may speak of the beauty *of* the good and *of* the true, indeed of goodness and truth *as* beauty; in other words, we may extend art to every activity and beauty to cover work, yet without falling foul of aestheticism.

In this formativity common to all the aspects of spiritual life resides the inevitably "artistic" side of every human operation, which, just as it does not oblige us to state that all spirit is undoubtedly art, likewise ensures that art in the strict sense is guaranteed the possibility of not being confused with other activities, and of constituting an autonomous and specific operation. And the principle of such autonomy and specification must be sought out and defined with care, with the awareness that it is because art could never emerge if the entire spiritual sphere had not already prepared it with its common formativity, for art must be sought in a sphere where that formativity may acquire a particular and distinct character, with its own specification and an insuppressible autonomy.

4. Specification and Concentration of Human Activity in Every Operation

The issue of the autonomy and specification of art cannot be addressed without at least a passing mention of the more vast and complex issue of the unity and distinctness of human activity. If art is determined as a specification of the formativity common to all spiritual life, there is an element of *distinction* between the activities, according to which it is *a* distinct activity, and its operation is *not* that of science, of philosophy, of morality; if formativity, the specification of which gives rise to art, is inherent in all forms of spiritual life, it is because there is an element in *unity* between the activities, and so every operation, whatever the specific activity may be, nevertheless involves the deployment of *all* the others.

If human activities cannot be performed except by making operations of them, these operations in turn cannot be defined if not as an act which both separates and conjoins the activities. Every human operation is always *either* speculative or practical *or* formative, but whatever its specification may be, it is always a combination of thought and morality and formativity. An operation is not determined except by specifying an activity *among* others, but it cannot do so unless by concentrating all the other *combinations* in itself. In every operation there is, in combination, the *specification* of *one* activity and the *concentration* of *all* the activities: this is the structure of operating, in which the specification and concentration of activities go hand in hand, meaning that there is not one without the other.

The specification of activities does not by any means imply their original "distinctiveness," nor is their concentration limited to there being a "co-presence" of them in the spiritual sphere. The specification consists in stressing an activity to the point of making it *prevalent* over the others and *intentional* within an operation: the remaining activities are *subordinate* to that which is thus specified, conspiring in its intention. Nevertheless, even if they thereby forego being concretized in a specific operation, they do not therefore cease to act according to their own nature; indeed, however *subordinate* they may be, they are still *constitutive* of the specified activity which, as a specific operation, cannot do without their contribution. No human activity may be specified within an operation without the cooperation, contribution, support, and control of all the others, each of which—in the very act of subordinating itself to it—continues regardless to act in line with its own character: thinking is not possible without both acting and forming, nor is acting without both thinking and forming, and nor is forming without both thinking and acting. Depending on the condition in which they find themselves within a given operation, human activities always therefore become specific or common, prevalent or subordinate, intentional or constitutive.

The need for the concentration of all activities within a specific operation is guaranteed by the unitotality of the person, who as the creator of his own operation, puts himself into it entirely, with all his potential and aptitudes. On the other hand, if the exercise of an activity calls for it to be specified in an operation, this is not possible without an act of the person that actively impresses onto the whole of his spirituality a specifying direction, identifying within it a task to which to devote himself. Only a philosophy of the person is capable of resolving the problem of the unity and distinctness of such activities, for on the basis of the indivisibility and initiative of the person, it explains how every operation always calls for both the specification of an activity and the concentration of all the others: if the operation were of the absolute spirit, there would be no reason to distinguish between the activities, and they would all be reduced to one.

5. Art as Pure, Specific, and Intentional Formativity

That's why formativity, despite covering the entire spiritual sphere, may be specified in an intentional operation, and thus give rise to art in the true sense.

Every human operation is always formative, and even a work of thought or a practical work call for the deployment of formativity. A virtuous action must be invented as required by moral law in that given circumstance, and it must be performed and implemented at the same time with a movement that devises the best way to actualize it. In posing and resolving a problem, in deducing the consequences from a starting point, in carrying out a demonstration, in connecting reasonings within a systematic complex, we need to perform movements of thought, and with an act of invention, discover what reason requires in that specific case, and then to expressly formulate thoughts. Productive strength and inventive capacity are therefore demanded of thought and of action, for speculative and practical operations are made up of a formative activity which—in the specific field—carries out and produces works at the same time as it invents the way they are to be made.

But in art this formativity, which envelops the whole of the spiritual sphere and makes the deployment of other specific operations possible, is specified in turn; it is accentuated through a prevalence that subordinates to itself all other forms of activity: it takes on an autonomous tendency, an independent path, a specific direction, and instead of supporting the other activities in the deployment of their respective operations, it supports itself, becoming intentional and an end unto itself. In art, it is not that the person does not feel the need to form in order to think and act, but he thinks and acts solely so as to form and to be able to form. In speculative and practical works, forming is subordinate and constitutive, for in them we form in order to think and act, and it is necessary to form in order to be able to think and act. In the work of art, on the other hand, forming is intentional and prevalent, for in it we form in order to form, and thought and action are subordinate to the specific aim of formation. While every operation is always *formative,* in the sense that it cannot be itself without forming and we cannot think or act if not by forming, the artistic operation instead is *formation,* in the sense that it intentionally sets out to form, and within it, thought and action intervene exclusively so as to make it possible for it to be nothing but formation. The artistic operation is a process of invention and production deployed not in order to create speculative or practical works or whatever they may be, but only for itself: forming in order to form, forming solely by pursuing the form for its own sake: *art is pure formativity.*

Of course, "intentionality" has nothing to do with practical desire, insofar as it is not enough to wish to make art in order to manage to make it, nor may we rightly say that in order to be able to make art it is necessary to wish to make it. Naturally, being an act of personal initiative, desire also plays its role, but it is a profound and total act, one which resonates not only in the moral field but also throughout the spiritual sphere. It is an act by which the whole life of the artist is placed at the service of formativity: thoughts, reflections, actions, habits, aspirations, and loves—in other words, every aspect of his experience takes on a formative direction, pursues formative intention, and acquires formative capacity: the artist thinks, feels, sees, and acts for the sake of form. Of "desire for art" we may therefore speak only in the sense that, once the artist has impressed a formative direction onto his own spirituality, all his actions are directed toward the goal which is that of art: pure formativity, the pursuit of form as an end unto itself, forming in order to form.

6. The Intervention of Other Activities in the Artistic Operation: Thought and Morality in Art

But the act by which formativity is specified in the artistic operation entails all the other activities intervening as well. Just as in speculative and practical works, one forms in order to think and to act, and it is necessary to form in order to be able to think and act, so not only does the artist think and act for the sole purpose of forming, but in order to be able to form, it is also necessary to think and act. Forming, as is required by thought and action, cannot be pure forming if it is not supported—or indeed, constituted—by thought and morality which, despite being subordinated to the purposes of formation, do not cease to act in accordance with their own nature. In brief, the artistic operation, in order to be such—that is, pure formativity—requires thought and morality, and it includes them as constituent elements, without which it would not exist. Furthermore, it includes them as unadulterated thought and morality, not as elements resolved in the formation underway, which would be as if to say dissolved: no longer recognizable in terms of their own function.

Art is constituted of thought because pure formativity manages to carry out its own specific operation only if supported and controlled by the watchful deployment of critical thought. Without the intervention of thought, the production of the artwork would not even be possible, for while it is true that the guide to the production process cannot but be the formative intention in art, and that therefore the only criterion of judgment is the work of art itself, what connects and compares the various attempts, what judges the outcomes, discerning success from failure, what puts the possibilities to the test as they are chosen, checking them against the formative intention, what achieves the effect on the basis of the needs of the work, what weighs up the already done against the yet-to-do, and the yet-to-do against the already done at all times, what judges where it is necessary to cancel, how a correction should be made, and what must be put in its place is always thought, and at that, thought in its most pure and genuine form: that of critical judgment. The artist is the primary critic of himself, and would be unable to move forward in the formation process of the work were he not to constantly subject his own work to the judgment of critical thought, deployed not in the pauses between bouts of formation but within it and throughout its expression.

No one has ever thought of contesting the deployment of this critique within the formation of the work of art, given how clearly it emerges from the testimony of all artists; instead, it was believed that it might be reduced to figuration itself, as if it were a matter of inflexions that figuration adopts in its own exercise independently of thought. But on closer inspection, it is a matter of critical judgment and thus of unadulterated thought, which as thought, is deployed *within* the figuration, making its autonomy possible. Of course, this is not thought as an end unto itself, made intentional in the exposition of a philosophical meditation or of a scientific study, but one of thought subordinate to formative intention and regulated by the criterion of pure formativity, and which may have no other aims than to add its own *contribution* to the result of formation. However, it still remains a thought, one that does not cease to carry out its own critical function, in keeping with its own nature and character.

On the other hand, there is a constitutive morality in art, in the sense that in people's actual lives, the act of specification of art takes on a practical relevance, because it contains the individuation of a task to which to dedicate oneself and the commitment to dedicate oneself to it in the way required for its completion. Morality not only accompanies but also constitutes the artistic operation, just as it constitutes every other specific operation, meaning that a necessary condition for the realization of any form of value is morality, and every value insofar as it is deployed by a person is also a moral value. The artwork thus entails a practical commitment and a moral decision, to the point that if the artist falls short of these conditions and does not consider his art a task to be carried out in the way that it calls for as a work, as well as an artistic disvalue, he produces a moral disvalue too.

In the personal commitment to dedicate oneself to an artistic task lies acceptance of the rules and norms of formation as genuine moral laws, which the artist must observe, for he has made that initial commitment to it. Nor may it be said that in this case ethical law is resolved without a trace in aesthetic law, in the sense that it prescribes nothing if not for the artist—to be considered as such—to be an artist, that is, he must make art and nothing else. In actual fact, it is a matter of the exact opposite, that is, of poetic laws that in the concrete and personal exercise of art, become ethical laws and are made and endowed with moral significance, taking on the aspect of rules that the artist cannot violate with impunity, not only because he would cease to be an artist but also because the task to which he freely devoted himself would be compromised, and the commitment that he initially took on under his own responsibility would be betrayed.

7. Two Issues: The Contents and the Material of Art

However, here two issues arise which, if left unsolved, risk jeopardizing the whole inquiry, for one concerns the presence of the entire spiritual sphere within the artistic operation, and the other the very possibility of an autonomous artistic operation: one which is self-standing, without being subordinated to the purposes of other activities.

Speaking of a constitutive intervention of thought and morality in art, I was ultimately referring to that amount of thought and morality that the artistic operation requires as such, that is, to those particular *acts* of thought and morality that the *exercise* of art demands as a condition—one which is necessary, albeit not sufficient alone—for the realization of artistic value. But thought and morality are always the concrete thought and concrete morality of a single and unrepeatable person. They represent a personal way of thinking and acting, a particular interpretation of reality and a particular attitude toward life, an unrepeatable *Weltanschauung* and a quite singular *ethos*, whether that *Weltanschauung* remains an unconscious conception of reality, more experienced and felt than reasoned and thought through, or if it is expressed in a conscious and explicit philosophy, and whether this *ethos* emerges from an unconditional accentuation of traditional customs or from the free and original invention of a lifestyle. In other words, it concerns the whole life of the person, his particular and concrete spirituality, his single and irreplaceable experience which—on the basis of the principle of the concentration of all the activities in the specific operation—must in some way come under the concept of art, thereby posing the issue of *contents* in art: in what way do thought and morality—in the very act by which they are actively deployed—constitute the artistic operation from the inside, and in terms of personal and concrete spirituality, how do they become artistic contents?

Art is specific and intentional formativity, as we mentioned before; however, it is now necessary to establish how that specification is actually possible. And indeed, the doubt may reasonably arise as to the actual possibility of specifying formativity in a given and distinct operation. The formativity common to all spiritual life is always constitutive of a particular operation, and it seems impossible for it to be uncoupled and deployed on its own account: forming entails creating particular and specific works, that is, speculative or practical works as they may be, in such a way that it would seem there could be no art that were not the art of some particular activity, nor a form that is not the success *of* some specific operation. In this case, we would have an art of thinking, an art of living, an art of producing and so on, and the achieved works to which these arts give rise would be forms, just as unquestionably occurs after all, but there would be no art in the true sense: art that is simply art, without an ensuing genitive, that is, art as an end unto itself. In order for there to be art, it is necessary for formativity to be specified, and for forming to be no longer concerned with forming thoughts, reasonings, systems, or actions, virtues, characters, or objects useful for some predetermined end, but instead with form only, and for form to be such not as a speculative or practical work, but merely as a form which intends to be a form and nothing else. Art in the true sense therefore needs matter to form, in which to bring form into existence: otherwise pure formativity would be a mere abstraction bereft of body and consistency; it could not be deployed as a particular operation; it would not concretize in single formation processes and it would not give rise to real and existent works. Naturally, this matter must be such as not to reconvert artistic formativity into common formativity, and not to add a genitive form to art but, once formed, it must be presented as pure form: that is, form which is nothing but form. Pure formation, therefore, to confirm its own autonomy and to guarantee its own potential, must define a matter for forming, and thus we come to the issue of the *material* nature of art.

Translated from the Italian by Bennett Bazalgette, with the help of Lucy Conticello

Formativity: A Philosophy of Making

Gilles A. Tiberghien

Art theory and the philosophy of art often focus on problems which, fundamentally, either did not interest artists or which only concerned them very indirectly. Problems dealing with the judgment of taste, for instance, may be essential in criticism but appear rather ancillary to creators. This fact was already noted by John Dewey in a lecture given at Harvard in the early 1930s that he expanded into a book, *Art as Experience*, published in 1934. For Dewey the emphasis on experience is relevant as much to the work completed as to the work in process. As he wrote at the beginning of his study: "the trouble with existing theories is that they start from a ready-made compartmentalization, or from a conception of art that 'spiritualizes' it out of connection with the objects of concrete experience."[1]

In spite of the idealistic sources of an aesthetics that springs from a critical dialogue with Benedetto Croce, the idea recurs with Luigi Pareyson. Indeed, in places Pareyson is careful to point out his debt to Dewey. But prior to returning to this point I would like to demonstrate the originality of Pareyson's thinking and his contribution to the field that interests us here. This exposition will be split into six parts of varying length.

1. Formativity

In his major study *Aesthetics. The Theory of Formativity*, Pareyson reflects on what is customarily termed *creativity* with respect to artistic production—though he himself prefers to keep this term for God, since he is of the opinion that the image of the creative artist as God's equal or of God as the great artist of the cosmos are empty metaphors. As he contends: "whereas creation is absolute activity, thus unthinkable as such in humankind, formativity is an activity with a receptive character and is composed of trial and error, to the point that it becomes inoper-

1 John Dewey, *Art as Experience* (New York: Perigee, 1980), 11.

able if it is not sparked by an impulse, an impetus [*spunto*] and remains incomplete if it does not culminate in a success, something certainly unthinkable for God."[2] This receptive quality lies at the heart of actuation in the field of human creativity, a notion that can have little meaning in the theological realm.

Formativity is thus a complex movement relating at once to aesthetic reception and to activities of *poiesis*, understood as the producer of its object. On the formative side, as it were, the issue here is not a theory of formation in which to form would be limited to producing something conceived upstream. Neither is it a question of realizing a preplanned project for which it is enough to observe a series of ordained rules. In question here is a pattern of thought around making and/or doing that does not operate by following a matrix or a predetermined mold but by inventing its own way of making and the rules it obeys. One may then, Pareyson writes, call an operation formative insofar as one can say of its result that it is well made, not because it followed the rules, but in that it forged its own rule instead of applying a preexisting one. This definition leads to that of "forming," a definition which imposed itself in Pareyson's thinking from the outset and which he will continue to employ almost altered in all his writings dealing with it: "'To form' means to make, but to do so in such manner that, while doing so, it invents its own way of making."[3]

The definition as stated needs to be unpacked to avoid falling into a number of misinterpretations or erroneous meanings that would make formativity into a theory that treats solely of art or what is customarily called art. The theory in fact concerns every sphere of human activity, even if it applies especially aptly to art. This is the case because all human activity is a production of forms—technical, moral, historical, etc.

"Every operation," writes Pareyson, "implies first of all a 'making': there is no operation if not through completing, performing, producing, and building (*realizzando*). There are operations in which this executionary and constructive (*realizzativo*) aspect is visible, if not indeed on full view, as in the production of objects; less evident, yet not for this reason less effective, is its presence in other operations, such as in those for example which are only concerned with thinking or acting: even the exercise of thought and moral activity call for a 'making', without which they would not be expressed in concrete practices or thoughts."[4]

Thus, a properly artistic quality exists in any human operation worthy of the name and in whatever domain, because there is always execution and invention. Basically: "It takes art to do anything: in all fields it's a matter of 'making *with* art', that is, of fueling with inventiveness and ensuring the success of any 'making' present in a given operation. In other words, from the most humble of techniques right up to the greatest of inventions, there is the deployment of formativity, and therefore the need for art."[5]

Whether one is doing the cooking or the housework, repairing pipework or rewiring, whether one is sorting out files or pondering a treatise on style, a certain power of invention is mobilized within oneself on which the execution of each task undertaken depends. Each of us has our own way of doing things, however stereotyped the gestures we have learned in our chosen trade. Yet despite this it is from the unique fashion in which such gestures are appropriated that stems

2 Luigi Pareyson, *Esthétique. Théorie de la formativité*, trans. Gilles A. Tiberghien and Rita di Lorenzo (Paris: Editions rue d'Ulm, 2007), 278.
3 Luigi Pareyson, *Esistenza e persona* (Genoa: Il Melangolo, 1985), 222; see also Pareyson, *Esthétique*, 59.
4 Luigi Pareyson, "The Specification of Art", in this anthology, 31.
5 Ibid., 32.

from an authentically inventive character and on which their success relies. As John Dewey puts it: "art is a quality of doing and of what is done. When we say that tennis-playing, singing, acting, and a multitude of other activities are arts, we engage in an elliptical way of saying that there is art *in* the conduct of these activities, and that this art so qualifies what is done and made as to induce activities in those who perceive them in which there is also art."[6] With the proviso that one must understand that this is so only because human beings participate in this product, that is, because behind it, there stands a person, Pareyson would say.

Now the marked artistic quality of all human activity does not mean that each of these activities is (an) art, or that everyone is an artist. What Pareyson wants to bring out is that there is an operative character in all human activity—a term that tries to translate Pareyson's *operosità*, with which he designates every human activity, not only real but also virtual—everything that relates to the way in which humans make works, as well as their capacity to do so. This operosità can also be defined as a making, a doing that implies at the same time the drive and the need to make, since both are integral to human beings. Any operation, artistic or no, implies trial and error and aims at a result, that is, at its execution. Every operation has its laws and pursues an end: its processes must be regulated in accordance with such laws and in view of such finalities. The work is accomplished only insofar as it conforms to this frame of laws and to this finality. Yet, at the same time, since they are formative, these operations, while the work is in the course of execution, require that an individual rule be invented: in this, it necessarily proceeds by increments. For the legitimacy or the finality of the work to become the individual rule during an operation calls for an act of invention that progressively reveals the way in which work must and can be made whilst it is being made. This discovery, however, occurs gradually—that is, by devising a range of potential solutions until the most appropriate to the situation and to the rational imperative of the maker emerges. Thus, writes Pareyson: "The *attempt* passes from the sphere of research to that of discovery, from the field of free inventiveness to that of rational necessity, precisely when the laws and the rational specific to the operation intervene to sanction the putative solution."[7]

In a formative movement, invention and attempts always go hand in hand and it might even be said that what characterizes formativity is that it is always an inventive "tentative" (a neologism designed to translate *tentativo*). The same applies to nonartistic operations, but there the result has to conform to the aims of a specific operation. In cooking, for example, the leeway is large and the possibilities many, but in the end, we still want to succeed in preparing a given dish. To do so will also require art—or skill. Even when the task is simply to put into practice an already formed idea, writes Pareyson, or to carry out a predefined project, "formativity intervenes in a certain manner, not only because it is a question of 'knowing' how to create, and of inventing ways in which the idea is to be executed, but also because all projects are tested and put through their paces during their realization and execution." Nothing can be done or made successfully unless, at some degree or other, it is made or done inventively.

This theory proves especially interesting, for example, for designers, architects, and landscapists. Landscape designers have a dynamic relationship with form without themselves being artists, in the sense that, since every activity is formative and thus landscaping is too, form is not its sole object. The project is a kind of

6 Dewey, *Art as Experience*, 213.

7 Pareyson, *Esthétique*, 63.

material metaphor, a physical vehicle for intuition. Techniques provide means of this transformation; it is intuition transforming or materializing itself. Pareyson demonstrates how generally the technique is imbued with the project, driven by inventive dynamism whenever it is not "the result of a mechanical and extrinsic application of preestablished rules." Because then, and as opposed to those who dissociate design and execution, "the person executing is not satisfied with *transferring* the project; they interpret it in an inventive way, truly making it live in the real."[8] Thus the techniques, just like the means of execution, form an integral part of the project, so the originator—in this case, the landscape designer—cannot entirely rely on another to undertake an implementation that otherwise risks becoming purely extrinsic and mechanical. "Execution should then be an extension of the very conception of the project, in the sense that it ought not only to interpret its operational capacity, but also condition it by modifying the idea in the course of realization."[9] Even where technology and the mastery of the means employed would seem to ensure the realization of the project, Pareyson states, there is still place for formativity. Thus, those activities that are often delegated to supposed specialists assumed to have no more than a technical and subordinate role whereas they are in fact an integral part of the process itself, also belong to world of formativity.

This is why this aesthetics is also highly pertinent to all other fields of making, whatever they may be: "The result is a vast and inexhaustible field of study for aesthetics, which until now has limited its scope narrowly to art due to a process of amputation as fatal as it is artificial." This state of affairs has deprived us of useful tools that would allow for a more acute appreciation of the role of formativity. Conversely, by taking into account activities regarded as accessory with respect to art, or even simply completely devoid of art, the field of formativity could rehabilitate "the world of 'arts and crafts,' which range from the efforts of the humblest workman to the masterpieces of the most skillful craftsperson—a world that is usually but wrongfully relegated to that of mere technique." It has to be understood, however, that: "Any production, when it is not simply standardized, sets aside, requires even, a certain margin for formativity, so that, above and beyond its products whose frosty, inert 'perfection' is merely the result of a mechanical, extrinsic application of preestablished rules, there always remains the possibility of works, which, while still only the implementation of projects in accordance with acknowledged rules, betray a singular liveliness, an inherent vivacity."[10]

This is the case because the one who executes does not limit themselves to copying out the project: they interpret it inventively, making it live in reality so it becomes distinct from mass-produced objects in series or what Pareyson calls "servile implementations."

2. Person and Interpretation

To understand the theory under consideration, the central question of interpretation needs to be addressed, even if here cannot be the place to rehearse the entire hermeneutic tradition to which it is attached but from which it can be differentiated.[11] In the way the craftsman, handyman, or artist forms or transforms their object also stems from how they, like any person, is able to transform themselves.

8 Ibid., 65.
9 Ibid., 64.
10 Ibid., 78–79.
11 From Schleiermacher to Gadamer, via Heidegger and on occasion Paul Ricœur.

Formativity relates to knowledge derived from the senses, since to form is to know and one cannot know without forming. Yet one cannot know without interpreting, resulting in the following definition of interpretation: "interpreting is that form of knowledge in which, on the one side, receptiveness and activity are indissociable, and, on the other, what is known is a form and the knower a person."[12] For it is only by and through persons that interpretation is possible. A person is not the same as an individual or a subject: its identity cannot be definitively defined as regards external characteristics. Person is not a term, an end: it is a relation with self and others. Moreover, interpretation through engaging the person cannot be limited to the aesthetic field. Persons and works can exchange properties, since, as Pareyson writes in *Esistenza e Persona*, "every work draws its independence precisely from its character as a personality, while the person is in its turn work, or more precisely, work of and on the self, made from the self and constructed through its works."[13] Pareyson's theory contends that the knowledge of things as well as of persons is predicated on a constant dialogue. Thus, to argue that people speak about dumb objects is insufficient, since, on closer examination and considering them from the point of view of their plasticity, as singular, open and mobile, objects too might be regarded as strictly defined totalities, to the point that interpreting them becomes no more straightforward than interpreting people. To know a person implies exchange and reciprocity; it is both an encounter and an adventure. But to know a thing is also to question it, to cast on it "a gaze that is also an unspoken interaction."[14]

Thus, Pareyson argues: "Viewing 'things' as 'persons' offers corroboration of the impossibility of reducing people to 'things.'" In consequence, just as it is not possible to know a person if one reduces them to the status of pure object, "similarly it is not possible to know things if they are not personified, that is, if one does not regard them in their primal, animated independence."[15] Because any person is, for itself, a form in the process of being formed, and, to be understood, every form presupposes interpretation by a person. In the person as Pareyson considers it, "singularity and universality not only complement each other, they imply each other in essence."[16] At the root of this universal singularity lies initiative. It is initiative that bestows concrete value on the person by embodying it in action and providing it with a historical dimension. But initiative is not *sponte sua*. Initiative cannot initiate itself; it is as it were initiated, initiated by something else. And it is this that is the sign of our finitude. Only a God would harbor his own beginning in himself. It is now clearer why Pareyson reserves the term *creation* to Him alone. Initiative always proceeds from an activity and a receptivity qualifying it. It is with respect to one or another thing that I create and to create I need a starting point, the famous *spunto* to which I will return below. Humankind does not create ex nihilo: every initiative is always "sparked, suggested, set into motion" by something else. This does not mean that, as we form, we obey external causality. It is because we are already so inclined that we act as we do and what some might take for a cause is in fact only an occasion, an opportunity to develop what we already bear within us. "Otherwise stimulus and starting point would not be what they are and reception would not even exist: the stimulus is only a stimulus in so far as it is received, in a reaction, a starting point only if it is apprehended as an opportunity for developing something."[17]

Through initiative, such personal opportunity goes beyond the person and becomes work. The person is central because it lies at the heart of interpretation,

12 Ibid., 190.
13 Pareyson, *Esistenza e Persona*, 201.
14 Pareyson, *Esthétique*, 220.
15 Ibid.
16 Pareyson, *Esistenza e Persona*, 178.
17 Pareyson, *Esthétique*, 191.

without which formativity cannot be understood. Speaking of interpretation, one thinks at once of my, of your, of their interpretation. This shows that interpretation is inevitably interpretation by somebody, a personal activity by an interpreter. In the same way, it should also be stressed how the object of interpretation, because interpretation is always of something, is an activity that grapples with a specific object. And the truth of interpretation always lies in a continuous process diffracted as it were in the person of each interpreter. Both works and persons are thus involved in an unending process.

"The workingness [*operare*] of the person is a plasmatore, modeling forms [*plasmare forme*]," writes Pareyson in *Estetica. Teoria della Formatività*. "Indeed, if the person is a totality, infinite but defined, each of its operations aims to result in works that are in their turn defined and complete, which live a life of their own and which can develop on their own terms and generate new developments and fuel new processes. [...] It is precisely because a person is their own work, and thus form, that works that are the result of its operations are in their turn forms, complete, singular, and exemplary."[18]

3. Technics and Material

Though highly original, this theory has roots in the history of thought and philosophy, in authors such as Goethe and Schelling, with whom Pareyson dialogued during his whole life, as well as in a poet and art theorist like Paul Valéry, to whom he will devote two important articles on sound and meaning and on the creative virtues of rules.[19]

Concurring with a frequently repeated axiom of Valéry's, Pareyson writes that the point is not to "apply rules in their extrinsic normalcy, but to return them to their roots as *poiesis*, to restore their inventive character, to observe them in their operative effectiveness, while remaining conscious that, if rules inherited from an external world that has ceased living are dead letter, equally it is nonetheless true that nothing can be made, be done, without rules."[20]

In contrast to the idealist aesthetics of a Croce, who saw material solely as the locus of an objective manifestation of intuition-expression that alone can be subjected to aesthetic judgment, Pareyson ceaselessly affirms the importance of material. If, as Valéry rightly affirms, poetry is at once sound and meaning, no work can be thought of independently from the material composing it. This does not mean that the interlock between form and matter results from a priori adjustment, but rather that form can be found only by way of a series of attempts (*tentativi*), trials, approximations in the course of which it discovers the material corresponding to it and the techniques it calls for. Moreover, the work makes a virtue of necessity by embracing the constraints it encounters—even at the risk they may not always be overcome. Success here inevitably unfolds against the backdrop of potential failure, the inventiveness of the artist treating material resistance, and the obstacles encountered as a law presiding over the work's formation.

This idea recurs with Gaston Bachelard, for whom imagination itself is profoundly material and cannot be divorced from its means of execution. From this stems the distinction the philosopher draws between a purely intellectual project—a kind of

18 Ibid., 184.

19 In *L'esperienza artistica* (Milan: Marzorati, 1974), reprinted in *Problemi dell'estetica* (Milan: Mursia), as Opere complete, 2000, vol. 11; *L'esthétique de Paul Valéry*, trans. Ricardo Pineiri (Montpellier: Théétète, 2002). I published a first abridged French translation in *Recherches Poïétiques*, no. 5 (Winter 1997–98), and no. 8 (Spring 1999).

20 Pareyson, *Esthétique*, 81.

more or less vague intention or plan devised without account of the place and the means of its realization—and what he names a "material project." In the latter, the creative imagination truly engages with substance, in a manner entirely different from a purely intellectual plan. "The project undertaken with youthful energy flies like an arrow," he writes in *Earth and Reveries of Will*, "strikes its object, catches there, and holds. In the final analysis, the project in the process of execution (the material project) has a different temporal structure from the intellectual project. An intellectual project is often quite separate from its execution; it is conceived by someone who then supervises its execution by others."[21]

It is clear that, in formativity, there is no avoiding material, since matter is constitutive of the work. Of course, Pareyson concedes, "one can envisage the possibility of attaining a genuine artistic outcome in the exercise of other operations, as in cases where a moral experience or even a theoretical experiment becomes the 'material' of an exclusively artistic intention." This, though, is a case of matter without materiality, if one may put it like this. The same is true when someone endeavors to turn their life into a work of art; as this amounts to a kind of corruption of formativity, as it were applied to no purpose, to a lapse into aestheticism. In truth, an artistic operation can only be pure formativity if it incorporates the forming of physical matter, to the point that it can be said that physical manifestation is a necessary and constitutive aspect of art and not something inessential or additional, and to do solely with communication, as Croce contends. Thus, "to make a work of art, that is, a form that is only form, means making a physical and material object, as arises from the fact that no art can be exercised without the use of a physical substance, be it the words (which are sounds in addition to meaning) or sound itself, or color, marble, and stone, or the human body itself, as in mime and dance."[22] A formative intention is always in striving for its own matter from which it is moreover inseparable.

"Though entirely free, the choice of material cannot be regarded as arbitrary, since it is determined by the formative intention in which it is embodied and that adopts and modifies it to its intention." Yet, Pareyson goes on, there is not on the one side an empty intention preexisting the material selected and on the other a material that allows itself to be passively handled by that intention. The choice of a material and the definition of a formative intention are one and the same: "formative intention is defined as the adoption of a material, the choice of the material being settled upon as the advent of a formative intention." A true formative intention is that which selects its matter from the outset: otherwise it is but "sterile rumination and pointless proposition." Furthermore, Pareyson continues: "matter that fails to join with the formative intention that attracts it and which does not already harbor a formal tendency in itself is not the stuff of art, but a formless mass devoid of stipulations and potential."[23] Pareyson found the expression "formal tendency"—"vocation formelle"—in Focillon, an author he read and admired and whom he quotes on several occasions. Thus, in *The Life of Forms in Art*, Focillon insists on the fact that not only is the form incarnated, "it is invariably incarnation."[24] Focillon though distinguishes form from image. Everyone has, or can have images, and no more artists than anyone else. Yet, in general, these images suffice for themselves and by their own means, while those who have them are "made up of unknown arts that have their life exclusively in the twilight realms of the mind."[25] Creators of the twilight, "they do not need to leave this twilight to be complete." On the other hand, "form insists in withdrawing: its

21 Bachelard, *Earth and Reveries of Will*, trans. Kenneth Haltmann (Dallas: Dallas Institute of Humanities and Culture, 2002), 17.

22 Pareyson, *Esthétique*, 58.

23 Ibid., 60–61.

24 Focillon, *The Life of Forms in Art*, trans. Charles Beecher Hogan and George Kubler (New York: Zone Books, 1989), 10.

25 Ibid., 122.

very externality [...] is its innermost principle, and its life in the mind is simply preparation for its life in space. [...] Even before separating itself from thought and entering into extent, matter, and technique, form is extent, matter, and technique. Form is never nondescript. Just as each of various kinds of matter has its formal vocation, so has each form its material vocation."[26]

In this sense the matter referred to here is always thought of as being the matter of this form, a matter determined by a form, called up by it in some way. The raw material is thought within this movement and it is only through it that it becomes meaningful in a work. John Dewey expresses the same idea: "The fatal defect of [...] exclusively identify[ing] the matter of a work of art with what is objective [that] passes by the fact that objective material becomes the matter of art only as it is transformed by entering into relations of doing and being undergone by an individual person with all his characteristics of temperament, special manner of vision, and unique experience."[27]

4. Forming Form and Formed Form

"The process of art thus bears its direction within itself, since the trial [*tentativo*], being neither regulated in advance nor left to chance, is intrinsically directed by the harbinger of the work it generates," writes Pareyson.[28] One is here in a kind of anticipation that is not a simple presentiment or "vague shadow," even if it is difficult to explain. Artists do not start off with no idea where they are headed, even if they are far from able to say what the goal is that they may or may not reach. Pareyson often asserts that an artistic operation is an "adventure" because it "is a process where one undertakes or carries out without precisely knowing in advance what there is to do and how it might be undertaken, because it is discovered and invented progressively during the operations." Only afterwards can one describe each stage in the process and understand their sequence in a flow that stems rather clearly from what Bergson calls in *La pensée et le mouvant* "the retrograde movement of truth,"[29] and which consists in believing that what is real is first and foremost possible, whereas its possibility can be only deduced from its current existence. "As if," Bergson exclaims, "when it comes to a truly new form invented by art or nature, the thing and the idea of the thing, its reality and its possibility, were not created at the same time!"[30]

Turning back to Pareyson, it is only once the work is complete that one can clearly see that what has been done, what has been made, was precisely what one had to do, and that the manner in which it has been done is indeed the only way it could have been. However, as Pareyson declares, there is no other means of finding the form, that is, of knowing what has to be done and how it has to be done, then carrying it out. His conclusion is unambiguous: "an artist does not imagine his work as finished and later undertakes and produces it, because he designs it as he makes it."[31]

That said, even if artistic production is an adventure, it is not that trial and error in art advance without any guide. It is simply not a preestablished form or inner image employed as its model. Furthermore, taking such a route does not mean progressing entirely at random, for then we would end up with an "endless wandering." This would equate to considering artists as mere witnesses to their work,

26 Ibid., 119.
27 Dewey, *Art as Experience*, 287.
28 Pareyson, *Esthétique*, 90.
29 Henri Bergson, *La pensée et le mouvant* (Paris: PUF, 2006), 10.
30 Ibid., 14.
31 Pareyson, *Esthétique*, 83.

a notion Pareyson rejects. Something animates the artist and the work, and leads them to formation; this is the forming form. To understand what this is requires overcoming the prejudice that considers that a form exists only once it is formed and, even if this may be so, in treating a work as such only once it is finished. In effect, to say that form only truly exists once it is both invented and executed does not mean that whatever precedes its discovery is a mere pipe dream: "prior to the advent of form there exists something that foreshadows and prefigures it, which reaches out toward it and creates its expectation, which directs and orients the artist in their production. This something is the *spunto*, the starting point, whence form—though it will exist only once the process is complete—already operates and acts as a guide to a process from which it will emerge in all its fullness."[32] We are in the presence of something that imposes itself within the process with the quality of a necessity without however existing: "during the process of its production, form exists and does not exist: it does not exist, since, as it is formed, it will only exist once the process is accomplished; it does exist, since, as it is forming, it starts acting as soon as the process commences." Thus, the form is active even before it exists. Neither can it be said that formed form excludes everything that precedes it, nor that forming form suffices unto itself for it to be regarded as a work. Hence: "Those who forget that form does not exist before it is put into execution undermines understanding of the artwork; but no more so than those who fail to see that form is already present in its execution. Yet this is the mysterious process artists undertake: as they produce, they are guided by the very work they are making; they work toward an end that only becomes known once they attain it; they work at the work in accordance with successful results of operations they can foresee; obviously, they can only get to know the norm governing their acts once, when work is done, they no longer need it; they tentatively reach their goal by envisioning something that reveals itself only once it exists in total completeness."[33]

It is a conception that can be compared to that of Paul Klee, who thought a great deal about creativity and for whom the artist is not to be subjugated to the appearances of nature: "final forms," he writes, "are not the real stuff of the process of natural creation"; adding, "for he places more value on the powers that do the forming than on the final forms themselves."[34] Klee has a dynamic conception at once of creativity and of nature. The latter is not a mere amalgam of forms, however perfect and fascinating they may be. It is above all a potential for form. It is the artist's job to channel this power in a process that is itself formative, for, as Klee insists: "all ways meet in the eye, in an assemblage point from where they are converted into Form to lead to the synthesis of the external glance and the inner vision."[35] It is this way that determines the work and, for Klee, formation is primary. Hence his declaration: "Form is the end, death. Formation is life."[36]

5. The *Spunto*

In understanding this, it is worth making a short detour via the pragmatic philosophy of Dewey. The only real aesthetics adumbrated by that philosophical current he offers in *Art as Experience*, although from very different presuppositions, overlaps with Pareyson's thinking at various points. For Pareyson and Dewey share a processual conception of art and a marked interest in the organic character of form—as met with in Goethe[37]—a writer to whom both authors refer. In chapter 12

32 Ibid., 88.
33 Ibid., 91.
34 Paul Klee, *The Thinking Eye*, ed. Jürg Spiller, trans. Ralph Mannheim (New York: George Wittenborn, 1961), 45.
35 Ibid., 66.
36 Ibid., 169.
37 It is Goethe's organicist metaphor that drives his reflections on artistic creation. For the poet, Nature is "the model of all artistic form," opposing static form (*Gestalt*) with the mobility of organic forms that undergo perpetual metamorphosis (*Bildung*). See Goethe, *Zur Morphologie*, 1817.

of his study Dewey quotes the following text by Goethe: "Art is formative long before it is beautiful. For man has within him a formative nature that displays itself in action as soon as existence is."[38] Another strong parallel arises as regards the status of matter and its relationship to form. "The fact that form and matter are connected in a work of art does not mean they are identical," writes Dewey. "It signifies that in the work of art they do not offer themselves as two distinct things: the work is formed matter."[39] Pareyson subscribes to exactly the same idea: "The work is none other than matter given form."[40] Dewey's conception of form is profoundly dynamic. It is for him a shape "adapted"[41] to an environment or a use, for example, in a process of constant readjustment. Thus, Dewey argues: "Form, as it is present in the fine arts, is the art of making clear what is involved in the organization of space and time prefigured in every course of a developing life-experience."[42] "Form is a character of every experience that is an experience. Art in its specific sense enacts more deliberately and fully the conditions that effect this unity. Form may then be defined as the operation of forces that carry the experience of an event, object, scene, and situation to its own integral fulfillment."[43]

This formal dynamism means that any form starts with an "impulsion," as Dewey calls it: the "impulsion is the initial stage of any complete experience."[44] It is a movement toward the exterior of the form conceived as an organism enabling it to develop and perfect its balance. This cannot though occur without conflict, without meeting obstacles which it has to transform into facilitating agents, while remaining conscious of itself and of its own movement.[45] This impulsion corresponds closely to what Pareyson, for his part, calls the *spunto*, the starting point, already referred to above,[46] effected by a dynamism, a gradual, embryonic drive: "More often than not, matter puts up a resistance," he writes. "This though elicits and stimulates rather than obstructing or thwarting, since, in becoming matter for art, the formative intention transforms resistance into fertile *spunti*, into profitable opportunities; so that the better an artist succeeds in measuring up to his chosen material, the better he manages to render it ductile enough to attain his goal."[47] This starting point is also what Klee tries to describe in speaking of excitation or stimulation: "The word 'stimulated,'" writes the artist, "says everything necessary for the beginning of action. [It] suggests the prehistory of an incipient act, its connection with what has gone before, its bond with the past."[48] The artwork draws its value from the fact of equating, not to something else, but to itself, "so that the process of its formation consists precisely in the fact of attaining in the form formed the forming form."

In fact, Pareyson never fails to situate his argument simultaneously from the perspective of the artist and of that of the work. From the artist's standpoint, as he grapples with the work that is to be made, what is uppermost in his mind is the series of trials and errors, the oscillation between discovery and failure, and the awareness that the process must be directed towards fulfillment. Once the work is over and done, however, all these failed attempts are left behind, disappearing as if vaporized. From the point of view of the work, these are seeds, embryos: its development entails their expansion and growth, during which the process of formation determines and imposes inclusions and exclusions. Pareyson thus quotes an observation by Goethe in a letter to Zeller on November 9, 1829: "The older I get, the greater confidence I have in the law that makes the rose and the lily flower"—the implication being that it is at the same time the work that makes itself and the artist who makes it.

38 Dewey, *Art as Experience*, 281.
39 Ibid., 114.
40 Pareyson, *Esthétique*, 130.
41 Dewey, *Art as Experience*, 115.
42 Ibid., 25.
43 Ibid., 135.
44 Ibid., 58.
45 Ibid., 59: "In the process of converting these obstacles and neutral conditions into favoring agencies, the live creature becomes aware of the intent implicit in its impulsion."
46 The Italian word *spunto* suggests the idea of a brainwave, a source of inspiration, an outburst of productivity.
47 Pareyson, *Esthétique*, 62.
48 Klee, *The Thinking Eye*, 168.

Yet the starting point is in itself nothing. As such it is just an inert entity; to become something it needs to be identified. The *spunto* is a response to an expectation and without the latter it possesses no power whatsoever. "Otherwise, even admitting it does come, it would not even be noticed and would pass without consequences. Therefore, in this respect too, impulsion is nothing without the activity of the artist; it would not even emerge if it were not expected and prepared for, and it can present itself only by prolonging an expectancy it fulfills. Expectation requires its own impulsion."[49] It is a movement that obeys a "you won't find me if you've already sought me." The true artist, however, is one for whom everything or almost everything can play this role of *spunto* or impulsion; she finds *spunti* all about her without having to look for them deliberately, even if, unconsciously, she is always on the lookout.

In an artist, this capacity or receptivity corresponds to what Pareyson calls "formative intentionality"—that is, "a way of seeing while forming and of looking while constructing, which converts the slightest accidents into impulsions and which can be sparked at the least opportunity."[50] Thus the artist is confronted by this same starting point he has "not only waited for, but produced, not only elicited, but constructed." Thus—though only after the fact—it is by recalling her own efforts that the artist can appreciate how everything she sought was indeed necessary. "So," Pareyson concludes, "one might venture to say that the artistic process is that in which the aims of the person undertaking it is to adopt the point of view of the work they are making, and that a work is only successful and well-made if they do in fact succeed in occupying that position."[51]

6. Anthropological Extrapolations

With respect to the conception of the activity of making, anthropologist Tim Ingold's outlook verges relatively close to Pareyson's theory. Thus, when in *Marcher avec les dragons*, a collection of articles published in France in 2013, Ingold reflects on what inhabiting a place means, he shows that when one thinks of building a house, one traditionally thinks, in order to carry out the project, in function of some preconceived model. Thus, one generally reflects in terms of manufacture, of fabrication; this simultaneously affirms the exteriority of a tool with regards to the object it modifies, but without its having a relationship, either with this object or with whoever manufactures it—save for an entirely contingent relation. To make or do things well, however, Ingold contends, one should rather think in terms of cooptation, that is, of understanding how to adapt a material into a tool.

Coopting is a way for the user to associate in his mind an extant object with the conceptual image of its future use. A stone thus becomes a hammer when we need to drive in a nail. After making use of objects from our environment to achieve our goal, we then we modify them so that they serve our purposes more effectively. From a viewpoint rather like Heidegger's, Ingold, who refers to the philosopher's lecture "Building Living Thinking," shows that, to live in place means doing more than simply occupying it. Inhabiting is a way of being in the world, that is, a way of establishing relationships with the world other than those of pure exteriority. In short, people, he writes, do not import ideas, plans, or mental representations into the world, since that very world, to borrow a phrase from Merleau-Ponty, is

49 Ibid., 95.
50 Pareyson, *Esthétique*, 96.
51 Ibid., 94.

the "homeland of their thoughts."[52] It is in this sense that a house should to be designed in a dynamic that treats it as a thing transformed by a man whom in its turn it transforms. To build then, does not simply mean "to project a form onto a material," but "to connect materials in motion."[53] The operation needs to be thought of, "not as an assemblage of solid blocks, but more like weaving together flexible materials."[54]

In a recent study *Making: Anthropology, Archaeology, Art and Architecture*,[55] Ingold is interested in making as a process of growth that proceeds not by opposition to raw materials that have to be subdued, but on the contrary in a kind of collaboration with them. It is not thus a question of imposing something from without but of "interven[ing] in worldly processes that are already going on, and which give rise to the forms of the living world that we see all around us."[56] Making is not transposing an image on an object; it is conceiving the generation of the form as process. Thus, the supposed frontier between organization and artifact, or between what Kant calls in *Critique of Judgment* making and acting (§43), is overcome. Here, the difference between the two is no longer one of nature but of degree. Of course, the maker of an object can have a form in her mind as she is creating, but it is not this form that generates the object: the work is created through the engagement of the maker with her materials, because the whole form cannot be prefigured within the project—if it was, why take the bother of producing the form?

Here, Ingold concurs with Simondon and his critique of the hylemorphic model, taken up by Deleuze and Guattari. For all three, if matter and form is considered in exteriority, it is impossible to understand how matter can be formed at all and how form occurs in matter. There is in matter something like implicit forms that act in combination with processes of deformation. Consequently, it is a question of following the material, of following, for example, the wood, of "surrendering to the wood, following where it leads, by connecting operations to a materiality, instead of imposing a form on a matter."[57]

The point, writes Ingold, commenting on these authors in his turn, is that "the essence of matter, or the material, lie[s] in form-taking activity." It is a "correspondence."[58] This notion, together with the idea that the model does not preexist mentally but has to be searched for in the artifact itself, returns us to Pareyson's idea of the forming form and the formed form, even if Ingold never quotes Pareyson, quite probably because he is unaware of his work. Tim Ingold also has the same idea that the artwork is not an object, but a thing, that is, that it cannot be reduced to its physical properties, to an object standing before us—a *Gegenstand*. Things, we accompany; they belong to a whole to which we belong.[59] For this reason "the role of the artist is not to give effect to a preconceived idea but to follow the forces and flows of material that bring the work into being. To view the work is to join the artist as a fellow traveler, to look with it as it unfolds in the world, rather than behind it to an originating intention of which it is the final product."[60] This refers us back to Luigi Pareyson, when, in *Conversations sur l'esthétique*, he writes: "The work of art is certainly a thing, a produced object, but it is at the same time a world, a personal sense of things: what's mysterious in interpreting an artwork is precisely that one stands before a thing and that one discovers in it a world, that one grapples at the same time with the presence of a physical object and with the impenetrability of a spiritual world."[61]

52 Tim Ingold, *Marcher avec les dragons* (Paris: Zones sensibles, 2015), 173.
53 Ibid., 244.
54 Ibid., 245.
55 Tim Ingold, *Making: Anthropology, Archaeology, Art and Architecture* (London: Routledge, 2013).
56 Ingold, *Making*, 21.
57 Gilles Deleuze and Felix Guattari, *A Thousand Plateaus*, trans. Brian Massumi, (London: Continuum, 2004), 451.
58 Ingold, *Making*, xi and 25.
59 See Heidegger's meditations on *Das Ding, the thing*, etc. which imply the notion of gathering. See Ingold, *Making*, 85.
60 Ibid., 86.
61 Luigi Pareyson, *Conversations sur l'esthétique* (Paris: Gallimard, 1992), 125–26.

From the convergence of these thoughts, we can see that, though unfamiliar with the art of his time, a thinker like Luigi Pareyson had a powerful sense of the processes of the formation of the artwork and was able, through the theory of formativity, to produce a set of useful and fruitful observations that would enable us to understand the processes at work in the creation of forms, whatever domain they belong to.

Translated from the French by David Radzinowicz

Gestaltung: A Process of Transformation of Forms as the Dynamic of Creativity

Gaëlle Le Page

In the course of my research, the concept of Gestaltung, as it appears in the work of German psychiatrist Hans Prinzhorn, struck me as the essential wellspring of the movement of creativity. In his seminal work of 1922, *Artistry of the Mentally Ill: A Contribution to the Psychology and Psychopathology of Configuration*, Prinzhorn presents the characteristics and scope of *Gestaltung*, defining it as: "The expressive urge can be understood only as an ever-present atmosphere [fluid], like the erotic [...], the need for expression, which satisfies itself in configuration [*Gestaltung*], [and] has at its disposal all kinds of gestures and their concrete manifestations as a means of self-representation.[1]

It was Prinzhorn who first addressed the issue of the art of the insane. He was also the first to recognize authentic artistic qualities in the pictorial productions of schizophrenics, going on to assemble a collection of works by mentally ill patients numbering more than 5,000 works. Some have been on public exhibition since 2001 in the psychiatric hospital at the University of Heidelberg. Prinzhorn is an author who marked a turning point in the conception of both art and psychiatry at the beginning of the twentieth century.

Brief Notes on the Biography and Career of Hans Prinzhorn

To start with, so as to afford a better appreciation of the concept of *Gestaltung*, it seems advisable to give an outline of Prinzhorn's career and the context in which it unfolded. Hans Prinzhorn was born in Hemer, Germany, in 1886 and died in Munich on June 14, 1933. One of three children, he confessed that he never felt affection from his mother nor developed any particular admiration for his father, regarding them as alien to him. Prinzhorn sat for his school leaving certificate in 1904, and, if his father began by wanting Hans to take up a trade, in the end he allowed his son to study philosophy and art history.

1 Hans Prinzhorn, *Artistry of the Mentally Ill: A Contribution to the Psychology and Psychopathology of Configuration*, trans. E. von Brockdorff (New York: Springer, 1972), 14.

In 1908 Prinzhorn presented a PhD dealing with the fundamental aesthetic conceptions of Gottfried Semper on the psychological origin of artistic activity, the characteristics of the symbolic, and principles of configuration (*Gestaltungsprinzipien*).[2] He also took up music, developing close links with the Impressionist movement[3] and throwing his whole being into the life of that city of art, Munich.[4] In 1909 he took up singing in earnest. Three years later he married Erna Hoffman, who also studied singing. Just a few weeks after their wedding Erna betrayed signs of a mental disorder of which there had been harbingers before the marriage, sparked seemingly by the suicide of her former fiancé. In despair, Prinzhorn wrote to his sister that he had decided to take up a profession that obliges one to do good,[5] promptly embarking on the study of medicine. Finding it difficult to live together due to Erna's stints in the clinic, in 1922 the couple split up. Since 1919 Prinzhorn's medical studies had entailed working as an assistant in the University of Heidelberg psychiatric clinic under psychiatrist Karl Willmanns. The latter instructed him to investigate a series of drawings and paintings in the institution's collection by hospitalized schizophrenic patients, the study of which, at that time, was undertaken for its diagnostic value. Deciding to widen the corpus beyond the clinic, Prinzhorn turned to psychiatrists working in other asylums, gradually building up a large collection of writings, paintings, and sculptures by schizophrenics. Having spent two years collating these works, he advanced the hypothesis that, if mentally ill patients draw and paint in a peculiar and sometimes awkward manner, the aesthetic qualities of their productions can in certain respects prove attractive, stating: "The awkwardness and lack of discipline in the lineation of our scribblings in no sense allow us to find their origin in any pathological conditions in their authors. They simply indicate an unpracticed hand and a lack of elementary formal intention."[6]

Pathological Art

"Hygienist" psychiatrists had already made use of pictorial productions and writings by their patients in the nineteenth century. The works of "lunatic" or "degenerated" patients were, however, reduced to the status of pathological symptoms.

For Ambroise Tardieu in 1872, the writings and paintings of the insane might assist in refining diagnosis. Joseph Rogue De Fursac, in 1905, considered that drawings by lunatics, "convey, like their writings, unwholesome activity, haste, a propensity for joking, and obscenity,"[7] while César Lombroso in 1909 presented creative genius as an indicator of degeneracy. In 1911 Eugen Bleuler argued that "art is often employed to express delirious ideas and its unhealthy character can be recognized at a glance."[8] Commenting on this approach, Prinzhorn argues that "Bleuler merely touches on the question of 'pathological art.'"[9] In 1924 Jean Vinchon too explored the links between art and madness. In his book, *L'art et la folie*, he contends that this atypical art is not exceptional like that of an artist but closer to "primitive" art, since it is generated by the drive to symbolic representation he dubs "involuntary symbolism."[10] It is a discordant art, which, freeing itself from norms, may appear ungainly. Later, in 1956, Robert Volmat published a study entitled *L'art psychopathologique*, in which he refers to Prinzhorn, writing how, thanks to the psychiatrist, "for once, drawing was considered as an expression of the personality."[11] Without addressing the art as such, Volmat's intention

2 Marielène Weber, "Prinzhorn, l'Homme, la collection, le livre," in *Hans Prinzhorn, Expressions de la folie. Dessins, peintures, sculptures d'asile* (Paris: Gallimard, 1984), 3–4 (French edition of the above).
3 Jean Broustra, *Abécédaire de l'expression. Psychiatrie et activité créatrice : l'atelier intérieur* (Toulouse: Érès, 2015), 28.
4 Ibid., 4.
5 Ibid., 5.
6 Prinzhorn, *Artistry of the Mentally Ill*, 231.
7 Joseph Rogue de Fursac, *Les écrits et les dessins dans les maladies nerveuses et mentales* (Paris: Masson et Cie, 1905), 276; see Prinzhorn, *Artistry of the Mentally Ill*, 41.
8 Eugène Bleuler, *Demencia praecox oder Gruppe der Schizophrenien* (Leipzig/ Vienna: Franz Deuticke/ Handbuch der Psychiatrie, 1911), 72.
9 Weber, "Prinzhorn, l'Homme, la collection, le livre," 21.
10 Ibid., 82.
11 Robert Volmat, *L'art psychopathologique* (Paris: P.U.F, 1956), 172.

was to account for artistic behavior among the ill. In this perspective, however, these unusual productions were primarily analyzed from a medical point of view, being basically thought of as psychological indicators. Nevertheless, this art was soon to be taken up elsewhere, in particular in the artistic field itself.

Modern Art Among the Insane in the Early Twentieth Century

Thrown into turmoil by the upheavals of the early twentieth century, modern art broke with the conventions of the classical and sought inspiration in creative innovation, including so-called pathological art, that of the insane.

Writer, art critic, and collector Wilhelm Uhde, who, in 1912 and again the following year, did much to promote now famous works by Henri Rousseau and Séraphine de Senlis, was part of this process of emancipation. Uhde was an enthusiastic defender of these unique productions created by autodidacts. Unrecognized and unacquainted with one another, they of course did not form a movement in the manner of the Impressionists. If Uhde remarks that the common characteristic of these painters lies in the fact that their art bears the stamp of an awkwardness those not accustomed to it might perceive as "clumsy handling,"[12] he sees it as "the inevitable corollary of the highest qualities."[13]

In the wake of Uhde, Prinzhorn and Marcel Réja reflected on what this clumsiness of line teaches us about the essence of expressivity and its prolongation in the creative act. According to Prinzhorn, an artist's talent is not to be reduced to mere skill or competent production, since, as he states in concluding his observations of the drawings of the mentally ill, it is a way of making that channels an "inner need."[14]

Far from being pejorative, this articulation aims to bring out an artistic dimension in the process that resonated particularly with Prinzhorn's contemporaries, themselves artists, such as Max Ernst, Paul Klee, and Salvador Dalí, all initiators of the Surrealist movement, together with André Breton and Louis Aragon.

By presenting the drawings and writings of schizophrenics as artworks, Prinzhorn comforted the Surrealists in their idea that art ought not to be dependent on a line of thought, but be defined as a movement incorporating the whole process of creation and expression and deploying all the psychic forces at work, "in the absence of any control exercised by reason, exempt from any aesthetic or moral concern,"[15] as André Breton proposed in the first *Manifesto of Surrealism*. Holding Hans Prinzhorn's work as a collector in high regard, in 1948 Breton wrote in a letter to his friend Jean Dubuffet: "Hans Prinzhorn, by revealing [works of the ill ...] and, for the first time, ensuring a display worthy of them, has promoted their confrontation with other contemporary works."[16]

Recognizing these shadowy creators devoid of artistic culture as their peers, many envisaged the productions of the insane as a welcome release from the rules defined by art history and the art schools. As Jean Starobinski observes: "Barriers fell and the field of art (under the unwonted term, *Bildnerei*, that is, the visual work or, almost, imagery) broadened in a staggering fashion."[17] It was against this effervescent backdrop that Art Brut emerged, placing the art of the insane in an

12 Wilhelm Uhde, *Cinq maitres primitifs: Rousseau - Vivin - Bombois - Bauchant - Séraphine* (Paris: Philippe Daudy, 1949), 21.
13 Ibid., 21.
14 Prinzhorn, *Artistry of the Mentally Ill*, 77.
15 André Breton, "The Manifesto of Surrealism" (1924), in *Manifestos of Surrealism*, trans. Richard Seaver and Helen R. Lane (Ann Arbor: University of Michigan, 1972), 26.
16 André Breton, "L'art des fous, la clé des champs" (1948), in *La clé des champs* (Paris: Sagittaire, 1953), 224–27.
17 Jean Starobinski, preface to Hans Prinzhorn, *Expressions de la folie*, vii.

artistic category in its own right. The father of the movement, Jean Dubuffet, took up the idea of exploring the world of the psychiatric hospital for his own ends. In 1945 he started to assemble a collection of works of art by psychiatric patients incorporated into the concept of Art Brut, defined as "an immediate, unpracticed art."[18] His own collection featured several works by "artist patients" at Heidelberg from the Prinzhorn collection. As Dubuffet remarked: "There is no more an art of the insane than an art of the dyspeptic or of people with knee problems."[19]

In the course of an extensive program of research, Dubuffet came across the remarkable work of Dr. Léo Navratil, a psychiatrist working at the Klosterneuburg psychiatric hospital near Vienna in Austria, who had initiated an original experiment. With support from the director of the institution, Dr. Aloïs Markstein, he founded an "artists' house": "a wing [...] allotted to the group of creative patients and inaugurated on June 9, 1981."[20] The unit was not to be a place for indulging in ergotherapy to practical ends, since by the 1950s Léo Navratil had reached the same conclusion as Dubuffet that the creative process is inherent in every individual, sick or healthy. Alluding to "social legitimacy,"[21] Navratil's thesis was that promoting the creative process among his patients would further their social cohesion.

Several patients became acknowledged creators in Art Brut. Johann Hauser, for example, invented a script and a coding of subjective reality far more expressive than all the secondhand languages one is usually confronted with.[22] Or Oswald Tschirtner, the patient O.T., to whom Navratil devoted a detailed monograph in his work, *Schizophrénie et art*. Reacting to Navratil's study, Michel Thévoz wrote of the visual vocabulary of painting.[23] In the wake of this vogue for a singular art, many artists—drawing, painting, or carving away up in prisons, hospitals, attics, or farms—gained recognition and made their way in the cultural scene and even into the history of art. Becoming artists in the true sense, they contributed to liberating the vision of art, society, and politics at the time. For the artists themselves, however, the consciousness of being an artist did not exist and they were unconcerned with ideological progress. Often extremely isolated, they were also estranged from social concerns. As Dubuffet observed, they create like autists, their art was a response to an inner imperative.

Prior to his interest in this new kind of art, Prinzhorn had engaged in various investigations into the creative drive. On the methodological level he especially studied the evidence schizophrenia provides about the processes of creativity inherent in humanity. Making art is envisioned as the seminal factor exemplifying a creative dynamic, resulting in a new way of considering the work of formalization in a process of generalized form-giving he dubs *Gestaltung* (configuration). His approach revealed a process worth identifying and demarcating for what it can teach us about the dynamic of form and its intrinsic impulsion. In this regard its definition lies beyond both the artist and the physician as phenomenologist.

The Origins of Gestaltung and the Most Significant Authors to Inspire Hans Prinzhorn

In founding his theory of *Gestaltung* Prinzhorn took inspiration from many writers in domains such as phenomenology, philosophy, art, and psychology. We will treat here only of those who made a significant impact on Prinzhorn's

18 Jean Dubuffet, *Guide d'un petit voyage en suisse* (Paris: Gallimard, 1947), 20.
19 Jean Dubuffet, "L'art brut préféré aux arts culturels" (1949), in *Prospectus et tous écrits suivants*, vol. 1 (Paris: Gallimard, 1967), 202.
20 Collectif Art Brut 12, *Art Brut 12: Gugging*, vol. 25, no. 12 (Lausanne: Collection de l'art brut, 1982), 6.
21 Ibid., 6.
22 Ibid., 25.
23 Ibid., 66.

development of *Gestaltung* and on his thought generally. They include Marcel Réja, Karl Jaspers, Sigmund Freud, Ludwig Klages, and Walter Morgenthaler. In parallel our examination will enable us to pinpoint certain concepts significant for Prinzhorn, such as expression, flow, rhythm, and the various levels of *Gestaltung*.

In 1907 Marcel Réja had already considered artistic productions by the insane as a pathological expression whose artistic dimension derives from an isolated event. His innovation lay in his interpretation of the phenomenological sign, not only as diagnostic indicator, but also as a tool for the further understanding of the relationship between the human and creativity. Thus, Réja attempted to identify elemental signs that might clarify the ontology of artistic creation. Associating the concept of creativeness with human development, Réja sees the art of the insane as examples of the untutored forms of art in their raw, primary expression. Referring to such works as spontaneous, he draws a parallel between drawings by mental patients, children, and "savages," underlining spontaneity as their common characteristic. This analogy led Réja to become interested in art produced by children. What the child draws, he says, "is thrown down whole, the mental image inscribed on the paper."[24] Describing children's drawing in the light of this dynamic, he divides its development into periods, such as formless scribbling and the symbolic period. Prinzhorn took these categories as a basis for defining various stages in the drawings by the schizophrenic patients he studied, grading their degree of *Gestaltung* that can be more or less organized, more or less elaborate and symbolized.

Prinzhorn too refers to disordered, nonfigurative scribbling, to playful drawing dominated by the tendency to organize and reproduce, to imaginary visual worlds, and, finally, to increased expressivity and symbolism. Hypothesizing a differential, even evolutionary principle in the degree of expressiveness, Prinzhorn does not theorize stages of development, as Réja had done in his studies of children's drawings. He concentrates instead on the unfolding of an increasingly refined artistic awareness among schizophrenics, who use drawing as a tool to defuse threatening intrapsychic phenomena.

Prinzhorn was also interested in the theories of philosopher Karl Jaspers, who in 1913 published a vast study entitled *General Psychopathology*, in which he develops a psychology of expression referred to as the "expression of the psyche."[25] For Jaspers the expression of the psyche connects psychic and physiological phenomena: "expressions of the psyche [...] consist of the human physiognomy, involuntary gestures, speech and writing, artistic productions and conscious purposeful behavior."[26] Regarding artistic productions as expressive phenomena, Prinzhorn concurs with Jaspers. The latter explains how "all psychic manifestations are pervaded by an expressive atmosphere,"[27] while for Prinzhorn *Gestaltung* derives from a process characteristic of all human beings, ebbing and flowing inside in endless flux. Jaspers distinguishes two domains of expression: that channeled directly through the body, unconscious and involuntary; and indirect expression mediated by language, work, thought, and action, which Jaspers presents as objectified in consciousness. His reference to direct (*sinnlich*) expression and indirect, intelligible (*sinnhaft*) expression is echoed in Prinzhorn's characterization of various degrees of *Gestaltung* which tend toward formalized expression, more or less organized and complex. Prinzhorn also took inspiration from

24 Marcel Réja, "L'art chez les fous, le dessin, la prose, la poésie" (1907), in *La nudité de l'Art* (Nice: Z'éditions, 1990), 6.
25 Karl Jaspers, *General Psychopathology*, vol. 1, trans. J. Hoenig and Marian W. Hamilton (Baltimore: Johns Hopkins University Press, 1997), part one, chapter IV, section 1.
26 Ibid., 251.
27 Ibid., 252.

Jaspers in his exploration of the varieties of expression and of its emergence in the most primal and most unforeseen forms. However, for Prinzhorn, if the forms are gradually organized, becoming more and more complex to compose "a kind of alphabet of expressive movements,"[28] he parts company from Jaspers when arguing that there exists from the outset no planned, anticipated finality. Unlike Jaspers, Prinzhorn finds no place for voluntary expression and adheres to a definition of the phenomenon dependent on the drive for expression in which we discover "the core of the impulses to configuration [*Gestaltung*],"[29] rather than considering it as a conscious, expressive aim with a given goal. Prinzhorn writes of "a tendency, a compulsion, a need for the expression of the psyche [...] compulsive vital processes which are not subordinated to any outside purpose but directed solely and self-sufficiently toward their own realization."[30] He identifies an involuntary component of the subject who does not know what will occur from the start and rightly observes that art by schizophrenic subjects reflects an inner compulsion, the artist creating above all for, and thus in, himself. To the dimension of expression, he also adds the concept of expressive gestures "subordinated to one purpose: to actualize the psyche,"[31] which plug into the process, rather than the finality of expression, which systematically designates something interpretable. Regarded as primary, this impulse offers evidence of a will to transform that involves the progressive modification of form and of the meaning the latter may take. Meaning is contemporary with form. Prinzhorn's position is not that of the comprehension of expression, as advocated by Jaspers, but that of the expression in becoming. He thus conserves intact the enigmatic side of the artwork—that which, *in fine*, produces an effect on the being of whoever undertakes a process of *Gestaltung*.

Prinzhorn is to be hailed for opening fresh perspectives in the field of research into human expressive processes, particularly with his description of the operations of form-giving ("configuration") and which we will call the "urge to form" (*poussée à la forme*). Prinzhorn's aim was to develop a theory derived from a detailed study of all the phenomena of pictorial expression. With this in mind, he centered his study on the observation of schizophrenic patients, focusing on the vital force at work among them, rather than on pathological phenomena, though the term *schizophrenic Gestaltung* does appear. On this point, he goes beyond the notion of the pleasure associated with such activity to concern himself with the urge (*poussée*) as a vital need obeying a distinct logic. Hence, he places the phenomenon of creativity in resonance with his observation of schizophrenia. He identifies a "specifically schizophrenic symptom, [...] the devaluation of the external world and the dissolution of reality and unreality."[32] Intrigued by how, in schizophrenia, the mind is split, cleaving to withstand the illness and further the emergence of a form of expression deriving precisely from this *Spaltung*, Prinzhorn defends the idea that the condition presents a dysfunction of the associative mechanism, which, in his view, promotes the "associative loosening"[33] that sustains *Gestaltung*. Prinzhorn's aim is to locate what in the psychic phenomenon of schizophrenia might underpin a capacity for *Gestaltung* and further the emergence of forms that may reach back to the archaic through primitive, primordial processes. The schizophrenic's autistic attitude to the world may lead to an arrangement of latent psychic contents that can provide form through expressivity to an impression predicated on the archaic, on traces. "The autistic [...] schizophrenic," he adds "creates for himself an entirely different, richer world [...] whose reality he does not establish for himself by logical conventions or

28 Prinzhorn, *Artistry of the Mentally Ill*, 40.
29 Ibid., 6.
30 Ibid., 13.
31 Ibid.
32 Ibid., 241.
33 Ibid., 39.

reconciles with the impressions of others."[34] By acting concretely on the world surrounding him, the subject, bolstered by an autocracy of the ego that pays heed solely to its own desires, can start creating.

On this point Prinzhorn was to be durably influenced by Morgenthaler, publishing his work on *Gestaltung* just a year after the latter's study. Morgenthaler was the author of a work published in 1921 with the title *Ein Geisteskranker als Künstler: Adolf Wölfli*. Dealing with intriguing cases not widely referred to at the time, Dr. Morgenthaler presented works by one of his patients, Adolf Wölfli, from an entirely new angle. Addressed to an uninitiated public unfamiliar with traditional scientific publications, the study envisions Wölfli's art as intimately dependent on his schizophrenia. Extending to more than 25,000 pages, the subject's output is composed of poems, prose texts, drawings, and paintings, as well as an entirely invented musical writing. All these art forms appear to be marshaled in the service of a single, unitary oeuvre that passes seamlessly from drawing to text and on to musical composition. The rhythm of the words and a musical linguistic quality irrigates Wölfli's entire production, imparting sonority and presence to what is an individual and vivid language. Focusing on an output expressive of the subjective and dynamic qualities of the subject, Morgenthaler and Prinzhorn alike concur with the aims of psychoanalysis that treats of pathological characteristics that lead the subject into the living heart of his intimate experience.

With regard to psychoanalysis, Prinzhorn entertained reservations as to the approach of Freud and his contemporaries, adopting a critical stance. He diverges from an analytical method that studies artworks in order to delve into the author's psychic world, regarding such a process as "vulgar and sensational"[35] and alien to genuine art. Prinzhorn also argues that, if psychoanalysis is interested in works by great masters, he is more concerned with the stammering of form; for him then it is just as important to deal with scribbles as with symbolically accomplished works. He will though draw on Freud in consideration of this primitive aspect of *Gestaltung*, calling Freud's *Totem and Taboo* "a decisive work"[36] for its comparisons between the psychic operations of the child, the primitive, and the mentally ill. The invariability of the human psyche "appl[ies] to all forms of affective processes as they occur in humans in all stages of evolution and all periods."[37] Symbolic expression, the need for symbols, already manifest among primal peoples, demonstrates that it "is a final, irreducible psychological fact—an urge in man [...] to impress [...] traces of his existence."[38] Prinzhorn also acknowledges that psychoanalysts have been alone in having "prepared the ground for a theory of symbols"[39] and ascribing an adequate role to "compulsive desire."[40] It is the case though that for Prinzhorn the common characteristic, its "essence,"[41] resides "at the level of immediate vision, where we intuitively have the revelation of expressive values,"[42] not in sensory qualities or in the qualities of the *Gestalt*.

This universal principle intrinsic to the human he identifies as drive (impulse). The term recurs on several occasions in Prinzhorn's discussion. This notion of impulse includes an activity sufficing in itself. He prefers, however, the word urge, speaking of an "active urge" and noting how it "first appears in physical movement."[43] He distinguishes six urges: the ornamental urge, the ordering tendency, the tendency to imitate (copying urge), the need for symbols (significance), urge to play (active), and finally the expressive urge, defining them as the psychological foundations of all *Gestaltung*. For Prinzhorn the urge for expression, the

34 Ibid.
35 Ibid., 271.
36 Ibid., 254.
37 Ibid.
38 Ibid., 21.
39 Ibid., 240.
40 Ibid., 262.
41 Prinzhorn, *Expressions de la folie*, 354.
42 Ibid.
43 Ibid., 14.

active urge, and the impulse to impart form converge in *Gestaltung* characterized as a constant force in the psyche that compels the individual to project the inner stimuli outward. He adds that individuals at an early age show a disposition to *Gestaltung*, which is readily identifiable in the delight a child takes in drawing, logically associating the tendency to *Gestaltung* with a pleasure principle.

Moreover, if *Gestaltung* articulates its satisfaction within a movement, it is also necessary to consider the repetition borne by this movement. Within repetition, Prinzhorn distinguishes rhythm and reproduction. In an attempt to refine the notion of repetition inherent in instinctual urges, he addresses the tendency to order identical elements and seriate them as a characteristic of the *Gestaltung* principle. Nonetheless, repetition does not equate to reproduction, since it underlines instead how pleasure is obtained through the rhythm impelled by the flow of *Gestaltung* correlated with its intensity. A remark by Henri Maldiney makes this idea clearer: "Rhythm lies in the ripples on the water, not in the flow of the river."[44]

To explore this idea further it is worth introducing Ludwig Klages's notion of rhythmic flow to which Prinzhorn also alludes. Showing immense respect for his work, the psychiatrist regarded Klages as the founder of a general theory of expression, relying on his analysis to determine the characteristics of form-making and *Gestaltung* as exemplary of all acts of expression. Klages compares rhythm to the infinite motion of waves that ebb and flow but which do not conform to any metric logic. Distinguishing rhythm and rate, he concedes how there can be no rate without rhythm as long as the latter remains correlated to a movement that produces an effect of continuity and envelops the whole subject. Klages opposes the rule of rate as a regular beat (a creation of the industrial era and its machines) to rhythm considered as unique to the living. If oscillatory movement is indeed repetitive, it can never be reproduced entirely identically since it is not a mechanical movement but a pulsation comparable to a heartbeat. Prinzhorn discerns this pulsating power in the urge to *Gestaltung*. Moreover, for Klages, the pleasure inherent in rhythm is fundamental; the pleasure of a rhythm, be it created by the subject or perceived by him, arises from the fact that the perception of rhythm seizes the individual—both the beholder and the creative artist: "I can then experience rhythm only insofar as I am gripped by it."[45] This idea of being gripped is essential for our argument since it points to how, if rhythm brings with it renewal, it is also relayed in physical, felt experience, affording consistency to the movement that makes presence itself through gesture.

Following this account of the sources of *Gestaltung* and of the authors who inspired Prinzhorn, it is time to address the essence of the concept: a process of expression directed at artistic creation which circulates in each of us as flow.[46] *Gestaltung* is structured from a flow that is to be thought of as an organized, rhythmical movement like a pulse. "It has become common to call the succession of similar [expressive] elements rhythm; not only is music called rhythmic, but quite generally the formed development of a gesture is called 'rhythmic' because of the original meaning, which is 'flowing.'"[47] Moreover, *Gestaltung* is a value in itself as an impulse to form-making whose sole goal is to actuate its own process.

It is our contention that in this fashion the principle of *Gestaltung* introduces a new way of envisaging the emergence of supple, dynamic, expressive, and artistic forms which are shaped and then distorted. *Gestaltung* is to be thought of as a

44 Henry Maldiney, *L'esthétique des rythmes* (Lausanne: Editions l'Age d'Homme, 1967), 12.
45 Ludwig Klages, *La nature du rythme*, trans. Olivier Hanse, 4th ed. (Bonn: Bouvier Verlag, 2000), 94.
46 Ibid., 80.
47 Prinzhorn, *Artistry of the Mentally Ill*, 22.

general process of forming, which, rather than being confined to the production of objects, is to be defined in terms of vectorization. As we see it, a literal translation would be the process from which something is formed, created in a genetic and perpetual movement of constructing and deconstructing form. *Gestaltung* operates immediately on the emergence of the first trace, the first imprint, and is directed toward the constitution of an innovation that is revealed and then channeled through the plurality of the forms, while at the same time it is a process that encompasses the instinctual urge, movement, and the transformation of forms.

If *Gestaltung* was not at the outset embraced by the field of psychology, which takes its cue from psychoanalysis, Prinzhorn's conception has imposed itself as a powerful pattern of thought in practical and theoretical fields alike, be they artistic, aesthetic, phenomenological, or psychoanalytical.

As the links between madness and art remain a burning question today, this concept could certainly be a valuable tool in addressing the problem, and, beyond this, the genesis of any creative act. The concept of *Gestaltung* can teach us much about the function that an object in the process of becoming (a pictorial one in particular) can take for the subject creating it. It seems to us that the artistic endeavor at work in configuring forms incorporates a facet of subjective truth whenever a subject enters in resonance with the object, during the process of fashioning it. Its effectiveness lies much more in the process itself, in the movement of *Gestaltung*, as Prinzhorn declares, "directly, without the interposition of a purpose or any other rational instance."[48]

On this point Prinzhorn agrees with the ideas later advocated by the psychiatrist Léo Navratil, whose critique opposed head-on the ideas of the philosopher Joseph Gabel, who categorized creativity as being dependent on dialectical thought. Far closer to Prinzhorn, Navratil defines associative loosening as the condition for the "urge to form." Prinzhorn quotes Leonardo to the effect that: "Through entangled and undefined things the mind is opened to new inventions," adding that "thus the artist is inspired to let latent formal preconceptions come alive within himself."[49] Thus, as he sees it, to start creating, the artist draws upon inner movements like the schizophrenic. The subject is then receptive to the active urge with respect to their psychic state and what is "presensed"—that is, prior to formal representation—demands to acquire form. This is what, dealing with the subject of *Gestaltung*, Jean Oury terms the *fabrique du "pré"* or mechanism (manufacture) of the "pre." The "pre" is situated on the side of emergence: "There is no work, no motivation, there is no psychology, no representation. This is the 'pre.' And this modifies something."[50] Delimiting the process included beneath the principle of *Gestaltung* Jean Oury adds that one might also speak of: "The 'Weg,' the path, in the sense of a path being walked out; the path paced out [*le chemin cheminant*]. The character of the pathway [*cheminement*] of thought. This place, this *topos*, with the characteristics of the 'pre,' 'pre-specular,' 'pre-representational' [...] is seized in an ongoing process of construction of creativity."[51]

Gestaltung in this sense precedes *Gestalt*; it is more circulation, the "way," the progress of forms or, to use Jacques Lacan's expression, a "trickle-down" (*ruissellement*)[52] than a formation of forms. This argument places at the center of the present subject the question of the pliability of forms as an essential quality.

48 Ibid., 7.
49 Ibid., 19–20.
50 Jean Oury, *Création et schizophrénie* (Paris: Galilée, 1989), 64.
51 Ibid., 60.
52 Jacques Lacan, "Lituraterre," *Littérature*, no. 31 (October 1971): 4.

Kunstwollen

We have crossed *Gestaltung* with the concept of *Kunstwollen* defined by Aloïs Riegl—literally meaning "art wanting," one could characterize it as an "(in-)becoming"—in order to better understand the issue behind this dynamic. For our part, we will speak of "form wanting," which to us seems closer to Prinzhorn's thinking. Riegl offered the following definition: "*Kunstwollen* means neither artistic will nor a will to art, neither intention nor artistic intentionality, neither artistic impulse nor aesthetic impulse, neither intentional form, nor will to form, but exclusively and literally 'art wanting.'"[53] He added, "The artwork is not only an artistic work but anything formed by man [...], the product of visual art in the broadest sense [...] visual art in its primal sense, that is, an activity giving form to a substance."[54]

This wanting is not to be confused with the will; it does not include thought or any faculty, nor a conscious motivation predicated on external causes, forming instead part of internal processes within the subject himself. In this sense *Kunstwollen* is nothing to do with a voluntary act; it is a desire for art. "Desire, inclination, force whose orientation or object remains generally instinctive and unintelligible [...]. A wish for art whose object is almost unwanted and which is embedded in a context of wanting."[55] We can then compare this wish for form as an unconscious psychic process to the function of figurability met with in the dream work. Our dreams may appear inane to us, absurd and without apparent logic, but they are rich in sensations and impressions conveyed through images, like seeds of representation. This idea converges with one of the characteristics of *Gestaltung*, which is to integrate the notion of imprint into the process of artistic creation. As Céline Masson remarks in this connection: "At the beginning of art there was borrowing and imprinting, the visual appropriation of form and its transfer onto a different support."[56] Echoing Leroi-Gourhan's study on the links between gesture, word, and the birth of the graphic, she notes that early in the paleoanthropic era, "motricity conditions expression, in the figurative language of the most recent hominins, reflection determines the graphic."[57] Moreover, "lines incised in bone"[58] testify to "the emergence of figuration and rhythmicity."[59] Figuration and motion, physical movement and rhythm were involved at the birth of human expression and imply a wish for form that starts with the observation of nature before being transposed into different media and becoming a symbol. This is concretized, as Prinzhorn states, in the earliest graphic traces. Thus, it exists well before *Vorstellung* (representation), in a pre-state Freud terms *Darstellung* (figurability, presentation). It is an object's potential for figuration, the result of a rhythm that fostered the emergence of the initial traces. In fact, Freud writes in the dream work of the emergence of the first mnemic traces. Movement is not engulfment, that is to say, a covering over of the trace, but emergence. And, however abstract the trace, as origin it paves the way to a potential for "forming"; it calls upon a form containing within it a wish to create borne by the power of *Gestaltung*.

Maldiney's remarks with regard to the genesis of the visual artwork are enlightening: Paths to form are "moving paths," currents without banks. Far from being a vector, locatable and calculatable with respect to a permanent frame of reference, an aesthetic form creates its own frame of reference at every decisive instant of its autogenesis. A form and a work function like a world. They do not exist in space and time; but—as they are in the world—space and time are within them.[60]

53 Jacques Boulet, préface to Aloïs Riegl, *Le Culte moderne des monuments* (1902), trans. Jacques Boulet (Paris: L'Harmattan, 2004), 28.
54 Ibid.
55 Ibid.
56 Céline Masson, *Fonction de l'image dans l'appareil psychique* (Paris: Erès, 2004), 60.
57 Ibid.
58 Ibid.
59 Ibid.
60 Maldiney, *L'esthétique des rythmes*, 11.

As Jacques Lacan observed for his part: "the function of the painter is something quite different from this organization of the field of our representation [...] what is crucial, essential [are] those strokes that rain down from the painter's brush."[61]

Hence, *Gestaltung* appears to us as a fundamental process that harbors the germ of potential creativity. Art fits into a dialectic between *Gestaltung* and creativity, between a being in becoming and the object being created, between self and the other encountering the thing created.

According to Heidegger the work is installing (*ein-richten*);[62] it takes up its place in the world, installing itself (at the same time) as it creates itself. From a similar point of view, Claude Lecoq has written of painting that it "makes clear that not everything is named and that its object tends to make visible that which does not have a name."[63]

If art bears within it something irreducible rather than susceptible to interpretation, its expression should be considered as that which "compels us to invent a new language."[64] A remark of Pierre Soulages too should be pondered: "To paint means constantly escaping from a project."[65] We cannot then confine creativity to the mere production of objects sometimes described as artworks; it needs to be apprehended as a fundamental process stemming from a sudden emergence for the subject himself, in the here and the now.

Lastly, if creativity no longer corresponds to a subjective logic, its value might potentially be reduced to that of an object. As production or reproduction, it risks being considered uniquely in respect of how well it replicates the world. It would thus be reduced to its function as a *lathouse object*, a term coined by Jacques Lacan that designates gadgets and the whole host of objects meant to satisfy our consumerist appetites, products of the contemporary technological arena.[66] To view creativity through the prism of *Gestaltung* obliges us to stand this logic on its head: the work that creates and is created is not part of a finality; it does not lead anywhere; it is simply presence to itself, and this is why it is so moving to us. *Gestaltung* moreover commits us to treating the conditions of the emergence of the trace lying at the origin of form as essential. In that tension between form and the void at which it hints—"in this fundamental character of the work-being as argument is the root of the need for what we call 'form,'"[67] declares Heidegger. A form delimits an edge; it allows a glimpse of the world but does not portray it—not completely in any case. The artist is someone who, Maldiney argues, "as Dante says, possesses the habit of art and a trembling hand."[68]

Conclusion

In conclusion, I would like to refer briefly to a number of patients who have been the subjects of detailed study: Isis, a schizophrenic, with her floral patterns and the significant discovery of a "personal interpretation" that enables her to strike out into subjectivity where before she had been limited to copying. It is she who does the interpreting and no longer the invasive Other who used to scrutinize her inquisitorially and prevent her from exhibiting her artworks under her own name. Unburdened by judgment, she has adopted a personal style that prompts a movement of creation in which the forms unfold; the constant plea-

61 Jacques Lacan, "Les quatre concepts fondamentaux" (1964–65), in *Séminaire, livre XI* (Paris: Seuil, 1973), 126.

62 Martin Heidegger, "Origin of the Work of Art," in *Off the Beaten Track*, trans. Julian Young and Kenneth Haynes (Cambridge: Cambridge University Press, 2002), 202.

63 Claude Lecoq, *La peinture et la traversée du pire. Création, savoir, soin* (Paris: Acéphale, 1996), 7.

64 Ibid.

65 Ivan Toulouse, *Clair-Obscur, essai sur la pensée créatrice* (Paris: L'Harmattan, 2012), 61. Ivan Toulouse notes that Pierre Soulages made this remark in a film shot by the painter Jean-Michel Meurice in 1980.

66 Jacques Lacan, "L'envers de la psychanalyse" (1969–70), in *Séminaire, livre XVII* (Paris: Seuil, 1991), 188.

67 Martin Heidegger, "L'origine de l'œuvre d'art," in *Chemins qui ne mènent nulle part*, trans. W. Brokmaier (Paris: Gallimard, 1962), 21 (French translation of the first version).

68 Maldiney, *L'esthétique des rythmes*, 18.

sure she gains from painting allows her to relate to others and forge social bonds. There is Tania, a young patient with autism who circumscribes the eruption of raw instinct in circles—her "anger bubble"—protecting her from outpourings of aggression toward herself and others without forcing her to abandon her characteristic anger. The circle becomes a malleable form she develops from drawing to drawing, forming and distorting it, sampling it in one place and reinjecting it in another. She has discovered the pleasure of play and the fluidity of a movement that alleviates her relations with others, all while keeping them far enough away to avoid literally crashing into them. Working on the question of the edge, of the fringe, she has delimited a horizon that encircles the void. Thus, she can remain on the edge and keep the terrifying effects of reality at bay. Then finally there is Raoul, who wards off his descent into melancholy by spontaneous architectures and poetic writings that circumscribe a space he can inhabit.

If one can talk of therapy in the case of these patients it would be of "*Gestaltung* therapy"—not to be confused with Gestalt therapy. This detour by *Gestaltung* has changed the direction of my work as a psychologist practicing psychiatry. It is an interest that leads me today to undertake many collaborative workshop experiments with artists as key partners in the generation of the movement inherent in creativity and in the transformation of form.

Translated from the French by David Radzinowicz

Form in the Sphere of Design[1]

Pierre-Damien Huyghe

The notion of form is a recurrent one in the history of design. My assumption in the following text is that the notion remains useful, in spite of the prevailing pattern of contemporary discourse. Here I examine four landmark formulations of this notion during the history of the discipline, presenting form as one element in a tension that underpins the industrial world. Neither categorically predetermined nor hosted by a specific body of knowledge or skill, and rarely mobilized as a solution, form is framed mainly within a logic whose values are option and relation. Thus, what is under discussion here is the emotional capacity—or the attraction—of the technical dynamic with which in any event all human industry is employed.

A Field of Tension

Historically in industrial society the issue of design has generally been defined in terms of scarcely more than three or four expressions. My hypothesis is that these formulations remain valid today: every time design comes into play it always articulates a particular standpoint within the field of tension these expressions make it possible to circumscribe. Admittedly, superficial terminological developments have occurred. If, for instance, less credence is given today to the vocabulary of "function," much is made of "uses" and "services." These various designations themselves, however, include areas that may overlap with the more ostensibly historical notion of "functionality." This kind of slippage in the lexicon of reference, by and large a rather recent phenomenon, is obviously not without consequences for the essence of work. Still, the point at hand is insufficiently understood if one concedes that a priori it is little more than a movement emerging from the core of design, from the nerve center of its activity. The contrary assumption should at least be considered—one that defines current discourse in terms of the harbingers of an external influence that has settled on the fringes of the field. There it siphons off its potential energy, as it were dragging it out of its

1 The present text derives from an article published in the chapter "La notion de forme dans le champ du design" in Pierre-Damien Huyghe, *Travailler pour nous* (Saint-Vincent de Mercuze: De l'incidence éditeur, 2020), which is the third in a series of reissued and significantly expanded books (Pierre-Damien Huyghe, *À quoi tient le design* [Saint Vincent de Mercuze: De l'incidence éditeur, 2014]). The text was then published under a slightly different title: "Formel et relatif."

natural space of gravitation and inducing it to abandon—in the absence if this is indeed the case of all other poles of attraction or magnetization—its specific medium.

I am aware that the vocabulary—"field," "tension," "gravitation," "attraction," "magnetization"—with which I have just addressed the question of "design," possesses a metaphorical dimension. Is proceeding in this manner wrong methodologically? I leave it to the reader to judge hereafter. The issue is to make clear that the global term *design* covers operations which, although not arbitrary, have not yet been "stabilized"—nor probably are they conducive to stabilization. This is why, for this subject (or, better, for this field), it has proved impossible to devise a watertight methodology capable of ensuring absolute effectiveness, and why, on the contrary, the proximity to the relative but essential indetermination that culture has gradually vouchsafed to the word *art* remains crucial.

In these conditions, the first task, methodically speaking, consists in establishing the nature of the tension within which design was formerly confined and which has historically constituted its field of operations. Such an undertaking demands that we return to the three expressions quoted at the start—not in order to fix them forever as if in a museum, but to reveal the resistance at their conceptual core. If, as I believe, these three expressions constitute genuine polarities, it should be possible to locate in the heart of the field they define an element under tension because it is magnetizable. Hovering as if between the forces of attraction of two magnets, this element is in itself relatively indefinite, or else definable only within a logic of tension or as a rapport, a relation. This element, as we will see, is *form*; it is the approach to the concept of form, the relationship of form to something that is not formal, but which, by dint of its distance from the register of form, helps to produce the potential tension without which design would not exist. What I want to highlight in this study of the three formulations referred to above is the character, the dynamic condition of the field. The essential thing here is how it is split between two poles—its relative irresolution, the very fact there is divergence. All this implies that, in all human undertakings and industries concerned with design, it is finally less a question of solutions than of options. It is interesting to note how such and such an option—once reflected in a text—gives life so to speak to the term *form* by associating it with a statement of the relevant issues or goals that a more a priori, more specific, more artistic study, or one less bound up with the notion, would not necessarily have revealed.

"Design for Life"

The first of the aforementioned expressions that interest me transpires in a notion proposed in a text by László Moholy-Nagy published in 1947 which I will interpret here rather freely.[2] Design, the title says, is intended "for life." It strives to make us, city-dwellers for the majority, become more active, more alert, more vigilant, more aware. Why? Because the usual pace of modern life and its spurts of production (*poussées productives*) do not necessarily result in our being in phase with what surrounds us. Such growth (*poussées*) is not immediately obvious, far from it. It has infiltrated our everyday life without our becoming aware of its nature. Thus, in the modern world we generally come and go burdened with audio and visual information, but unconcerned about the aesthetic qualities of this information. In

2 László Moholy-Nagy, "Nouvelle méthode d'approche. Le design pour la vie," in *Peinture, photographie, film et autres écrits sur la photographie*, trans. Jean Kempf and Gérard Dallez (Paris: Jacqueline Chambon, 1998), 242–74.

our eyes they constitute a kind of atmosphere or fog; often paying scant attention to them, our mind drifts elsewhere. It is basically rather simple: the idea of design "for life" presupposes that, if the deployment of the production capacity of industrial society demands the specific activities of design, this is precisely because such deployment is not spontaneously organic, because it does not form organically.

But what does *organic* actually mean? The most explicit definition is probably to be found in remarks by Frank Lloyd Wright, though it doubtless also occurs in Moholy-Nagy (and not just in the text explicitly devoted to design).[3] In lectures devoted to modern architecture given in 1930, which Moholy-Nagy might well have been aware of, Wright states that "industry must educate designers instead of making craftsmen."[4] Production capacity formerly dwelt in the bodies of expert workers; today, in the main, it resides in machines. The challenge it is to get "these formidable craft-engines" to do their work better. "[B]eyond mechanical skill," the plan must be to find the "cadences of form."[5] In other words, where there is no design, contemporary mechanical production lacks a formal rhythm. And it is within this deficiency that an industry has developed which is not as well developed in its formation as it might be considering the mechanical apparatus it deploys. It is this industrial state that, to Wright's mind, is not "organic." He goes as far as to allege that is not even "organized." The problem though, as the architect himself counters, is that the term *organic*, if "taken too biologically, is a stumbling-block. The word applies to 'living' structure—a structure or concept wherein features or parts are so organized in form and substance, as to be, applied to purpose, *integral*."[6]

Comparatively well-known, these remarks are more involved than they may appear. To understand the nature of a "living structure" which is not overly "biological" is far from easy. This, however, is the task at hand. My thesis is that Frank Lloyd Wright and with him Moholy-Nagy level their critique at the possible existence of an industry in which the product's components—its features, its structural outline—can be disposed and thereby presented to perception without, however, forming a "whole." Under the cover of words of Latin origin (*disposition, administration*) introduced to the analysis here at my own behest, I am alluding to another term, Greek this time: *economy*. If, in Wright and Moholy-Nagy's view, a product's components may be arranged incongruently, and if it can, by this very fact, be described as inorganic, its economy is not in proportion: ill-adapted, it proliferates. It produces, but it also incorporates into the finished article interests other than those of the product; it is not simply the production of a product. Understood in this fashion, such propositions might be compared to the perspectives opened up a little later by Victor Papanek.[7] Read in parallel with another text by Wright himself, they can be understood as follows: the nonorganic state of industry consists in producing an "entity" that is not "integral" or "intrinsic" at all.[8] These "entities" are thus produced, or released into the world, for reasons other than the typical, characteristic, and specific capacities by which they are put into operation. Instead of being treated for what they might offer, instead of being worked in view of their specific purpose, they are employed as a means, as utensils, instruments, so that their raison d'être lies elsewhere than in their being.

It is important to understand that Wright and Moholy-Nagy, though thoroughly critical of the advance of industry in the world, do not recommend jettisoning

3 See Frank Lloyd Wright, *The Future of Architecture* (New York: Horizon Press, 1953).
4 Frank Lloyd Wright, *Modern Architecture: Being the Kahn Lectures for 1930*, ed. Neil Levine, Facsim. ed (Princeton NJ: Princeton University Press, 2008), 29.
5 Wright, *Modern Architecture*, 29.
6 Ibid., 27 (emphasis in the original).
7 Victor Papanek, *Design for the Real World: Human Ecology and Social Change* (New York: Pantheon Books, 1971).
8 I here use the terms Frank Lloyd Wright employed later in "The Language of Organic Architecture" (1953); in Wright, *The Future of Architecture*, esp. 322.

every possible deployment of modern technicity. In principle, moreover, no design is in contradiction with technical progress (*poussées*). The problem is how to manage this progress so that the objects resulting from the production capacities active in each particular epoch attain a certain quality of presence, a certain look—that of the aforementioned "formal cadence." Neutral-izing or reducing aesthetic power is thus not precisely what is at stake. On the contrary, the challenge is to awaken whatever is striking in the way objects appeal to each of us. In the final analysis, the adversary is that state of intellectual passivity in which, as I indicated above, many are accustomed to living with dynamic growth without ever explicitly embracing it. It is true—this at least is the creed of "for life" designers—that this same state is not entirely unmotivated: those who take refuge in habitual living are, as I have said, led to do so because progress has not managed to present its own formal possibilities to itself, because it has not completely assured its quality as such. Progress is not serene with regard to itself; at root, and not without reason, it is riddled with self-doubt. So it tries to slip in unnoticed, make itself amenable without attracting attention; no-one adopts it wholeheartedly. Maintaining illusions as to its nature, it prevents itself from being perceived: it does not even perceive itself. Hence, in reaction, the ambition of design "for life," when it is not dedicated to establishing—as it may well also seek to do—forms of new functions but rather new forms for preestablished functions, for those already endowed with a certain tradition: to make formally perceptible—by ensuring suitable conditions—how an object manufactured in the materials and with the techniques of its time cannot look as it might have in earlier times without eliciting a kind of lassitude. Why for example is plastic used as the material for a chair and why is molding (the formative mode technically adapted to this material) used when the aim is a seat that adopts the forms of yesteryear—less its period sheen? The feet or stretchers bearing chairs and stools constructed out of something other than join wood can easily be made to look different from their predecessors. The task for design is surely rather to devise and to create designs for seating and shapes inherent in the potential and dynamic properties of the materials and textures of our era.

"Ugliness Doesn't Sell"

The above precept defines the notion of design held by the second approach I would like to refer to. The expression is also taken from a text, rather better known and in any case more readily compatible with the expectations and justifications of the modern economy: *La laideur se vend mal* (Ugliness doesn't sell).[9] This axiom, which I will once again interpret freely, was that of another designer, Raymond Loewy, who explicitly stated that he worked in an industrial "aesthetic" register. Of course, as I have just implied in so many words, the leitmotif of collusion with the forces and the rationale of commerce is practically audible. But this is not what I would like to stress and discuss initially. I am more interested in how the polarization of design proposed and advocated above has to deal with surfaces and envelopes. Unlike the preceding proposition, the chief concern here is not so much to authenticate the advances in form of any given period; neither is it to celebrate the materials, textures, and expertise that underpin these advances. No, the point is chiefly to lodge these materials, textures, and capacities in the mind for pecuniary advantage: determining the "satisfactory" amount of ostenta-

9 See Raymond Loewy, *Never Leave Well Enough Alone* (Baltimore: Johns Hopkins University Press, 2002), published in French as *La laideur se vend mal*.

tion and ornament becomes a matter of business. This character of "satisfactory" ornament I might call "elegance"—the elegance of seduction, in fact. Loewy spoke for his part of "simplification."[10]

This concept bears stressing since it can result, indeed has resulted, in a misunderstanding of the aesthetic qualities inherent in the two axioms I have been analyzing up to this point. Loewy (as I just remarked, this is one of the components of his vocabulary) pleads for a certain formal simplification, or, putting it differently, a certain rightness or aptness as to pattern. Yet if, in substance, Loewy recommends reining in outward show, it is not because he wants to expose the technical nature or period texture of the objects concerned: it is simply to attract clients, to entice buyers more effectively.

Moreover, it can scarcely be a coincidence that Loewy's account of how ugliness doesn't sell opens with a story of seduction. Loewy frequently couches the aesthetic positions he defends or criticizes in terms of physical appeal and attraction. Thus, writing of a Gestetner duplicator he found himself responsible for refurbishing: "Unwrapped and standing naked in front of me, it looked like a very shy, unhappy machine. [...] It was a sad machine, really, in spite of some gold striping that failed to lift its morale. Besides it smelled." If the register is no less organic than in Moholy-Nagy's diktat, the perspective is utterly different. Here, design is surgical or medical, so implying a normative conception of the living. "After locking at my patient for a while, under operating room floodlights," continues Loewy, "I decided it was too far gone for a complete redesign job [... in] only three days. [...] So I decided to limit my efforts to amputation (the four legs) and plastic surgery on the body. By this, I meant a 'face-lift' job. I would simply encase all the gadgety organs of the machine within in a neat, well-shaped, and easily removable shell."[11]

Above and beyond such rehabilitation work on the general shape, when the goal is to create and not merely revive a formal element, Loewy defends, in the name of his conception of industrial design, a course of action he sums up as follows: the astute industrial designer is the one who is clear-sighted enough to detect the "shock-zone"[12] in any particular problem. At this point, a piece attains what Loewy calls the MAYA (Most Advanced Yet Acceptable) stage, which in fact designates the relative gap between a novel avant-garde form and a "norm in its own field." Any new form deviating too abruptly from this norm, Loewy contends, "involves risk to the manufacturer."[13]

The distinguishing characteristic of Loewy's approach is the substantial relationship to habitual behavior and to the norm I have just highlighted. Though design may consist in deviating from one or the other, it is nonetheless freighted with both and continues to embody them. Raymond Loewy is neither a modern nor a modernist, he is a modernizer;[14] that is, an originator who advocates the measured emergence of technological advances. I write "emergence" since I wish to imply that Loewy's consent is proportional, not to the principle of technical modification, but to the degree of its appearance in experience, its presence in the—aesthetic—register of phenomenality. Thus, Loewy encourages designers to mitigate innovation through outward appearance. This is partly the reason behind the attention they are to give to the housing, body, and panels of a product—the Gestetner duplicator being one example among many. Thus,

10 Ibid., 211.
11 Ibid., 82–83.
12 Ibid., 278.
13 Ibid., 281.
14 On the nature of and issues behind this terminological distinction, see Pierre-Damien Huyghe, *Modernes sans modernité (éloge des mondes sans style)*, Collection "Fins de La Philosophie" 4 (Paris: Lignes, 2009), 22–24.

even if Loewy did not practice exactly what I am talking about here, his way of thinking acknowledges that design is able to plug into the production of certain imaginary contents on the formal level. Seduction is perhaps impossible without the production of a self-image. By extension, in the pampered world of design objects, as promoted by thinkers like Loewy, a transparent plastic chair cannot be just what it is: a seat visibly of its time. No, its looks may well betray an allegorical, symbolic, or signifying element which can, in spite of its banal function, render it attractive. By stylish formal features in its legs, feet, or back—historically locatable and for this reason bound, by habit, to a perceptive norm—a chair can be enhanced by allusions to some respectable formal vocabulary, even if this vocabulary emanates from an earlier period. Such a practice implies a sense of outward show absent from the idea of design mentioned above. While the latter implies formal rupture, the former finds room if required for implications and connotations. Rather than seeking to confirm to a productive paradigm, it modulates a culture. In the final analysis it opts for a principle of variation that allows a modern or modernized technicity to plug into values of imagination and appreciation already in place.

"Form and Function"

In what is an inevitably polemical section in his book—a passage devoted moreover to a eulogy of simplification that erects simplicity into a template for imagining objects—Loewy attacks the third of the adages I would like to refer to, one whose best-known expression is that of Louis Sullivan in the late nineteenth century. It is, however, not exactly to that famous formulation ("form follows function") that I will refer now, but to a substantially corrected version which we owe once again to Frank Lloyd Wright: "form and function."[15] Sullivan's axiom was articulated in a particular historical context: that of the battle against industrial products that imitated handicraft. Its goal was first and foremost to make apparent, to deliver, and then render admissible, the potential for unadorned, unvarnished beauty in modern industry. As I see it, in adapting the axiom Wright is drawing attention to the fact that design wholly dedicated to function—in reality, to functional purification—would lack something essential, something he, and, after him I too term "form." To a point, it designates one of the central tasks of design—that of selecting, among all the possible functions and operations, those which can be bound to a formal value, to a certain quality of aspect, in its turn inextricably linked to a functionality, which can, in the end, never be superfluous. The implication is that, if an object, space, or situation does not fulfill a function, if it does not simply function, then it is alien to design. But it also means that not everything of this functional order necessarily attains the level of what Wright calls "form." Hence design cannot exist just anywhere and for anything: it has conditions of possibility. Not every technical practice is a potential subject for design simply by dint of its existence. There has to be something "formable" in it.

15 Such an alteration of Sullivan's diktat is clearly assumed by Wright in the aforementioned essay of 1953, "The Language of Organic Architecture," though it is also latent in earlier texts by the architect.

It is precisely this relationship with the "formable" that Loewy's offensive leaves out in favor of a conception of design that is at root decorative. How can such an assertion be valid? Decoration does not necessarily imply opulence in appearance. Actually, when pleading for simplification in design, Loewy meant no more than this. Reading him, I recall that the Latin etymological axis (*decus*, *decet*), the root of the notion of decoration, also incorporates values such as decency and decorum. Even if Loewy does not employ such a vocabulary, he certainly strove to ensure a suitable (fitting, minimal, economical) appearance in every object he concerned himself with. In so doing though Loewy always basically thinks in term of appearance. What interests him is the sheer veil, the thinnest cover that might allow an object—that is, in this context, its functions—to seduce without shocking, to attract without extravagance. For Wright form is of a different nature. It operates on the level of the actual conditions of its presence, of its coming into being.

It is an approach that has at least two consequences. On the one hand, since the connection between form and function is reciprocal, it is not enough for the design materializing this connection (this was the horizon of Sullivan's diktat) to make (the) form "follow" (the) function: it will in some way affect the thrust of these functions. In addition, once the concept of functionality is no longer regarded as neutral, or as sufficiently defined by and of itself, design forestalls the unlimited deployment of functions. In consequence, the intersection between humanity and technical advance is not determined solely by the logic of functionality. Functionality only emerges as applicable when confined to a limit—that of a potential form.

Generally speaking, it is thought that the techniques with which the designers work can be directed at will. These techniques may proceed in the direction of what Wright calls "form," but they may just as easily not go down this path and give rise in consequence to the presence of formless objects, pieces, situations, and spaces. This point is crucial. It admits that at the root of design there lies, together with a certain capacity for distinction, a principle of technical undecidability. As rectified by Wright, Sullivan's maxim does not assign one and one form only to each given function in a predetermined fashion. In point of fact all this is entirely paradoxical, since it admits that the much-vaunted form craved by all emerges only through difference; it contends that design exists only differentially, owing to how, for the same function, there may exist a range of presences in which formed productions may be associated with productions possessed of less form or even with no form at all. This is why I insisted at the start on the idea that design needs to be understood in reference to a field of tensions. Design is possible only because it is not systematic. It relies on elements of orientation and selection. Functionally, whatever fulfills such and such an option might just as well do without it: a concern with form is thinkable only within a range of ostensible functional modes.

Form as a Relative Element

By and large, explicit commitments to the particular expression "form and function" have been few and far between. To the complexity it highlights, prevailing historiography has tended to prefer Sullivan's version as simpler, easier to classify, though it too is rarely analyzed in the context of its utterance. The personal closeness of the two architects (Wright worked for Sullivan for a time) has done the rest and is mobilized as an argument to situate their thinking in the same lineage. Similar methods that take insufficient account of the precise wording of texts often result in associating standpoints that are actually at variance. For example, Sullivan (once again) is yoked to Adolf Loos, then Loos to Walter Gropius and the Bauhaus—as if the Bauhaus itself presented a self-evident unity of thought, as if this unity might without further ado be linked back to the name of its first director, and as if, finally, Gropius's own thinking had not undergone evolution, alteration, or (why not?) contradiction. Reading these texts and building a subtler representation of the way in which they orbit around one another should, however, result in a different pattern of thought. Likewise, the attentive examination of their works. In truth, both the concept and the reality of design—though it cannot be coupled with just any functional operation, and remains neither boundless nor always applicable—have constantly wavered in both its concept and in its reality. Admittedly, as with any oscillation, the amplitude of these differences may appear minimal. Genuine differences—variations in standpoint—exist and they are far from inconsequential.

If, as I contend here, "design" does not indubitably exist, if it proceeds from a non-systematic economy of production, and if in these conditions it succeeds in creating in every domain it is applied to states of form without which it could not be present, it is because its chief purpose in the industrial world is to give rise to situations of possible preference. Opening onto questions concerning the forms of functions (notice I do not write "functional forms"), it has and should still be able to make it possible to exercise taste with respect to the things of this world. A concern with the formal, however articulated, adds to industry. It enlarges it. It is in this manner that the effect of design in the relatively unspecified unity thereby constituted fuels the attraction of the world of production, its emotion-creating capacity.

Emotion, literally, etymologically, implies the existence of movement. Formerly, "to move" meant "to disturb the calm of." Why promote the idea of such a "move" today? In the absence of all emotional disturbance, absolute calm is the state of a perfectly unaffected being—sheltered, for sure, and completely protected from having to express a preference, but inert as well. What human would accept, in their own life, the calm never to be "moved"? Any relationship to the world we can adopt—and not submit to or yield to by force of circumstance—excludes such uniformity. Such adoption does not proceed as much as is believed from the sovereignty—the arbitrariness—of the subject; it arises primarily from the particular presence surrounding a being which we do not ourselves cause but which arouses our consciousness. This is the case with spaces, situations, and objects that owe their existence to the implementation of productive capacities channeled through human activity, but which are most of the time presented to us as fully realized entities, as things whose processes of production we have not witnessed. How can this receptivity not fall back into passivity? How can industrial products be apprehended? Globally, for design, in the very diversity of the few articulations applicable to it, the mission amounts to the following: to counter the uniformity or inertia that technical experience is liable to and which can be borne only in the passivity of reception. By expressing through one or another of these formal preferences the fact that there can be no cast-iron industrial formula or productive "solution," in consequence it furthers the possibility of appreciating the existence value of the objects it produces.

At the same time, though, design would lack consistency if the states of form with which it is concerned, under the pretext of depending on the genius, discretion, or simply the caprice of the designer, were thought of as free to be varied ad infinitum. The response of an industrial system intent on forcing through the uptake of its products lies precisely here: in the ceaseless variation of appearances, that is, in the purely superficial negation of uniformity. By invariably associating thinking about the element of form with some other element (form and organicity, form and simplification, form and function), historical design has not confined itself to this negation. In all probability, in this fashion it touches upon the very dynamic of the industrial world, for such a task can only have been accomplished by each time considering form, whatever formulation is deployed to enhance it, as relatively variable.

Neither categorical nor arbitrary: such is the formal principle of design.

Translated from the French by David Radzinowicz

First There Is Form
Some Critical Remarks about the Belief That Form Follows Function

Jörg Petruschat

The present text will focus on the idea that function follows form. This is diametrically opposed to one of the overriding dogmas in architecture and design since the end of the nineteenth century, which states that form follows function. In many discourses this phrase is attributed to the architect Louis Sullivan, as if he were the first person to have hit upon it. But this is wrong. Sullivan himself made use of analogies to developmental processes in nature to back up his arguments, and saw his ideas as akin to those of the philosophers Horatio Greenough, Henry Thoreau, and Ralph Waldo Emerson.[1]

The history of the idea that form follows function is, in fact, considerably older. Aristotle was an early and firm advocate of this position. He insisted in a dispute with his fellow philosopher Anaxagoras that humans have hands because they are the most intelligent of all living organisms.[2] In Aristotle's philosophy, hands were a form of intelligence. Form follows function.

Anaxagoras claimed the opposite on this point. He believed that intelligence preceded the hands. Humans, he argued, have intelligence because they have hands.[3] For him, the function is an event of the form. And this is the line of argument I shall follow as well.

Anaxagoras was not the only proponent of a primacy of form. In Germany, for example, Gottfried Wilhelm Leibniz led the way in rejecting Aristotelian arguments that form was preconditioned by function. Leibniz regarded reality as the result of inherent possibilities of action in each substance. In his opinion, form is one of the inbuilt characteristics of the living substance, with an infinite number of different attributes. Each substance has a dynamic force which contains an inexhaustible abundance and gives rise to a multiplicity of living beings.[4] Some

1 Elisabetta di Stefano, "Form follows function? Misunderstanding and Value of a Sullivan's Concept." In *Wolkenkuckucksheim* 17, no. 32 (2012): 38–44.

2 Aristoteles, *Zoologische Schriften II: Über die Teile des Lebewesen* (Berlin: Akademie-Verlag, 2007), 108.

3 Anaxagoras cited in Jaap Mansfeld and Oliver Primavesi, eds., *Die Vorsokratiker* (Ditzingen: Reclam, 2012), 635.

4 Ilse Jahn, Rolf Löther and Konrad Senglaub, *Geschichte der Biologie. Theorien, Methoden, Institutionen, Kurzbiographien* (Jena: VEB Gustav Fischer Verlag, 1985), 221.

years later the French mathematician, geodesist, astronomer, natural science researcher, and philosopher Pierre Louis Moreau de Maupertuis took up Leibniz's basic idea but formulated it in a more mechanistic way. He argued that the innumerable diversity of forms of individual living creatures was based on the random combination and characteristics of formal elements. However, only a small number of these randomly structured individual animals had the appropriate construction of their body parts to be able to satisfy their needs. In the case of "another, far larger number, there is neither adaptation nor order: all these latter animals died; animals without mouths could not live, and others that lacked reproductive organs could not reproduce themselves. The only remaining ones are those for which order and adaptation existed; and species that we see today are only a tiny proportion of those that were produced by a blind fate."[5] Maupertuis believed that it was the combination of elements that led to the diversity of life-forms, and it was the function of survival that determined the continued existence of these combinations.

The following is divided into three sections: In the first, I shall indicate that evolution follows the primacy of form and not the primacy of function, as Louis Sullivan and many other architects and designers with a rather weird view of evolution argued and still argue to this day. In the second section, I shall show that form is also the primary and decisive element for creative thought, rather than function or meaning or logic—these three elements all taken together are also seen as practice from which creative thought may emerge but which it must surmount to arrive at changes. Third, for agents that want to design things, I shall show how, once we disregard the functions, the capacity can be developed to recognize form as form and to explore its potential.

1. Form in Evolution

No one who claims today that evolution developed forms of life with functions that serve the purpose of survival would suggest that evolution was deliberately aiming at these functions and is therefore teleological. Biologists discussed this topic around eighty years ago when rejecting the Aristotelian concept of entelechy. In the first place it was the Neovitalists around Hans Driesch who regarded the functionality of life-forms as explicable only with reference to this Aristotelian concept. Nowadays biology has very largely discarded this kind of metaphysical assumption. Nonetheless, the idea of *telos*, the purposeful origin of biological forms, has not completely disappeared. It survived in the concept of teleonomy.

Those who speak of teleonomy no longer mean that the whole of life is permeated or overarched by a metaphysical principle of purposefulness, or is somehow mysteriously oriented toward this principle. Those who speak of teleonomy today are referring to empirically verifiable processes. When forms are reproductive, and thus fit for survival, their creation must be oriented toward this functionality—or not?

The concept of teleonomy was developed by the British biologist Colin Pittendrigh. He saw the functional directionality in the behavior of an organism or its parts as the effect of programs. In his day that was absolutely modern, a kind of cybernetic thinking.

5 Pierre Louis Moreau de Maupertius, *Œuvres* (Lyon, 1756), part 1, 11–12, translated by Karen Margolis. The original reads: "dans un autre infiniment plus grand, il n'y avoit ni convenance, ni ordre: tous ces derniers ont péri; des animaux sans bouche ne pouvoient pas vivre, d'autre qui manquoient d'organes pour la génération ne pouvoient pas se perpetuer: les seuls qui soient resté sont ceux qui se trouvoient l'ordre & la convenance; & ces especes, que nous voyons aujourd'hui, ne font que la plus petite partie de ce qu'un destin aveugle avoit produit."

Not long afterward the French biologist and Nobel laureate Jacques Monod described every functional adaptation of living organisms, and the artifacts they created, as "teleonomic" because every structure, every performance, and every activity within them contributes to the success of "projects" for the maintenance and reproduction of the species.[6] This repositions the argument of the primacy of function in the evolutionary event: every form finds its justification for existence in the function of an individual survival. Although Jacques Monod tried to deny the basic arguments for any ideology which teleologically explained what happens in the universe, the argument of the primacy of function returned at the level of the organism. This results from Monod's cybernetic perspective. According to him, "the functional coherence of so complex a chemical machine, which is autonomous as well, calls for a cybernetic system governing and controlling the chemical activity at numerous points."[7]

It is noteworthy, however, that the regulatory functions are not based on cybernetic systems but on simple reciprocal relations. "We may say," Jacques Monod wrote, "that any teleonomic performance or structure in a living being—whatever it may be—can in principle at least, be analyzed in terms of stereospecific interaction involving one, or a very large number of proteins."[8]

The stereospecific property on which the cybernetic effect of enzymes is based refers to relationships that are at least bilateral. These at least bilateral relationships occur when a molecule enters into a relation with other molecules. It is the potential of this relation that gives rise to the stereospecific effect.

We should point out that what Jacques Monod called a "stereospecific property" is not a characteristic that simply belongs to one of the two sides. It is a property that is actualized on the one side only by the existence of other sides. Monod defined the faculty of an enzyme or a protein to react to a substrate or another protein as "a microscopic discriminative [...] if not 'cognitive' faculty."[9] In using this term he was fully aware that it was not a matter of some mysterious attribute of molecules but a situation for which the cybernetic repertoire evidently lacked an appropriate terminology. Nothing was regulated here. Relationships were constituted here—and indeed, from the bottom up, not from the top down.

Jacques Monod's observations in the microscopic field concurred with those he found in the composition of macroscopic structures. He wrote, "Order, structural differentiation, acquisition of functions—all these appear out of a random mixture of molecules individually devoid of any activity, any intrinsic functional capacity other than that of recognizing the partners with which they will build the structure. [...] These epigenetic processes therefore consist essentially in this: the overall scheme of a complex multimolecular edifice is contained *in posse* in the structure of its constituent parts, but only comes into actual existence through their assembly."[10] Only the affiliation made reality of the functional potential of the elements inherent in it. Only "the sum, or rather the cooperation of a multitude of noncovalent intramolecular interactions that stabilizes the functional structure of the protein—which in turn enables it to form—electively—stereospecific complexes (likewise noncovalent) with other molecules."[11] First the form, then the function.

I use the term *self-designing processes* (*Selbstgestaltungsprozesse*) to describe the interplay of elements. They are based on elementary forces that arise from

6 Jacques Monod, *Chance and Necessity: An Essay on the Natural Philosophy of Modern Biology* (New York: Vintage Books, 1972), 14–15.
7 Ibid., 45.
8 Ibid., 46.
9 Ibid., 46.
10 Ibid., 86–87, emphasis in the original.
11 Ibid., 91.

the relations of elements to each other. In these processes, molecules, enzymes, and proteins act on each other above and beyond their characteristics of *Gestalt* (*Gestalteigenschaften*). For their part, in affiliating they create a constellation of a higher order, as it were, which in turn, appears as a *Gestalt* itself in its relation to others: as a *Gestalt* above *Gestalten*.

In fact, Jacques Monod represented everything that functions in the cybernetic vocabulary. But at the same time, in terms of information theory the calculation in the cybernetic model posed a limit for his attempts at cognition. He himself called this limit a limit of decipherability. In a fundamental passage, he wrote: "In the ontogenesis of a functional protein are reflected the original and descent of the whole biosphere. And the ultimate source of the project that living beings represent, pursue, and accomplish is revealed in this message—in this neat, exact, but essentially indecipherable text that primary structure constitutes. Indecipherable, since before expressing the physiologically necessary function which it performs spontaneously in its basic make-up it discloses nothing other than the pure randomness of its origin."[12] First the form (*Gestalt*), then the function.

I use the German word *Gestalt* as a term and concept when it is a matter of grasping relationships in which one actualizes and engenders the other, in which the characteristics of the one result from the characteristics of others. I do this because the term *Gestalt* is itself a relational concept.[13] The one actualizes its *Gestalt* by means of the other's *Gestalt* which is actualized by the one. This is the deep etymological meaning of the term in German and the methodological value that this concept can have for cognitive processes. The German term *Gestalt* derives from a converse to-be-positioned. What I want to say is that the characteristic of things to have a *Gestalt*, a shape or form, is not only a human event, as proven by the school of cognitive perception at the beginning of the twentieth century.[14] The character of *Gestalt* is by nature universal. In the characteristics of *Gestalt* cosmic relationships find their connections. This basic assumption I am making here can be manifested and proven for everything that is observable, whether a situation or a process. It is a precondition of every kind of cognition to establish a reality, to register it and to make it into an object (*Gegenstand*). Observation is always intermingled with already established things.

What we call form represents what the human capacity for understanding has recognized as effects in relationships of form (*Gestalt*).[15]

For practical work in experimental systems this would mean abstracting as far as possible from the purposes of the experimental systems and perceiving the forms they create in their potential for creating shape (*Gestalt*)—and this means being able to see them aesthetically.[16]

Relationships of *Gestalt* (*Gestaltverhältnisse*), and thus potentials of forms for function, impact at every level of the evolutionary process. They are found in the creation of Eukaryota, which emerge as a kind of hybrid organism from a Eubacterium and an Archaebacterium and thus constitute a starting point for the development of every complicated and complex living organism such as plants, fungi, and animals. The evolutionary biologist Ernst Mayr wrote, "the first step toward multicellularity is an increase in size such as that found in more than a dozen groups of unicellular protists, algae, and fungi. This usually leads to a division

12 Ibid., 98.
13 Jörg Petruschat, "Von Grund auf: Einige Bemerkungen zum Experiment im Design," in *Experimentieren: Einblicke in Praktiken und Versuchsaufbauten zwischen Wissenschaft und Gestaltung*, ed. Séverine Marguin et al. (Bielefeld: transcript, 2019), 227–46.
14 See Christian von Ehrenfels, "Über Gestaltqualitäten." In *Vierteljahrsschrift für wissenschaftliche Philosophie*, year 13 (Leipzig, 1890), and Max Wertheimer, *Über Gestalttheorie*. Sonderdrucke des Symposiums 1 (Erlangen, 1925).
15 Jörg Petruschat, "Das Leben ist bunt," *Form+Zweck: Zeitschrift für Gestaltung* 21 (2005): 100–111.
16 Jörg Petruschat, "Routinen und ihre Überwindung. Einige Bemerkungen zur Evolution von Formen," in *Serie und Serialität: Konzepte und Analysen in Gestaltung und Wissenschaft*, ed. Gerhard Scholtz (Berlin: Reimer, 2017), 95–136.

of labor among the cells of such aggregations, eventually merging into genuine multicellularity."[17] First the form, then the differentiation in functions, which actually occurs in the mode of reciprocity.

A glance at the great pattern of evolution confirms this: Since Charles Darwin, evolution had been modeled as a process of rejection, a process in which budding repeatedly occurs. *Budding* means that the majority of new strains originate in a side branch of a major strain to which, within a relatively short period, they become so dissimilar that their affinity can only be demonstrated by molecular biology processes.[18] At the origin of this budding is a form that subsequently becomes functionally differentiated, embedded in its environment.

One of the most spectacular events in which forms were starting points for diverse functional differentiations is known as the Cambrian Explosion. In the late pre-Cambrian and early Cambrian period, around 70 to 80 basic structural body plans appeared on the projection surface of evolution. No new additions to them have appeared since then.[19]

To conclude this section on the primacy of form in evolution, I would like to mention Adolf Portmann. I am grateful to Patricia Ribault for this reference. Portmann writes extensively about the many dimensions in which animal forms are found. "For many people the view is still often obscured by a one-sided, functional method approach," he writes.

> They are only prepared to see horns as weapon or as a sexual character. Both these explanations are true; but they forget that this view does not enable us to grasp fully the peculiar shape and position of these structures. The slender limbs of many hoofed mammals are viewed merely as instruments for running, for speedy flight in forest or steppe. This is undoubtedly correct—but in addition to that, they are also part of a higher grade of differentiation. This need not be a functionally more efficient one; when it becomes further developed it may finally contribute to the extinction of the species. We must get beyond the functional conception, which judges only according to purpose and performance, and arrive at a concept of the animal which, while never ignoring the functional point of view, yet for that very reason also realizes how much wider and greater is the full significance of the animal form.[20]

This is Portmann's key idea: The form *enables* the function. Its development is not driven solely by impositions and challenges that we attribute to it when we operate with a functionalist gaze, modeling evolution only as an increase of efficiency in adapting to the lifeworld of organisms. Referring to the evolution of mollusks, Portmann writes that

> it is in the lower types that the shell formation appears more complicated than in the higher ones. Higher organization within a type does not mean an all-round increase in the elaboration of all the features and of all the activities, but a one-sided, specially oriented increase of certain performances, a promotion in one direction with a corresponding sacrifice of other rich possibilities. In the types of lower rank the mode of form production of the molluscan body might be characterized as "extensive,"

17 Ernst Mayr, *What Evolution Is* (New York: Basic Books, 2001), 53.
18 Ibid., 61.
19 Ibid., 64–65.
20 Adolf Portmann, *Animal Forms and Patterns: A Study of the Appearance of Animals* (New York: Schocken Books, 1967), 86.

> directed toward the greater unfolding of external forms; conversely, this mode might be described as "intensive" in the higher types of mollusc, where an outward simplicity is correlated with considerable internal complexity and with greater possibilities of a richer relationship with the environment. Nothing points more clearly to the hidden greatness of the creative life-forces than the fact that animals with a rather simple organization can produce structures which man spontaneously compares with the works of his artistic creations.[21]

The more an animal is seen as highly developed, the more rigorously its forms are integrated into functional relationships. Given this, it is not surprising that today experiments are being made in design with fungi, bacteria, and enzymes, and not with cats and dogs.

2. The Form in Thinking

Are the hands, as Anaxagoras thought, the organs that facilitate reason and that are involved in its creation? In evolutionary and ontogenetical terms? There is no doubt that hands are unique and remarkable organs. They reveal to us the world that lies before us, as they have always done, even back in the age when hands were flippers paddling on the side of our bodies in water. Our hands help us to connect to the matter of our existence. They support us when we are in danger of losing our position. With our hands we can feel our reality and simultaneously observe ourselves with our eyes. The eyes see what the hands are doing, what they are manipulating, what they are identifying and touching. This reciprocal distance and referentiality of seeing and touching (comprehension; *Begreifen*) makes us aware of our reality, our capacity to act. For the hands not only perceive our reality, they intervene in it and change it.

While the muscular system in the eye makes the eyeball turn, bends the lens of the eye, and thus brings the object of interest into sharp focus, separates it out from other things, and distinguishes between foreground and background, it is the hands that make this selection process into a palpable reality and attract the gaze of the eyes. At the place where the sensors in the finger feel an edge, at this same edge the eye registers the breaking up of the effects of light. At the level of the brain, the signal pattern from these two sensory procedures lead to resonance relationships and, in the resonance of their vibrations, guarantee the self the reality of its perceptions beyond all possible delusions that may arise from just one sense alone. The *Gestalt* of the hand is the *Gestalt* of the eyes, and conversely.

Indeed, the truly remarkable things about the hands, the eyes and, incidentally, all the other sensory organs, is that they are able to let go of the things their attention is focusing on. They are equally capable of turning toward something and turning away. This makes the sensory organs a universal form in relation to the particular situations individuals are in, and in which each of them experiences their own concrete meaning. It is the universal character of the sensory organs that allows individuals to experience the special nature of their situatedness, to demarcate differences and to memorize them. The brain is a growth of the sensory organs, and not conversely.

21 Ibid., 106–7.

We have known ever since Rudolf Arnheim's research on the connection between perception and thought that human thinking is a visual thinking.[22] Frank Wilson's research on the connection between the hand and consciousness has told us that our thought owes its structure, its grammar to anatomy, to motoric logic and the play of the hands.[23] In this context it is not only as the ancient sensualists imagined, that the material in which and with which we think is only a delivery/product of the sensory organs, and the intellect can do as it pleases with it. In terms of the principles with which they process the contents of memory, the brain and the intellect follow the mode of functioning of the sensory organs. Although the neurons in the brain are constructed and organized in a very special biochemical way, the neuronal networks mimic the composition of the body.[24] Thinking is a function of the bodily form, it is an embodied thinking.[25] In recent years, the investigations by Antonio Damasio in particular have shown that our consciousness is constructed on the feeling of the sensory organs, that feeling is the genuine basis of our self and not merely a companion phenomenon of it.[26]

To put it briefly: the sensory forms of our perception provide the pattern in which our thinking is organized.

I am distinguishing here between two forms in creative thought: a weak form and strong one. The weak form is usually understood in the context of the solution of tasks. I define the solution of problems as the strong form of creativity. Tasks differ from problems in the sense that the definition of the task already contains the shape of its solution. This is the case for almost all mathematical and geometric figures: they can be logically evolved and solved. Simple mathematical tasks do this with the equals sign. On the other hand, I define problems as constellations in which the factors of a relationship may be summarized but are not interrelated in a logically functional way, and do not separate logically.

It is possible, of course, to find tasks problematic as well. The mathematician and epistemologist Horst Rittel used the term *tame problems* for what I describe here as tasks. He called problems whose solution does not emerge from a logical sequence of factors *wicked*.[27] The spectrum of human challenges ranges between tame problems and wicked problems.

But when does a connection between factors and elements become problematic in a strong sense? My answer is that problems arise when routines fail in the constellations they create.[28]

Problems are constellations in which the agents come to a standstill with their habitual knowledge and when the routines that these constellations produce no longer work for the agents within them, but become counterproductive, destructive, or otherwise no longer satisfactory. A car can become a problem when it runs badly. But it can also become a problem because its industrial production releases toxic substances or takes place under working conditions that destroy people.

Yet how are problems solved that do not simply contain the shapes of their solutions in their definition of the task? I have observed that this occurs in two steps: first, the *Gestalt* in which the problems come to light is dissolved by critical thinking. In the process, the problematic situations collapse into a heap of elements or factors. What was previously a functional relationship loses its

22 Rudolf Arnheim, *Visual Thinking* (Berkeley: University of California Press, 1969).

23 Frank R. Wilson, *The Hand: How Its Use Shapes the Brain, Language, and Human Culture* (New York: Pantheon Books, 1998).

24 Antonio Damasio, *Self Comes to Mind: Constructing the Conscious Brain* (New York: Pantheon Books, 2010).

25 George Lakoff and Mark Johnson, *Philosophy in the Flesh: The Embodied Mind and Its Challenge to Western Thought* (New York: Basic Books, 1999).

26 Antonio Damasio, *Descartes' Error: Emotion, Reason and the Human Brain* (New York: G. P. Putnam, 1994); and Antonio Damasio, *The Feeling of What Happens: Body and Emotion in the Making of Consciousness* (New York: Harcourt Brace & Company, 1999).

27 Horst Rittel and Melvin Webber, "Dilemmas in a General Theory of Planning," *Policy Sciences* 4 (1973): 155–69.

28 Karl Popper, *The Logic of Scientific Discovery* (New York: Basic Books, 1959); Petruschat, "Von Grund auf."

previous existential logic and becomes random and free. The second step consists in gathering these elements or factors into a new whole, a new *Gestalt*. In doing this, some individual elements are discarded, others are altered or varied, and elements are often added from other contexts. The production of a renewed integration, the solving of the problem, does not have to be a logically constructed process. With hindsight this is true in most cases. This is what makes creative thinking so similar to the evolutionary event. In retrospect it seems logical to say that "evolution produced this bird." But it could not have been predicted in advance. Spiders do not spin webs to catch flies. They catch flies because they spin webs.

For the pooling of individual factors and elements in a new *Gestalt*, patterns are brought into play that are intrinsically meaningless and have no function of their own before they integrate this constellation in a novel way and consequently solve the problem. It is only their potential for gathering the disparate factors and elements into a structure and a totality that makes them into the form for these functions.

When Charles Darwin wanted to clarify the process of evolution, he used the model of branching. When Watson and Crick wanted to bring the molecular structure of nucleic acids into a probable structure, they built a spiral staircase in the room.

The theorist of science Karin Knorr-Cetina argues in her fundamental study *The Manufacture of Knowledge* that such metaphors and analogies have a key meaning in the production of processes of scientific knowledge. Although she herself expresses critical objections to the use of metaphors and analogies in scientific processes, she cannot deny their unrestrained usage in every area of formulation of knowledge. She emphasizes the importance of the semantic origins of these metaphors and analogies for their functionality and recommends researchers to engage in "reasoning from analogy." She argues this will help them to a deeper understanding of the knowledge that emerges.[29] I do not share this view. Charles Darwin did not make the analogy to branching because he thought evolution had deep roots that bear fruit, and Watson and Crick did not use the figure of the spiral staircase for their structural arrangement of DNA in order to climb upward. It was solely the form of these metaphors, abstracted from their semantic content, that provided the researchers with a formal solution for their hodgepodge of factors. In the case of Watson and Crick it was simply prototyping with laboratory equipment.

Formal solutions for wicked problems usually come from contexts that are extrinsic to the data scientists were attempting to arrange for scientific research. Anything else would be mere tasks.

The decisive process for solving wicked problems consists in the capacity of thinking to adduce forms for the arrangement of data or factors that give this arrangement shape and totality. For this purpose, these forms must be empty of their own meaning as far as possible. This is the only way they can exploit the functional potential in the pooling of elements and factors without interference. And this, in turn, means that thinking contains the ability to garner these kinds of forms that are empty of meaning and make them available.

29 Karin D Knorr-Cetina, *Manufacture of Knowledge: An Essay on the Constructivist and Contextual Nature of Science* (Oxford: Pergamon Press, 1981), 59–60.

To understand this creative process properly we have to discard the idea that the brain functions like a computer. The production of consciousness does not occur in a linear or parallel way but in complex patterns. As in evolution, what happens in the brain is organized by the selection principle. Out of a very complex data stream that converges from all parts of the central nervous system, the only data that are selected and emerge as dynamic core processes are those whose integration simulates a viable setting for the self.[30] Consciousness is not an additional performance over and above the data the body provides, but the selection and degeneration of these data. I am not claiming that the dynamic cores that Edelman and Tononi identified through magnetic resonance imaging in neuronal firing are the same as the patterns that synthesize factors into a form in creating solutions to problems. I do not mean that this is a way humans can be seen in the process of thinking. But the patterns in the synchronous oscillation of neurons that Edelman and Tononi could detect are equivalents in terms of consciousness. In both worlds—the physiological world of brain activities and the psychological world of thought—creative processes are organized according to similar principles. The constructiveness in thought and creating follows principles that are also decisive for the evolution of creatures. They are principles for which a form is the organizing factor.

3. Form in the Development of the Ability to Change Routines (Gestaltungsvermögen)

In 1921 Johannes Itten invited students at the Bauhaus Academy in Weimar to share his analysis of an altar painting by Meister Franke, *The Adoration of the Magi* from 1426.

Itten overlaid the original painting with an arrangement of basic geometric forms. This geometric layer made it possible to identify principles of composition, tensions between individual elements, their proportionality and harmony. The Virgin Mary's halo is created from the form of a circle in the center of the picture, while the axes framing the mutual tension created by the other visual elements result from a triangular composition. What appears as an analysis is the discovery of deeper underlying relationships created by the picture. In other words, the reality of art is a material evolution of basic formal constellations; universal forms precede concrete meanings and invoke reality.

In another exercise of Itten's foundation course, the student Paul Citroen made a color analysis of a painting of the Madonna. The results showed a juxtaposition of color fields with a relatively even grid forming a kind of frame for the Madonna figure. While Paul Citroen's analysis led him to an abstraction of color fields, the student Max Pfeiffer-Watenphul's analysis becomes a picture by itself, a colored rhythm study. This picture no longer illustrates or reproduces any kind of reality. It is intended to create a rhythm flowing into the observers' bodies. The color paper artwork is supposed to create a movement in the eyes of the observers that makes them vibrate and shows them something about themselves.

Many art historians still see the Bauhaus as a style that captures the functions of everyday life in abstract geometric forms. The opposite is the case. The functions are produced from an arrangement of forms.

30 Gerald M. Edelman and Guilio Tononi, *A Universe of Consciousness: How Matter Becomes Imagination* (London: Penguin Books, 2000).

For the students to practice producing functions with abstract forms, they have to learn to abstract these formal patterns from past experiences. To achieve this, Johannes Itten made his course students do loosening-up exercises. Humorously described as "figure skating on paper," big sweeps involving the whole body were to be drawn on paper, nudes were to be sketched "rhythmically," the students were instructed to practice feeling textiles or to use linear interplays to express experiential traces of the war that had just ended.[31] Wassily Kandinsky also required students in his foundation course to nurture the capacity for abstraction. Lines to be seen by the eyes were simultaneously intended to be lines of sound paths. Kandinsky himself experimented with such synesthetic correspondences between the eye and the ear.[32]

This achieved an arsenal of forms that went far beyond the evocation of emotional states. It was an exercise in the ability to cleanse forms, step by step, of all individual semantic memories. They were supposed to facilitate a universal experience. What is involved, in my opinion, is the key ability for solving problems, that is, the provision of forms that are suitable for gathering disparate factors into a *Gestalt*, a form that allows these factors diverse functional relationships.

What is called *functionalism* has its social dimension in the question of what to design for. Yet the deepest reason for *Gestaltung* is to be found in the form, not the purpose.

Translated from the German by Karen Margolis and Uli Nickel

31 Friederike Holländer and Nina Wiedermeyer, eds., *original bauhaus: übungsbuch* (Munich: Prestel, 2019).
32 Wassily Kandinsky, *Point and Line to Plane* (New York: Dover Publications, 1979).

No Deviation, No Life
Fine Arts and Symmetry[1]

Horst Bredekamp

1. Nefertiti's Asymmetry

The bust of Nefertiti in the Neues Museum on the Museum Island is considered Berlin's Mona Lisa.[2] Aside from the unfinished left eye, the portrait of the Egyptian queen from the final years of the reign of her spouse Akhenaton (1353–1336 BC) appears to be the epitome of perfected beauty. Strictly frontal photographs of Nefertiti refer the regularity of her features to their bilateral mirror-image composition (fig. 1).[3] This presents Nefertiti as satisfying the concept of symmetry as defined in 1794 by Johann Georg Sulzer: division of a work into two equal and similar halves.[4]

On closer examination, however, a disconcerting detail challenges this impression.[5] Facing the bust, the bottom right edge does not lie flat but instead hovers strangely in the air. The first extant photograph in which this anomaly is visible from the side is the 1945 portrait of the American monuments officer Captain Walter I. Farmer (fig. 2), one of the so-called Monuments Men. The photograph shows him as the director of the Wiesbaden Collecting Point, with the bust resting on a dark pedestal.[6] At the lower short end one can see the shadow of a gap created by a wedge placed underneath the side of the bust. The slant of the lower edge, as indicated in the 1954 photograph, is the result of the same wedge (fig. 1). It lifts the bust roughly 8 mm on that side at an angle of approximately 3 degrees. This finding is remarkable.

Ever since first being displayed in public in 1924, Nefertiti has never been positioned in line with this slightly oblique base, as is also the case with its most recent presentation in the New Museum. The pedestal is tilted so that the bust is perfectly plumb. In a now-famous photograph of German chancellor Angela Merkel, the base onto which Nefertiti has been mounted is practically a ramp (fig. 3).

1 This text is, in large part, a translation of Horst Bredekamp, "Ohne Abweichung kein Leben: Die bildende Kunst und die Symmetrie," *Nova Acta Leopoldina*, no. 412 (2016): 187–209.

2 On the basic history of her discovery and preservation see Rolf Krauss, "1913–1988: 75 Jahre Büste der Nofretete – Nefret-Iti in Berlin.," *Jahrbuch Preußischer Kulturbesitz*, part 1, vol. 24 (1988): 87–124; and Bénédicte Savoy, ed., *Nofretete: Eine deutsch-französische Affäre* 1912–1931 (Cologne: Böhlau, 2011).

3 Rudolf Anthes, *Die Büste der Königin Nofretete* (Berlin: Gebrüder Mann, 1954), 13.

4 "Symmetrie," in *Historisches Wörterbuch der Philosophie*, ed. Walter Kambartel, vol. 10 (Basel: Schwabe; Darmstadt: Wissenschaftliche Buchgesellschaft, 1998), col. 745.

5 On the following in detail, in part verbatim, see Horst Bredekamp,

Fig. 1

In 2010 the bust was examined by the Rathgen Research Laboratory in Berlin's Altes Museum, and on this occasion I had the opportunity to examine Nefertiti more closely. When she is not mounted on a wedge, her disposition changes (figs. 4, 5). The central axis of her face tips the aforementioned roughly 3 degrees to the right as we face her. As a result, her slightly raised right shoulder is displayed more prominently, introducing a kind of torque that creates a vitalizing thrust. Her left eyebrow appears broader than her right one at its outer area, and the folds in the upper lids commence at different heights. Assuming a central vertical axis, the individual facial elements are not at a uniform distance to it. The inclined Nefertiti loses her impression of flawless mirror symmetry but gains a touch of inner vitality due to the minimal disruptions.[7] This effect is even enhanced in the rear view. In the tilted position, the neck and shoulder lines contrast with each other, and the shift from a vertical to a tilted position (figs. 6, 7) releases a small surge of vitality.

Ever since Nefertiti has been on public view, her absolute verticality has always reinforced the scholarly consensus that Egyptian art pursued a normative mirror symmetry. This aesthetic prejudice sacrifices her own refinement in bringing forth her inner vitality through the interplay of symmetry and a break in symmetry. For this reason, I will focus here all the more on this shifting.

Fig. 2

Fig. 3

Fig. 4

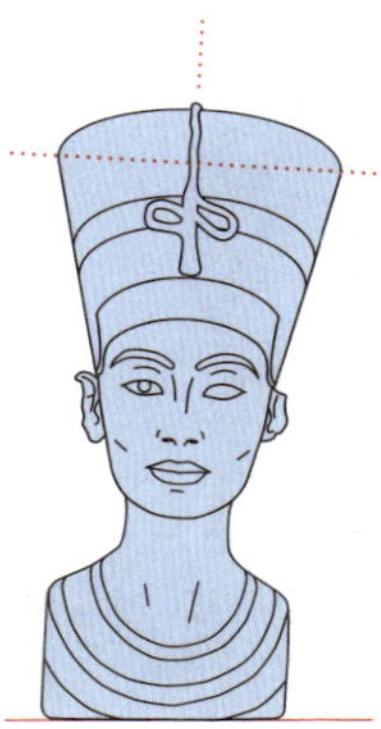

Fig. 5

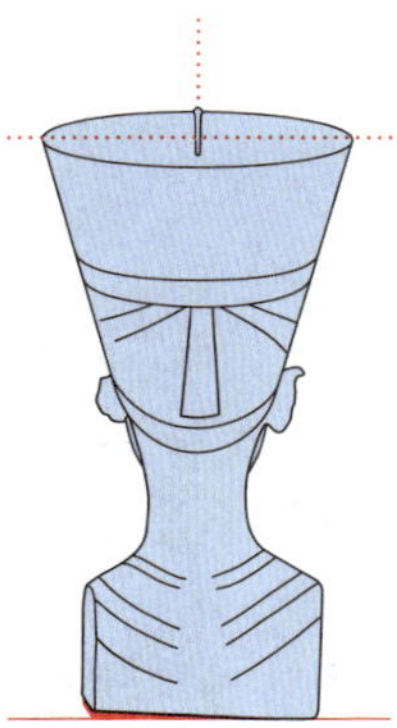

Fig. 6

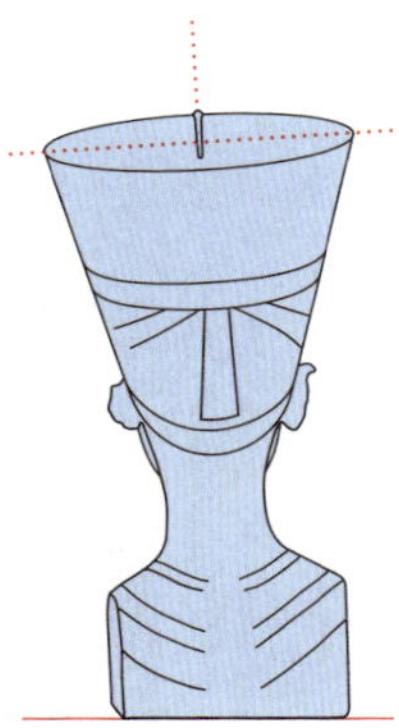

Fig. 7

Fig. 1: Bust of Nefertiti, Amarna period, c. 1340 BC, painted stucco-coated limestone, photographed in 1954.

Fig. 2: Walter I. Farmer with the bust of Nefertiti, Wiesbaden, 1945.

Fig. 3: Angela Merkel with Michael Eissenhauer looking at the bust of Nefertiti at the re-opening of the Neues Museum in Berlin, 2009.

Figs. 4 & 5: Frontal view of Nefertiti with and without supporting wedge.

Figs. 6 & 7: Back view of Nefertiti bust with and without supporting wedge.

"Der Keil der Nofretete, oder: 8 mm entscheiden die Welt," in *Synergies in Visual Culture: Bildkulturen im Dialog: Festschrift für Gerhard Wolf*, ed. Manuela De Giorgio, Annette Hoffmann, and Nicola Suthor (Munich: Fink, 2013), 579–590.

6 Walter I. Farmer, *The Safekeepers: A Memoir of the Arts at the End of World War II*, revised and with a preface by Klaus Goldmann (Berlin: de Gruyter, 2000), 86, 228.

7 Rolf Krauss, "1913–1988: 75 Jahre Büste der Nofretete – Nefret-Iti in Berlin," part 2, *Jahrbuch Preußischer Kulturbesitz* 28 (1991): 123–56, here 144–45.

8 For an early criticism of this interpretation see Jan Assmann, "Flachbildkunst des Neuen Reiches," in Claude Vandersleyen, *Das Alte Ägypten*, Propyläen Kunstgeschichte 17 (Berlin: Propyläen, 1985), 304–17; and Dietrich Wildung, "Grundstrukturen der Ägyptischen Kunst," in Heinz Herzer, *Ägypten und moderne Skulptur: Aufbruch und Dauer* (Munich: Lipp, 1986), 35–47. The methodological problem is developed on a larger scale by

Caris-Beatrice Arnst and Regine Schulz, "Vorwort," in *Typen, Motive, Stilmittel*, ed. Caris-Beatrice Arnst and Regine Schulz, Beiträge zur altägyptischen Kunst 1 (Heidelberg: Propylaeum, 2021), 7–11.

9 Lyvia Morgan, "Enlivening the Body: Color and Stone Statues in Old Kingdom Egypt," *Source: Notes in the History of Art* 30, no. 3 (Spring 2011): 4–11, here, 4.

10 In the sense of this new overarching understanding of the Mediterranean region see *Fremdheit – Eigenheit. Ägypten, Griechenland und Rom: Austausch und Verständnis: Symposium of the Liebieghaus, Frankfurt a. M., 28–30 November 2002 and 16–19 January 2003*, ed. Peter Cornelius Bol, Städel-Jahrbuch, n.s., 19 (Munich: Städel Museum, 2004), and the superb *Ägypten – Griechenland – Rom: Abwehr und Berührung*, ed. Herbert Beck, Peter Cornelius Bol, and Maraike Bückling, exh. cat., Liebieghaus, Frankfurt am Main (Tübingen: Wasmuth, 2005). For an English review see also Beatrix Gessler-Löhr, "Egypt, Greece, Rome: Rejection & Contact," *Minerva* 17, no. 1 (2006): 21–24.

11 Among a few other ancient authors quoting Polykleitos, Philo of Alexandria has passed on a key statement: "Perfection, he said, comes about little by little (*para mikron*) through many numbers." Philo, Mechanicus 4.1, 49.20, cited in Andrew Stewart, *One Hundred Greek Sculptors, Their Careers and Extant Works* http://www.perseus.tufts.edu/hopper/text?doc=Perseus%3Atext%3A1999.04.0008%3Apart%3D2%3Achapter%3D2%3Asection%3D3. Arguing along the same lines, Galen (*de plac. Hipp. et Plat. 5*) has written that beauty consists "not in

2. Proportionality and Disruption

Nefertiti's vertical orientation adjusted this figure to the familiar notion of Egyptian art as a consistently strict symmetrical and stylized art.[8] The bust in a non-wedged form supports all the more forcefully an alternative view that sees Egyptian sculpture as the epitome of lived individuality.[9] The interplay of symmetry and disruption as laid out here thus reinforces the connection to Greek art, which is usually viewed as an antithesis.[10]

As an original concept of Greek art theory, symmetry as proportionality generally gained meaning as the relationship between the parts of a work according to a common measure. This definition can in essence be traced back to the legendary *Canon*, a lost text by the Greek sculptor Polykleitos.[11] The dimensional ratios that Polykleitos had incorporated into the model figure of *Doryphoros* (fig. 8) consisted of clean fractions: The face accordingly makes up one-tenth of the entire body; the head, one-eighth; the mid-chest to the crown, one-quarter; and the length of the foot, one-sixth (fig. 9). The dimensions of the individual appendages are also determined according to this model.[12]

In *Timaeus*, Plato argued that this kind of symmetry is a proportional interplay of parts of a structure. This definition has continued to be accepted to the present day.[13] Plato's point of departure was the relationship between tone and number in music, but he took fine arts, which he was known to fear, no less into account. One must imagine what processes were meant—also and in particular with an eye toward an awareness for proportion and symmetry—when the inhabitants of the Greek cities were surrounded by more statues of symmetrical bodies than by actual residents (fig. 10).[14] Each and every step was like an exercise in commensurability and proportionality as conditions of symmetry.

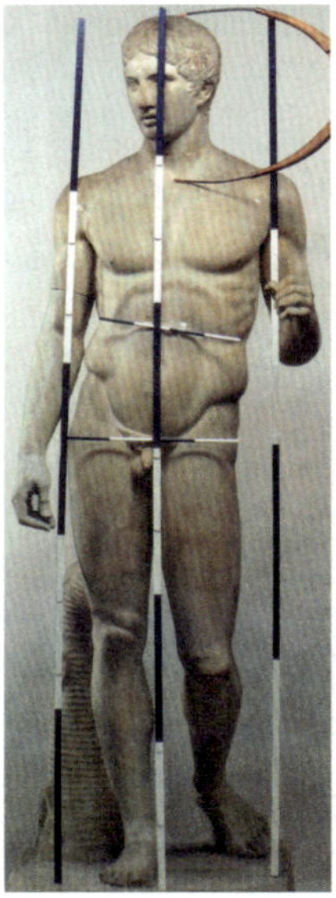

Fig. 9

Fig. 10

3. Proportion and Its Disruption

Disruption, however, was also systematically introduced into this principle. The proportionality of the spear bearer can be juxtaposed with Aphrodite of Cnidos (fig. 11), which was created between 350 and 340 BC by Praxiteles and was no less celebrated than Polykleitos's *Canon* figure, but for the opposite reason: Aphrodite confronts the observer with her slightly disproportionate form.[15]

Her narrow shoulders and the corresponding breasts, which indicate an adolescent age, contrast with the impression of her large and excessively curved, matronly lower torso. This disproportionate composite character of the body is carried over into her psychological ambivalence. Her head conveys an air of indecision with its slight tilt, and also the hand gestures appear ambiguous: Her left hand does not reveal whether she is laying down her robe to undress, or if she is picking up the fabric to cover herself. Correspondingly, it is unclear whether the right hand aims to cover her pubis or to reach for her robe.

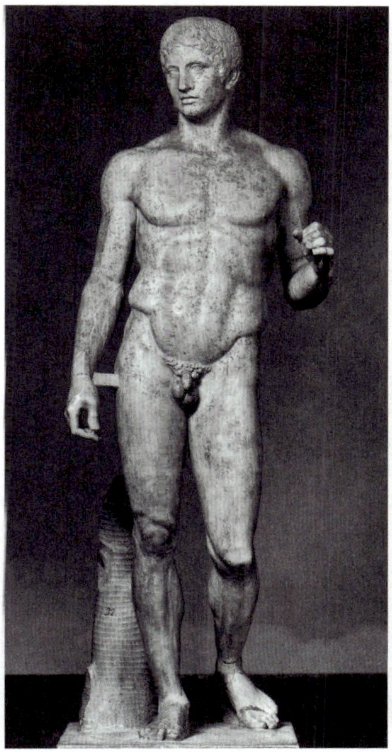

Fig. 8

Fig. 11

Fig. 8: Roman copy of Polykleitos's *Doryphoros*, 1st century BC, marble, Naples, Museo Archeologico Nazionale.

Fig. 9: *Doryphoros*, Naples, with segmentation into quarters, fifths, and sixths.

Fig. 10: Two spear bearers in the *Serial Classic* exhibition, Milan 2015.

Fig. 11: *Venus Colonna*, Roman copy of Praxiteles's *Aphrodite of Cnidos*, 350–340 BC, marble, Rome, Vatican Collections.

the commensurability of elements, but in the commensurability of the parts/members ... and all of these with the whole, as it is set forth in the Canon of Polykleitos," cited in Richard Tobin, "The Canon of Polykleitos," *American Journal of Archaeology* 79, no. 4 (1975): 307–21, here 308–9. See also Diels, 40 B 2; and Jürgen Fredel, "Ideale Maße und Proportion," in *Die Beredsamkeit des Leibes: Zur Körpersprache in der Kunst*, ed. Ilsebill Barta Fliedl and Christoph Geismar (Salzburg: Residenz, 1992), 11–42.

12 Ernst Berger, "Zum Kanon des Polyklet," in *Polyklet: Der Bildhauer der griechischen Klassik*, ed. Herbert Beck, Peter Cornelius Bol, and Maraike Bückling, exh. cat., Liebieghaus, Frankfurt am Main (Mainz am Main: Von Zabern, 1990), 156–84, here, 169. On this and the following, see in detail, cited in part verbatim: Horst Bredekamp, "Das Ideal der Proportion und die Kontingenz des Lebens," in *Die Verfassung als Aufgabe von Wissenschaft, Praxis und Öffentlichkeit: Freundesgabe für Bernhard Schlink zum 70. Geburtstag* (Heidelberg: C.F. Müller, 2014), 311–21.

13 Gernot Böhme, "Symmetrie: Ein Anfang mit Platon," in *Symmetrie in Kunst, Natur und Wissenschaft*, vol. 1: *Texts*, ed. Bernd Krimmel, exh. cat. (Darmstadt: Mathildenhöhe, 1986), 9–16, here, 10.

14 Babette Babich posed this question in "Die Naturgeschichte der griechischen Bronze im Spiegel des Lebens: Betrachtungen über Heideggers ästhetische Phänomenologe und Nietzsches agonale Politik," in *Articles and Chapters in Academic Book Collections*, paper 1 (2008), http://fordham.bepress.com/phil_babich/1.

It was this interplay of contrasting motifs that agitated an unidentified author of the second century AD to assert that "the hard unyielding marble did justice to every limb,"[16] presenting them as supple and alive. I believe that herein lies the decisive source. Through her vitality, the slightly disproportionate Aphrodite figure develops an erotic valence that drives a series of young men to madness.[17]

Doryphoros, the spear bearer (fig. 8), embodies a relationship of proportions that Aphrodite violates. And while Doryphoros generates the detachment of a well-nigh unattainable norm, Aphrodite—in her broken proportions—unleashes a desire that grows to insanity. The two statues realize their impact in different ways: the spear bearer through his normative proportions, and Aphrodite through her disruption of the dimensional ratios, which seems to give her life. As with Nefertiti, the break in the harmonic proportions connotes a vitalizing if not eroticizing effect.

4. Leonardo's, Dürer's, and Michelangelo's Dissonant Harmony

In the teachings of Pythagoras, the cosmos was configured according to the principles of commensurability, and this appeared to correspond to the proportionality of the human being. In Book III of his *Ten Books on Architecture*, Vitruvius, military engineer serving Caesar and Augustus, presented a chapter on the proportions of the human body in the sense of the *Canon* of Polykleitos. According to Vitruvius, the natural central point in the human body is the navel. With hands and feet extended, the navel is the center of both the circle and the square.[18] From the *convenevolezza*—or decorum, suitability—of this interplay of body and geometry, a sort of formula for everything resulted. What astrology claimed on the basis of the correspondences between the stars and human fates, the Vitruvian Man seemed to base on more rational and mathematically founded principles.[19]

This conviction was also met with both acceptance and criticism. Early on, Francesco di Giorgio Martini, Leonardo's teacher, visualized Vitruvius's assumption with the nonchalance of an intuitive certainty that ideal proportion and vital reality could never be brought into complete and total correspondence (fig. 12). His Vitruvian figure avoids the rigid frontality in order to allow the arms to swing slightly. By deviating from Vitruvius's provision, it defends the mathematics of vitality. The human being literally steps out of the bounds set by the dimensions of the circle. In the autonomy characterized by this insight lies the bewitching quality of this small drawing by Martini.[20]

Leonardo too by no means displays, as is consistently claimed, the ideal of the consonance of cosmic and human proportions, but rather the impossibility of implementing this (fig. 13). After a series of studies he recognized that the Vitruvian figure of proportions cannot be realized as the squaring of the circle. Symmetry is already broken by the fact that the feet at the center are not placed frontally, but instead face to the side, in order thereby to turn the lower body slightly. To form a circle, he angles the arms of his Vitruvian man slightly upward and displays the legs correspondingly. The square, on the other hand, is formed by straight legs and arms extended horizontally. The human is inscribed in the circle and the square, but the core of Vitruvius's statement is discredited, since the human being now has two centers: while the navel represents the center point

On the seriality of antique sculpture, see Serial Classics [sc]. *Multiplying Art in Greece and Rome*, ed. Salvatore Settis, exh. cat. (Milan: Fondazione Prada, 2015).

15 This is extant in copies, such as the version in the Vatican museums. On the history of the veneration of the statue of Praxiteles, see Berthold Hinz, *Aphrodite: Geschichte einer abendländischen Passion* (Munich: Hanser, 1998). On the figure itself see Peter C. Bol, ed., *Die Geschichte der antiken Bildhauerkunst*, vol. 2 (Mainz: Von Zabern, 2004), 329. Photograph taken from Adolf Heinrich Borbein, ed., *Das alte Griechenland* (Munich: Bertelsmann, 1995), 275.

16 Lucian, *Amores: Affairs of the Heart*, ed. and trans. M.D. Macleod, Loeb Classic Library 432 (Cambridge, MA: Harvard University Press, 1967), 169–71; see also Hinz, *Aphrodite*, 17–21.

17 Translation from the German edition: Lukian, *Erotes: Gespräch über die Liebe*, trans. Hans Licht (Munich: G. Müller, 1920), 13, 69–70.; on this see also 16, 73 (English: Lucian, 1967, 175–77).

18 Vitruvius, *The Ten Books on Architecture*, trans. Morris Hicky Morgen (Cambridge, MA: Harvard Univ. Press, 1914; New York: Dover, 1960), 72–73, "On Symmetry," no. 3: "Then again, in the human body the central point is naturally the navel. For if a man be placed flat on his back, with his hands and feet extended, and a pair of compasses centred at his navel, the fingers and toes of his two hands and feet will touch the circumference of a circle described therefrom. And just as the human body yields a circular outline, so too a square figure may be found from it. For if we measure the distance from the soles of the feet

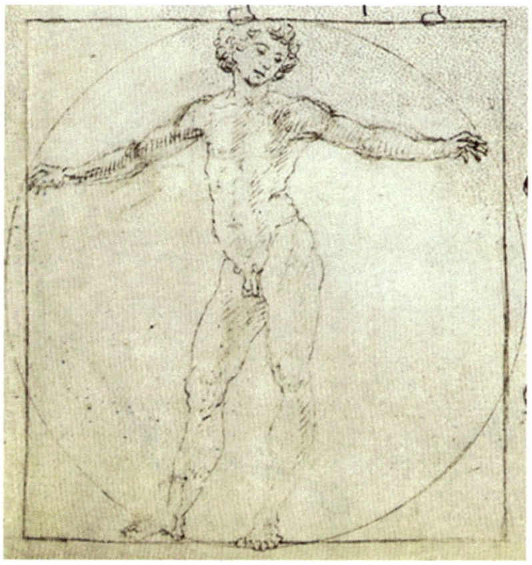

Fig. 12

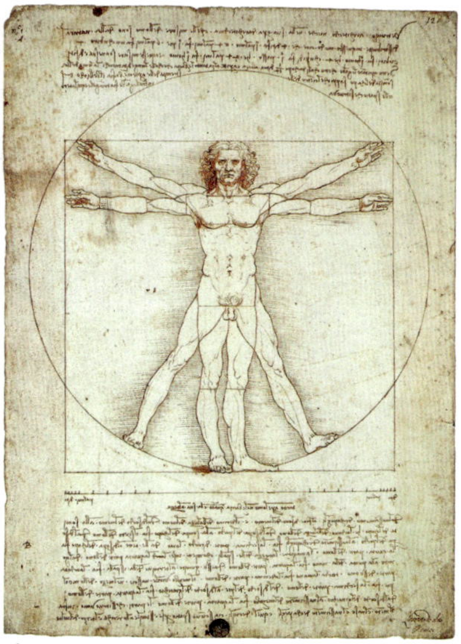

Fig. 13

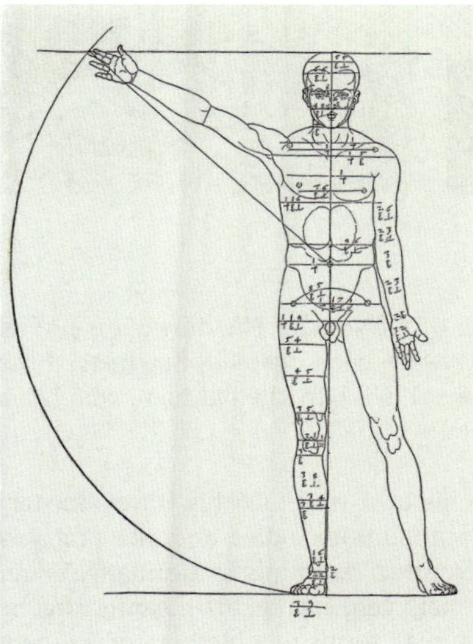

Fig. 14

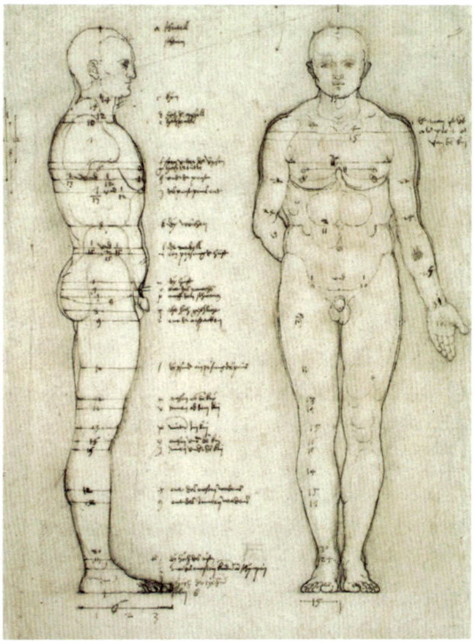

Fig. 15

Fig. 12: Francesco di Giorgio Martini, Vitruvian Man, drawing based on Vitruvius, *De Architectura* III.1, c. 1475, Florence, Biblioteca Laurenziana, Codex Ashburnhamianus, no. 361, fol. 5r.

Fig. 13: Leonardo da Vinci, Vitruvian Man, drawing based on Vitruvius, *De Architectura* III.1, c. 1492, pen and brown ink drawing, watercolor, on paper, Venice, Galleria dell' Accademia.

Fig. 14: Albrecht Dürer, *Study on Human Proportion*, woodcut, in Dürer, *Vier Bücher von menschlicher Proportion (Four Books on Human Proportion)*, vol. 2 (Nuremberg, 1591), fol. 55 verso.

Fig. 15: Albrecht Dürer, *Study in human proportion*, male body (profile and front views), pen and brown ink drawing, 1531, Vienna, Albertina.

to the top of the head, and then apply that measure to the outstretched arms, the breadth will be found to be the same as the height, as in the case of plane surfaces which are perfectly square."

19 The Vitruvian Man became the symbol of the "mathematical sympathy between microcosmos and macrocosmos"; Rudolf Wittkower, *Grundlagen der Architektur im Zeitalter des Humanismus* (Munich: Beck, 1969), 21. On Wittkower's criticism, see Frank Zöllner, *Vitruvs Proportionsfigur: Quellenkritische Studien zur Kunstliteratur im 15. und 16. Jahrhundert* (Worms: Werner, 1987), 8–22.

20 On this and the following see Bredekamp, "Das Ideal der Proportion und die Kontingenz des Lebens."

Fig. 16

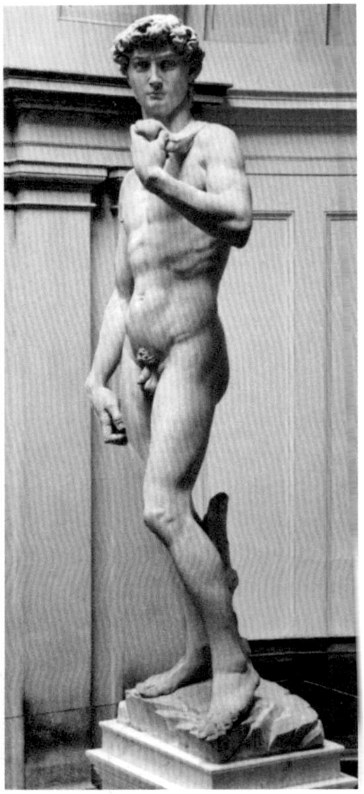

Fig. 18

of the circle, the genitalia are at the center of the square. The drawing is not an illustration of the Vitruvian Man, as has always been claimed, but instead the refutation of the rule it is based on. Perhaps this is why the old man, who has a young body, has such a grim expression.

Albrecht Dürer pursued a similar path in his own way.[21] On his travels in Italy from 1505 to 1507, he dealt intensively with proportion studies, and thus probably also with Leonardo's Academy drawing.[22] After returning to Germany, Dürer "measured" two to three hundred people of both genders (fig. 14), meaning that he experimented in drawing and measuring human forms in a plethora of different variations.[23] Unintentionally he shattered a normative concept of beauty that is contingent on proportion. His statement, "What beauty is, I know not,"[24] marked the beginning of a number of different, yet more or less consistent options for describing human proportions (fig. 15). Like Leonardo, Dürer too did not propagate a formula of ideal proportions, but rather the impossibility of specifying them.[25]

Michelangelo's *David* also depicts the difference as compared with the spear bearer (fig. 16). The body is resting on the right standing leg, as in the spear bearer, and the left hand is raised toward the head, with his glance looking intently at something at the same height. The frontal view, at least, seems disproportionate, as if the body were too small to carry the head.

21 His theory of proportions was misunderstood as a norm-obsessed presentation of jointed puppets; consequently, Michelangelo judged them, saying the figures seemed "straight upright like poles." Ascanio Condivi, *The Life of Michelangelo*, ed. Hellmut Wohl, trans. Alice Sedgwick Wohl, 2nd ed. (University Park, PA: Pennsylvania State University Press, 1999), 99.

22 In October he sent a letter to Germany, saying that he wanted to go to Bologna to learn the "secrets of the art of perspective, which a man is willing to teach me." William Martin Conway, *Literary Remains of Albrecht Durer* (Cambridge: Cambridge University Press, 1889), 58. This can refer only to Luca Pacioli, mathematician and friend of Leonardo's, whose *De divina Proportione* (1509), which appeared with illustrations by Leonardo, examined the traditional canon on proportions. See also Fredel, "Ideale Maße und Proportion," 21.

23 See Albrecht Dürer, *Vier Bücher von menschlicher Proportion (1528): Mit einem Katalog der Holzschnitte*, ed. Berthold Hinz (Berlin: Akademie Verlag, 2011).

24 "Waß aber dy schonheit sey, daz weis jch nit." "Van Schonheit," in Albrecht Dürer, *Schriftlicher Nachlass*, ed. Hans Rupprich, vol. 2 (Berlin, 1966), 100, here, 53–54; Albrecht Dürer, *The Writings of Albrecht Dürer*, ed. and trans. William Martin Conway (New York: Philosophical Library, 1958), 180, 199.

25 On this and the following see Zöllner, *Vitruvs Proportionsfigur*, 88–103.

In view of this disproportion, the figure as a whole faced criticism; once eyes started seeking violations of an internal coherence, the arms have been considered too long, the right hand too large, and the standing leg too short.[26]

This criticism identifies a true phenomenon without knowing the reason. Michelangelo did not want to equal his ancient sources of inspiration, the *Apollo Belvedere* and the *Horse Tamers* from Quirinal Hill, he wanted to surpass them by means of a disruption. Michelangelo's *David* resists the norm of the ancient proportion theory. This effect was also achieved because Michelangelo had to make use of an inferior, discarded narrow block of marble, but he did it on principle.

The quality of the entire figure is concentrated in his right hand (fig. 17). It appears relaxed, almost casual, but its structure of powerful veins and sinewy tendons and muscles reveals the possibility of action and grasping. This hand turned out to be too large, like the overpowering head.

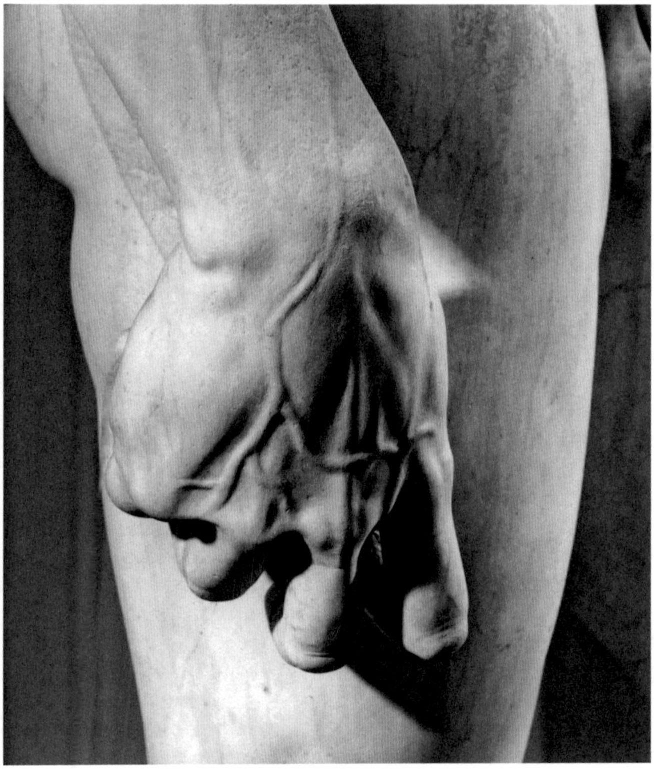

Fig. 17

Fig. 16: Michelangelo, *David*, marble sculpture, 1503, Florence, Accademia di Belle Arti.

Fig. 17: Right hand of *David*.

Fig. 18: *David* from half right.

26 In his typical rhetorical style, Jacob Burckhardt characterized in *The Cicerone* the problems of the figure with some sarcasm. Michelangelo, he said, "chose a young boy as a model for a young man, and consequently all the proportions got confused. It would be possible to rectify this by pointing a backwards telescope on him. 'When looking through a reducing glass, *David* profoundly gains beauty and life, with the exception of the head.'" Cited in Franz-Joachim Verspohl, "Michelangelo und Machiavelli: Der David auf der Piazza Della Signoria in Florenz," in *Städel Jahrbuch*, n.s., 8 (1981), 204–46, here 206.

Fig. 19: Antonio da Sangallo and Michelangelo, Palazzo Farnese, 1514–49.

Fig. 19

This moment of potential action seems particularly strong when the figure is viewed slightly from the right, from where the oversized hand comes forward (fig. 18). The figure is standing firmly on the right leg, but as the left foot prepares to move forward, it seems as if the weight will be shifted in the next moment. The firm stance also has a sense of something springlike, lurking, that gives the casual sleekness of the body a sense of something threatening. The planar unfolding of the body is bound here into a narrow axis that concentrates the centers of relaxation and energy, of defense and potential attack.[27] The figure's inner extremes are reinforced and concentrated here in the narrowest of space. The compelling vitality of this statue arises from the linking of its canonizing perfection and the breaks of its disproportionality.

5. Symmetry and Asymmetry in the Renaissance

It could be argued that this principle of the vitalizing break in harmonic proportion pertains largely to figurative art, whereas architecture is fundamentally, or almost exclusively, designed according to symmetry. Symmetry does in fact have an indispensable status in the history of architecture, but the principle of the life-giving disruption does not apply here any less. The Palazzo Farnese in Rome can serve here as a paradigmatic example (fig. 19). Since 1516, when it was built by the architect Antonio da Sangallo for the later Pope Paul III, the building has exhibited a puristic, unadorned architectural concept that is rigorously oriented along classical rules.[28] The facade is captivating in its spartanly frugal use of just a few modules such as the segmentally curved and triangular pediments, which the architect derived from the aediculae of the Pantheon. This design is flawlessly mirror-symmetric and in principle it is boundless, both upwardly and to the sides. All the more spectacular was that Paul III commissioned Michelangelo with the completion of the palace in the mid-1540s. Through interventions that were at first hardly noticeable, Michelangelo altered the character of the facade. He retained Sangallo's central window, but crowned it with a huge Farnese coat of arms that encroaches into the pedestal zone of the upper level (fig. 20). He augmented the

27 Ibid., 210–11.

28 Christoph Luitpold Frommel, "Sangallo et Michel-Ange (1513–1550)," in *Le Palais Farnèse*, vol. 1.1 (Rome, 1981), 127–74. See also Horst Bredekamp, "Michelangelos Modellkritik," in *Architekturmodelle der Renaissance: Die Harmonie des Bauens von Alberti bis Michelangelo*, ed. Bernd Evers, exh. cat., Kunstbibliothek, Berlin (Munich: Prestel, 1995), 116–23; and Emmanuela Ferretti, "Palazzo Farnese," in *Michelangelo: Architetto a Roma*, ed. Mauro Mussolin with Clara Altavista, exh. cat. Musei Capitolini, Rome (Milan: Silvana, 2009), 158–67.

wall above the windows in order to prepare a massive, three-and-a-half-meters-tall, overhanging cornice that seems to give the structure wings. Sangallo supporters agitated against this departure from the classical order, claiming that the entablature would not be able to support the main cornice, and the substructures of the palace did in fact have to be reinforced in order to bear the weight of this massive stone roof.

With only few interventions, Michelangelo transformed the mathematically sophisticated structure into a vertically accentuated sculptural mass that was weighted at the base with overhanging extensions. The architect was working as a sculptor. By overemphasizing the upper level, Michelangelo reversed the relationship between load and support, and here he created an inner tension that indicated a break in symmetry along not the vertical axis, but the horizontal. By raising and overhanging the cornice, the construction was stretched and pulled upwardly and to the sides. Michelangelo's interventions thus impart a sense of movement and life to Sangallo's clear pre-Cartesian grid and proportional order.

6. Symmetry and Disruption in Modernity

Symmetrical architecture as perfected by Sangallo was optimized in 1803 through the introduction of graph paper (fig. 21).[29] From that moment on, it was possible—already in the model—to prepare the mirror-symmetry down to the smallest detail. Jean-Nicholas-Louis Durand at the École Polytechnique in Paris developed an abundance of motifs out of a square and other shapes, which displayed perfected symmetry. Karl Friedrich Schinkel, in his plans for the palace on the Acropolis (fig. 22) for King Otto of Greece, formulated an invective against this requirement for rigorous symmetry that largely determined further developments. Schinkel vehemently advocated a departure from "neo-French maxims in which a misunderstanding of the concept of symmetry especially has produced so much hypocrisy and boredom and achieved such deadly dominion."[30] What he had in mind with his consistently asymmetrically designed palace complex also

Fig. 20

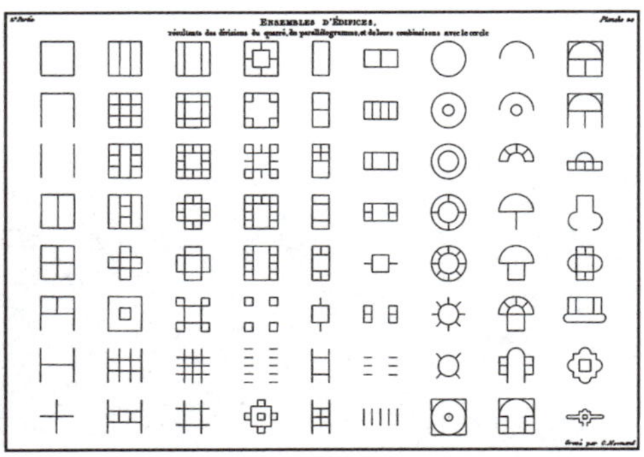

Fig. 21

Fig. 20: Central tract of the Palazzo Farnese.

Fig. 21: Jean-Nicolas-Louis Durand, Patterns of Geometrization, in Durand, *Précis des leçons d'architecture*, 1802.

29 Sandra Schramke, "Das autonome Quadrat: Zum Gebrauch von Millimeterpapier in der Architektur Oswald Mathias Ungers," in *Bildwelten des Wissens*, vol. 11, *Planbilder: Medien der Architekturgestaltung*, ed. Sara Hillnhütter (Berlin: de Gruyter, 2015), 42–50, here 45–46.

30 Schinkel to Crown Prince Maximilian of Bavaria, January 24, 1833, cited in Rand Carter, "Karl Friedrich Schinkel's Project for a Royal Palace on the Acropolis," *Journal of the Society of Architectural Historians* 38, no. 1 (1979): 34–46, here 41.

Fig. 22: Karl Friedrich Schinkel, Project for a Royal Palace on the Acropolis: Southern view, 1834, pen/reed pen and watercolor on paper, Munich, State Collection of Graphic Art.

Fig. 24: Mark Rothko, *Blue and Gray*, oil on canvas, 1962, Basel, Beyeler Foundation.

Fig. 22

spoke to Leo von Klenze in support of irregularity as a sign of unhindered development of individual and community.[31] This well-nigh irresistible argument was decisive for much of modernity—the watershed as it were between the symmetrical classicisms of totalitarian systems and trust in the stimulating force of disruptions and tensions.

This impulse had an impact even in painting. Of particular significance were the geometrically designed works of Barnett Newman (fig. 23) and Mark Rothko (fig. 24). They are vitalized, so to speak, inwardly and outwardly: resisting a planar fixation, they autonomously spring back into the depth of the space or out to the viewer. In this they create a break in the two-dimensional symmetry.[32] This can often lead to the most intense reactions. Barnett Newman's works have been attacked numerous times (fig. 25),[33] and viewers never break into tears so involuntarily as before the works of Rothko.[34] These are examples of quasi-metaphysical breaks in symmetry that occur beyond geometric-symmetrical forms.

Fig. 24

31 Leo von Klenze, *Aphoristische Bemerkungen gesammelt auf seiner Reise nach Griechenland, mit einem Tafelatlas* (Berlin: Reimer, 1838), 355–56; see also Adrian von Buttlar, "Griechische Analogien: Zur historischen Semantik der James-Simon-Galerie," in *James-Simon-Galerie Berlin*, ed. Martin Reichert, for David Chipperfield Architects (Cologne: Walther König, 2019), 43–59, here 52.

32 Marion Lauschke, "Bodily Resonance: Formative Processes in Aesthetic Experience and Developmental Psychology," in *The Body in Relationship: Self, Other, Society*, ed. Courtenay Young (Stow: Body Psychotherapy Publications, 2014), 175–96.

33 Dario Gamboni, *The Destruction of Art: Iconoclasm and Vandalism since the French Revolution* (London: Reaktion, 1997), 208. See also Angela Matyssek, "Überleben und Restaurierung: Barnett Newmans *Who's Afraid of Red, Yellow, and Blue III* und *Cathedra*," Max-Planck-Institut für Wissenschaftsgeschichte, preprint 398 (Berlin, 2010).

34 James Elkins, *Pictures and Tears: A History of People Who Have Cried in Front of Paintings* (New York: Routledge, 2001).

Fig. 23

Fig. 25

Fig. 23: Barnett Newman, *Who's Afraid of Red, Yellow and Blue III*, 1967–1968, oil on canvas, Amsterdam, Stedelijk Museum.

Fig. 25: Barnett Newman, *Who's Afraid of Red, Yellow and Blue III*, 1967-1968, after it was attacked in 1986, oil on canvas and slash marks, Amsterdam, Stedelijk Museum.

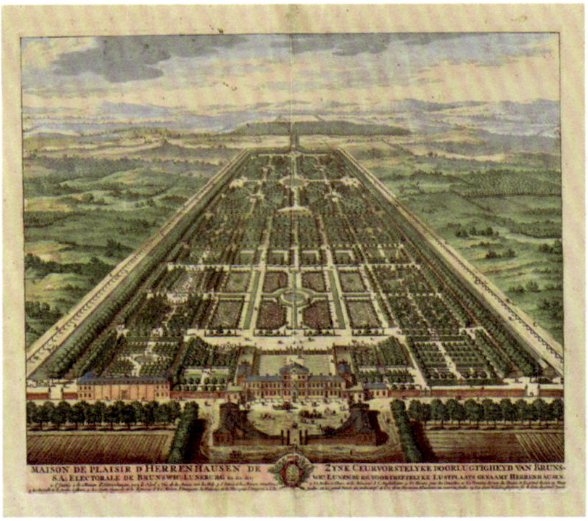

Fig. 26

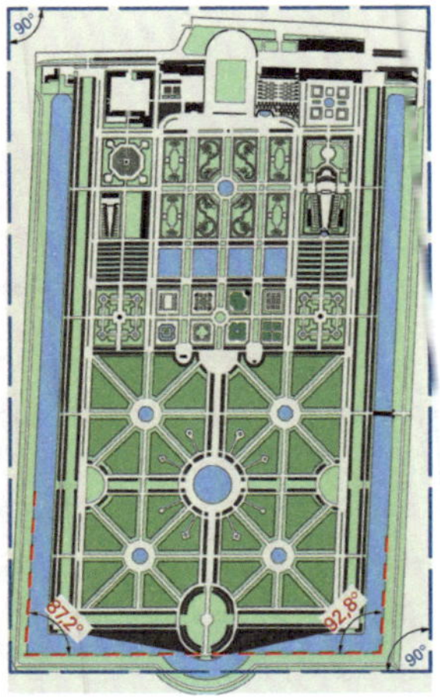

Fig. 27

Fig. 26: "Maison de Plaisir d'Herrenhausen de S. A. Electorale de Brunswic Luneburg," bird's eye view of the Great Garden from the north, colored copperplate engraving, c. 1708, Hannover, Gottfried Wilhelm Leibniz Bibliothek - Niedersächsische Landesbibliothek, XIX, C, 178 b.

Fig. 27: Reconstruction of the angular deviation of the Garden of Herrenhausen by Hans Georg Preißel, in H. G. Preißel, "Über die Wahrnehmung des Unbewussten im Großen Garten. War Leibniz der Urheber einer Winkelverschiebung?" *Herrenhäuser Gärten* 4, 4–8 (2003).

7. Lucretius's *Clinamen*

My final example brings together what I think can be reconstructed for the fine arts in general. It is the Garden of Herrenhausen, which has a special form that is key to our present subject (fig. 26).[35]

Since his time in Paris in the 1670s, Gottfried Wilhelm Leibniz valued the principle of surprise as a defining moment of thought-inspiring education. He likely welcomed the peculiarity that the corners of the Garden of Herrenhausen deviate by 2.8 degrees from a precise perpendicular to the axes of the palace building (fig. 27).[36] Leibniz presumably did not intentionally arrange for this effect, but he moved about in this garden for decades, planning and reflecting.

The idea for this deviation (fig. 28) might have been inspired by the *clinamen* of the Roman Epicurean Lucretius, which has enjoyed a history of unremitting validity right up to quantum physics.[37] As a minute swerve, the clinamen encompasses irregularities of atoms and thus the principle of all life and all creation that results from self-will and deviation.[38] Without bodies deflecting slightly from their straight course, according to Lucretius, "nature would never have created anything."[39] The minute deviation can be seen in the Garden of Herrenhausen on a grand scale, and this ambiguity of symmetry and disruption can be understood as expressing the basic approach of Lucretius, whose *De rerum natura*, as versified natural philosophy, also represents a comprehensive theory of art. Lucretius's natural philosophy is also a sublime art theory on the interplay of symmetry and asymmetry on a cosmic scale.

When the diagrammatic maps of the most remote areas of the cosmos received considerable press coverage a couple of years ago, it brought to mind the Herrenhausen Gardens and Lucretius's theory of cosmic deviation. Aside from confirming the model of symmetry, the maps also exhibit anomalies. They show the patterns of the distribution of matter that according to the Big Bang theory must have been spread only a few 100,000 years after this hypostatized event (fig. 29).

35 On this and the following, see Horst Bredekamp, *Leibniz und die Revolution der Gartenkunst. Herrenhausen, Versailles und die Philosophie der Blätter* (Berlin: Verlag Klaus Wagenbach, 2012).

36 Hans Georg Preißel, "Über die Wahrnehmung des Unbewussten im Großen Garten: War Leibniz der Urheber einer Winkelverschiebung?" *Aus den Herrenhäuser Gärten*, no. 4 (2003): 4–8.

37 Ernst A. Schmidt, *Clinamen: Eine Studie zum dynamischen Atomismus der Antike* (Heidelberg: Universitätsverlag Winter, 2007). See also Michel Serres, *La Naissance de la physique dans le texte de Lucrèce. Fleuves et turbulences* (Paris: Editions de Minuit, 1977), 214–37.

38 Lucretius, *De rerum natura*, II, 292–93, see *Lucretius: On the Nature of Things*, trans. and annotated by Martin Ferguson Smith (Indianapolis: Hackett, 2001), 42.

39 "ita nil umquam natura creasset." Lucretius, *De rerum natura*, II, 224–225. see Smith, *Lucretius: On the Nature of Things*, 41.

According to the reports, the model was largely confirmed, except for a series of anomalies that have not yet been accounted for. On this pointilist field, confusing clusters of matter appear again and again that cannot be properly explained. The reports show that it is these deviations that led to cautious confusion.[40]

To Lucretius, this existence of exceptions would be a reason not for confusion, but for corroboration, as he would have found this to confirm his theory that asymmetry is the basic condition for any creation, any life, and any work of art.[41] Symmetry without disruption in and of itself is not even possible as a thought construction, according to Lucretius.

In my opinion, this is the core of what can be said about the fine arts. I therefore see this diagram of the cosmos also as a work of art of our times. When Yoichiro Nambu and his team received the 2008 Nobel Prize for physics, the jury said: "We are all children of broken symmetry." This key aspect of Lucretius's teachings should be understood as a basic principle of the fine arts. It necessarily focuses on the tension between symmetry and asymmetry.

No form semantics can develop without symmetry, but all design that keeps a strict mirror and proportional symmetry retains an emptiness.[42] The concept of symmetry has been influenced over millennia by the fine arts and music, and developed in almost all areas of life. The conceptional framework it created from mirror to proportional symmetry has also largely determined the natural scientific claims to knowledge.

The uniqueness of fine arts lies in the fact that they have systematically incorporated the disruption, and the concepts of vitality are connected to them. Deviation is the prerequisite for art's coming to life. Symmetry and a break in symmetry are definitive, mutually conditional, and coactive basic determinants of all art that confronts the viewer as a living counterpart. Disruption conveys to the work the *energeia* that is captivating as a pseudo-vitality. This in turn explains an asymmetrical network of relationships between the image and the viewer. That, however, would be a subject of its own.

Translated from the German by Allison Brown

Fig. 28: Hedge alignment in the Great Garden of Herrenhausen.

Fig. 29 (overleaf): European Spacecraft Planck (NASA), The SMICA CMB Map, 2013.

Fig. 28

40 P. A. R. Ade, et al., "Planck 2013 results. Overview of products and scientific results," in *Astronomy & Astrophysics*, manuscript no. PlanckMission2013 (June 6, 2014), 26, fig. 15. https://arxiv.org/pdf/1303.5062.pdf.

41 If the atoms, all of which fall parallel in similar paths, all persist ad infinitum in this structure, then in principle nothing exists, as the uniform movement is devoid of resistance, of space, of time. It is the *clinamen*, the minute swerve, that generates the disruption, turbulence, vortices, and condensations, and with which the thereby resulting tension causes an infinite form of momentum, on which, together with the processuality, all life depends. Lucretius recognized the foundation of the cosmos not in the uniformity of the expansion, but in the disruption in a few isolated areas.

42 Ingo Rentschler, Martin Jüttner, Alexander Unricker, and Theodor Landis, "Innate and Learned Components of Human Visual Preference," in *Current Biology* 9, no. 13 (1999): 665–71.

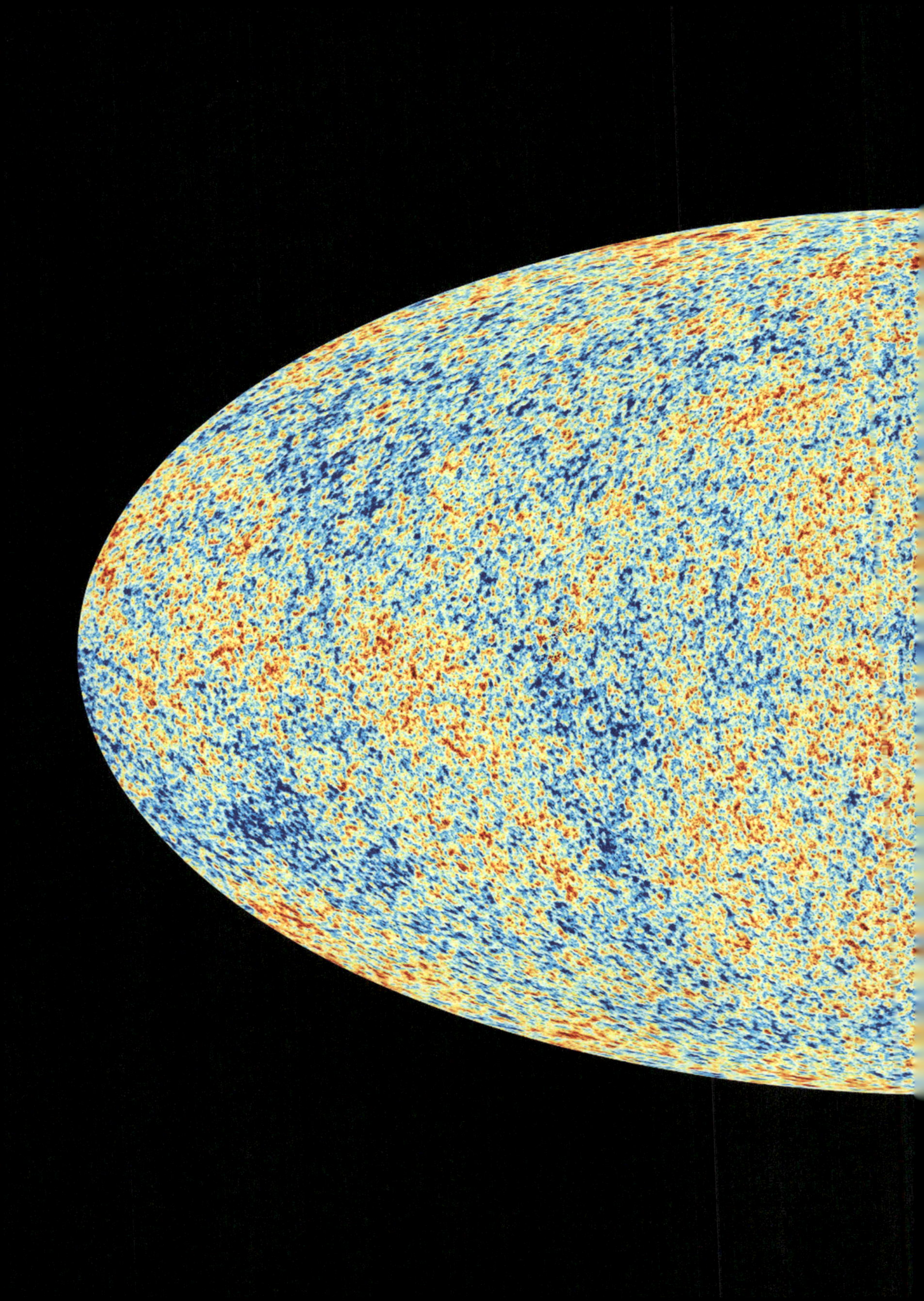

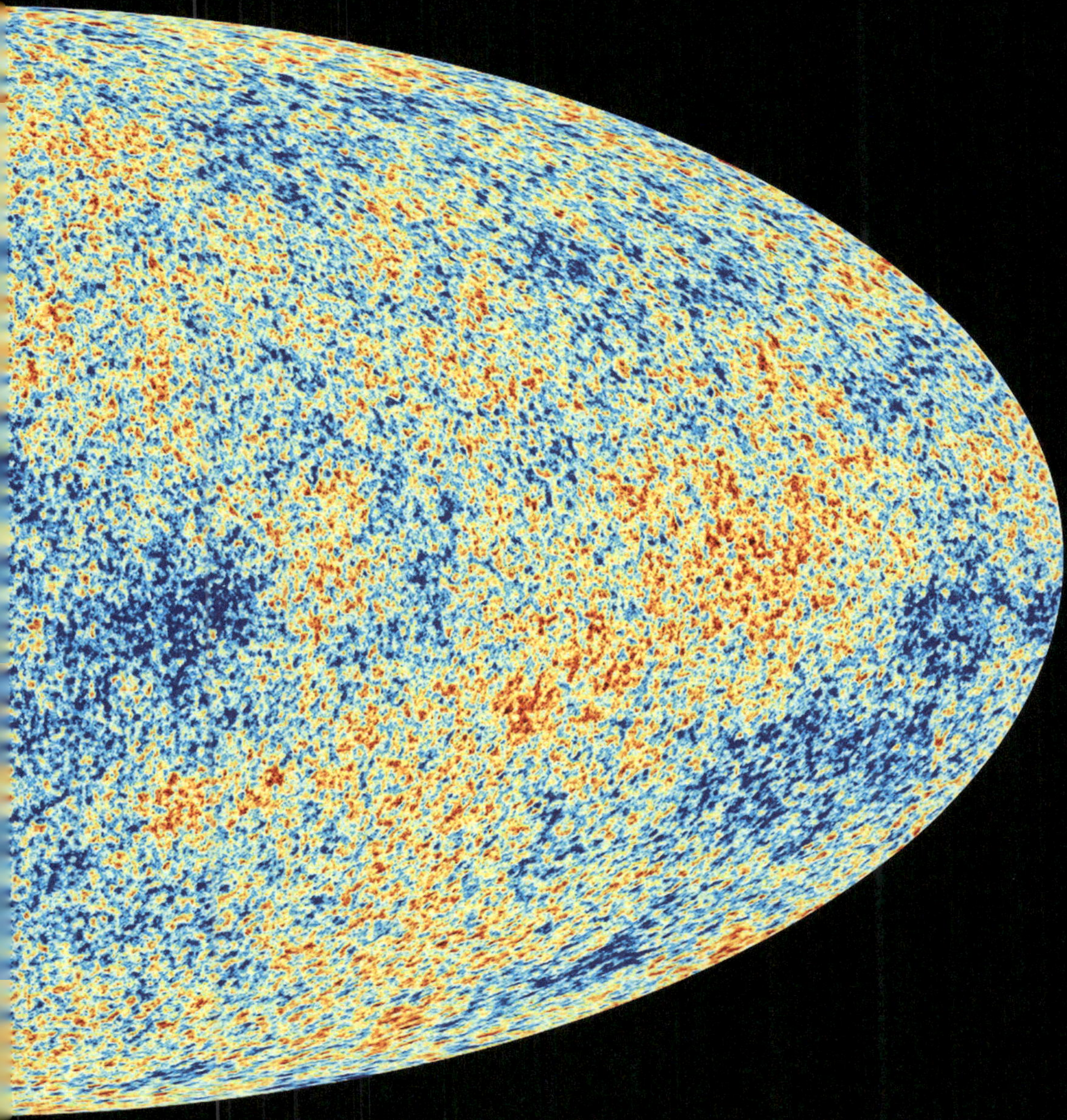

Bricology: An Anthropology of Making Art

Thomas Golsenne

Artistic Operational Chains[1]

As everyone is aware, art is not synonymous with technique. It can even be said that art loathes technique. Tim Ingold, who has written extensively on the subject, sums it up perfectly:

> An object or performance could be a work of art, rather than a mere artifact, to the extent that it escapes or transcends the determinations of the technological system. And its creator could be an artist, rather than a mere artisan, insofar as the work is understood to be an expression of his or her own subjective being. Where technological operations are predetermined, art is spontaneous: where the manufacture of artifacts is a process of mechanical replication, art is the creative production of novelty.[2]
>
> Indeed the opposition between art and technology has, in recent times, become such an established part of contemporary thinking on the "human condition" that we are inclined to use it as a window through which to view practices of all kinds, past and present, Western and non-Western, human and animal.[3]

We also know that it has not always been this way. It would appear that, among the Greeks, *tekhne* meant any artifact-producing activity, whether utilitarian or aesthetic; it is also believed that the word was translated by the Romans by *ars*, in the sense of an activity requiring skill, as in the "arts and crafts."

Likewise in late Antiquity various authors separated the mechanical arts (manual arts) from the liberal arts (intellectual arts), and that from fifteenth century in Italy intellectuals started to incorporate into the liberal arts manual practices such

1 The present article appeared as an introduction to *Essais de bricologie. Ethnologie du design et de l'art contemporain*, gen. eds. Thomas Golsenne and Patricia Ribault, *Techniques & Culture* 64, no. 2 (2015): 18–31.
2 Tim Ingold, "Beyond Art and Technology: The Anthropology of Skill," in *Anthropological Perspectives on Technology*, ed. Michael B. Schiffer (Albuquerque: University of New Mexico Press, 2001), 18.
3 Ibid., 29.

as painting, architecture, and sculpture (painting as "*cosa mentale*" as Leonardo da Vinci expressed it); that these arts were gathered together as "arts of *disegno*," exploiting the two meanings of the Italian word (both *drawing* and *design*, in the sense of "intention"); then into "fine art" or "the fine arts" in the eighteenth century, the period Ingold contends marks the final divorce between art and technique (as a symptom he cites the exclusion of engravers from the Royal Academy of Arts); then, a final phase, a single conceptual category was forged in the nineteenth century, that of Art, conceived of by Hegel in particular as an activity of the mind manifested in the realm of the senses.

In this perspective, twentieth-century art has further entrenched the split. Since Manet, the reproach leveled at avant-garde art by a public accustomed to traditional criteria in appreciating artworks (craftsmanship, time at work, the story depicted, etc.) is always the same: "my five-year-old son could have done that." Avant-garde artists themselves, in rejecting the lessons of the academy and taking inspiration from "works of *art nègre*," as the primal arts were called in the early twentieth century, folk art, drawings by children and the insane, left themselves open to such criticism.

Relying on chance as a compositional method (Arp), employing machines such as the camera to produce images (Man Ray), or, in the extreme case of Duchamp, doing no more than inscribing a signature on an object purchased in a department store, were just some of the methods artists deployed to undermine the value of skill, craft, and, in short, technique. A New York artist of the 1960s–70s Paul Thek, stated the case very clearly, in remarking about his own work, *The Tomb* (1967):

> The body pieces began appearing because I was trying to figure out how to make a full bodycast. I'd never done moulds or anything like that before. I was working with dentists' moulage, which is used for open wounds and is extremely quick-setting. I had a studio filled with imperfect limbs, covered with different colored wax, to test the tinting, so it was an easy, natural thing to make use of them. If I have an aesthetic, it's rooted to some extent in pragmatism. If you have something around, you might as well try to make something of it.

Thek though did not consider technique as paramount and when he was described (by Pincus-Witten) as a "master technician," he balked: "That's absolute nonsense and an insult: you don't call an artist a master technician—that's somebody else."[4]

Thek's fierce opposition to technique can be seen as reinforcing the modern dichotomy between conception and realization, the artistic dimension residing entirely in the former. The period also saw the development of Conceptual art, influenced on the one side by Duchamp, and on the other by literature, a domain where the traditional bonds between work and artist had been dissolved. Lawrence Weiner, Sol LeWitt, and Robert Filliou, with his "principle of equivalence"—well made, poorly made, not made—placed further doubt on the role of artists in making their own pieces and the relevance of quality of execution. This rejection arose from an ethics of economy, in the sense that for conceptualists making an object (as is generally expected of an artist) was a problem, a noxious vanity even in a world already saturated with pointless things.

4 Richard Flood, "Paul Thek: Real Misunderstanding," *Artforum* 20, no. 2 (October 1981); reprinted in *Paul Thek: The Wonderful World That Almost Was: Snap! Crackle! Pop! Was! Touch Me Not!*, ed. Roland Groenenboom (Rotterdam: Witte de With Center for Contemporary Art, 1995), 107.

This linear account of the continuous "spiritualization" of the arts, paralleled by an increased focus on a unique transcendental concept, is the story wheeled out each time one needs to explain why art goes beyond technique. This has had effects on various domains of knowledge: art historians, for instance, take little interest in the techniques employed by artists, leaving this field to restorers. Tim Ingold's summary is eloquent: the common view is that technique functions, while art signifies.[5] Art historians, who study the meaning of artworks, can thus be justified in their neglect of the technical domain. The question they ask of works and artists is: "Why?" and only seldom "How?"

This account is not entirely untrue, far from it. But it leans heavily on a hylemorphic conception of the production of artifacts inherited from Aristotle: to produce is to *in*form—that is, to endow matter with a *form* (an idea), as the female vessel is filled by virile form [*sic*]. From this point of view, matter remains passive, or at best resistant. Then man (in both senses of the word) deploys his secret weapon: the tool. Faced with a tool, matter is revealed as impotent. Technique, according to the hylemorphic schema, is an auxiliary of information: it facilitates it; it is purely instrumental. It adds nothing to meaning: it simply if gently instills it into matter.[6]

If this schema has begun to date, it still lurks in the minds of many art historians. Some great names in twentieth-century art history and aesthetics, however, had already subjected it to a critique. Henri Focillon,[7] Pierre Francastel,[8] Etienne Souriau,[9] and Gilbert Simondon[10] in philosophy, to quote only French examples, defended the idea that matter was not something inactive that the artist had to force into his form; instead he had to conciliate with it. The form of the work of art results rather from a compromise or an alliance between artist and material than from a struggle or a kind of domination. As for technique, far from being solely instrumental, it can lead the artist down paths he cannot entirely control. Even if one handles a tool to perfection, there are things one cannot ask of it: with Bruno Latour,[11] one might say that a tool is full of "affordance," as James Gibson has called it: it enables us to make use of it in such and such a way, and not in any way, though it remains rich with the promise of unexpected uses. In anthropology Tim Ingold has also used *affordance*, although critically, as a substitute for the form/matter couple *force* and *material*, inspired by the work of Gilles Deleuze: objects are no longer described solely by their function or utensility, but by their actual use.[12] Thus a stone is a shelter for the crab taking refuge underneath, but a plate for the rambler who balances his sandwich on it. Form, intention, idea do not encounter some neutral, meaningless matter-object: they emerge rather by reacting to the affordance of material things.

The continuance of hylemorphism as the fundamental theory of art history seems all the stranger today, since, for more than a hundred years, the modernist definition of art, namely to treat the medium (the means) as an end in itself, has become largely dominant. Whether the artistic medium be defined as the material support of the work (the painter's canvas), by the tool employed (film), by the technique (assemblage) is of little import here, since in each case, form no longer precedes materialization in the artist's mind: it results from it. And in fact, for a century art's relationship to materials, tools, and techniques has continued to become richer and more complex. To visit an exhibition of contemporary art today is not so much to be confronted with a critical or unexpected vision of the world: it is rather to observe experiments on substances, unusual uses of instruments,

5 Tim Ingold, "Beyond Art and Technology," 19.

6 Aristotle, *The Generation of Animals*, book I, ch. 20, 729a10–730a5. See also Fredrika H. Jacobs, *Defining the Renaissance Virtuosa: Women Artists and the Language of Art History and Criticism* (Cambridge: Cambridge University Press, 1997), 27–33.

7 See Henri Focillon, *The Life of Forms in Art*, trans. George Kubler (New York: Zone Books, 1989).

8 See Pierre Francastel, *Art and Technology in the 19th and 20th Centuries*, trans. Randall Cherry (New York: Zone Books, 2000).

9 See Etienne Souriau, *The Different Modes of Existence*, trans. E. Beranek and T. Howles (Minneapolis: Univocal, 2015 [1943]).

10 See Gilbert Simondon, *L'individuation à la lumière des notions de forme et d'information* (Grenoble: Éditions Jérôme Millon, 2005).

11 Bruno Latour, "Morality and Technology: The End of the Means," *Theory, Culture and Society* 19, no. 5/6 (2002): 247–60, here 250.

12 Tim Ingold, "Being Alive to a World without Objects," in *The Handbook of Contemporary Animism*, gen. ed. Graham Harvey (London: Routledge, 2015), 213–14.

Fig. 1: Frank Stella, *Bonin Night Heron No I*, from *Exotic Bird Series*, 1976. Acrylic on aluminum, 275 × 350 × 65 cm.

technological subversions, which enrich our relationship to the concrete. And even if contemporary artists no longer dialogue with matter like the painters or sculptors of the first half of the twentieth century did, their rapport to technique is only the more fruitful.

To take an illuminating example, at the beginning of the 1960s in New York artist Frank Stella made his mark on abstract painting with large-size, radically sober pictures of geometric design offering a clean break with the preceding generation's Expressionism. To produce an original painting without psychological outpouring: such was his ambition. Then, in 1975, his practice took another turn: he introduced curves, twisted forms that intersect. The earliest drawings and pictures of this new kind were entitled *Exotic Birds* (fig. 1). For the most part art critics saw these as manifesting the artist's need to "fly away" from the art milieus of New York and renew his severe style by an excursion into baroque. But the painter himself saw it differently. In 1975 he recounted how he bought a set of the irregular templates known as French curves (known in French as *perroquets* [parrots]), which gave him the idea for these curving forms.[13] From this perspective, the shapes Stella painted changed but his methods did not: as ever, he employed tools to dictate the forms. Previously it was ruler and set-square; now, French curves. Far from being a total rupture, the *Exotic Birds* series is an extrapolation of his previous work in a new direction. Incorporating or ignoring technique in an analysis of such pieces warps their interpretation.

The situation is the same in anthropology as in the history of art. It has long been and still is dominated by the search for meaning, by the question Why? Why do people perform the practices they do? Why did they develop such beliefs? It was long thought that the ultimate answers could be discovered in analyses of myths

13 Frank Stella, *Working Space* (Cambridge MA: Harvard University Press, 1986), 153.

and social structures. The anthropology of techniques, in the wake of André Leroi-Gourhan, casts a different light on the cultures studied: meaning no longer resides in myths, rites, beliefs, and structures, but in the way in which objects were manufactured, in physical techniques, in "how." Anthropologists of technique devised concepts and analytical methods that describe the facts they study and provide cultural content. Though on the face of it art history, due to its hylemorphist ideology, is not so well equipped to understand the role of the techniques employed by contemporary artists, it is likely that the anthropology of techniques might furnish the tools it lacks. But first these tools have to be tested for purposes and on materials for which they were not intended. It is by no means certain that all will function. Let us start though by taking five tools from the anthropologists' toolbox.

Skill

Tim Ingold[14] contends that the split between art and technique emerged from industrial modernity and so proves unsuited to the study of the manufacture and appearance of artifacts produced in societies that are not modern. The art/technique dichotomy occurs, as he sees it, when humankind no longer uses tools to produce artifacts, but machines. As Ingold has it, if the use of tools necessitates know-how, skills that mobilize the craftsman's perception, intelligence, and experience, machines can be operated by any of a series of interchangeable workmen, independently of their level of expertise. Consequently, making objects becomes a purely mechanical action, entirely divorced from the design process that presupposes a priori scientific and rational knowledge of the physical laws of matter, detached from the experience of manufacture and its contingencies. This is how art was born—in opposition to the mechanical and purely technical action of the workman, like a new incarnation of craft. Indeed, one can consider painting, sculpture, drawing, and the other visual arts carried out with the hand as avatars of craftsmanship, for which the tool is less complex than the expertise exerted to use it.

Ingold's considerations can be summed up in five points about proficiency and skill:

1. Skill is "both practical knowledge and knowledgeable practice," expertise that implies an intellectual as much as a physical scope.
2. Skill is not just a technique of the body, in Mauss's sense, by which the latter would still be thought of as a passive, mechanical tool, but the total engagement of the human being, body and mind, in its perception and its action, and in its relation with the object and its environment.
3. Skill is not the application of a subject's will on an object, but "care" for this object, a way of "feeling" it.
4. Skill is not transmitted by writing or by fixed formulae, but by the facilitation of opportunities for perception and action.
5. Skill is not the correct implementation of a mental intention, an idea or form, but creativity immanent in the very act of making.

This enriched definition of skill can serve for studying many preindustrial artifacts, whether they originate in New Guinea or the Italy of the Renaissance.

14 Ingold, "Beyond Art and Technology," 21–22.

Since contemporary artists, however, often employ industrially made products, whatever it is in their activity that makes it art cannot reside (solely) in manual dexterity. The tool of "skill" then appears somewhat inadequate—unless it is redefined above and beyond the schism between craft and industry. If one can extricate oneself from the basically traditional association between skill and manual dexterity, then Ingold's concept can be seen as entirely operational with respect to contemporary design and art in that it characterizes ways of being intensely receptive to things, artifacts, or materials, and to the processes of their transformation. Extrapolating from the philosophy of Michel Foucault and work on material culture and processes of subjectivation undertaken by the "Matière à penser" group of Jean-Pierre Warnier and his colleagues,[15] one might perhaps add that this "skillful" rapport to things and materials defines a form of subjectivation specific to craftsmen and artists.

Agentivity

In the anthropology of art, the concept of agentivity owes its definition and application almost entirely to Alfred Gell, the aftershocks of whose posthumously published *Art and Agency* (1998) continue to resonate in the worlds of anthropology and art theory.[16] Originating in cognitive psychology, the concept itself is not Gell's coinage: it defines the capacity of a being, human or not, to act; or, more specifically, as Gell employs it, it designates a supposed power humans, in certain conditions, invest in objects. To attribute agentivity to an object is to consider it as an active member of a social relation. Or rather, the object points to an external agent; but, since this agent is remote, invisible, or unknown, the real relationship is with the object, which is thus freighted with agentivity in and for itself. Thus, the child who plays with her doll as if it were a real baby, the man in a hurry who insults his car because it stalls, the poor wretch railing against the landmine that blew up beneath his feet, the congregation venerating a statue of the Virgin because she/it "performs miracles" all, in their own manner, attribute agentivity to objects. It is this kind of relationship, through objects, that Gell calls *art*. Art is no longer a particular human activity relating to a specific kind of artifact (works of art in museums), but the fact that one endows an object with an importance, a status, comparable to that of an agent. Resolutely anti-hylemorphist, this theory opens the door to a serious approach to all those circumstances in which humans cease considering the world surrounding them as a reservoir of passive and inert objects. It also makes it possible to consider works of art—in the usual sense of the term—from a new angle: they become indices of an agent, in general the artist, whose technique allows the piece to attain autonomy. Be it a *kolam*, a decorative doorstep in southern India, or a Vermeer, the artist's virtuoso technique is impressive enough for the work to appear "magical."

Faced, however, with a Duchamp readymade or with many contemporary artworks in which virtuosity is the last quality, such enchantment risks being short-lived. And indeed, when Gell applies his theory to a piece by Duchamp, he reverts to a "classical" form of art history. This though does not invalidate the theory itself and the concept of agentivity can be used fruitfully to illuminate the work of certain artists. To quote just one, it would make it possible to treat seriously the expression used by Joseph Beuys when he talked about "conversations" between the objects he arranged in his purpose-built vitrines. If there exists one category of people for whom objects and materials are partners rather than inert, it is surely artists.

15 Marie-Pierre Julien and Céline Rosselin, gen. eds., *Le sujet contre les objets... tout contre: Ethnographies de cultures matérielles* (Paris: CTHS, 2009).

16 Alfred Gell, *Art and Agency: An Anthropological Theory* (Oxford: Oxford University Press, 1998).

Style

The concept of style might also serve to bring together art history and the anthropology of techniques, because it was long deployed in structuring discourse in various disciplines. The same opposition between two interpretations of style always transpires, however.[17] Either style is interpreted as a choice made along an operational chain that changes nothing material in the expected functional result, concerning as it does something arbitrary, gratuitous, nonfunctional. A style is thus recognized before it signifies: belonging to an infra-semiological cognitive level, it is more a kind of feeling. Or else, on the contrary, style is interpreted as a choice in the operational chain that has its relevance as cultural significance. At root, in art history, we have an opposition between style as an assertion of a singularity against a backdrop of norms, style as rupture, as a corporeal or cultural unconscious, which leads to style as the individual expression or *Kunstwollen* of a people, inexplicable but unique—what Leroi-Gourhan for his part called the "*ethnic indefinable*"; and style as the assertion of the most significant features of a culture, precisely those that best represent it, that constitute its norms; and this leads to iconology and to "symbols" in Ernst Cassirer's sense.[18] The anthropological or iconological approach to style also always implies a sociological interpretation—style as the expression of a social group, ethnic or no. This presupposes a kind of stylistic constant that might be summarized in archaeologist Gustav Kossinna's rather rough-and-ready equation: pots equal people. This equation has inevitably been called into question (what is a people? the same people may adopt several different styles in various fields, etc.). Structuralist anthropology tends to emphasize systems of transformation affecting forms, rather than invariants (Lévi-Strauss on Caduveo painting or "split representation," Alfred Gell on tattooing in the Pacific, inter alia). Still, these transformations comprise a system because those performing them remain the same. The goal of anthropology in such cases is to establish analogies between stylistic transformations and social transformations. It is the same type of analogy that Erwin Panofsky establishes between Gothic architecture and scholasticism or between perspective and modern rationality.

The concept of style, however, will not help us adumbrate an anthropology of techniques for contemporary art. For two reasons. The first is that today this concept has become irrelevant to definitions of the artist's work. Since the 1960s artists have been busy destroying anything and everything that might connect their practices to the notion of style. Associated with the expressionist narcissism of their predecessors, style became something to offload at a time when Duchamp's dictum, "it's the beholder that makes the picture," found an echo in Barthes's assertion that the reign of the author had been succeeded by that of the reader. Artists no longer think of themselves as higher beings, as geniuses towering above society, but more as mediators, facilitators, producers. And this more modest conception of the artist's role corresponds to a utopian ideal of art reconciled with life.

And today, if this ideal is no longer the credo of the younger generations of artists, it is still the case that style remains an inoperative category for appreciating their work, since every contemporary artist, or almost, handles a number of media in parallel, and sometimes the same medium in a different way. Moreover, at the present time, it seems impossible to define the style of the 1990s, of the

17 Bruno Martinelli, "Style, technique et esthétique en anthropologie," in *L'interrogation du style. Anthropologie, technique et esthétique*, ed. Bruno Martinelli (Aix-en-Provence: Presses de l'Université de Provence, 2005), 40.

18 Erwin Panofsky, *Studies in Iconology* (New York: Harper & Row, 1972), 8.

Fig. 2 (opposite):
John Baldessari, *Commissioned Painting: A Painting by Elmire Bourke*, 1969.
Oil and acrylic on canvas, 150.5 × 115.6 cm.

2000s, such has been the growth in the numbers of artists and the diversity of their artistic practice—unless, that is, the analysis is restricted to artists who have created the most noise over these years. It is enough to visit any major contemporary art biennial to appreciate the challenge faced by those whose task it is to capture the "zeitgeist" at this kind of event. Artists no longer have a style but means of expression they adapt to the project or else visual signatures they apply repeatedly like rubber stamps.

The second reason arises from the anthropology of technics itself, in its critique of the relevance of the concept of style. One can follow the example of Pierre Lemonnier:[19] He remarks how style, as Leroi-Gourhan sees it, defines the peripheral properties of an artifact, those on the margins of more intractable "tendencies" determined by the materials that limit the range of technical options. Thus, style (and, by extension, aesthetics, that is, the cultural values specific to each population) does not relate directly to the techniques employed themselves. The examples he supplies, however, underscore how cultural preferences are already present in the initial technical options, including the choice of materials, during stages in the operational chain that will not necessarily be perceptible in the end result, in the appearance of the artifact.

The Operational Chain

This concept might perhaps constitute a more effective tool than style. Coined by Leroi-Gourhan and popularized by his students, one should recall that it arose from the idea that an artifact bears cultural significance not so much due to its appearance, its visual qualities, in short, its style, as to the technical choices and materials that govern its manufacture and use. Constituted as a "syntax," the operational chain is unavoidable and obeys rules that lie partly beyond the purview of the user. In other words, the existence of an operational chain signals the presence of a technical grammar belonging to a social group, that is, the existence of a culture. The individual does not have to reinvent every gesture made when manufacturing an object; he masters them, is conscious of them, as when one makes coffee or has a wash. Be it "mechanical" or "periodic," the existence of an operational chain articulates the individual within the group, by means of the collective memory in which the chain is stored. In spite of the idea of a "program" or an unchanging corpus, operational chains evolve, because individuals play an active and conscious role in manipulating them: they have to adapt to contingent circumstances, correct errors, repair damage, and these interventions become a source of innovation.[20]

Analysis of the artistic operational chain is something very rarely undertaken by art critics and historians. For that reason alone, the concept might surely prove singularly useful for our enterprise. One must, however, add that, in the case of the modern or contemporary artist, the articulation of the individual in the group by way of operational chains is no longer self-evident: their specificity (in opposition to craftsmen and to traditional artists) resides in the fact that they do invent their operational chains; and it is this, rather than their style, that is the focus of their singularity. Thanks to a tool such as the "operational chain," it can now be understood how a succession of actions, the use of objects which, taken in isolation, are not artistic, can be induced to produce a work of art.

19 Pierre Lemonnier, "Objets sacrés sans 'style'. Circulez, y'a rien à voir" in Martinelli, *L'interrogation du style*, 250.

20 André Leroi-Gourhan, *Gesture and Speech*, trans. A. Bostock Berger, An October Book (Cambridge, MA: MIT Press, 1993), 232–34.

A PAINTING BY ELMIRE BOURKE

We will call bricology the study of operational chains resulting in the production of a contemporary work of art.

By the same token, certain apparently anti-technical postures adopted by conceptual artists and by artists who delegate the production of their pieces to technicians can also be understood "bricologically." Delegation is one of the processes artists most frequently employ so as to dispense with style. John Baldessari is a prime example (fig. 2). In the 1960s he abandoned an Expressionist yet paradoxically not especially personal painting, to replace it with cooler pictures inscribed with phrases to which he sometimes added photographs transferred onto canvas. Initially he painstakingly wrote out the letters himself, but later he had them produced by a specialist sign painter. The picture is thus totally devoid of the artist's manual expression. In 1969 he went further. He commissioned about fifteen Sunday painters to produce paintings based on photographs he had taken all showing an index finger pointing to some nondescript object or zone.

The remarkable thing is the complex relationship established between the artist who selects (the pointing gesture is a metonym for this) and the painter who executes, but whose name is writ large on the work in place of a title or signature. Baldessari, moreover, was inspired by the widespread practice of "treasure painting"—that is, pictures painted from a personal photograph so as to enhance its value. Delegating in this manner does not simply mean rejecting technique: it is a bricological choice in the sense that it implies a social relation between at least two actors, a reflection on art as both professional occupation and amateur pastime, as an instrument for telescoping "high" and "low" culture.

Bricolage

As is only fitting, let us conclude with the conceptual tool most utilized and commented on by contributors to these *Essais de bricologie*: "bricolage," to which Lévi-Strauss gave its letters of nobility in some famous pages in *The Savage Mind*.[21] Like delegation, "bricolage" can be considered as a certain type of artistic operational chain much employed today. I would like here to rehearse just one essential point of this theory. For Lévi-Strauss, one has to distinguish the artist from the bricoleur and the engineer. The artist finds himself or herself so to speak in an intermediate position between the other two opposite poles; between the former, who salvages anything useful and adapts his or her project according to what he or she has in stock, and the latter who, as a faithful follower of Aristotle, starts from the project and then searches for the tools and materials required to carry it out. The value of this distinction, for Lévi-Strauss, is that it unpacks a form of non-Aristotelian rationality, founded, not on abstract categories, but on the observation of the environment: it means thinking, not abstractly, but concretely. "Bricolage" could serve as a preliminary metaphor for the "savage" thinking Lévi-Strauss's book went on to describe at length. The idea of bricolage as a form of thought has met with phenomenal success; François Jacob, for example, famously applied it to the field of evolutionary biology.[22] It should be understood though that bricolage does only equate to thought metaphorically: if Lévi-Strauss's theory remains of interest in our eyes it is because the actual practice of bricolage can produce thought; the thinking, in point of fact, of artistic invention.

21 Claude Lévi-Strauss, *The Savage Mind* (Letchworth: Weidenfeld & Nicolson Ltd., 1966), 16–33.

22 François Jacob, "Evolution and Tinkering," *Science* 196, no. 4295 (June 1977). I thank Frédéric Joulian for having alerted me to this.

It is striking to see how, if, referring to bricolage, Lévi-Strauss cites the Facteur Cheval, surrealist poetry, and Breton's "objective chance," but when he evokes art he thinks of a perfectly classical portrait by Jean Clouet. It is on record that Lévi-Strauss did not think much of the visual art of his time. This is all the more regrettable since he could have found in it any number examples of his definition of the bricoleur. Since the 1920s the art of recycling and assemblage—the handyman's bread and butter—has developed continuously, reaching a high point in the 1950s and again today.

Moreover, bricolage also is the artistic practice that equates best to Tim Ingold's definition of skill qua creativity in the act of production itself. Unlike artists who plan their work upstream and subsequently ask technicians to carry it out, dispensing with other forms of collaboration or experimentation, the artist-bricoleur creates in the hiatus between the formative idea and the end result. This gap opens up due to the contingency of the materials salvaged. Thus, for artists who like to recycle unassuming materials they find in the street, bricolage has nothing to do with random "botching," with a lack of technique. It is again a "bricological" choice: that of making things with the means at hand. For the artist, against the backdrop of an ongoing crisis in the consumer society, bricolage constitutes an ethical and political, as much as an aesthetic, choice. It is in this manner that the singularity of the operational chains artists implement can nonetheless acquire broader cultural import and mediate with the interests of the group from which they emerge: the more artists act as inventive and original bricoleurs, the more they will constitute a source of inspiration for others. The bricoleur artist appears as a model for all adepts of "do-it-yourself," for all those combating the obsolescence—planned or not—of commercial products, for all the "poachers" of culture—to use Michel de Certeau's term—intent on developing "tactics" for resisting the neoliberal spirit and the culture of the supermarket.[23] By attending to the bricological aspect of an artwork makes it possible—far more effectively than the analysis of its discourse—to fully integrate politics into artists' praxis, that is, to think of them as participating in the life of a community, from which, willingly or not, they are sometimes—indeed all too often—excluded.

The toolbox of contemporary ethnology contains far more than these five tools. Each school, each current has developed its own. Some will prove inoperative when applied to contemporary art. A number of contributors to these *Essais de bricologie* have adroitly mobilized others. There remains, however, much to do.

In launching this expanding field of research, we hope that other researchers, on reading the present volume, will be urged to explore it further.

Translated from the French by David Radzinowicz

23 Michel de Certeau, *The Practice of Everyday Life*, trans. S. Rendall (Berkeley: University of California Press, 1984).

The Threshold of Invention
Design Processes in Light of Some Methods of Projection

Tiago da Costa e Silva

The main objective of this essay is to inquire into the specific, all-encompassing projective activity intrinsic to the process of design. I am considering the term *design process* as one describing a formative, purposeful, form-giving process, including its interactive mental and material aspects. This purposive, projective action of a design process is characteristic of several fields of knowledge and forms production, such as architecture, design, material sciences, engineering, and the arts, as well as occurring in a myriad of other fields as a method of projecting.

But how can one grasp such an abstract concept, one which describes a general process at play in every form of design? Can this general process be described at all? And if it can, how does it relate to every form of concrete design processes?

In order to solve this problem of the relationship between an abstract and very general description of design processes and the concrete, particular occurrences of projecting, it is necessary to describe the operation of design processes, as I understand it here, as precisely and as generally as possible within a theoretical and philosophical framework.

1. The Hypothesis and the Theoretical Framework for Design Processes

My leading hypothesis states that a generated idea, leading trigger, or general purpose sets off a flowing stream of new formative processes, including the dialogue inherent to every process shaping materiality according to a particular purpose within a given design context. This generated idea is not only a mental feature of a dominating brain. Here, *idea* involves the mental and synthetic aspects of setting forth a new associative process as well as the material aspect, especially the ability to enable discoveries by operating synthetically with a myriad of materialities, material processes, medial vehicles, and embodied languages—the latter include, for instance, visual, diagrammatic, musical, audio-visual, and material languages. Whereas this synthesis refers to a form of disclosure or discovery of new possibilities, the operation with materiality enables the conditions for aesthetic discoveries. Therefore, synthesis is a phenomenological perception, though in this case it requires constant dialogue with material and medial operations. Reciprocally, the more development that is unfolded within this process, the more the generated idea itself becomes developed. This flowing stream of a given design context drives the formative process toward new processes and new discoveries of processes. Proportionally, the more this flowing stream drives the formative process, the more it is heuristically developed. This proposition may seem strange at the outset. But in what follows, I will argue for this dialogical and simultaneous approach in light of the concept of formativity as a characteristic feature of design processes.

The philosophical position informing the present reflection is objective idealism, as it was formulated by the German Idealism movement, especially by Friedrich Wilhelm Joseph Schelling (1775–1854) and Georg Wilhelm Friedrich Hegel (1770–1831). Objective idealism is a metaphysico-cosmological hypothesis stating that there is a seminal identity in which nature (*Natur*) and mind (*Geist*) are in their genesis so completely merged that the reality of both harks back to an absolute origin. This absolute point of origin is considered as a pure point of indifference that can only be apprehended by aesthetic contemplation or by a form of intuitive feeling. In the case of Schelling and Hegel, it can be apprehended by intellectual intuition (*Intellektuelle Anschauung*). There is, therefore, no genetic difference between mind and matter; they differ not categorically, but in their states. Matter is, accordingly, a highly specialized form, or effete Mind.

Objective idealism is one of the main theoretical backgrounds for the theory of *formatività*, as formulated by the Italian philosopher Luigi Pareyson (1918–1991). Also in this tradition is the philosopher, mathematician, chemist, and logician Charles S. Peirce (1839–1914). For Peirce, "the one intelligible theory of the universe is that of objective idealism, that matter is effete mind, inveterate habits becoming physical laws."[1] Moreover, Peirce stated that he would not take it hard if his philosophy were identified as an updated variant of Schellingism, that is, a variant of the objective idealism proposed by Schelling. More important for our reflection is the objective-idealistic thesis defended by Peirce that "ideas really influence the physical world, and in doing so carry their logic with them" in the form of embodied relations; and when embodied, these relations become open to further phenomenological interactions.[2]

Pareyson, also in the tradition of German Idealism and based upon Schelling's thesis of objective idealism,[3] formulates his theory of formativity as a constant dialogue with mutually interacting, synchronized processes between ideality on the one hand and materiality, mental powers, material potentialities, and embodied actions on the other. For he states that productive force and inventive capacities alike are required by thought and by action in order to carry out a given plan. He justifies this simultaneity by contending that speculative and practical operations are constituted of a formative activity. This formative activity, or *formativity action*, articulated within a specific field, executes and produces works at the same time as it, formativity, invents the very manner in which these works will be carried out.[4]

1 Charles S. Peirce, *Writings of Charles S. Peirce: A Chronological Edition*, ed. M. Fisch et al., six volumes now completed (Bloomington: Indiana University Press, 1982–). References are abbreviated as "W" followed by volume and page numbers. W8: 106.

2 Charles S. Peirce, *The New Elements of Mathematics by Charles S. Peirce*, vol. 4, ed. Carolyn Eisele (The Hague: Mouton Publishers, Humanity Press, 1976), 31.

3 Observe here the studies made by Pareyson regarding the philosophical position of objective idealism taken from German Idealism, being here specially influenced by Schelling's thought. Two important texts from Pareyson attest this claim: "Federico Guglielmo Schelling," published in the work *Grande Antologia Filosofica* (1971, pp. 1–340), and his book *L'estetica dell'idealismo tedesco* (1950).

4 Luigi Pareyson, *Esthétique. Théorie de la Formativité* (Paris: Éditions Rue d'Ulm, 2007).

It is with this philosophical position and with the theoretical background related to it, the theory of formativity, that I approach design processes. While the articulation of objective idealism and the theory of formativity seeks to unveil deeper properties of design processes, there are still some considerable difficulties to overcome. The most difficult issues to tackle while inquiring upon design processes at this theoretical level are certain aspects of projective and creative processes embedded in inventive mental and operative activities such as, for instance, the projection of a newly formed concept, its exteriorization, and the mental continuity between all the inferential kinds involved in the process.

2. Design Process as *Entwerfen*: Forming with Relations, Projecting with Materiality

Design processes, as a general procedure of a projecting mind, encompass the specific mindset of proposing projections and creating strategies to conceptualize and execute these proposed projections, thus concretizing the mental projected forms into formed relations. The term *design process* is used as a technical term in a very general manner. Therefore, I propose to integrate the German concept of *Entwerfen*. I hold the latter to be better qualified to describe, in a very general sense, a purposive action and its embodiments within the scope of a certain project or design, as well as its materializations. These are here not mere sequences of separate, stage-like events, but are kinds of operations of a larger relational scope. *Entwerfen*, in its turn, carries the meaning of a process during which, in the activity of projecting and designing, a first conception is generated from a new idea. This first conception, upon being projected, develops itself into certain forms, which unfold as possibilities for realizations. That is to say, there is a close relationship between the mental realm, the realm of ideas and idea generation, and the operations with materiality. In this specific process, the projectivity and the materiality are not necessarily exclusive of one another. They are simultaneous operations and require the particularities of both realms—the ideal and the objective.

During the course of design processes, these realizations will take the shape of mediated phenomena, that is, they will be embodied in different mediative supports. As such, they will be, potentially at least, articulated within a given language, through which the realizations will be given a certain *Gestalt*—a shape, a form. These projected forms thus become more defined and grow, for their embodiments allow certain observations and analysis which, in turn, lead to modifications and improvements. These modifications and improvements enable processes leading to the discovery of newly formed relations between elements. This process is led by a projective power, which projects its potential into the future, aiming at the generation of more complex systems. For such purpose, it must be embodied in some medium and also codified in some language so as to be able to transmit its intended power of signification. Only then can projective power transform its potential intention into actual power to create a system with a more perennial and pragmatical structure.

More precisely, the term *language*, which I consider here in its broadest sense, means not only the codified verbal languages but also general forms of nonverbal languages with different degrees of codification. Being in the world and being surrounded by an intricate net of languages forces interpreting minds to communicate with the world through the reading (decodifying) and writing or graphing (codifying) of forms. These forms are in their vast majority codifications and proto-codifications of nonverbal languages, for example noises, images, visual signs, acoustic signs, odors, gestures, facial and corporal expressions, social movements, clothes, cultural aspects and movements, natural signs, and so on. Through the interactive processes of translation, interpretation, rearrangement, and resignification, and through successive acts of association, rearrangement, and resignification in distinct contexts, the vast set of nonverbal signs can spark further codified languages. Through this process, languages can grow. The well-known codifications, such as literary languages, photography, graphic languages, music and its varieties, cinema, and digital audiovisual to mention just some of them, are examples of languages that, through a process of constant interaction, have achieved well-structured codification as languages, thus becoming referential. These codifications also constantly interact with each other, and this provokes interchanges and modifications within languages, which thereby continuously grow and enrich each other.

3. *Entwerfen*: Embodied Relations as Agencies

Because of its triggering force and its formative capacities—both of which lead to invention and discovery within a given frame of reference in a design context—I propose to frame the design process as an agency. From this perspective, while engaging in design processes, the projecting mind forms purposive conceptual projections which lead it to imagine, to combine, to discover, and to guide actions connected to this mindset so as to carry a particular plan into execution. There will always be an experimental aspect, also including a great deal of improvisation and invention in the making—at least potentially—connected to this conceptual projection, which may become an active agency to propose a given line of conduct. In this perspective, therefore, the technical and the practical are not separate from the mental but are still connected. The scope of design processes is thus broadened by the symbiotic articulation of processes of inventing and discovering, form-giving, rule-finding, and conducting experiments. Furthermore, the whole design process is viewed not as discrete stages, but as continuous.

In relation to *Entwerfen* and its connection with projective activity and design processes, it is important to cast an eye upon the multifaceted spectrum of meanings presented by this concept. The concept *Entwerfen*, which in the past may have denoted the tossing movement of a ship on high seas, became aggregated with the meaning of the French word *projet*,[5] thus acquiring a more symbolic meaning of *projecting* as an intellectual and artistical act of projecting mental images. In turn, the French concept of *projet* gained, at the beginning of the fifteenth century, the meaning of "plan," "draft," "schema." The French *projet* is a derivative of the Latin verb *proicere*, which, in classical times, meant literally "throwing something forth"—from *pro*, "forward," and *iacere*, past participle form of *iactus*, "to throw." Thus, the idea of mentally projecting is embedded in the general concept of *Entwerfen*.

The German dictionary of the Grimm brothers[6] has an entry on *Entwerfen*. This concept, connected to the French word *projet*, includes the meanings of two Latin concepts normally used in an architectural context: *adumbratio* means "contour,"

5 Barbara Wittmann, "Papierprojekte: Die Zeichnung als Instrument des Entwurfs," *Zeitschrift für Medien- und Kulturforschung* 1, no. 12 (2012): 123–38.

6 Compare with Jacob and Wilhelm Grimm: *Deutsches Wörterbuch*, vol. 3 (Munich: Deutscher Taschenbuch Verlag, 1984), 655–56.

"profile," "outline," and also "sketch"; the entry simultaneously refers to the word *informatio*, which means "the action of producing an image" from a first input in the mind. Further definitions enrich the term *Entwerfen*. The Ancient Greek terms *diagraphice* and *diagraphé*, that is, the projective work of and with geometrical constructions, have also been articulated within the contexts of architecture, arts, and engineering. Goethe probably had these conceptions in mind when he formulated another name related to the project maker, or *Entwerfer*: the *Skizzisten*, that is, the agent who graphically translates ideas into form conceptions.[7] Similar to the modern concepts of *disegno* and *dessin*, the concept of *Entwerfen* began, in an analogous manner, to denote the conceptual arrangement of an idea which will lead to its realization, relating both to artistic and technical processes—a sort of *animo concipere*, that is, to plan something in the mind and accordingly carry it into execution.

However, an important definition remains unformulated: the aspect of form-giving, that is, the formative aspect of design processes. Before I formulate this point in-depth, I stress the simultaneity of both aspects of design processes, the projective and the formative. As aforementioned, they do not oppose each other but rather are complementary and simultaneous.

4. Interactivity within Design Processes

Every purposive projective action of design processes and its consequent performance carries out a projected content in the field of disciplines generally related to the creative or inventive. These, in their turn, bring about novelty, both technically and culturally. I contend that from a specific projective context involving a specific projective purpose, something new, not previously conceived can be born. In this attitude of mind, which allows discovery to come into play, a process of invention of new elements, of new concepts, and the formation of new systems becomes operative. This is presented to the perceiving mind, becoming defined as a generated idea, as it persistently insinuates itself into the mind. If this idea is adopted as one worth being pursued, it invades the conscience, thereby setting off further potential mental procedures approaching the definitions of conceptions and conceptualizations. Some of the conceptions will then be selected as courses of action. Those selected will, in their turn, guide conduct and action by carrying the projected design, project, or artifact into performance, with the realization of this particular projective process having been driven by the first conceived idea. The effectuation of design processes takes place in a series of embodiments, that is, in attempts at conceptualizing and exteriorizing forms and sequences of this projected, first-outlined conception, that is, the first conception inscribed into different mediative supports, with different materiality, and also codified with language or thereby developing the potential to create new languages. This series of successive embodiments and replications carry the projective process further. In this whole process, the process of invention plays a central role. Invention not only takes place at the beginning of a projective process. It pervades the whole process, which is a form of invention in the making, whereby the creative, the inventive, and the procedures of embodying and of testing occur *pari passu*, that is, simultaneously.

7 Wolfgang Pircher, "Entwerfen zwischen Raum und Fläche," in *Kulturtechnik Entwerfen: Praktiken, Konzepte und Medien in Architektur und Design Science*, ed. Daniel Gethmann and Susanne Hauser (Bielefeld: transcript, 2009), 103.

Perhaps one of the most illustrative examples is that of Jackson Pollock's work. By constantly and incessantly searching for a visual language to express the concrete qualities of liquified paint he was striving at, Pollock devised in the making this specific concretion of qualities, that is, the concrete qualities of stains of paint dripped over a surface, while also using, as medium or vehicle to that effect, his body movements to throw the liquified, dripping paint over the horizontally placed canvas. One good example is his 1952 work *Convergence*.[8] Projects and designs are the products of a concatenated effort—even if this effort is rather spontaneous, as in Pollock's case—that occurs over a certain period of time and involves preliminary conceptualizations, a myriad of medial translations, definitions, subsequent embodiments of the concepts, corrections, and improvements, until the concept becomes mature and can thereby be developed into the defined shape selected for the project, including all the planning and the spontaneous variations that appear as part of the design process. Generally stated, the whole procedure that engenders invention and discoveries is described—and circumscribed—by the design process. This process introduces something not previously given. Even if the premises of a certain project are well established, the subsequent unfolding of a conception is neither controllable nor predictable in advance. When a design or project is being developed, new aspects appear, at least partially. These new aspects can reveal and determine new directions for the whole process or can potentially reshape the course of its development by calling for a whole new procedure or new sets of procedures.

The newly formulated conceptions will unfold the projections into new forms and new contexts: they will demand to be carried into execution with distinct materiality, occupying a mediatic space, delineated by certain forms, and articulated with specific languages. The conceptions that gave impetus to this process will then be embodied in some media with the chosen materiality. That materiality and the specific mediatic and language articulations will act, in their turn, as defining instances given the fact that their possibilities and limitations will require specific actions in order to establish a dialogue. In this case, design processes assume a dialogical character: the interactors must deal with properties of materiality, media, languages, and technology so that the concept can be thereby embodied. This embodiment is the result of the dialogue. In fact, the aspect of formativity characterizing design processes highlights the pragmatic character of the latter.

5. Formative and Dialogical Aspects of Design Processes

The act of projecting is one of unfolding as a dialogue, in which the conceptions created are shaped, translated into a more developed concept, embodied in different media, and articulated in different actual or potential languages. A design process is thus dialogical, for it takes into account the activities and agencies of the involved plans, elements, and material instances. Dialogue is understood as a concept that functions in relational terms within design processes. That is to say, the projective activity driven by a mind needs to dialogue with the active and relational characters of the materiality, the active and relational aspects of technology, and whatever fields of knowledge are related to design processes in order to carry the project's conception into execution. This dialogue that pervades the entire design process can also be called *semiosis*. Semiosis, in Charles S. Peirce's terms, is the translation of a sign into another, more developed sign,

8 Entitled *Convergence*, this huge canvas (241.9 × 399.1 cm), produced in 1952, can be seen at the Albright-Knox Gallery in Buffalo, NY.

called the interpretant of the first sign. It is a developmental process, a process of translation, in which the concept represented by the sign grows. A design process thus involves a specific mental procedure on the part of an agent—a designer, a project maker, or a *Skizzisten*.[9] This agent is situated in a peculiar state of uncertainty, for he or she operates in an epistemological in-betweenness, that is, exactly at the threshold between the unknown, the insecure place with unknown order, and already established, well-accepted knowledge. His or her position marks directly the transition between critical predicament and an undecided—still to be formed—future. His or her task consists of stating the unthinkable to render something feasible. This epistemological in-betweenness has the power to constitute an arena for playing, a space for intellectual freedom where experiments of thought can take place, conceptions can be tested, the elements of these conceptions and the conflating of parts of ideas assembled, and elements of ideas separated to better perceive their particularities and specific nuances. In this context, plans for the specific courses of actions can be drawn from these experiments of thought and their embodiments into mediative supports.[10]

This is the case, for instance, with the troubled—but quite revealing—production of Steven Spielberg's 1975 film *Jaws*. The original plan was to produce a monster film in which the overgrown great white shark would appear much more frequently. The main concept, as it was written in the earliest drafts of the screenplay and later transformed into a rather primitive storyboard, focused on the terror created by the sight of the shark and the reaction of the actors. This formula, however, could not be put to work due to innumerable flaws with the mechanized shark and also due to various difficulties with the production. The film needed to be readapted to overcome such difficulties. There were times when no one could foresee what the best course of action would be to ensure the continuation of the film's production. To make sense, the narrative of the film had to be completely reorganized so that the giant shark does not simply appear but is characterized and represented by a theme song and by the movements of the camera. The result of this forceful and necessary adaptation was—and this was a true discovery for everyone involved—the creation of a true horror/thriller that became a landmark for upcoming cinematographic productions.

This process of discovery was triggered by a constant process of revision, of mediatic and language—therefore semiotic—translations that eventually led the way from a first plan to the film that came to have a completely new cinematographic meaning. This transformation means constantly transforming, reinterpreting, and improving upon the first parameters. It is also important to say that in the case of *Jaws* there was an almost complete loss of control of the process.

6. Gestalt, Form-Giving, and Embodiments

For the sake of clarity, I will use the terms *idea*, *conception*, and *conceptualization* to respectively imply here, in the context of the logic of design processes, first, the generated idea that appears to the perceiving mind through an abductive, synthetic process; second, the representation of this idea in a more defined manner as the triggering idea is developed with different materials, for instance in a sketch on paper or canvas, from a screenplay to a storyboard, or from the storyboard to the first audiovisual sequences, to serve as a registration of these

9 This rather untranslatable word, as coined by Goethe, describes the one who produces sketches (*Skizzen*) with the aim of developing them into more complex forms until a work is sufficiently done and can exist by itself.

10 See Markus Krajewski, ed., *Projektemacher: Zur Produktion des Wissens in der Vorform des Scheiterns* (Berlin: Kultur Verlag Kadmos, 2004).

first impressions emerging in the mind, and third, the representations aiming at a determined representation and realization, which are also constantly contrasted with the first generated idea. It is important to note also that this contrast between the first generated idea and the further conceptualizations does not imply that the first generated idea will be simply copied into conceptions and articulated in subsequent conceptualizations. I stated earlier that the first generated idea is of the nature of a mental appearance—or mental phenomenon. The insistence of this mental phenomenon reveals a certain purpose—even if it is still quite uncertain—and this purpose will be subsequently further developed by the interplay of possible lines of thought and conduct, that is, a formative process that includes the dialogue inherent to every design process and which shapes the materiality according to this purpose. And, reciprocally, the more this development is unfolded and takes shape, the more the first generated idea itself becomes developed. In this context, it is possible to realize how the plan, the purpose, and the further development of this purpose operate simultaneously.

As I am using the terms here, *conceptions* and *conceptualizations* bring about a very peculiar notion, similar to the concept of the German term *Gestalt*, that is, the idea of a spreading form-giving process triggered by and reciprocally enabling the growth of an idea. Similarly to how I consider the term, and in connection with the aforementioned concept of *Entwerfen*, Maurice Merleau-Ponty (1908–1961) considers *Gestalt* to involve general principles of distribution that become integrated into a constellation that spans space and time.[11] In this sense, *Gestalt* is something general manifesting itself in several objective fragments or embodiments within several media. The entirety of the form-giving principle that characterizes *Gestalt* cannot be reduced to the sum of its generated parts. There is a dialogue between the phenomena of *Gestalt*, the principles that trigger them, and the actor or subject interacting with them. In this interaction, neither the objective realm of the things outside, the fragments, nor the subjectivity of an individual actor is primary. Accordingly, in such an environment a sort of "involvement in circumstances" occurs in which the individual actor becomes totally absorbed. Through this, the individual actor interacts with this environment with a different understanding and it is exactly this that allows a myriad of heuristic moments to appear.

In this context, the effectuation of the design process arises and takes shape in a succession of embodiments, that is to say, in successive endeavors to conceptualize and exteriorize forms and sequences of the projected first-outlined conception. Otherwise stated, the first conception, which was provoked by the first emerging idea, will be inscribed into different mediative supports, shaped with different materiality, and also articulated within a certain language or thereby develop the potential to create new languages. The successive embodiments and replications, guided by more developed conceptions, carry the projective process further. The first conception, developed from the aforementioned generated idea, thus becomes refined and improved in the subsequent conceptions and conceptualizations.

7. General Bases for Invention within Design Processes

From the analysis of relations performed hitherto, it follows that invention, as a vital component of design processes, does not take place only at the beginning of a given projective activity. It is present and operative in every step of the whole

11 Maurice Merleau-Ponty, *The Visible and the Invisible: Followed by Working Notes* (Evanston: Northwestern University Press, 1968), 204–5.

design process and possesses a formative character, for invention and the procedures of embodying new conceptions and conducting experiments occur simultaneously to the whole projectual development. At first glance, the present formulation fulfills its function of presenting a broader and more detailed operation of the projective action in a synthetic manner, referring as it does to the continuity of events, its pronounced nonlinearity, and the simultaneity of operations, as well as the abductive processes that commence new, future-oriented operations and purpose-oriented experimentation. The general comprehension of design processes includes the future-orientedness signalized by every form of projective action.[12]

Invention in the light of abductive processes is a key element. Being a correlative process within the simultaneity between projection and formative processes, it follows that invention is not a singular occurrence, but that it may occur continuously in virtually every new unfolding of a given design process. Thus, the property of inventiveness is an ingredient of a broader phenomenological process, a process that initiates further processes and, at the same time, promotes the unfolding of formative, that is, form-giving processes that may be developed further under a given set of circumstances.

When the logic of events of a certain process starts unfolding, the creation of new elements that will be embodied in subsequent conceptions of the process influences the development of the process itself in a specific manner: the newly introduced ideas propose new conceptions which, in their turn, thereby introduce new logical perspectives to the whole design process. That is to say, these newly formed conceptions carry their own logic with them into the whole process, and for that reason, demand specific ways of being dealt with.

At this point, it is possible to draw an important conclusion. In every process of determination, in every form of seeking for a more clarified and specified embodiment of the leading idea through the development of subsequent conceptions, there will be a myriad of accompanying processes of discovery: the sought properties need, indeed, to be discovered. They need to become open to experience in the process of making. These newly found properties are then the subject of further abductions taking place simultaneously with the formative process. Moreover, this process of discovery always occurs *pari passu*, that is to say, concomitantly with a specific form-giving process.

The most important idea of formativity in Luigi Pareyson's theory concerning design processes is that it integrates into the form-translating process the heuristic moment, the inventive process, for, as he states, the productive force and the capacity for invention, the ingenuity implied in and pervading all of the process, are then requirements displayed by thought and conduct. In this case, whenever thought and conduct are articulated in a self-controlled manner to achieve a general purpose, speculative operations and practical articulations are pervaded by formative principles which, within the scope of the specific project, craft the production and the execution of certain shapes simultaneously with the invention of the manner in which these shapes are being produced.

In accordance with this broader view of abductive processes concerning aesthetic principles, Luigi Pareyson affirms that the predominance of the aesthetically interpretable—or, in a pragmatic sense, conceivable—allows innumerable ways

12 For a deeper analysis of the logic of relations operative within invention and discovery, see Tiago da Costa e Silva, *The Logic of Design Process: Invention and Discovery in Light of the Semiotics of Charles S. Peirce* (Bielefeld: transcript, 2018).

in which things can be accessed, grasped, and captured.[13] This multiplicity of ways of accessing, grasping, or capturing things does not imply a sort of sensual relativism or a skepticism, but rather denotes the inexhaustibility of this kind of active, heuristic dialogue, which is capable of awakening further processes and bringing forth a series of semiotic processes. A design process becomes open to every trained mind which engages in this interpretative process and establishes this form of dialogue. It thus allows one to continually replenish oneself with originality and freshness again and anew while engaging in an act of formation as a plasmator,[14] a modeler of forms, proposing the exteriorization of concepts and conceptualizations that, because these concepts and conceptualizations gain their own reality and existence, feed back to the mind in an active form of pragmatic, and also aesthetic, dialogue.

The present essay has unveiled the phenomenological, formative, and pragmatic dimensions of design processes following the processuality of the design process in light of formativity. With this specific focus, I have presented the practical relationship between aesthetic principles and abduction, defending the idea that abductions are operative in determinate practical aesthetic contexts. This is of importance because the generation of new ideas and of new concepts results from the formation of generative mental habits in which aesthetic contexts are predominant. Otherwise stated, aesthetic conditions enable more abductive mindsets to arise and take place, thus propelling inventiveness within design processes.

13 Luigi Pareyson, *Conversations sur l'esthétique* (Paris: Gallimard, 1992).

14 Luigi Pareyson coined a new term in Italian, *plasmatore*, which has been translated into French as *plasmateur*, meaning the *creator of forms*. Here, I have translated it as *plasmator*, for I think that this term can convey a very close meaning to that intended by Pareyson in his original text. According to the French translator, Gilles Tiberghien, the Italian verb *plasmare* means *modeler*, the one who creates or models forms.

From *Gestalt* to *Gestaltung*
A Conversation with Giovanni Anceschi[1]

Emanuele Quinz

Cofounder of the Gruppo T at the end of the 1950s, Giovanni Anceschi (born 1939) is a pioneer of kinetic and programmed art, having grown up in close contact with the Milanese, Italian, and international avant-garde. In the 1960s, he attended the Hochschule für Gestaltung in Ulm, where he studied and collaborated with Tomás Maldonado, Gui Bonsiepe, Max Bense, Abraham Moles, Otl Aicher, and Martin Krampen.

On his return to Italy, after working for three years as a design director for the Algerian national oil company, he focused on design, teaching communication disciplines in various universities, including the Milan Polytechnic and the IUAV in Venice.

Anceschi's diverse career, emblematic in terms of the experimental and liberatory tension underpinning it, allows us to consider the historical phases of the passage from the research stage of the 1960s, examining the relationships between perceptional models and formal/informational structures—which would come to a head in the range of Programmed Art practices—to a theory of design based on an equilibrium between empirical experimentation and the analysis of complexity, and which would develop the bases laid down by the *Grundkurs* of the Bauhaus and the *Grundlehre* of the Hochschule für Gestaltung in Ulm: how to pass from *Gestalt* (a "tendency toward wholeness") to *Gestaltung* (a "configurative formational process").

EMANUELE QUINZ: I would like to start from *Miriorama*, the cycle of events that marked the entrance on the arts scene of the Gruppo T—which you founded in 1959 with Davide Boriani, Gabriele Devecchi, Gianni Colombo, later joined also by Grazia Varisco—and which officially opened the season of Programmed Art, long before the exhibition of the same name curated by Bruno Munari and

1 A shorter version of this interview has been published in Italian, in Emanuele Quinz, *Contro l'oggetto: Conversazioni sul design* (Macerata: Quodlibet, 2020), 19–30.

Giorgio Soavi in the Olivetti space in Milan [1962]. In *Miriorama 1* [1960], you presented the *Grande oggetto pneumatico, ambiente a volume variabile* [Large Pneumatic Object, Environment with Variable Volume], a system made up of seven tubular elements in polyethylene, which inflate and deflate cyclically thanks to a photoelectric cell linked to an air compressor. When the system is entirely inflated, it takes up almost the whole environment, squashing the onlooker. According to the programmatic declaration of the Gruppo T, *Miriorama* explores the dimension of "dynamism as a variation of the phenomenological world"; "every aspect of reality, color, form, light, geometric spaces and astronomical time is a different aspect of how space-time is given, or rather, a different way of perceiving the relationship between space and time..."[2]

With this clear-minded declaration, the bases were laid down for the "research condition"[3] which over the years to come would characterize the various animating principles of Programmed Art: drawing on scientific methods despite maintaining an aesthetic effect as the goal of artistic operation. What was the philosophical background that marked the birth of the Gruppo T? (figs. 1a, 1b)

GIOVANNI ANCESCHI: The Gruppo T started out in 1959, and it is generally believed to have come to an end around 1968, although the members of the group would continue to work together in subgroups even beyond this date, and in actual fact, the Gruppo T never formally disbanded. But while Boriani, Devecchi, and I stayed together, even though we soon abandoned the art market to do other things—design, teaching, business ventures, journalism etc.—Grazia Varisco and Gianni Colombo, who stubbornly but bravely chose to remain inside the market, decided to give space to their own individual artistic figures, thus unilaterally declaring the end of the shared experience. As far as I'm concerned, I believe that despite everything, Colombo's work remained most faithful to the outlook of the group. His last environment, the *Spazio diagoniometrico* [Diagoniometric Space, 1992], with its twelve large misaligned cones, rotating and hanging from the ceiling, generates a heavily invasive modification of the viewer's behavior, very much akin to that provoked by the *Grande oggetto pneumatico* (figs. 2, 3).

We presented our first kinetic works in 1960 in Milan: works that called on the public to participate: they were to be turned upside down, rotated, manipulated, etc., followed soon afterwards by the animated works, that is, those set in movement, motorized. Our thinking set out from a declaration of aesthetic theory based on the notion of becoming, on the registering of the continuous transformation of the world, on the *panta rei*. On the broader contemporary scene, Kinetic and Programmed Art were instead hastily pigeonholed as one of the many subcurrents of the Optical movement, with an often-exclusive accent placed on perceptual aspects. In actual fact, as the New Tendencies demonstrated, perceptual experimentation goes hand in hand with constructive, kinetic, and programmed research.[4] On our part, the notion of variation, implied by the movement of the work, was initially conceived in ontological terms, or rather "ontic" ones: like a variation that arises in concrete terms in material and which art isolates and makes visible, from powdered metals reacting to magnetism, to falling granules to dripping liquids. The interest in the processes of reception/perception did not start out at all as the glorification of Gestalt psychology or geometry, as Giulio Carlo Argan claimed, tending to force us into a neo-Constructivist or even essentialist approach.[5]

2 Gruppo T (Giovanni Anceschi, Davide Boriani, Gianni Colombo, and Gabriele Devecchi), *Miriorama 1* (1960), published on the occasion of the exhibition at the Galleria Pater in Milan and republished in *Il Verri*, no. 22 (October 1966). See also *Il Gruppo N: La situazione dei gruppi in Europa negli anni 60*, ed. Italo Mussa (Rome: Bulzoni, 1976), 188.

3 Giulio Carlo Argan, "Arte come ricerca," in *Nova Tendencija 3* (Zagreb, 1965), 20, reprinted in *L'ultima avanguardia, Arte programmata e cinetica 1953–1963*, ed. Lea Vergine (Milan: Mazzotta, 1984), 193–97.

4 For the history of the New Tendencies, see Margit Rosen ed., *A Little-Known Story about a Movement, a Magazine, and the Computer's Arrival in Art: New Tendencies and Bit International, 1961–1973* (Cambridge MA: MIT Press, 2011).

5 See Giulio Carlo Argan, "La Ricerca Gestaltica," *Il Messaggero* (August 24, 1963): 3.

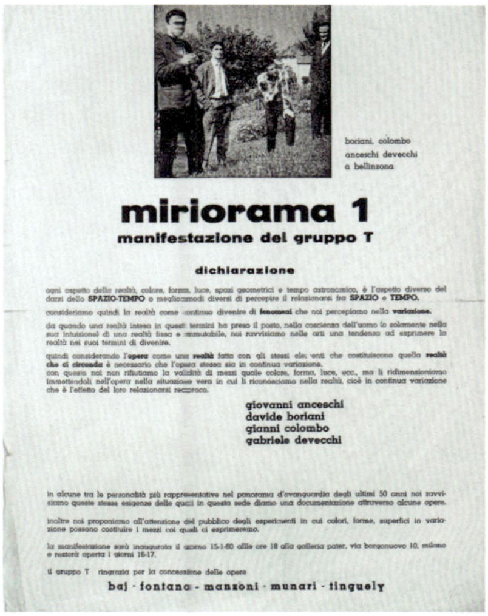

boriani, colombo
anceschi devecchi
a bellinzona

miriorama 1

manifestazione del gruppo T

dichiarazione

ogni aspetto della realtà, colore, forma, luce, spazi geometrici e tempo astronomico, è l'aspetto diverso del darsi dello **SPAZIO-TEMPO** o meglio modi diversi di percepire il relazionarsi fra **SPAZIO** e **TEMPO.**

consideriamo quindi la realtà come continuo divenire di **fenomeni** che noi percepiamo nella **variazione.**

da quando una realtà intesa in questi termini ha preso il posto, nella coscienza dell'uomo (o solamente nella sua intuizione) di una realtà fissa e immutabile, noi ravvisiamo nelle arti una tendenza ad esprimere la realtà nei suoi termini di divenire.

quindi considerando l'**opera** come una **realtà** fatta con gli stessi elementi che costituiscono quella **realtà che ci circonda** è necessario che l'opera stessa sia in continua variazione.
con questo noi non rifiutiamo la validità di mezzi quale colore, forma, luce, ecc., ma li ridimensioniamo immettendoli nell'opera nella situazione vera in cui li riconosciamo nella realtà, cioè in continua variazione che è l'effetto del loro relazionarsi reciproco.

giovanni anceschi
davide boriani
gianni colombo
gabriele devecchi

in alcune tra le personalità più rappresentative nel panorama d'avanguardia degli ultimi 50 anni noi ravvisiamo queste stesse esigenze delle quali in questa sede diamo una documentazione attraverso alcune opere.

inoltre noi proponiamo all'attenzione del pubblico degli esperimenti in cui colori, forme, superfici in variazione possono costituire i mezzi coi quali ci esprimeremo.

la manifestazione sarà inaugurata il giorno 15-1-60 alle ore 18 alla galleria pater, via borgonuovo 10, milano e resterà aperta i giorni 16-17.

il gruppo T ringrazia per la concessione delle opere

baj · fontana · manzoni · munari · tinguely

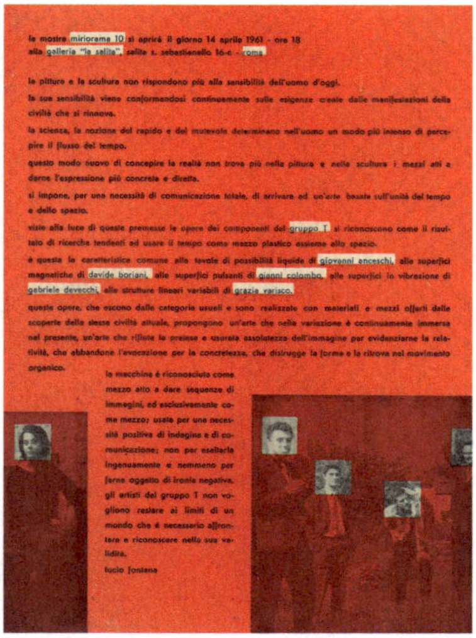

la mostra miriorama 10 si aprirà il giorno 14 aprile 1961 - ore 18
alla galleria "la salita", salita s. sebastianello 16-c - roma

la pittura e la scultura non rispondono più alla sensibilità dell'uomo d'oggi.

la sua sensibilità viene conformandosi continuamente sulle esigenze create dalle manifestazioni della civiltà che si rinnova.

la scienza, la nozione del rapido e del mutevole determinano nell'uomo un modo più intenso di percepire il flusso del tempo.

questo modo nuovo di concepire la realtà non trova più nella pittura e nella scultura i mezzi atti a darne l'espressione più concreta e diretta.

si impone, per una necessità di comunicazione totale, di arrivare ad un'arte basata sull'unità del tempo e dello spazio.

viste alla luce di queste premesse le opere dei componenti del gruppo T si riconoscono come il risultato di ricerche tendenti ad usare il tempo come mezzo plastico assieme allo spazio.

è questa la caratteristica comune alle tavole di possibilità liquide di giovanni anceschi, alle superfici magnetiche di davide boriani, alle superfici pulsanti di gianni colombo, alle superfici in vibrazione di gabriele devecchi, alle strutture lineari variabili di grazia varisco.

queste opere, che escono dalle categorie usuali e sono realizzate con materiali e mezzi offerti dalle scoperte della stessa civiltà attuale, propongono un'arte che nella variazione è continuamente immersa nel presente, un'arte che rifiuta la pretesa e usurata assolutezza dell'immagine per evidenziarne la relatività, che abbandona l'evocazione per la concretezza, che distrugge la forma e la ritrova nel movimento organico.

la macchina è riconosciuta come mezzo atto a dare sequenze di immagini, ed esclusivamente come mezzo; usata per una necessità positiva di indagine e di comunicazione; non per esaltarla ingenuamente e nemmeno per farne oggetto di ironia negativa. gli artisti del gruppo T non vogliono restare ai limiti di un mondo che è necessario affrontare e riconoscere nella sua validità.

lucio fontana

Fig. 1a (left): Printed invitation *Miriorama 1*, Gruppo T, Milan, Galleria Pater, Milan, 1960.

Fig. 1b (right): Printed invitation *Miriorama 10*, Gruppo T, Galleria La Salita, Rome, 1961.

Fig. 2: Gianni Colombo, *Spazio Elastico* ("Elastic Space"), 1967. Fluorescent elastic cords, electrical motors, Wood's lamp, 400 × 400 × 400 cm.

Fig. 3: Gabriele Devecchi, Giovanni Anceschi, Davide Boriani, Gianni Colombo with Lucio Fontana and Piero Manzoni (back turned) at the opening of the Anceschi, Boriani, Colombo, Devecchi exhibition at Galleria Pater, Milan, 1959.

Fig. 4: Cover of the catalogue *Arte Programmata, Arte cinetica. Opere moltiplicate. Opera aperta*, Umberto Eco and Bruno Munari (eds.) (exhibition curated by Bruno Munari and Giorgio Soavi, Showroom Olivetti, Milan), Officina d'Arte Grafica A. Lucini & C, Milan, 1962.

EQ: Right from the beginning, you rejected Argan's definition of "Gestalt art," setting against it the distinction put forward by Max Bense between Gestalt and structure. In 1974, in your introduction to the translation of Bense's *Aestetica*, which you edited, you wrote: "In Italy, the term 'Gestalt art' performed the role of an emblematic flag behind which to bring together all those who, in the field of the plastic arts, operated either by drawing on a more or less thorough knowledge of Gestalt psychology, or more simply, those wallowing in melancholic neo-Constructivist laments, or otherwise, those generically exploiting unusual technical devices, so-called leftover materials." Fairly minimal requisites, I might say. Bense, on the other hand [...] introduces the term *Gestalt conception* as an opposite concept to the term *structural concept*, and makes a more usefully classificatory use of both of them: on the one hand, those works that tend to produce globality (*Gestalt*); and on the other, those works that tend to produce iterative series (structures)."[6]

GA: Yes, because unlike the stance adopted by Argan, for us, the interest in perception was instrumental: it was rooted in the process of artistic ideation, in the need to deploy an aesthetic control over the inevitable repetition caused by the use of technologies. In particular, the electromechanical motors generated repetitions that risked becoming boring, and therefore called for variations in order to obtain an intriguing effect of nonrepetition, that is, of originality. Speaking of effects may seem surprising, because *effect* is a Baroque term, but it's also a keyword in our research. At that time, the expression *perceptual present* was used by Abraham Moles when exploring the possibility of a *perception esthétique*,[7] referring to the density and the stratification of the present. Our theoretical move thus consisted in acknowledging the fact that if we ensure that the repetition outstrips the confines of the perceptive present, our minds are tricked into no longer

6 Giovanni Anceschi, "Intorno all'estetica di Bense," in Max Bense, *Estetica*, trans. G. Anceschi (Milan: Bompiani, 1974), 21.

7 Abraham A. Moles, *Théorie de l'information et perception esthétique* (Paris: Flammarion, 1958).

noticing the mechanical action which is reproduced in monotonous, unchanging cycles. The repetition is no longer perceived as such, but appears unpredictable in its development.

There's another point I believe to be important. We in the Gruppo T viewed the artist as an intellectual, one who expresses his aesthetic theories through his works, but also in his programmatic declarations. And we believed it to such a point that we generated a new form of artistic literature: the systematic description of a series of our artworks in which the time component was strongly present, and which we published in *Il Verri* in 1966.[8]

In terms of my own training, during my studies at the faculty of philosophy I happened to meet Enzo Paci, a student of Antonio Banfi. Paci, the philosopher of relationism, was closely tied to the Husserlian current of phenomenology. With the Gruppo T, we felt very close to the phenomenological outlook of Husserl and later of Merleau-Ponty insofar as perception is thought of as a process, and at the same time the hub of the reflection is shifted onto the notion of temporality. Our manifesto *Miriorama 1*, which once more starts out from the Bergsonian term *becoming*, is imbued with phenomenological aesthetics. At the same time, our works of the 1950s and 1960s, which—as always happens—went beyond our programmatic intentions, aiming for novel approaches which then became the norm, such as demanding participation on behalf of the public, as represented very successfully in Devecchi's *Scultura da prendere a calci* [1959], and the environmental character, exemplified by the *Grande oggetto pneumatico*, as Munari renamed our collective work, which we instead had defined explicitly as the *Ambiente a volume variabile* (fig. 4).

EQ: Taking up a position in favor of kinetic and programmed works, Argan defended a potential enhancement in the quality of art through scientific technologies. Unlike Neo-plasticism, which was driven by a metaphysical faith in mathematics and geometry, what Argan defines as "Gestalt art" draws on a scientific methodology based on a project, an *experimentation* and a *verification*. The idea of a *verifiable art* is taboo today, and yet at the time it was at the heart of the debate, as a means by which to break out from the subjectivistic vagueness of the informal and from Croce's idealism. Argan insists on how this technical dimension may become a political program, a sharing of media and results with the public, as the only chance for art to have a social bearing, concretely contrasting the alienating action of the crowd and the solitary fate that awaits the alienated man in industrial society.

GA: Giulio Carlo Argan's prospectives are part of that theoretical-critical avalanche which had overwhelmed the artistic debate in that period. A substantial scientific optimism was rife, one of a materialist and neopositivist nature. Nowadays, it's hard for me even to do so much as try to don that hat again. But it's important to underline that our kineticism, our introduction of material movement into the artwork—unlike what Argan thought—did not stand in contrast to the informal but in a sort of dialectical continuation. Most of all, if you think of the mysterious material collapses of Boriani's magnetic filings [*Superficie magnetica*, 1959–62], or even the dripping of my own *Tavole di possibilità liquide* [1959], which we jokingly referred to at the time as "Pollock in movement," and even of the glimmering of the *Superfici in vibrazione* [1959] by Gabriele Devecchi…

8 See the texts by the members of the Gruppo T in *Il Verri*, no. 22 (October 1966).

EQ: The notion of program was essential at the time. How would you define it?

GA: If we're talking about the early days, around the turn of the 1960s, the word and the notion of programming were not yet present: there was some talk of electronic calculators and a few hints at cybernetics, but nothing about IT, especially not in the artistic context.

The one who launched the use of this expression in art was Bruno Munari,[9] even though to tell the truth his definition was a bit flimsy: "By programming, we mean a kind of planning which allows for infinite or multiple variants on the same theme."[10] The expression *Arte Programmata* appeared for the first time in the pages of the *Almanacco Bompiani 1962*, edited by Umberto Eco, with the help of Munari.[11] Although those concerned have never admitted it, my impression is that Munari and Eco, always very much with an ear to the ground, were already aware that in 1960 Max Bense, founder of informational aesthetics, had published a book titled *Programmierung des Schönen* [*Programming the Beautiful*].[12]

In the *Almanacco Bompiani* (fig. 5), several of our graphic projects were published: from the sequence by Gianni Colombo, which foreshadowed the "inbetweening" of photograms, to the diagram by Devecchi presenting the results of an operation of figural subtraction, etc. With the Gruppo T, what we defined as *Grafica Programmata* [Programmed Graphics], started life as a "handmade" form of programming, with compass and ruler. Boriani's case was truly exceptional: starting from the subdivision of an image into little squares, and attributing a number value to every little square on the basis of a given morphological criterion, Boriani anticipated what would later be called the pixel and preempted image processing, that is, graphic production starting out from an analogue image and digitizing it, elaborating it and transforming it through algorithms. My own work on Programmed Graphics, on the other hand, introduced the definition of a program of figural generation, programmed through a combinatorial process: a playing field is defined, made up of places, elements, and rules of transformation. The title of the work describes the program: *In dieci tempi nove rettangoli orientati verticalmente decrescono da 9 a 0 mentre nove rettangoli orientati orizzontalmente crescono da 0 a 9, secondo schemi diversi, 1961/2009* [In ten stages, nine rectangles set vertically decrease from 9 to 0, while nine rectangles set horizontally increase from 0 to 9, on the basis of different schemas]. The strip published in the *Almanacco Bompiani* is the forced exemplification of just one of the possible metamorphic paths. Today with digital technologies, I can show the exact implementation—in the form of an interactive iPhone app [Innovetempi], which puts the infinite random potential of the program into the hands of the spectator/interactor.

But perhaps the most "programmed" of the artists to appear in the *Almanacco Bompiani* is not a figural but a verbal artist: Nanni Balestrini. At the time, Balestrini—whom we envied enormously—was messing around with punch cards and Univac in order to produce his *Tape Mark One* [1961]: a combinatorial poem which randomly mixed together fragments of sentences. *Tape Mark One* was then presented—the only Italian work—at the exhibition *Cybernetic Serendipity*, staged by Jasia Reichardt at the ICA in London in 1968.

9 G. Anceschi's note: The interview was published in the catalogue of the remake show of the original *Arte Programmata* (Negozio Olivetti, Galleria Vittorio Emanuele, Milan, 1962); and in Marco Meneguzzo, *Arte Programmata 1962*, ed. Stefano Fumagalli, exh. cat. (Bergamo: Galleria Fumagalli, 1996). The 1996 remake was perfect. However, the remake of the remake was instead full of strained philological notions; see Marco Meneguzzo, Enrico Morteo, and Alberto Saibene, eds., *Programmare l'arte: Olivetti e le neoavanguardie cinetiche* (Milan: Johan & Levi, 2012).

10 Meneguzzo, *Arte Programmata 1962*.

11 *G. Anceschi's note*: Sergio Morando, ed., *Almanacco Letterario Bompiani 1962: Le applicazioni dei calcolatori elettronici alle scienze morali e alla letteratura* (Milan: Bompiani, 1961). On the contents page, above the list of the featured artists, the term "Arte Programmata" already appears. The list included: Giovanni Anceschi, Davide Boriani, Enrico Castellani, Gianni Colombo, Gabriele Devecchi, Karl Gerstner, Enzo Mari, Bruno Munari, Dieter Rot; Soto, Grazia Varisco. Although only the members of the Gruppo T had been called upon by Eco and Munari to produce works created "according to cybernetic criteria."

12 Max Bense, *Aesthetica*, vol. 4, *Programmierung des Schönen: Allgemeine Texttheorie und Textästhetik* (Krefeld/Baden-Baden: Agis, 1960).

EQ: In 1962 you set off for Ulm where, at the Hochschule für Gestaltung, you met Tomás Maldonado, Abraham A. Moles, and Max Bense, whose *Aesthetica* you were to translate into Italian a few years later. Moles and Bense were trying to reconcile the principles of the theory of information with art, in order to found a rational form of aesthetics, in which the effects of art would not only be programmable but also verifiable.

This theory was pretty much in line with the scientific and positivist theories of art which, ever since Helmholtz, Fechner, or Lipps, had attempted to empirically and quantitatively determine the perceptual effects of a work of art. The most noteworthy historical example is the formula of aesthetic measurement by the American mathematician Birkhoff, scrutinized by Bense, who aimed to capture the compositional norms that preside over a completed artwork in a logarithm. The fundamental premise of this scientific aesthetic is not so much that the distribution of the formal elements in the work induces effects that respond to precise physiological or psychological laws, but that there exists a symmetrical and univocal relationship between stimulation and sensation. On the other hand, the idea of the measurability of the effects of art is part of a eudemonistic conception that sees art as a configuration that aims toward order and harmony. The same principles are taken up in the *Gestalt* theory. On the other hand, the informational aesthetics of Bense and Moles, starting out from the notion of entropy, is based more on the tension between order and disorder, for has we have said, information is linked to disorder. Likewise, from descriptive it becomes prescriptive (fig. 6).

Fig. 5 (below right): Cover of *Almanacco Letterario Bompiani 1962, Le applicazioni del calcolatori elettronici alle scienze morali e alla letteratura* ("Applications of the electronic calculator in the moral sciences and literature"), Sergio Morando (ed.), Bompiani, Milan, 1961.

Fig. 6 (below left): Cover of the first issue of *Bit International Magazine* (edited by Bozo), Zagreb, Galerije Grada Zagreba, 1968.

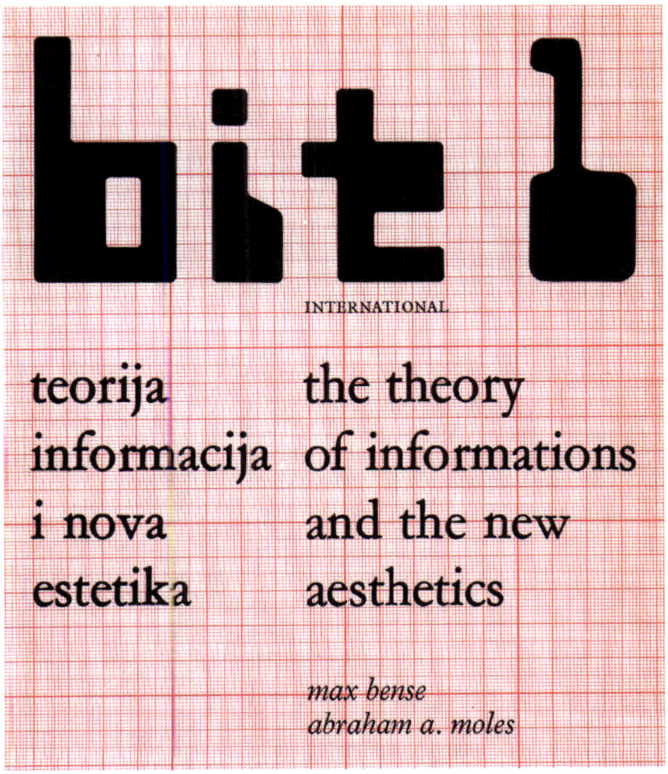

Fig. 7a: Giovanni Anceschi, Davide Boriani, *Ambiente per un test di estetica sperimentale* (Environment for an Experimental Test of Aesthetics). Drawing, 1965.

Figs. 7b & 7c (below): View of the environment on the occasion of the exhibition *L'Œil moteur. Art optique et cinétique, 1950–1975*, Museum of Contemporary Art, Strasbourg 2005.

GA: I think it's something of a scandal that such extraordinary anticipators like Max Bense, Abraham A. Moles, and even Kurd Alsleben in our current world, where their prophecies are known far and wide and have been confirmed in technical terms and implemented through technology, haven't been given their due acknowledgment. Nobody knows who they are anymore. The first reason, and perhaps the main one, lies in the fact that their elaborations and their foresight were formulated in German and French, and not in that universal jargon, in that *lingua franca* of the scientific disciplines that English has become. The second reason lies instead in the fact that the theory of information, which had entered the scientific and cultural discourse in the wake of cybernetics, had an expansion which I would not hesitate to define as explosive and all-inclusive. Indeed, so explosive as to burn up—as it were—the forerunners and anticipators along with all their triumphs and also their initial uncertainties.[13]

EQ: In actual fact, even in Italy, the introduction of the Aesthetics of Information, by Dorfles, Eco, and yourself, made it possible to counter the monopoly of Croce's idealist aesthetics with scientific methodologies, allowing you to discern and analyze the materials and forms of art in their compositions. At the same time, as you explain in the previously mentioned introduction to the Italian edition of Bense's *Aesthetica*, the experimental dimension of this approach also made it possible to open up the analysis—and creation—to other types of practice, such as graphics, advertising, and design, and to valorize the technical dimension of creative processes.

The *Ambiente sperimentale* [1965] which you created with Boriani constitutes one of the main examples of the application of informational aesthetics and at the same time, one of the first achievements of the emerging field of environmental aesthetics.[14] How would you define the notion of environment (figs. 7a, 7b, 7c)?

GA: The research aim behind the *Ambiente per un test di estetica sperimentale*[15] consisted in exploring the relationship between aesthetic information and the structural complexity of the visual message. One by one, the spectators are introduced into an environment structured with luminous, pulsating, colored strips. The programming produces twelve different sequences that follow on from one another, progressively more and more complex. When the spectators leave, they are handed an evaluation form, compiled on the basis of the semantic analysis of the aspects, which makes it possible to compare the statistic values of time measurement—duration of the time spent inside the environment—as values of enjoyment. The project was presented three times: in Zagreb in 1965, in Strasbourg in 2005, and in Rome in 2006,[16] but in none of the three cases was the analytical protocol completed, due to the fact that the three institutions were unwilling to invest in an activity of a scientific nature in terms of staff, time, and costs: for them, like for the spectators, the environment had to remain a work of art and nothing more. ... In actual fact, the procedure proposed a shift away from the field of artistic production in order to move to all effects into that of scientific research. In the 1960s, in the area of the New Tendencies, there was much talk of research, even with the risk of falling foul of forms of categorial incoherence, confusing experimentalism—that is, a rational methodology of artistic production [Programmed Art]—with scientific

13 See Umberto Eco, ed., *Estetica e teoria dell'informazione* (Milan: Bompiani, 1972); and Volli Ugo, ed., *La scienza e l'arte: Nuove metodologie di ricerca scientifica sui fenomeni artistici* (Milan: Mazzotta, 1972).

14 See Emanuele Quinz, "From Program to Behavior: The Experience of Arte Programmata (Italy, 1958–1968)," in *Practicable, From Participation to Interaction in Contemporary Art and New Media*, ed. Samuel Bianchini and Erik Verhaegen (Cambridge MA: The MIT Press, 2016), 91–111.

15 Giovanni Anceschi and Davide Boriani, "Ambiente per un test di estetica sperimentale," produced for *Nove tendencije 3*, Muzei Umjetnost i obrt, Zagreb, 1965.

16 In Zagreb, Galerija suvremene umnietnost, *Nova tendencija 3*, August 13–September 19, 1965; in Strasbourg, Musée de l'art moderne et contemporain, *L'Œil moteur. Art optique et cinétique, 1950–1975*, May 13–September 25, 2005; and in Rome, Galleria Nazionale d'Arte Moderna, *Gli Ambienti del Gruppo T: le origini dell'arte interattiva*, December 15, 2005–May 1, 2006.

research in the true sense, along with all its protocols and paradigms. Only François Molnar from the French group G.R.A.V. developed a genuine activity as a "scientist of aesthetic research."[17] It was however our own *Ambiente di estetica sperimentale* that constituted the only—but alas incomplete—case, constructed explicitly on the basis of a conscious orientation towards the production of knowledge—science—and not the application of more or less rational methodologies: the project.

To answer your previous question, in actual fact, as a student and then teacher from 1962 to 1967 at the Hochschule für Gestaltung in Ulm, I was influenced by the Information Aesthetics of Bense and Moles, and by the theoretical and epistemological framework of Tomás Maldonado, who called for thoroughly scientific ingredients and methodologies to be introduced in the planning process. The idea of a theoretical field dedicated to experimental aesthetics is basically derived from Bense's aesthetic theory, while to Moles we owe the concept of a structural complexity which, by linking up to perceptual processes, produces specific aesthetic effects in the spectator. Instead, the idea of comparing the values produced by the behavioral test with those produced by a qualitative verbal one is derived from another teacher at Ulm, Dölf Zillmann, in the wake of the semantic differential theories of Osgood, Suci, and Tannenbaum.[18]

When we produced the *Ambiente per un test di estetica sperimentale*, neither Boriani nor myself were informed at the time of the existence of a branch of aesthetics, known as that of preference, or prohairetic, aesthetics. It wasn't until 1973 when Gillo Dorfles published a book, *Dal significato alle scelte*, which took stock of the scientific panorama and put forward new hypotheses on the issue.[19] But our research was certainly moving in that direction (figs. 8a & 8b).

EQ: Let's move on to design. One of the most characteristic specificities of the programmed experience is to be found in the strong relationship which was established, right from the start, between the world of the arts and that of industry. And it was on that terrain that the research into techniques, materials, processes, and machines thrived greatly. Once Programmed Art had been established, both the theoretical and practical bases were laid out for the development of industrial design, marking the start of the golden period of Italian Design. Suffice to recall the fact that the first exhibitions of Programmed Art were held not in art galleries but in commercial and industrial spaces managed by the Danese and Olivetti companies; but the use of the replica should also be remembered, that is, of the multiple, promoted by Programmed Art, which paved the way toward the serialization of design. Even in 1960, in the Danese showroom in Milan, together with the Gruppo T you presented the publication in ten numbered and signed copies of the *miriorama* objects, including your own *Abstract video*, a *Giradischi ottico-magnetico* by Boriani, a *Rotoplastik* by Colombo, a *Miramondo* by Devecchi, a semi-double *Sferisterio* by Grazia Varisco. These works led Munari to observe that "the preconception of the unique item no longer makes sense."[20] How did you pass from art to design?

GA: I heard the word *design* uttered for the first time by Bruno Munari, while we were drawing together the great white circles on the poster for the exhibition *Oltre la pittura oltre la scultura* [1963].[21] But the real turning point for me was the HfG in Ulm. I had gone to Ulm in the belief that I would find

17 *G. Anceschi's note*: See François Molnar, "À la recherche d'un langage plastique ... pour une science de l'art," in *Vasarely*, ed. Denise René, exh. cat. (Paris: Galerie Denise René, 1959); and Molnar, "Towards Science in Art," in *Data: Directions in Art, Theory and Aesthetics*, ed. Anthony Hill (London: Faber & Faber, 1968), 204–13. The case of Manfredo Massironi of the Gruppo N is yet more different: he became an esteemed perceptologist and then cognitive psychologist.

18 *G. Anceschi's note*: Zillman published his research, which I personally took part in: Dölf Zillmann et al., *Test der Validität der semantischen Aspektanalyse*, Abteilung Visuelle Kommunikation/Institut für Kommunikationsforschung (Ulm/Zurich, 1965). This line of thought starts out from Charles E. Osgood, George J. Suci, Percy Tannenbaum, *The Measurement of Meaning* (Urbana: University of Illinois Press, 1957).

19 Gillo Dorfles, *Dal significato alle scelte* (Turin: Einaudi, 1973). As Dorfles explains, "prohairetic semantics"—from the Greek *proairesis*, "preference"—corresponds to "a search for meaning based first of all on our (or others') preferences, an attempt to identify the semantic aspects linked to a preferential factor and thus closely conditioned by motivations and impulses, by expectations and by the preference-based decisions" (p. 15). Preference, which transcends the historical notion of "taste," is understood by Dorfles "as a decisive element not only of every choice but of every meaning," and at the same time "as the subversion of age-old

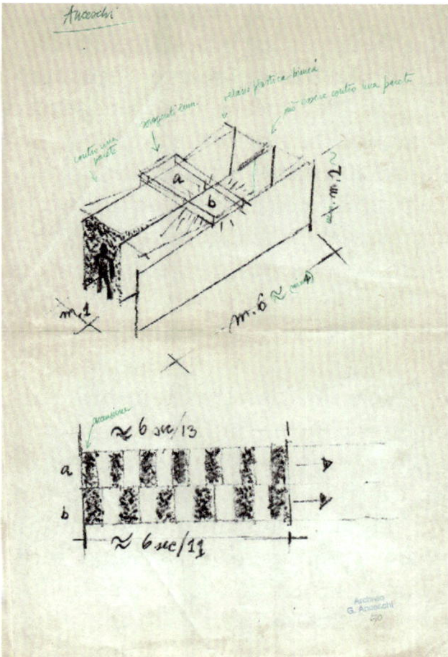

Figs. 8a & 8b: Giovanni Anceschi, *Ambiente a shock luminosi* (Light Shock Environment), 1964, drawing / Giovanni Anceschi in *Ambiente a shock luminosi* at the exhibition *Arte programmata e cinetica 1953–1963: the last vanguard*, curated by Lea Vergine, Palazzo Reale, November 4, 1983–February 27, 1984, Milan.

a school that was the heir to the Bauhaus, based on the merging of art and design. Instead I found a school where—at least in a certain fundamentalist wing that it had—it was even forbidden to speak of art, let alone make it. ... It was a matter of the stance adopted, ultimately justifiable in part, by a discipline—design—which in late modernity had to state its own independence and which was therefore attempting to sever its own umbilical cord. But this is another story. ...

My choice of design, setting out from the perspective of art, was then also a choice I would define as one of political commitment. The idea going around at the time was that design was art dissolving into real life, as De Stijl had advocated in its day: the genuine "art for all," far beyond the programs of multiplied art. A commitment which, after Ulm, came to a head in the decision to work in the third world—in Algeria, to design the image of the Societé Nationale du Pétrole Algerien—and then, on returning to Italy, to work for the extra-parliamentary left, designing the weekly publication *Potere Operaio*.

EQ: In the text *Confini: design e arte* [2008], you attempt to define the frontiers between art and design when you write: "from the Modern period onwards, art appears to pursue autonomous goals, while design seems to move toward the achievement of heteronomous aims."[22] Is the difference therefore to be sought out in terms of function rather than of form?

GA: It's not a matter of function but of teleological status. It's the aim that distinguishes art and design today. Put simply: design is such in the presence of a third protagonist, the client, alongside the designer and the receiver/user. Basically, the designer comes across as a figure comparable to that of the translator. A technician with access to the knowledge necessary for the realization of others' intentions, be it an advertising campaign or the production of goods.

preferentiality in the wake of the identification of a particular autogenetic semantics, which attributes value and meaning on each occasion to objects, events, and situations, which it itself chooses" (p. 18).

20 Bruno Munari, "I giovani del Gruppo T," *Domus*, no. 378 (May 1961): 53.

21 *Oltre la pittura oltre la scultura: Mostra di ricerca di arte visiva* (Milan: Galleria Cadario, 1963).

22 Giovanni Anceschi, "Confini: design e arte," in *Made in IUAV 2001–08*, exh. cat., XI Biennale of Architecture, Venice (Udine: Dindi Editore, 2008).

Be that as it may, it's foolish to think you can draw the line between art and design once and for all: it would ultimately be the undue hypostatization of a historically determined circumstance. The idea that we are interested in—that art is autonomous—is the result of history. This means it has been in force only since that great watershed moment around the turn of the twentieth century, when the notion emerged in culture at large of *l'art pour l'art*.

Be that as it may, more than noting the differences between the two disciplines, it's interesting to note what crosses them and unites them. The word *design*, evoking that of *drawing*, seems to indicate a derivation from the paradigms of representation, leading to a blunder which struck and which continues to strike architects above all. In actual fact, the genuine heart of the discipline lies elsewhere. There is in fact in this role a skill which we might define by the term *configuration*, which translates the German word *Gestaltung*. *Configuration* is not a synonym of *design*. Configuration is a particular element of design, absolutely constitutive yet partial. *Gestaltung* is the set of knowledge and skills that provide the operator with the ability to attribute a certain form to objects of everyday use, communicative artifacts as well as technical systems. And even to events, processes, etc. etc. But in such cases, given that we are dealing with not only plastic but also choreographic phenomena, I would suggest using the term *directorial*.[23]

After all, on close inspection, the configurative tendency is in equal measure an essential part of artistic activity. An artist must necessarily be a *Gestalter*, in the sense that he must master the ways of forming. And it must also be noted that the developments of design managed to generate a specific disciplinary branch which focuses on configuration and its pedagogy. This was the role of the *Grundkurs* [basic course] at the Bauhaus, which in Ulm would be called *Grundlehre* [basic discipline], and in the wake of the American diaspora, was to take the name of *basic design*: constituting training tools to teach that which represents what is absolutely specific to design, which is not so much or just solving problems, producing innovation, piloting technologies, etc., as the capacity to attribute a particular form to what is designed. Basic design deals with forms without in any way being the product of a formalist ideology. For in design, the form must always be the right one, the most suitable in the given situation, or as they say in jargon, to the given "brief" (fig. 9).

EQ: So you differentiate between the notion of *Gestaltung* and that of design? Could it not be linked, for example, to the notion of formativity theorized by Pareyson and then taken up by Umberto Eco?

GA: I think ultimately it's very clear: *Gestaltung*—that is, formativity, according to Pareyson/Eco—is a subset of what we might call design in general. *Gestalten—Gestalt* = form, appearance—is a way of designing which focuses on, or rather, which radically bears in mind the fact that the practices of configuration, of shaping, etc., produce a very concrete result, an outright figural effect. Engineers design things; instead, graphic artists, designers, architects, urbanists, etc., attribute a particular *Gestalt* to what has been designed.

Milan, March 2014, April 2017, January 2019
Translated from the Italian by Bennett Bazalgette

23 "The designer of communication and interaction as a director, a design director capable of coupling with practical and highly specialized planning skills, a way of viewing the project as a strategic activity, the ability to solve complex problems, to plan advertising campaigns, to develop and coordinate far-reaching projects, to devise goal-directed sequences of communication events and to guide their programming and implementation. The professional and researcher is therefore a figure at the same time specialized and capable of moving in a transversal manner": Giovanni Anceschi, "Retorica verbo-figurale e registica visive," in *Le ragioni della retorica*, ed. Umberto Eco et al. (Modena: Mucchi Editore, 1986).

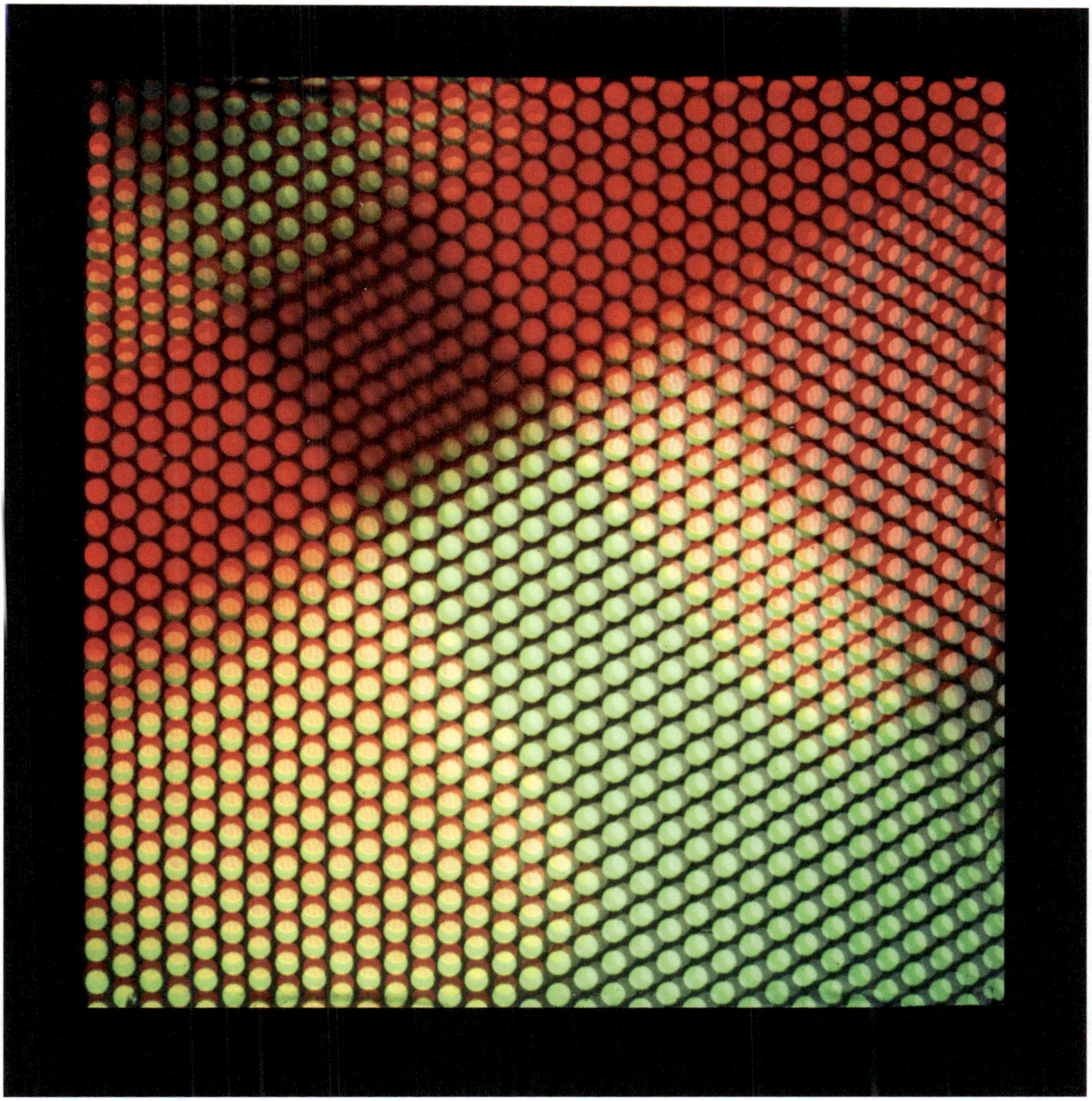

Fig. 9: Giovanni Anceschi, *Struttura tricroma* (Trichrome structure), 1964. Various materials, motor, 51.5 × 51.5 × 51 cm.

From Invisible Design to Post-Optimal Objects
Interface Design and Discourses of Dematerialization since circa 1960[1]

Claudia Mareis

The following text discusses selected positions within the field of design theory on the relation between materiality and visibility in the design of everyday objects, particularly technical devices and apparatuses. Starting from these objects' very concrete physical housings, it addresses the extent to which ideas of form, materiality, and functionality mutually influence and determine one another in the interplay between designed transparency and opacity. In this context, the concept of the interface—as an enabling operative instance between different actors and dimensions—also becomes important. Thus, a starting point for such a design theoretical consideration begins with the devices and apparatuses themselves.

It is no coincidence that iconic devices such as Braun's pocket radio and the Apple iPod, which both epitomize the technical progress of their times, are characterized by simple, opaque-glossy, and hermetic surfaces and housings (fig. 1).[2] Beneath the clean lines of their brilliant white exteriors, wires, batteries, circuit boards, and diodes lead a secret life hidden from the view of the user—not merely as materials but as "technicities" that are capable of "producing or undergoing [a technical] effect in a determinate manner."[3] Irrespective of their internal technical complexity and formlessness, the product-semantics of such "white boxes" convey the promise of effortless handling and "intuitive" interaction. The multiple operation modes and use options of such devices are revealed to the user mostly only superficially via reduced user interfaces such as buttons, switches, and touchscreens. The view to the inner workings—to the supposed actual functioning of the device itself—however, remains barred by the housing.

1 This text is an updated, abridged translation of Claudia Mareis, "Unsichtbares Design und post-optimale Objekte: Interface-Design und Entmaterialisierungs-diskurse seit circa 1960," in *Gehäuse: Mediale Einkapselungen*, ed. Christina Bartz et al. (Paderborn: Fink, 2017), 93–114.

2 On the stylistic similarity between these two devices, see Friedrich von Borries, "Ein Deutscher entwickelte die Apple-Vorgänger," *Die Welt*, May 21, 2010, http://www.welt.de/kultur/article7728575/Ein-Deutscher-entwickelte-die-Apple-Vorgaenger.html.

3 Gilbert Simondon, *On the Mode of Existence of Technical Objects* (Minneapolis: Univocal Publishing, 2012), 75.

Fig. 1: Pocket radio by Braun (1958) and iPod by Apple.

Fig. 2 (below): The Swiss Werkbund's 1949 catalog *Die gute Form* (The Good Form).

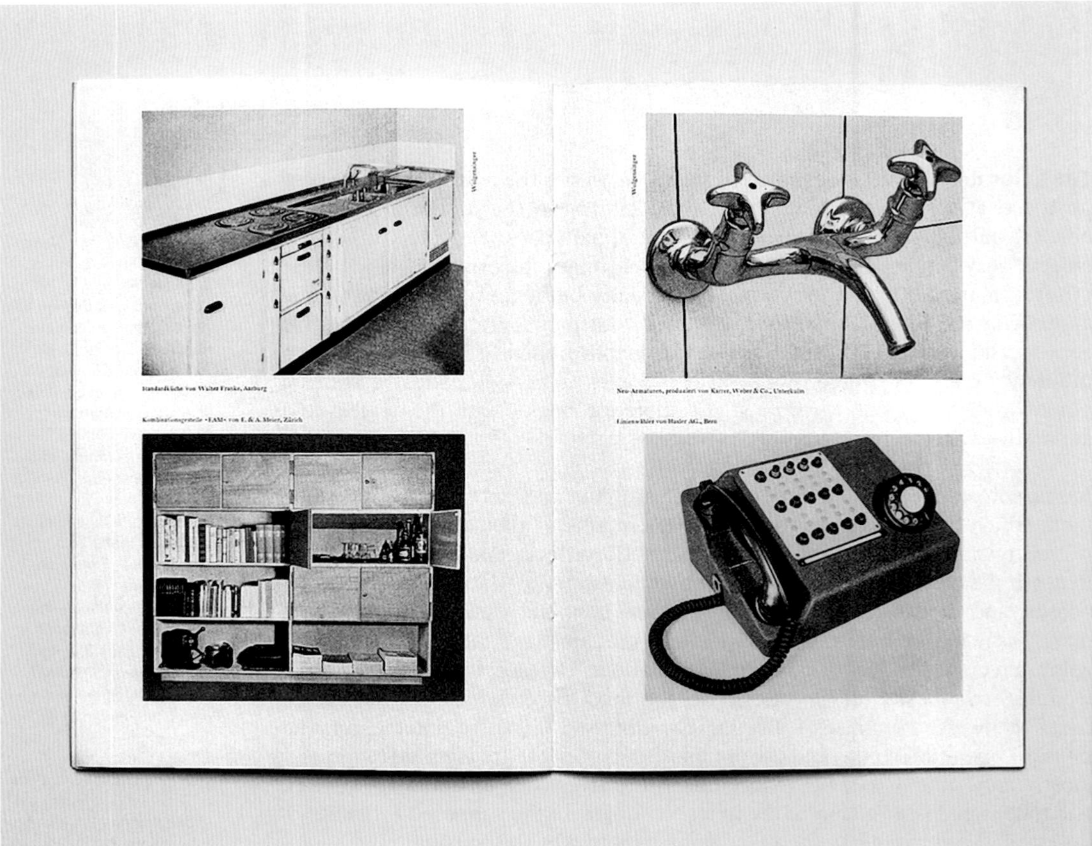

And yet the attractive but mute surfaces and housings of many technical devices are much more than a mere "make-up of the machines,"[4] promising users maximal power of use coupled with minimal technical know-how. And they go beyond the deliberate concealment of technical functionality or purely commercial marketing strategies. Rather, they bring together and reify strategies for the representation of technical knowledge and sociomaterial narratives. For the view on the housing of technical devices and apparatuses not only reveals various formal vocabularies, uses of materials, and stylistic choices; it points beyond this to different regimes of visibility and usability that imply by whom and in what way "technology" should be understood, used, and narrated. Particularly in the case of more recent intuitively operated electronic and digital devices, the semantic dimension and poetic content come to the fore. In this connection, the British designer Anthony Dunne speaks of "post-optimal objects," which are linked to the alleged disappearance of technical resistance: "In a world where practicality and functionality can be taken for granted, the aesthetics of the post-optimal object could provide new experiences of everyday life, new poetic dimensions."[5]

In the following, the interplay between form, materiality, and functionality that runs through the design and implementation of everyday objects, particularly technical devices and apparatuses, will be discussed in three stages. Moreover, different positions in the theory of design from the postwar period to the present will be examined that address the subject of interface design—in part before the term as such was even in use.

1. From Visible to Invisible Design

In the early 1980s, when the personal computer was establishing itself in the workplace as a technical tool and new type of physical furnishing, a trend toward a peculiar discourse of dematerialization can be observed in design theory. The focus here was no longer on visible, material design objects but on supposedly immaterial processes of interaction and on the understanding of design objects via "invisible" systems. Around 1980, the Swiss sociologist and architectural theorist Lucius Burckhardt introduced the concept of *invisible design* into the design discourse. He pointed out that, alongside visible objects, design is always also concerned with "the *invisible* overall system comprised of objects and interpersonal relationships," which it should "consciously take into account."[6] What is meant here are systems of an organizational or infrastructural kind, such as bureaucratic workflows, public transport timetables, business hours, urban planning decisions, etc., and thus the design of the basic programs of everyday life. In this connection, Burckhardt believed that traditional design practice was fatally attached to the development of single material objects rather than invisible systems,[7] and therefore that new devices were continually being designed without questioning whether a different—systemic—view of their use context would not render these devises obsolete.

In Burckhardt's design conception, one can clearly see the influence of conceptual approaches found in cybernetics and systems theory, which in the postwar period are common not only in computer science, sociology, and urban planning but also in design theory.[8] Moreover, his concept of invisible design also referred critically to the modernist and functionalist design ideals propagated for example at the Ulm

4 Peter Sloterdijk, "The Right Tool for Power: Observations on Design as the Modernization of Competence," in *The Aesthetic Imperative: Writings on Art* (Malden: Polity Press, 2017), 89.

5 Anthony Dunne, *Hertzian Tales: Electronic Products, Aesthetic Experience, and Critical Design* (Cambridge, MA: MIT Press, 2005), 20.

6 Lucius Burckhardt, "Design Is Invisible (1980)," in *Lucius Burckhardt Writings: Rethinking Man-Made Environments: Politics, Landscape and Design*, ed. Jesko Fezer and Martin Schmitz (Boston: De Gruyter, 2012), 165.

7 Ibid., 153–54.

8 On cybernetics, see Michael Hagner, "Vom Aufstieg und Fall der Kybernetik als Universalwissenschaft," in *Die Transformation des Humanen: Beiträge zur Kulturgeschichte der Kybernetik*, ed. Erich Hörl and Michael Hagner (Frankfurt: Suhrkamp, 2008), 38–71.

School of Design (1953–1968) and in the Good Form (Die gute Form) movement. Drawing on the tradition of Bauhaus modernism, the Good Form movement set out to create timeless, functional everyday objects, such as lamps, chairs, kitchen units, and electronic devices and apparatuses, that would be able to survive changing fashions and short-lived trends. Through the elimination of superfluous detail, these objects should be reduced to their "essentials," which is to say, to their genuine functionality. Further characteristics of the movement were the choice of durable, sustainable materials and the use of simple, minimalist forms. Nevertheless, the Good Form movement did not merely have an aesthetic agenda; it also had an educational mission. Through the matter-of-fact, functionally designed objects, it was hoped that the affective Nazi propaganda of the past could be overcome and the people of postwar Germany could be educated to adopt a democratic outlook and sustainable consumption. For Max Bill, following on the heels of earlier educative aesthetic programs concerned with the rejection of ornament,[9] the task of the Good Form movement was "to dispense as much as possible with 'appearance' [*Schein*] and focus instead on what is modest, true—even good" (fig. 2).[10]

Bill's criticism of the beautiful but deceptive exteriors of designed objects was principally directed against the American fashion of streamline modernism of the 1920s to 1940s. *Streamline* here refers to the design of buildings and vehicles such as ships and cars, but also of common household appliances and devices such as irons and vacuum cleaners, that on a formal-aesthetic level were intended to simulate aerodynamics, without these objects actually possessing aerodynamic properties. The minimalist design of the famous Ulmer Hocker, which Bill developed in 1954 in collaboration with Hans Gugelot, expresses the ideal of a functional design reduced to its essentials. This multifunctional stool, which can be used as a seat, occasional table, or tray, is still celebrated today as the prototype of an "honest," supposedly timeless design whose strength comes from the reduction to function rather than from a "deceptive" decorative surface design (fig. 3).

For Lucius Burckhardt, however, Bill's critical view of design did not go far enough. In Burckhardt's opinion, Good Form was just another aesthetic style, a "functionalism without a function"[11] in which greater importance was attached to the formal impression of functionality than to the actual handling of the object when using it or its systemic examination within a larger social context. For Burckhardt, what was problematic about the prevailing modernist design practice was that it was overly focused on the design and improvement of single objects and did not pay enough attention to overarching contexts and systems. Burckhardt considered the design phase to be overvalued, while the actual use and consumption were marginalized. Moreover, he saw in the focus on single objects a reductionist limitation to single problems that prevented a consideration of the larger contexts from which these problems arose.[12] As Burckhardt concludes, design must embrace "socio-design: a way of thinking about and resolving problems that results from coordinated changes made both to roles and to objects."[13]

Despite the marked differences in the positions of Lucius Burckhardt and Max Bill, each in its own way was the expression of a radically new definition and evaluation of design in the second half of the twentieth century. This period saw a shift in focus from product design to systems design, and from the design context to the use context of designed objects. This was further accompanied by a shift

9 For example, Adolf Loos, "Ornament und Verbrechen (1908)," in *Theorien der Gestaltung*, ed. Volker Fischer and Anne Hamilton, Grundlagentexte zum Design (Frankfurt: Verl. Form, 1999), 114–20.

10 Max Bill, "Good Form," in *Max Bill's View of Things: Die gute Form: An Exhibition 1949*, edited by Lars Müller in collaboration with the Museum für Gestaltung Zürich (Zurich: Lars Müller, 2015), 146–47, here 146. Originally published in *Die gute Form: Wanderausstellung des Schweizerischen Werkbundes*, Wegleitung 183 (Zurich: Kunstgewerbemuseum, 1949).

11 Lucius Burckhardt, "Invisible Design (1983)," in *Design is Invisible: Planning, Education, and Society*, ed. Silvan Blumenthal and Martin Schmitz, trans. Jill Denton (Basel: Birkhäuser, 2017), 28.

12 Burckhardt, "Design Is Invisible 1980," 160.

13 Ibid., 162.

Fig. 3: Ulmer Hocker by Max Bill and Hans Gugelot from 1954.

from an interest in materiality to an interest in concepts. While the Good Form discourse in no way neglected the material aspect of product design, with its normative surface critique and functionalist aesthetic, it nevertheless prepared the way for a widely influential discourse of dematerialization in design, reflected in particular in the concept of interface design that emerged in tandem with the rise of computer technologies.

Whereas over the decades single design objects such as Braun's pocket radio mentioned at the beginning and Bill's Ulmer Hocker became icons of simple, functional design, in the postwar period the discussion and reflection on design drifted away from specific design objects to a systemic economy of use and interface far removed from considerations about objects and materials. In particular, Burckhardt's postulate of a context-sensitive design that attempts to take account of systemic contexts and interrelations, from "the phase of the actual design or planning through to production; and the consumption phase, up to and including an object's disposal on the trash heap, or in a museum,"[14] bears a close resemblance to design approaches typical of the postwar period in which design came to be understood as a general—and thus abstract—immaterial process of planning and problem solving. These approaches, often labeled as "design methods," led to a lasting transformation and expansion of the practice and understanding of design.[15] Through the application of systematic design methods, the activity

14 Ibid., 159.
15 For more on this subject, see Claudia Mareis, *Design als Wissenskultur: Interferenzen zwischen Design- und Wissensdiskursen seit 1960* (Bielefeld: transcript, 2011).

of designing should be understood from the ground up, it should become more comprehensible and controllable and meet the requirements of interdisciplinary cooperation. In the course of the increasing transformation of the workplace and lifeworlds by cybernetic thinking and computer systems, design methods were increasingly formalized and opened to planning- and systems-theoretical considerations.[16] However, this transformation had a far-reaching effect on how design was thought. What had previously been central aspects of design, such as form, surface aesthetic, and truth to materials, now gave way to a systemic conception that believed it had everything in view, but eventually lost sight both of the human users and of the materiality of things.

2. From Artifacts to Interfaces

Parallel to the rise of computer technologies, beginning in the late 1960s the concept of the interface grew in prominence in the field of design theory and contributed to the systemic and dematerialization tendencies already established there. In contemporary interface debates, theories of artificial intelligence and human–machine interaction were combined under the catchword *synthesis* with an updated model of artifacts, indeed of the artificial in general. Considered the paradigmatic representative and initiator of this development was the computer itself.[17] In his book *The Sciences of the Artificial*, published in 1969, the economist and "artificial intelligence" researcher Herbert Simon outlines the foundations of the new sciences mentioned in the title.[18] These include economic behavioral theory, the psychology of cognition and learning, social planning—and design.

The common starting point for these different disciplines was the diagnosis of an irreducible, constitutive artificiality of the human environment and lifeworld. As Simon concluded: "The world we live in today is much more a man-made, or artificial, world than it is a natural world. Almost every element in our environment shows evidence of human artifice."[19] Here, in addition to technical constructions and material infrastructures, Simon was also thinking of the field of symbolic and linguistic production, which he understood as "strings of artifacts."[20] The diagnosis of a dominant artificiality was aimed primarily at the fields of engineering and design: "As soon as we introduce 'synthesis' as well as 'artifice,' we enter the realm of engineering. For 'synthetic' is often used in the broader sense of 'designed' or 'composed.' ... The engineer, and more generally the designer, is concerned with how things *ought* to be—how they ought to be in order to *attain goals*, and to *function*."[21]

Following on from this, Simon formulated a definition of *design* that, due to its general validity, is still widely accepted today. It states that everyone is a designer who "devises courses of action aimed at changing existing situations into preferred ones."[22] And thus: "The intellectual activity that produces material artifacts is no different fundamentally from the one that prescribes remedies for a sick patient or the one that devises a new sales plan for a company or a social welfare policy for a state."[23] With the approach of establishing design as a "science of the artificial," Simon's first aim was to improve the academic standing of practice-oriented disciplines such as design and engineering. Second, he strove to give the description and practice of design a scientific basis by developing systematic

16 For more on this subject, see Jesko Fezer, "A Non-Sentimental Argument: Die Krisen des Design Methods Movement 1962–1972," in *Kulturtechnik Entwerfen: Praktiken, Konzepte und Medien in Architektur und Design Science*, ed. Daniel Gethmann and Susanne Hauser (Bielefeld: transcript, 2009), 287–304.
17 Fernando Winograd and Terry Flores, *Understanding Computers and Cognition: A New Foundation for Design* (Norwood: Ablex Pub Corporation, 1986).
18 Herbert Simon, *The Sciences of the Artificial* (Cambridge, MA: MIT Press, 1996).
19 Ibid., 2.
20 Ibid.
21 Ibid., 4–5 (italics in original).
22 Ibid., 111.
23 Ibid.

design methods and new modal logics. Third, he aimed for a new definition of artificial objects—and thus artifacts—that would do justice to their specific epistemological and pragmatic properties.

Simon understood artifacts as "meeting point[s]," as interfaces that mediate between an "inner" and "outer" environment. Here, *"inner" environment* referred to "the substance and organization of the artifact itself," and *"outer" environment* "the surroundings in which [the artifact] operates."[24] He illustrated this relation as follows: "Whether a clock will in fact tell the time depends on its internal construction and where it is placed. Whether a knife will cut depends on the material of its blade and the hardness of the substance to which it is applied."[25] Accordingly, an adequate description of artifacts would need to take account of their "functions, goals, adaptation."[26]

Awareness of this distinction should finally guide and optimize the design and construction process itself inasmuch as the "inner"—that is, technical—functioning of an object and its "outer" environment—that is, the context of its use and the desired functional objectives—are optimally coordinated. The purpose of this optimization for Simon was the creation of an adaptive, self-regulating technical system that should function as independently as possible from parameter changes in the outer environment. By redefining the concept of artifact as a systemic interface, the logic and practice of design should be brought together and synthesized. Moreover, Simon's "functional description"[27] of artifacts reflects the overlapping and combining of biological and machinic models so productive for cybernetics. Hence, one focus of the Simonian concept of artifact lies in the reciprocal naturalization or technization of inner and outer modes of functioning and processes. Inner—technical—modes of functioning are equated with "natural" phenomena, whereas influences of the outer, biological-physical environment are subjected to parameterization with a view to the desired operability and stability of the system.[28] Accordingly, Simon sees the main task of inventors, designers, and engineers as being the description and coordination of "organization and functioning," and thus the design of the "interface between inner and outer environments."[29] In this sense, constructedness is no longer a category that follows an artisanal or material model but a conceptually and systems-theoretically guided design.

To sum up, Simon conceived artifacts as interfaces whose limits should not form the concrete material limits of the objects—and even less their physical, apparative housings or material surfaces—but the interactions linked with the objects. The inner environment—to some extent the "inner life"—of technical apparatuses and devices should ideally be so stable, friction-free, and independent of external influences that their optimal functional state becomes one of "invisibility"—whereby *invisibility* in this context means closure or stability rather than transparency.

Thus, whereas in Simon's artifact model concrete objects and their material specificity are replaced by a desired or prognosticated functionality and interaction, larger actant complexes and artifact ecologies come into view that today we would perhaps understand in Karen Barad's sense as an "agential realist understanding of apparatuses," which asks whether "the outside boundary of the apparatus [is necessarily] coincident with the visual terminus of the instrumentation."[30]

24 Ibid., 6.
25 Ibid.
26 Ibid., 5.
27 Ibid., 9.
28 He remarks that the "inner system is an organization of natural phenomena capable of attaining the goals in some range of environments." Ibid., 11.
29 Ibid., 9.
30 Karen Barad, *Meeting the Universe Halfway: Quantum Physics and the Entanglement of Matter and Meaning* (Durham: Duke University Press, 2007), 142, 145.

However, not only does the object's materiality—its material specificity—become obscured in Simon's interface model, but so too do the artifact's human users. To put it more precisely, in the self-regulating cybernetic loop that the interface ideally generates, human users are reduced to the role of subservient and ultimately invisible problem solvers and passive operators.[31]

3. From Interface Design to Post-Optimal Objects

The cybernetic model of artifacts as interfaces advocated by Simon in the late 1960s was taken up in the following decades by several design theorists addressing the topic of interface design. They initially expanded this model to include human-centered design, and in a further step, in the mode of Critical Engineering or Critical Design, criticized the hermetic housings of electronic apparatuses and digital devices. Exemplary for the continuation of the interface discourse following Simon is Gui Bonsiepe's *Interface: An Approach to Design*, first published in Italian in 1995.[32] For Bonsiepe, a former graduate and lecturer at the Ulm School of Design, the new task of design was the development of interfaces in the emergent computer industry[33] without this being reduced to the "dressing up" of graphical user interfaces. Like Lucius Burckhardt before him, Bonsiepe strove to give design a new legitimacy that was not "primarily concerned with aesthetics,"[34] but would address possibilities of action.[35] Computer technologies should be made accessible to a broader public not through the design of graphical user interfaces but through comprehensive interactions with the computer. The concept of the interface as a universal category that is as open as it is vague appeared suitable to extend design's previous sphere of responsibilities from the design of trivial objects to the design of systems, interactions, services, and actions. While Bonsiepe advocated a concept of interface that drew explicitly on Simon, he differed from Simon by attempting more strongly to integrate users. As he wrote: "the interface is not a material object, it is the dimension for interaction between the body, tool and purposeful action. [...] The design of the interface determines the scope for action by the user of products. The interface reveals the character of objects as tools and the information contained in data.[36]

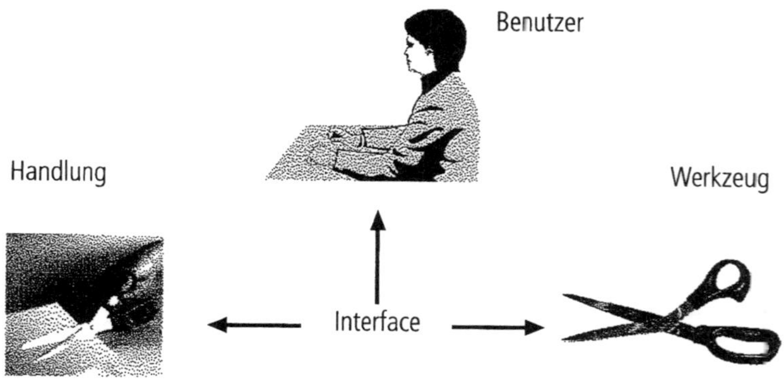

Fig. 4: Gui Bonsiepe: Ontological diagram of design.

31 This idealizing understanding of interfaces, which is far removed from actual practice, has been problematized for example by Lucy Suchman in her 1987 study *Plans and Situated Actions*, an ethnographic study of the use of photocopiers at Xerox PARC (Palo Alto Research Center). Suchman shows that the use of technical devices is in no way rational, methodical, or trouble-free; rather, human–machine interactions should be understood as asymmetric, contingent, and trouble-prone relations, which in the attempt to produce a shared sociomaterial world can be continually reconstituted, and in this way give rise to new kinds of human–machine reconfigurations. See Suchman, *Plans and Situated Actions: The Problem of Human–Machine Communication* (Cambridge: Cambridge University Press, 1987).

32 Gui Bonsiepe, *Dall'oggetto all'interfaccia: Mutazioni del design* (Milan: Feltrinelli, 1995).

33 Gui Bonsiepe, *Interface: An Approach to Design* (Maastricht: Jan Van Eyck Akademie, 1999), 42.

34 Ibid., 30.

35 Ibid., 34.

36 Ibid., 29.

Bonsiepe called the linking of the body, tool, and purposeful action in an immaterial since ultimately fictive relation—that is, in the interface—the "ontological design diagram" (fig. 4).[37] Although Bonsiepe's approach fully emphasizes the pragmatic dimension of interfaces, here too it is necessary to problematize an insufficient distinction between "material" design objects on the one hand and supposedly "immaterial" interactions and services on the other. In this relation, Bonsiepe pointed out that his intention was not to neglect the material dimension of design, but to go beyond "the duality of material/immaterial" and to bring together these supposed "opposites" through design.[38] Irrespective of this differentiation, however, what was strengthened in connection with his approach in the field of design was an inadequate understanding of the "immaterial" dimension of the interface and, connected with this, of an "immaterial" production of digital interaction.

A comparable concept of interface to that of Bonsiepe's was proposed by the design theorist Klaus Krippendorff, another graduate of the Ulm School of Design.[39] For Krippendorff, interfaces represent "a new kind of artifact," which as such encompass all interactions between users and (technical) devices "but have become objects of design only since their more obvious use in personal computers."[40] In his opinion, interfaces serve the purpose of making things accessible that escape the understanding of their users.[41] For their design, Krippendorff recommends a human-centered approach in order to design things that meet the needs and expectations of the users: "Designers must do their best to support the continued meaningfulness of these interfaces materially and in ways that come most naturally to the users."[42] The aim here is to create the most user-friendly, that is *trouble-free*, interaction possible. At the same time, the task of the designer is not to discipline others, but to "increase [their] options."[43]

However, in the interface approaches of Bonsiepe and Krippendorff, there is little problematization of the fact that while the design of trouble-free, expectation-conform interfaces facilitates the use of technologies, it nevertheless hinders access to a deeper understanding of technology. According to the cultural and media theorist Friedrich Kittler, user-friendly interfaces and "intuitive" graphical user interfaces promote an unfortunate "computer illiteracy,"[44] which leads to a conformist, planning-based use of computer technologies, including soft- and hardware.

In the field of design, the approaches of Herbert Simon, Lucius Burckhardt, Gui Bonsiepe, and Klaus Krippendorff discussed above provided an urgently needed sensitizing to context-relevant and systemic relations between artifacts and interactions. They have shown that interfaces have always been "the result of technical, societal, and individual design."[45] However, their contribution to the promotion of a well-grounded understanding of electronic apparatuses and digital technologies as an integral element of material culture remains somewhat problematic. Whereas media, cultural, and literary studies were prompt to address the sociomaterial effects of computer technologies and the role of programming,[46] this aspect has until recently formed a notable blind spot in design theory. It appears that Bonsiepe's wish that interface design should be more than simply a cosmetic addition to computer programs still awaits fulfillment. In many design courses today, one continues to teach what are essentially "analog" design methods and rules, but rarely programing skills or technical

37 Ibid., 28.
38 Ibid., 29.
39 Klaus Krippendorff, *The Semantic Turn: A New Foundation for Design* (New York: CRC/Taylor & Francis, 2006).
40 Ibid., 78.
41 Ibid.
42 Ibid., 84.
43 Ibid., 74.
44 Friedrich Kittler, "Computeranalphabetismus," in *Short Cuts* (Frankfurt: Zweitausendeins, 2002), 109–33.
45 Wulf Halbach, Interfaces: *Medien- und kommunikationstheoretische Elemente einer Interface-Theorie* (Munich: Wilhelm Fink, 1994), 14.
46 See Anthony Dunne, *Hertzian Tales: Electronic Products, Aesthetic Experience, and Critical Design* (Cambridge, MA: MIT Press, 2005), 16.

knowledge when dealing with computer hardware. Furthermore, traditional divisions between programmers, engineers, designers, and users still prove to be extraordinarily rigid and impermeable.

An exception is represented by new approaches such as Critical Engineering and Critical design, in which the accessibility, visibility, and designability of technical objects are made explicit objects of critique. Whereas the authors of the *Critical Engineering Manifesto* call for the acquisition of a broad knowledge and competence when dealing with electronic-digital technologies in order to "study and expose [their] inner workings, regardless of ownership or legal provision,"[47] Critical Design aims to highlight new narratives and design-based scenarios for an alternative use of technologies. Prototypes for fictional technical devices and potential technologies that are precisely *not* user-friendly, trouble-free, and expectation-conform are designed using techniques of aesthetic defamiliarization to be opaque rather than maximally transparent and visible.[48] Hence, Critical Design—also called Speculative Design—understands design artifacts and processes as a form of materialized critique,[49] and thereby breaks with the conventional demand for functionality and usability.[50]

In *Hertzian Tales: Electronic Products, Aesthetic Experience, and Critical Design*, Anthony Dunne, who established the Critical Design approach along with Fiona Raby around the turn of the century at the Royal College of Art in London, is critical of the way in which in most commercial design electronic objects are treated as uniform packages for incomprehensible technologies.[51] Instead of critically examining these technologies and creating new poetical narratives for them it merely develops market-conform "semiotic skins," reducing design to the level of mercantile sign production.[52] As an alternative to this affirmative, commercial handling of electronic-digital objects, Dunne suggests the production of so-called post-optimal objects. Rather than a commercial use or a concrete-technical or semiotic function, these should be situated "in the realms of metaphysics, poetry, and aesthetics" and promote alternative narratives, poetries, and aesthetic experiences in the use of technology.[53]

An example of this design practice is the work *New Needs in an Augmented World* (2011) by the designer Ludwig Zeller. On the basis of three fictional, electronic-digital devices, the Dromolux, Optocoupler, and Introspectre, Zeller addresses the speculative question of how in the future human senses will be both optimized and manipulated through technological means (fig. 5).[54] The devices he has designed exist on the one hand as single pieces in the form of highly finished prototypes, and on the other as aesthetically staged short films that demonstrate the intended application. What is striking about Zeller's fictional objects and short films is the minimalist and hyperaesthetic surfaces and mises-en-scène that combine to create a paradoxical impression of science fiction design and anachronistic Good Form attitude. Via the singular material-visual appearance and form of Critical Design objects, the specific temporalities of objects and discourses begin to converge. On the material, formal-aesthetic level of the objects, historical discourses on form and value, contemporary design debates, and future technological development appear to merge almost seamlessly.

Precisely this ambivalent impression is specific to Critical Design, which unlike historical precursor discourses such as Good Form, is not concerned with matter-

47 Julian Oliver, Gordan Savičić, and Danja Vasiliev, "The Critical Engineering Working Group, Berlin, October 2011–2016," http://critical-engineering.org (accessed February 2, 2020).

48 See Emanuele Quinz, "A Slight Strangeness: Objects and Strategies of Conceptual Design," in *Strange Design: From Objects to Behaviours* (Paris: Jehanne Dautrey and Emanuele Quinz, 2015), 10–43: 11.

49 See Claudia Mareis et al., eds., *Critical by Design? Potentials and Limitations of Materialized Critique* (Bielefeld: transcript, 2022).

50 See Matt Malpass, "Contextualising Critical Design: Towards a Taxonomy of Critical Practice in Product Design" (PhD diss., Nottingham Trent University, 2012), http://irep.ntu.ac.uk/id/eprint/280.

51 See Anthony Dunne, *Hertzian Tales: Electronic Products, Aesthetic Experience, and Critical Design*, (Cambridge, MA: MIT Press, 2005), 5.

52 Ibid., 1.

53 Ibid., 20.

54 See Ludwig Zeller, "New Needs in an Augmented World" (2011), https://www.ludwigzeller.net/projects/new-needs-in-an-augmented-world/ (accessed February 2, 2020).

Fig. 5: Introspectre, from the speculative design project *New Needs in an Augmented World*, by Ludwig Zeller, 2011.

of-factness or the greater transparency and permeability of technical devices and housings. Instead, the opacity and impermeability of the housing is taken as the material starting point to prompt new kinds of speculations and narratives about the secret, mostly invisible lives of electronic-digital objects.[55] The hyperaesthetic look should not only subvert the euphoric promise, smooth surface, and glossy housing with which electronic-digital objects are commonly associated and commercially advertised today; it should also give rise to an interface critique that is expressed and transmitted not in the medium of theory but via the object itself, its aesthetic surfaces and physical housings.

Finally, to sum up, in the multifaceted history and in the manifold practices and expressive forms of interface design, it is possible to identify reciprocal but thoroughly contradictory sites of the material negotiation of meaning, knowledge, and sociocultural interaction. What is shared by the positions addressed in this paper is the ideal that by means of design processes and artifacts the human lifeworld can be changed for the better—whether through the targeted production of useful, functional everyday objects or through the incorporation of invisible systemic relations. Another strategy that is being applied in this context is the attempt to elude the dictates of (supposed) usefulness and transparency and the related logic of commodification through strategies of poetic defamiliarization and "black boxing." The affirmative concealing and obscuring of something problematic become strategies of critical visualization. Black boxing, understood as both a design-related and epistemological desideratum can thus represent very different programs of action and constellations of interest. Ultimately, these can be understood less as a simple black and white contrast than as a series of transitions between numerous shades of gray—and many other colors.

Translated from the German by Ben Carter

55 See Anthony Dunne and Fiona Raby, *Design Noir: The Secret Life of Electronic Objects* (London: August/Birkhäuser, 2001).

The Will to Engineer
Synthetic Biology and the Escalation of Zoëpolitics

Martin Müller

As long as the genetic code for a particular trait is known, scientists can use CRISPR to insert, edit, or delete the associated gene in virtually any living plant's or animal's genome. This process is far simpler and more effective than any other gene-manipulation technology in existence. Practically overnight, we have found ourselves on the cusp of a new age in genetic engineering and biological mastery—a revolutionary era in which the possibilities are limited only by our collective imagination.[1]

The Promethean sciences of our day are marked by radical attempts to design life and the natural world. Transgressive practices and expressions of limitless possibility pervade the discourse in the technosciences, paving the way for a "culture of transhumanism." The world-generating techniques of these sciences are extending the idea of engineering not only into the smallest dimensions of (in) animate matter but also into vast planetary material cycles. Frédéric Neyrat has recently stated that the Anthropocene's drive to shape the world is evident most clearly in synthetic biology's will to create: "[T]he production of life has become the principal piece of a will toward a limitless terraforming."[2] Synthetic biology as currently practiced is developing new hybrid forms of life for industrial applications, seeking the resurrection of long-extinct species to preserve collaborative ecosystems, planning the redesign of entire genomes, and applying CRISPR (Clustered Regularly Interspaced Short Palindromic Repeats) in targeted ways to the human germline—as biopolitics and applied science overlap and merge to form a new paradigm.

Analyses of this new "will to engineer" reflect one of the most acute aspirations of the humanities in general and the cultural history of knowledge, media studies, and design research in particular.[3] Yet despite its evident topicality and

1 Jennifer A Doudna and Samuel H Sternberg, *A Crack in Creation: The New Power to Control Evolution* (London: Bodley Head, 2017), xiii.

2 Frédéric Neyrat, *The Unconstructable Earth: An Ecology of Separation* (New York: Fordham University Press, 2019), 52.

3 My diagnosis of a molecular "will to engineer" parallels Kevin Grove's work on the concept of resilience, in which the crucial *constitutivum* of discourse and practice is no longer the will to know but rather the respective means of construction and the premium on design. See Kevin Grove, *Resilience* (London: Routledge, 2018), 4.

urgency, biopolitical theory has yet to be placed into perspective from a contemporary point of view, which I will do here with the help of the term *zoëpolitics*.[4] It seems highly remarkable in this context that Michel Foucault's "faire vivre"—as the constitutive desideratum of *biopouvoir* around 1800—is undergoing extraordinary renewal as the distilled will of technoscientific striving. Or how else might the above citation by Jennifer A. Doudna, the cofounder of the CRISPR process, and its formula for a new age of "biological mastery" by means of engineering be understood?

My research takes the converse approach of placing synthetic biology and its zoëpolitical genealogy of making life at the center of discussion on giving form. If biologists view themselves as designers of future entities and novel evolutionary progressions, then imagination is revealed to be the core concept of synthetic biology. The engineering of life thereby appears as a discourse on formation and design, with biological life no longer manifest as a given form but rather as a molecular medium of control and production for the unmitigated materialization of human projects. However, the term *will to engineer* highlights the one-sided quality of the concept of bio-design as engineering. Contemporary synthetic biology consists for the most part of classical engineering as it has been applied and increasingly advanced since the nineteenth century: as the production, manipulation, and control of natural things. Seen in this light, Doudna's notion of mastery is to be taken quite literally, for it describes human domination over nature, which must bend to the will of the engineer. The contribution of design research to the synthetic turn in biology could be to shift the focus from destructive and hylomorphic mastery of living nature to fundamental questions about how to design. Reimagining novel ways of giving form to the living would be an eminently political contribution to the crisis of the Anthropocene and the exigencies of what it means "to make."

Engineering Tales

CRISPR originally referred to a molecular process involving an enzyme and RNA by which bacteria and archaea recognize and resist viral attacks. In other words a type of immune system in which cells are constantly repairing themselves by deleting and replacing undesirable elements and sequences from strands of DNA In 2012 Emmanuelle Charpentier and Jennifer A. Doudna succeeded in transforming this cellular molecular mechanism into a biotechnological tool. CRISPR can be used to edit entire genomes with unprecedented precision.[5] Applicable to all forms of life—including humans—it is seen as a new and universal tool of synthetic biology.

Yet the grand narrative of bioengineering consists of a bricolage of microstories, which I would like to term *engineering tales* with a nod to Donna Haraway.[6] Alongside the reprogrammed bacteria[7] now performing tasks such as filtering polluted water and producing valuable substances, synthetic biology has assumed an ecological-mythopoetic genre with nearly unlimited conceptions of feasibility. At a Harvard Medical School laboratory, renowned bioengineer George Church and his team are working to resurrect the woolly mammoth.[8] DNA from a carcass of this long-extinct Stone Age species recently found in the Arctic is to be prepared in such a way that an elephant cow—herself a distant relative of *Mammuthus*

4 The Foucauldian concept of *biopolitics* focuses solely on modern population politics and should only be used for this historical constellation. My concept of *zoëpolitics* addresses a deeper history of escalation that extends beyond modern constellations. I have incorporated Friedrich Kittler's historiographical concept of escalation into an approach to analyze different such events within the zoëpolitical history of power and knowledge: The "will to make life" and the vivification of power emerge around 1800, intensifying and escalating in specific ways in the molecular revolution and subsequently in the birth of synthetic biology. In near homology to this, Kittler's history of communications media reads as an iterative sequence of media-technical escalation(s): a "series of strategic escalations." Friedrich A. Kittler, "Geschichte der Kommunikationsmedien," in *Raum und Verfahren*, ed. Jörg Huber and Alois Martin Müller (Basel: Stroemfeld/Roter, 1993), 188.

5 Jennifer A. Doudna and Emmanuelle Charpentier, "The New Frontier of Genome Engineering with CRISPR-Cas9," in *Science* 346, no. 6213 (November 28, 2014): 1258096.

6 Donna J. Haraway, *Staying with the Trouble: Making Kin in the Chthulucene* (Durham: Duke University Press, 2016).

7 Stephen S. Fong, "Computational Approaches to Metabolic Engineering Utilizing Systems Biology and Synthetic Biology," *Computational and Structural Biotechnology Journal* 11, no. 18 (August 2014): 28–34.

primigenius—can be artificially inseminated and bear a calf. The aim of the project, made possible by the techniques of synthetic biology, takes a veritably eschatological approach to the climate: the majestic woolly mammoths are to be transported from the Harvard lab to the North Pole, where, as Church explains, hundreds are to roam freely as part of efforts to protect the fragile Arctic environment.[9] As spectacular as the project's staging may be, its actual uses are currently unclear.

In addition to de-extinction programs to preserve biodiversity, plans call for using CRISPR to manage the mosquito populations that transmit malaria. The plan is to encode resistance to the single-cell *Plasmodium* malaria parasite into the genome of *Anopheles* mosquitoes and release these insects into nature. Once introduced into the population, the mutation will be continuously passed on (gene drive). In subsequent generations only those mosquitoes without the parasite would then be able to reproduce. According to a study by the Department of Life Sciences at Imperial College London, "A CRISPR-Cas9 gene drive construct targeting this same sequence spread rapidly in caged mosquitoes, reaching 100% prevalence within 7–11 generations while progressively reducing egg production to the point of total population collapse."[10]

That bioengineers are no longer satisfied with reconstructing and ostensibly optimizing nonhuman life can be surmised from the following events involving CRISPR technology. Twin girls named Nana and Lulu were born in November 2018. He Jiankui, a biophysicist and researcher at the Southern University of Science and Technology in Shenzhen, had used CRISPR to edit their genome and germline. Before fertilization, He had "switched off" a receptor in the genome and thereby immunized the twins against HIV,[11] an action intended to make Nana and Lulu the first genetically edited humans. Outrage was predictably high when it was revealed that He had intervened in the germline and fertilization without authorization from the relevant authorities and in violation of Chinese law. Before publishing the data and documentation, he showed the procedure incognito on his YouTube channel on November 25, 2018.[12]

Diagnosing the techno-aesthetic condition of the present age begs the question of the contemporary composition of bio- and zoëpolitical theory itself. I will therefore now explore a constellation underlying this issue: using a critical examination of synthetic biology and the discourse surrounding CRISPR, the aim is to examine the positioning and historization of contemporary zoëpolitics with respect to technologies of power. The reading proposed here views the synthesis of biology and applied engineering pursued in institutionalized and globally active form since 2004 as the latest escalation of that propensity to "invest life through and through,"[13] whose genealogical predecessors are the vivification of power around 1800 and the invention of the genetic code in the 1940s.

Around 1800—Faire vivre: Vivification of Power

This critical examination of a contemporary constellation of power is prompted by historical-analytical and epistemological unease with current constituents of biopolitical theory and figures of thought. Can these still be considered powerful categories of analysis in our technoscientific, media-ecological,[14] post-metabolic,[15]

8 Beth Shapiro, "Mammoth 2.0: Will Genome Engineering Resurrect Extinct Species?," *Genome Biology* 16, no. 1 (December 2015): 1–3.

9 Neyrat, *The Unconstructable Earth*, 52.

10 Kyros Kyrou et al., "A CRISPR–Cas9 Gene Drive Targeting Doublesex Causes Complete Population Suppression in Caged Anopheles Gambiae Mosquitoes," *Nature Biotechnology* 36, no. 11 (November 2018): 1062.

11 CRISPR was recently used to remove the HIV pathogen from the DNA of living mice. Prasanta K. Dash et al., "Sequential LASER ART and CRISPR Treatments Eliminate HIV-1 in a Subset of Infected Humanized Mice," *Nature Communications* 10, no. 1 (July 2019).

12 Martin Müller, "Neues aus dem Menschenpark," *Frankfurter Allgemeine Zeitung*, September 11, 2019, N4.

13 Michel Foucault, *The History of Sexuality*, vol. 1, trans. Robert Hurley (New York: Penguin, 1978), 139.

14 Florian Sprenger, *Epistemologien des Umgebens: Zur Geschichte, Ökologie und Biopolitik künstlicher environments* (Bielefeld: transcript, 2019); Alexander Friedrich, Petra Löffler, Niklas Schrape, and Florian Sprenger, *Ökologien der Erde: Zur Wissensgeschichte und Aktualität der Gaia-Hypothese* (Lüneburg: Meson Press, 2018); Erich Hörl, "'Technisches Leben': Simondons Denken des Lebendigen und die allgemeine Ökologie," in *Black Box Leben*, ed. Maria Muhle and Christiane Voss (Berlin: August, 2017), 239–66.

15 Martin Müller, "Nach dem metabolischen Bruch," *Texte zur Kunst* 28, no. 110 (2018): 154–59.

Techno- and Anthropocene,[16] and now climate-eschatological present? The issue becomes even clearer upon considering the technicity and scope of this governance of life. The turn of the nineteenth century in European nation states saw the development of a post-sovereign, proto-cybernetic, cameralistic, and not least of all police-disciplinary type of power dedicated to the management of life spanning the spectrum from micro-dimensions of human bodily subjects to the collective body of the population. Human sexuality and reproduction served as juncture and pivot between these two poles.[17] The milieu surrounding body and population was also instrumentalized for the purpose of exercising power. In so doing, a crucial role was played by the process of reconfiguring urban space to enable its regulation.[18]

It is therefore no coincidence that the birth of biology and of zoëpolitics around 1800—that is, of the knowledge of life and the desire to regulate it—assume the same date in historical discourse. Once past this temporal threshold, the category of biological life is no longer seen in metaphysical terms. Instead, as Jean-Luc Nancy put it, *zoë* appears as *téchne*.[19] The technological appropriation of life causes the latter to lose its ahistorical quality while enabling new strategies in the form of technical and media-based procedures seeking to protect and monitor it, and ultimately also to enhance its vitality. With increasing strategic implementation, these natural-artificial procedures of augmenting and producing (human) life extend to the "geographic and climatic features of the milieu, which are to be integrated into societal functions in order to utilize their positive natural potential. Biopolitics proceeds with and not against nature."[20] As such, making life becomes the proto-cybernetic heart of a *zoë*-centered political economy of the modern age.

Michel Foucault, who placed bodies, sex, populations, and milieus into the context of power and production in the modern age, did not quite succeed in completing his history and theory of biopolitics. He nevertheless attempted to account for the application of power to life around 1800 by furnishing his own theory with a "predetermined rupture": a power that appropriates life in order to regulate, control, enhance, and ultimately "make" it will itself submit to the logic of perpetual escalation. Power as technology entails a continuous and productive incompleteness due to the quasi-living character of politics and the mechanisms it brings forth. "These mechanisms of power, these procedures of power, must be considered as techniques," he explains in *The Meshes of Power*, "which is to say procedures that have been invented, perfected and which are endlessly developed. There exists a veritable technology of power or, better, powers, which have their own history."[21] This processual and object-oriented openness in the concept of power over life is also its historical *constitutivum*. How else should this openness be understood today but as a call to theory?

Power over life escalates in the emergence of molecular biology. A new paradigm then appears with the arrival of a concept of life based on information theory and cybernetics. Although extending beyond the disciplining of bodies, the biopolitics of populations, and the modulation of milieus, it represents a continuation of the initial elements of making life. In my genealogical reading, the three paradigms sketched here do not simply succeed each other in a neat sequence. Instead, they are mutually contingent, parallel, and intersectional—they are "always co-present."[22] The biopolitics of populations remains pervasive to this day.[23]

16 Elizabeth A. Povinelli, *Geontologies: A Requiem to Late Liberalism* (Durham: Duke University Press, 2016).

17 Foucault, *The History of Sexuality*, vol. 1, 147.

18 Michel Foucault, *Security, Territory, Population: Lectures at the Collège de France 1977–1978*, ed. Michel Senellart, trans. Graham Burchell (Houndmills: Palgrave Macmillan, 2007), 19–21.

19 Jean-Luc Nancy, *The Creation of the World or Globalization*, trans. and with an introduction by François Raffoul and David Pettigrew (Albany: State University of New York Press, 2007), 93–96. The classical term *zoë* refers of course to physical corporeal life (Greek *zóon*: living being). It also denotes the quality of being alive, distinctive to plants, animals, humans, and gods. By contrast, the term *bíos* refers (only) to human life with respect to the capacity for the "good life" as an individual and in a community. See Martin Müller, "Zoë als Téchne: Zum Paradox möglicher Menschen in der Synthetischen Biologie," in *Potential Regieren: Zur Genealogie des möglichen Menschen*, ed. Antonio Lucci and Thomas Skowronek (Paderborn: Fink, 2018), 239–52.

20 Maria Muhle, *Eine Genealogie der Biopolitik: Zum Begriff des Lebens bei Foucault und Canguilhem*, (Munich: Fink, 2013), 236: "[D]ie geografischen und klimatischen Gegebenheiten des Milieus, die sie in den Funktionszusammenhang der Gesellschaft zu integrieren suchen, um so deren positive, natürliche Potenziale zu nutzen. Die Biopolitik geht *mit* der Natur und *nicht gegen* die Natur."

21 Michel Foucault, "The Meshes of Power," trans Gerald Moore, in *Space, Knowledge and Power: Foucault and Geography*,

Informatics of Control: Invention and Implementation of the Genetic Code

The second paradigm in the history of zoëpolitics can be discerned in the invention of the genetic code in the 1940s.[24] The genetic code becomes the prerequisite for a new zoëpolitical paradigm situated below the level of sexual reproduction, to use an image of Haraway's. The great narrative of the machine readability of life in a medium of those self-active molecular processes awaiting cultural-technical decipherment at the supposed foundation of matter reflects a radical escalation and intensification of zoëpolitical knowledge and power. Its iconic image is the molecular machine.[25] As Jacques Monod put it in 1970, "The organism is a self-constructing machine."[26]

A key genealogical moment in this code-based and universal concept of life can be traced to Erwin Schrödinger's thoughts on "What is Life?" in 1943 as the prologue to the current equation of "biology is technology."[27] Schrödinger's speculations about the physical, constitutive basis of living entities were influenced by the idea of auto-generation. The Austrian physicist postulated "some kind of code-script [that contains] the entire pattern of the individual's future development and of its functioning in the mature state."[28] The crucial actant in the search for the *prima causa* was the operative code itself. Or as one of Schrödinger's most striking passages reads, "The chromosome structures are at the same time instrumental in bringing about the development they foreshadow. They are law-code and executive power, [...] the architect's plan and the builder's craft."[29]

A further current of historical discourse arises in 1953 with the determination of the structure of DNA by James Watson and Francis Crick with contributions from Rosalind Franklin, and with the publication of the central dogma in 1958. During this period, which was marked by speculation and mathematization, it fell to François Jacobs and Jacques Monod to "insert" the discourse on genetic information into the regulative mechanism of cellular chemistry in the 1960s. Both the concept of life and the experimental exploration of its material processes thereby fell completely under the spell of cybernetics and information theory. The history of the techno-epistemic escalation of power over life, which begins with Schrödinger, was characterized above all by a molecular will to know, and was expected to proceed until the human genome was decoded.[30]

The second paradigm, which is embodied in discourse on the genetic code, is dominated by the idea of direct access to life, or *zoë* itself. The power over life began extending down under the world's skin—to borrow Max Bense's famous formulation—in the 1940s.[31] By 1970 François Jacob could state that "the genetic code is almost completely known today. [...] All organisms, from man to bacteria, seem able to interpret any genetic message correctly. The genetic code seems to be universal, and its key known to the whole living world."[32] With the descent into molecular dimensions and with postulation of both the symbolic and real universality of the genetic code, power now moves beyond a modern focus limited to human life and the microphysics of the body to establish a "much more potent field of operations."[33] This molecular-epistemic unleashing of power harbors enormous potential for expansion, extending out into life beyond the human species. While poststructuralist programs were seeking to extract metaphysical legacies from the humanities,[34] a new idealism was making its way into the ontologies, epistemologies, and

ed. Jeremy Crampton and Stuart Elden (Hampshire: Ashgate, 2017), 158.

22 Povinelli, *Geontologies*, 19.

23 Nikolas S. Rose, *The Politics of Life Itself: Biomedicine, Power, and Subjectivity in the Twenty-First Century* (Princeton: Princeton University Press, 2007).

24 Lily Kay noted—correctly—that the universal genetic code is an epistemological invention. The code as such was not simply discovered but rather written into life. See Lily E. Kay, *Who Wrote the Book of Life? A History of the Genetic Code* (Stanford: Stanford University Press, 2000).

25 Mathias Grote, *Membranes to Molecular Machines: Active Matter and the Remaking of Life* (Chicago: University of Chicago Press, 2019).

26 Jacques Monod, *Chance and Necessity: An Essay on the Natural Philosophy of Modern Biology* (New York: Vintage, 1972), 46.

27 Robert H. Carlson, *Biology Is Technology: The Promise, Peril, and New Business of Engineering Life* (Cambridge, MA: Harvard University Press, 2010).

28 Erwin Schrödinger, *What Is Life? The Physical Aspect of the Living Cell* (Cambridge: Cambridge University Press, 1992), 21. The monograph is based on a lecture of the same name given in Dublin in 1943.

29 Ibid., 22.

30 See Kay, *Who Wrote the Book of Life?*, 3–5.

31 "Die kybernetische Erweiterung der neuzeitlichen Technik bedeutet also ihre Erweiterung unter die Haut der Welt"; see Max Bense, "Kybernetik oder die Metatechnik einer Maschine," *Merkur 5*, no. 37 (March 1951): 205–18.

32 François Jacob, *The Logic of Life: A History of Heredity*, trans. Betty E. Spillmann (Princeton University Press, 1973), 276–77.

narratives of molecular biology.[35] Also in 1970, Jacques Monod drew an astonishing philosophical conclusion about the agency of the universal genetic code: "The biologists of my generation were able to unveil what amounted to the identity of cellular chemistry throughout the biosphere. Awareness thereof arose in 1950, and every new publication confirmed it. The hopes of the most committed 'Platonists' were more than fulfilled."[36]

At the same time, and herein lies an extraordinary heterodoxy, if life now appeared as molecular machinery controlled by a linear alphanumerical code, the concept of life was thereby radically reduced and stripped of complexity. In Lily Kay's assessment of the zoëpolitical scope of the genetic code, "Beyond the control of bodies and populations—in all their material messiness—the power of life was being envisioned within the new paradigms of communication. It was to be exercised on the pristine metalevel of controlling information flow, the sequence, the word, and the text."[37] With the concept of life linked to machine mentation, an epistemic approach to living bodies and systems now appeared capable of achieving the maximum reach via a minimal control code of quasi-metaphysical status that seemed the "origin and universal agent of all life."[38] Foucault termed the profound epistemic transformation advanced by Jacob, Monod, and other molecular biologists the "New Testament of biology."[39] *Zoë* now appeared as a molecular, code-based, and machine-readable téchne. Based on this concept of life understood in cybernetic terms, a new zoëpolitics arose which Donna Haraway sought to grasp with the term *informatics of domination*: "Foucault's biopolitics is a flaccid premonition of cyborg politics, a very open field."[40]

Although the concept of life in its universal technicity as sketched here was laying the foundation for a worldwide technoscientific bioeconomy,[41] a certain refraction in the second paradigm can be seen precisely at the dramatic zenith of deciphering the human genome in 2003. Although traditional concepts of the body and health had undergone profound change over the second half of the twentieth century, the results themselves of the sequenced human genome triggered a *crisis* in the concept of the gene. That molecular "bio-power, the power of genetic information [...] promised a great deal more than it can reasonably deliver."[42] In this moment of discursive crisis, a remarkable inversion takes place: at the start of the new millennium the all-encompassing concept of life, derived from DNA alone, was dropped, but the demonstrated molecular processes and mechanisms were promptly redefined as instruments, protocols, and standards of an applied biology that suddenly sought to affirm itself as a new science of engineering. References to an iconic "book of life" were to be replaced with the apodictic comment by hardware designer and nanoscience inventor Richard Feynman: "What I cannot create, I do not understand."

Making Life from Scratch? Synthetic Biology as Zoëpolitics

Emergence of the third paradigm of zoëpolitics can be localized and dated in historical discourse to 2004. That year saw the first international conference on synthetic biology, *SB 1.0*, held at the Massachusetts Institute of Technology. Recalling the *Macy Conferences* and attended by molecular biologists, computer scientists, chemists, designers, nanotechnologists, and cultural anthropologists, it established a new field of research.[43] Synthetic biology was then expected to diversify

33 Donna J. Haraway, *Simians, Cyborgs, and Women: The Reinvention of Nature* (New York: Routledge, 1991), 163.

34 Friedrich A. Kittler, ed., *Austreibung des Geistes aus den Geisteswissenschaften: Programme des Poststrukturalismus* (Paderborn: Schöningh, 1980).

35 Sigrid Weigel, Die *"innere Spannung im alphanumerischen Code" (Flusser): Buchstabe und Zahl in grammatologischer und wissenschaftsgeschichtlicher Perspektive* (Cologne: Walther König, 2006), 27–28.

36 Monod, *Chance and Necessity*, 103. On the momentous meeting of philosophy and (molecular) biology in France, see Onur Erdur, *Die epistemologischen Jahre: Philosophie und Biologie in Frankreich, 1960–1980* (Zurich: Chronos, 2018).

37 Kay, *Who Wrote the Book of Life?*, 30.

38 Ibid.

39 Michel Foucault, "Croître et multiplier," *Le Monde*, November 15–16, 1970, reprinted in *Dits et Écrits*, vol. 2, 1970–1975 (Paris: Gallimard, 1994), 101.

40 Haraway, *Simians, Cyborgs, and Women*, 150.

41 Melinda Cooper, *Life as Surplus: Biotechnology and Capitalism in the Neoliberal Era* (Seattle: University of Washington Press, 2008), and Eugene Thacker, *The Global Genome: Biotechnology, Politics, and Culture* (Cambridge, MA: MIT Press, 2006).

42 Kay, *Who Wrote the Book of Life?*, xvi.

43 Paul Rabinow and Gaymon Bennett, *Designing Human Practices: An Experiment with Synthetic Biology* (Chicago: University of Chicago Press, 2012), 18–20; on the origins of the discipline of (contemporary) synthetic biology, see Sophia Roosth, *Synthetic: How Life Got Made* (Chicago: University of Chicago Press, 2017).

and develop worldwide standards in the years to come. On May 20, 2010, the discipline witnessed a significant and much-discussed breakthrough when biotechnologist and entrepreneur Craig Venter announced to the global press that scientists at his lab had synthesized the first bacterial genome and thereby "created" new life.[44] He called the bacterium, which was named *Mycoplasma laboratorium* or *Synthia*, the first biological species to have a genetic code written entirely by humans at computers. With the human genome project still under the aegis of a genetic code to be read and deciphered, synthetic biology thereby took a major new step. Using CRISPR and other processes, entire genomes can now be extensively edited—or for that matter rewritten. The notion of writing and the logic of script led to an explosion of imaginative biological scenarios by the mid-2000s. Viewed as promising technical developments and Promethean projects, they are expected to break new ground and move from behind laboratory doors toward the midst of society itself.

The examples from the field of synthetic biology touched on here—from Venter's bacterium genome to the gene-drive mosquitos, from resurrecting the woolly mammoth to manipulating Nana and Lulu's germline—oscillate between milieus and individual bodies, between molecules and eco-spheres, between humans and nonhumans, between life and nonlife. The processes sketched raise the question of a common denominator of production, and of its principle of technicity. For the modern age, according to Foucault, this role was played by sexuality and the associated will to know. Today, however, control and regulation of the body and milieu are supplemented and at times replaced by the engineering of living bodies and environmental ensembles. This new spectrum of the third zoëpolitical paradigm is accompanied by what Frédéric Neyrat in the opening quote called a "limitless will," with the hyperbolic formulation referring to the compound *terraforming*. Setting "terra" aside for the moment, we arrive at the question of the technicity of (ostensibly) unlimited forming and designability. One possible answer leads us to George Church. In a work entitled *Regenesis*, he sheds light on synthetic biology's underlying concept of technicity which enables the will toward limitless forming of life.

The processes of synthetic biology substantiate a third paradigm of zoëpolitics, which in turn is based on an explicit understanding of the genome's textual form and molecular performativity. As Church and Edward Regis write, "[B]iological organisms could be viewed as a kind of high technology, as nature's own versatile engines of creation."[45] The authors do not shy from describing the natural history of the genome as a great narrative: "It's the story of a once invisible being, nameless for eons, now called 'the genome.'"[46] The genome (singular) here becomes the subject of a *longue durée inouïe*, which began billions of years ago with the emergence of planetary life:

> The appearance of DNA some 3,900 million years ago makes it the most ancient of all ancient texts. [...] The original ancient text is written in the genomic DNA of every being alive today. That text is as old as life itself, and over 10^{30} copies of it are distributed around the earth, from 5 kilometers deep within the Earth's crust to the edge of our atmosphere, and in every drop of the ocean. A version of this text is found in each nucleated cell of our bodies, and it consists of 700 megabytes of information (6 billion DNA base pairs). It contains not only a rich historical archive but also practical recipes for making human beings.[47]

44 Daniel G. Gibson et al., "Creation of a Bacterial Cell Controlled by a Chemically Synthesized Genome," *Science* 329, no. 5987 (July 2, 2010): 52–56.

45 George M. Church and Edward Regis, *Regenesis: How Synthetic Biology Will Reinvent Nature and Ourselves* (New York: Perseus, 2012), 4.

46 Ibid., 15.

47 Ibid., 38.

In this bioengineering narrative, DNA-based life appears as an aeonian, nonhuman technology and is described as a billion-year-old "engine of creation."[48] The conceptual figuration of life as high technology advances thereby to the core of a theory of synthetic biology. Reference to the genome takes concrete form when the idea of genetic programming comes into play: "Just as computers were universal machines in the sense that given the appropriate programming they could simulate the activities of any other machine, so biological organisms approached the condition of being universal constructors in the sense that with appropriate changes to their genetic programming, they could be made to produce practically any imaginable artifact."[49] Church and Regis declare an organism's genome to be a universal production technology, whose material output is controlled by an inherent genetic program: "A living organism, after all, was a ready-made, prefabricated production system that, like a computer, was governed by a program, its genome."[50]

In this line of thought, the production of life appears as a discourse on formation and design. Molecular coding processes are now taken as operative elements of a *command and control* approach to construction. On the genomic level, nonprogrammed biological entities are to use biological means to produce—from within themselves—artifacts conceived by humans.[51] In this paradigm, artifacts are made not by humans but by organisms:

> Given the profusion and variety of biological organisms, plus the ability to reengineer them for a multiplicity of purposes, the question was not so much what they can be made to do but what they can't be made to do, in principle. After all, tiny life-forms, driven solely by their own natural DNA, have, just by themselves, produced large, complex objects: elephants, whales, dinosaurs. A minuscule fertilized whale egg produces an object as big as a house. So maybe one day we can program an organism, or a batch of them, to produce not the whale but the actual house.[52]

What we find here can be construed as a resolute appropriation of Monod's description of life as a self-constructing machine. In the grand narrative of bioengineering, life no longer appears as a limited resource but rather as a medium of production for the unmitigated materialization of human projects. George Church's discourse is by no means limited to the realm of technological imagination. Instead, under his direction concrete engineering practices are being developed for the purposes of "radical redesign."[53] In April 2019 his team presented a new CRISPR process that can perform more than 13,000 programming actions at once in a single cell.

Outlook—Genomic Design and Anthropocene Eschatology

With the birth of bio- and zoëpolitics around 1800, life becomes the object of procedures to control and enhance it that function on the level of the population body and its surrounding milieu. The resulting biopower thereby succeeds (only) indirectly in controlling the *zoë*—by systematically linking knowledge with bodies. *Faire vivre* therefore has more to do with making a world in the sense of creating the optimal conditions for human life, health, and vitality to prosper. Moreover, this modern power over life is connected with the idea of reproduc-

48 In Drexler's (conceptual) figuration of the molecular machine, which is marked by the capacity to self-generate, an ideal model for nanotechnology is found: "In cells, molecular machines first transcribe DNA, copying its information to make RNA 'tapes.' Then, much as old numerically controlled machines shape metal based on instructions stored on tape, ribosomes build proteins based on instructions stored on RNA strands." Eric Drexler, *Engines of Creation: The Coming Era of Nanotechnology*, 2nd ed. (Oxford: Oxford University Press, 1990), 6.

49 Church and Regis, *Regenesis*, 4.

50 Ibid., 15.

51 Synthetic biology is characterized by classic code engineering because it literally encodes the symbolic into the material as instructions. For a contrary approach to design, which finds the (symbolic) operations in the material, see Wolfgang Schäffner, "Active Matter," in *23 Manifeste zu Bildakt und Verkörperung*, ed. Marion Lauschke and Pablo Schneider (Berlin: De Gruyter, 2018), 1–9.

52 Church and Regis, *Regenesis*, 7.

53 Cory J. Smith et al., "Enabling Large-Scale Genome Editing by Reducing DNA Nicking," *BioRxiv* (April 4, 2019), 1.

tion and therefore with the succession of generations. As such, life prescribes a temporal sequence to the procedures of enhancement. Life in its essence, as Foucault concluded, is apprehended in a permanent state of withdrawal and is constantly evading modern mechanisms of power.

The second paradigm of zoëpolitics, which begins to emerge with Schrödinger's speculations on the question of life, seems to meet the desire for directness in a new way when molecular biology, with its mathematical and subsequently experimental/empirical techniques applied to living cells, discerns something like a Platonic principle of formation in the guise of a subjectless code of genetic programming. By thinking in code, zoëpolitics reaches for the fundamental, molecular, universal, processual logical systems of life itself.

In the course of the third paradigm, the second paradigm's processual logical systems of auto-generation and knowledge become elements of a molecular engineering that now seeks access to planetary life as a whole. Whether this zoëpower in the sense of a radical type of engineering can fulfill what it promises under real-life conditions as well or whether it will be dismissed as misguided in a footnote to the history of technology and biology remains to be seen in the years to come, for instance in the case of the laboratory-modified mosquitoes: "On 1 July [2019], the group released a test batch of mosquitoes—genetically engineered but not yet equipped with gene drives—in a village in Burkina Faso."[54]

Synthetic biology has turned not only the human genome into a project but also nature itself as a living entity—from individual genomes to complete species and overarching environmental ensembles. CRISPR can be used to undertake changes in the human germline—thereby appearing to fulfill the *rêve de biopolitique moderne* in all its directness—and these changes can then be passed on as genetic traits to future generations. It suits the aspirations of bioengineers that the provenance of even fundamental genetic alterations made via CRISPR will subsequently no longer be apparent. The question thereby arising for the formulation of zoëpolitical theory is the following: What does it mean for the history of techniques to govern the human population and its milieus if power can encode its "will" directly into the germline? Doudna and Sternberg attempt to fit the zoëpolitical eventfulness of CRISPR into an account of progress, in which natural history suddenly becomes a history of technology:

> For the roughly one hundred thousand years of modern humans' existence, the Homo sapiens genome has been shaped by the twin forces of random mutation and natural selection. Now, for the first time ever, we possess the ability to edit not only the DNA of every living human but also the DNA of future generations—in essence, to direct the evolution of our own species. This is unprecedented in the history of life on earth. It is beyond our comprehension. And it forces us to confront an impossible but essential question: What will we, a fractious species whose members can't agree on much, choose to do with this awesome power?[55]

But that is not all: the emphasis on transversal and multiscalar constructability can also be perceived as an all-too-human response to a discursive emergency that confronts us in the term *Anthropocene eschatology*. The (zoë)poli-

54 Megan Scudellari, "Self-Destructing Mosquitoes and Sterilized Rodents: The Promise of Gene Drives," in *Nature*, 571, no. 7764 (2019): 160–62, here 160.

55 Doudna and Sternberg, *A Crack in Creation*, xvi.

tical sense of troubledness, which can be shared today with Donna Haraway, lies in an antagonism of powers, in the ominous intersection of two great narratives, namely the radical constructability of biological life at a time of eminent imperilment.

Translated from the German by Marlene Schoofs

The author acknowledges the support of the Cluster of Excellence »Matters of Activity. Image Space Material« funded by the Deutsche Forschungsgemeinschaft (DFG, German Research Foundation) under Germany's Excellence Strategy – EXC 2025.

Buckminster Fuller: In Praise of the Imperfect

Didier Semin

Among the many books published by Richard Buckminster Fuller, two continue to have a special resonance today, in this era of global climate change: *Operating Manual for Spaceship Earth* of 1963, and *Utopia or Oblivion*, which came out in 1969.[1] The essence of the author's argument can be summarized as follows: industry, fueled almost exclusively by oil resources and nuclear energy, is on the brink of turning a planet whose modest dimensions are comparable to those of a large spaceship into a wasteland. Fuller employs the dramatic but effective metaphor of a vehicle powered uniquely by batteries (here, oil), batteries that can only be recharged by burning bits of the vehicle itself (that is, nuclear technology). For Fuller, however, the solution does not reside in regressing to the preindustrial stage, in what is called today *degrowth*: in his eyes, on the contrary, everything depends on the development of automation designed to release that most precious resource, thought, for the benefit of all. In this way, a rational hypothesis would emerge concerning how best to escape this dead end. To forestall the social problems resulting from automation he proposes allocating a "fellowship income" to the unemployed. According to Fuller's thesis, just one inventor of genius among the hundred thousand anglers receiving such a "thinking" allowance would make the operation profitable. The spaceship *Earth* was delivered to us without the pilot's handbook by a didactic if humorous God—not personified in Fuller's vision—precisely so that we, its passengers, would develop that aptitude for thought that constitutes our chief asset. Fuller's appeal is for a world government of engineers and planners, who, far above the power struggles, would discover how to make more and more things with fewer and fewer materials: to maintain, and then to improve, the living standards of the planet's inhabitants, by exploiting renewable energies (solar, water, wind) with optimum effectiveness. Through the primitive accumulation of industrialization, fossil energies act as a stepping-stone to the exploitation of other, inexhaustible resources in the future; a mere kickstart, as Fuller saw it, on the cosmic timescale.

1 See Buckminster Fuller, *Operating Manual for Spaceship Earth* (New York: E.P. Dutton, 1963); and Fuller, *Utopia or Oblivion* (New York: Bantam Books, 1969).

Fig. 1 (opposite): Boris Artzybasheff, *Time Magazine* cover, 1964.

Such a vision may obviously appear naive and even questionable. Fuller's metaphors (which again borrow from the mechanical model outlined centuries before in La Mettrie's *Homme-Machine*, but more still from recent ideas in astrophysics or information technology) seem clumsy. His vision of a cosmos organized by intelligent design is reminiscent of the rearguard action now under way in the United States, even in spheres around the administration, against Darwinism. Fuller too believed a few rather absurd theses on evolution, being of the opinion, for instance, that the great apes were actually *Homo sapiens* which had, for some reason or another, regressed. ... Even if the recent discoveries of paleontologists (one thinks of the skeletons of the probably oldest human ancestors: Toumaï, Ardi and MRD) make the theory of evolution more and more complex, and could justify Fuller's doubts a posteriori, none obviously supports the idea that the apes would come from a decline of the human species. ...[2] His notion of synergy between scientists—synergy being a conjunction of talents, more productive than a mere accumulation—sheltered from political infighting will raise a smile among those with even a passing acquaintance with university life and with the jostling for position rife within it. And yet, nearly half a century after he expressed them, Fuller's concerns about the state of the planet appear more pertinent than ever; and his axiom (the dichotomy: utopia or death) has unfortunately lost none of its relevance.

So, who was this visionary whose extraordinary clairvoyance cannot be gainsaid? A lengthy feature in *Time* magazine in January 10, 1964, describes him as follows (fig. 1):

> He has been called "the first poet of technology," "the greatest living genius of industrial-technical realization in building" "an anticipator of the world to come—which is different from being a prophet," "a seminal thinker," and "an inspired child." But all these encomiums are fairly recent. For most of his life, R. Buckminster Fuller was known simply as a crackpot. He is also something more than the mere sum of his praise and criticism. He is a throwback to the classic American individualist, a mold which produced Thomas Edison and Thoreau.[3]

A crackpot? This scorn and ignorance can be readily explained: in Europe (and to tell the truth, alas for the author of these lines, especially in France) Fuller's outlandishness and his "inspired child" idealism has run up against an entrenched tradition of Voltairean skepticism. On this side of the Atlantic creative ingenuity is not freighted with the positive values it possesses sometimes in the American tradition. We tend to examine the great social utopias born in Europe from the literary angle rather than from the point of view of the changes they might bring in their wake. As Engels, referring to Fourier and Saint-Simon, gleefully remarked: "For ourselves, we delight in the stupendously grand thoughts and germs of thought that everywhere break out through their phantastic covering, and to which [...] Philistines are blind."[4] The self-proclaimed heirs of Marx and Engels, however, in order to pass Marxism off as a hard science, expended much energy in obfuscating the roots of the socialist thesis in the phantasmagoria of ideal worlds. Today the total failure of that masquerade—dressing Marxism up as a pure science—should encourage us to pay more attention and give more credit to futurological thinking long castigated as extravagant.

2 Thanks to Patricia Ribault for the many indications she gave me about the more recent researches in paleontology.

3 "The Dymaxion American," *Time Magazine* 83, no. 2 (January 10, 1964), cover story.

4 Friedrich Engels, *Socialism: Utopian and Scientific* (Sydney: Resistance Books, 1999 [1892]), 59.

TIME
R. BUCKMINSTER FULLER
Artzybasheff

The central idea of *Spaceship Earth*—that an initial fault or deficiency (forgetting to include the instruction booklet when the planet Earthy was delivered to humanity) is the very condition of progress—structures the entire edifice of Fuller's thinking. He even would often begin his lectures by introducing himself as "a successful failure." He would go on about this so often that it made his collaborators laugh. Yet, for the first thirty years of his life (he was born in 1895), his life story actually *was* one of handicaps and dramas overcome, of disaster followed by regeneration.

The first example he quotes: his very early discovery of the virtues of the tetrahedron, the first of the regular polyhedrons destined to become the basic building block of Fuller's architecture, which he ascribes to the acute but undiagnosed farsightedness that afflicted him. One day at primary school a teacher handed out some peas and toothpicks to Fuller's class, asking the children to build a house model using solely these elements. Unable to perceive distant objects clearly, Fuller had never really *seen* a house: feeling his way, he did his best to construct the most solid object possible, eventually obtaining, out of a triangle made of three peas and three toothpicks, a tetrahedron, that is, a volume comprised of four triangles fitted together. His construction proved much sturdier than those of his fellows, who had tried to imitate the cubic form that they knew by experience was the shape of a house: the fledgling engineer, who had come up with his original solution thanks to his visual handicap, was duly rewarded.

Subsequently, there came two successive dismissals from Harvard, his failure at the head of a real estate company (the Stockade Building Company), and above all the untimely death of his eldest daughter, which he never got over, compounded by alcoholism, which were to determine his vocation as a philanthropic engineer. "Vocation" is indeed the correct word, since Fuller traces his decision to devote his life to solving the overwhelming problems facing humanity back to a sort of mystical experience he had in Chicago—a mysterious call he heard when he was contemplating suicide by diving headfirst into Lake Michigan. *Post hoc* rationalizations? Memories reconstructed at a later date? Probably. Partly. But it so happens that the daydreams of a man who might easily be seen as a card-carrying crank, an unlikely cross between Joan of Arc and Le Corbusier, have not remained a dead letter. His *abstract utopias*—to employ a distinction made by Ernst Bloch—were soon to grow into *concrete utopias*, that is, into effective operating devices.

In 1928 he started working on plans for a metal house, inexpensive and transportable by air: the 4D House. He had been encouraged to ponder the possible applications of mass-production techniques to housing problems during his stint at the Stockade Building Company, where he had noted how technological innovation in the construction trade lagged behind the shipbuilding, aeronautical, and automobile industries. At that time his concerns overlapped with the *aesthetics of the engineer* vaunted by Le Corbusier in his review *L'Esprit Nouveau* (which appeared from 1920 to 1925)—though with Fuller, aesthetics is not the point. A priori, however, everything seems to situate Fuller in the functionalist current. His motto of "more-with-lessing," for instance, is close to Mies van der Rohe's "less is more."

But Mies van der Rohe's functionalism, like Le Corbusier's, is in the truest sense an *aesthetics* based on paring down. Fuller's functionalism is an *ethics*: he is not trying to make commodities sell by rendering them more attractive; he wants to make *more with less*, so as to save the planet's resources, and the form of his projects invariably results from technical thinking, combined with a concern that would be today called "ecological."

In this connection, it is enlightening to compare the project for the Citrohan House, a type of villa designed by Le Corbusier in 1922, with the plans for the Dymaxion House Fuller drew up in 1928–29 (figs. 2 and 3). The explicit model in both cases is the automobile, with even the division between the strictly functional spaces (kitchen, bathroom, toilets) and the living areas being derived from the distinction between engine and cabin (The name "Citrohan" was quite simply lifted by Le Corbusier from "Citroën"). Le Corbusier's construction though name-checks every characteristic of the functionalist aesthetics: walls at right angles, elegant overhanging awnings, rectangular openings. Fuller's project literally looks like nothing on earth: with something of the nacelle and something of a sailing ship, or suspension bridge, or teepee, or igloo: it appears to be just a roof bizarrely strapped onto a mast. Fuller's guiding principle was not the beauty of the house, or even, strictly speaking, its functionality, but its weight: three tons, compared to the 150 tons of materials the American Institute of Architecture regarded as standard for a five-occupant residence. It was that particular *less* that interested him. The project earned him a measure of recognition: a major Chicago company, the Marshall Field's department stores, proposed using it to attract customers (after the 1929 Crash anything and everything was deployed to this end—including wild imaginings around the "house of the future"). The word *Dymaxion* (the result of adding the words *dynamism* and *maximum* to *ion*) was coined by Marshall Field's marketing department. After they had copyrighted the brand name on his account, Fuller was to use it throughout his lifetime for the majority of his projects and inventions.

If the Dymaxion House of 1930 never got off the drawing board,[5] the car Fuller designed in 1933 along the same lines, the Dymaxion Car, reached the prototype stage, without, however, ever being mass-produced, due to a dramatic accident which occurred during a public presentation of the model. His researches were not, however, entirely fruitless and the remarkable similarity between the Citroën DS (the car Roland Barthes celebrates in his *Mythologies*)[6] and Fuller's prototype make one think that the engineers at Citroën might have taken inspiration from the latter. (It is equally conceivable that the creators of the 2CV at the same company may have thrown more than a cursory glance at Le Corbusier's drawings for the Voiture Maximum published in 1939: the resemblances are baffling.)[7]

During the Second World War—with the ingenious conversion of a model for a metal corn silo into a hut (the Dymaxion Deployment Unit)—Fuller was to enjoy his first industrial success. The first of his discoveries to meet with global recognition was, however, not a technical invention at all. It was the publication in 1943, in *Life*, of a world map established according to a highly original system of projection, which quickly earned him a surprising level of notoriety. Fuller had experience of the sea and of navigation, not only as a yachtsman, but also as a naval officer (he had served in the US Navy from 1917 to 1919). He had therefore been confronted at an early stage by the paradoxes of the Mercator projection that

5 Another version of the Dymaxion House, quite different, was to be designed in 1945 but only two prototypes were produced.

6 The DS (spelled in French, these initials are pronounced very exactly as the word *déesse* ["goddess"]) is a family car manufactured in France by Citroën in 1955. In his *Mythologies*, in 1957, in the chapter "La nouvelle Citröen" ["The New Citröen"], Roland Barthes described it as an icon of automotive modernity, smooth like a sci-fi aircraft. See Roland Barthes, *Mythologies* (Paris: Editions du Seuil, 1957).

7 Le Corbusier et al., eds., *L'Esprit nouveau: Le Corbusier und die Industrie 1920–1925* (Berlin: W. Ernst, 1987) 260–61.

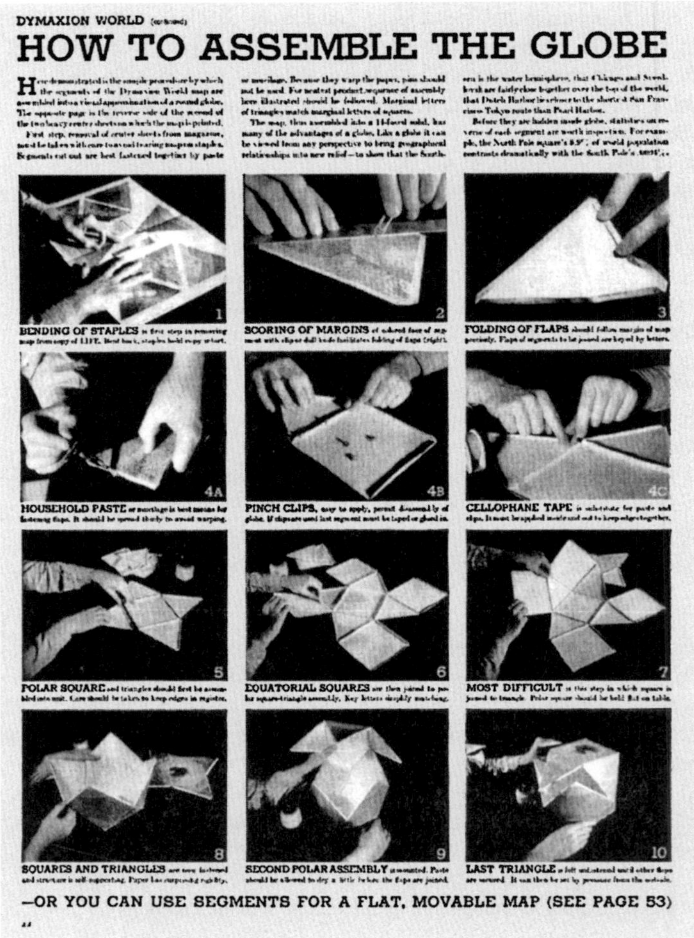
DYMAXION WORLD

HOW TO ASSEMBLE THE GLOBE

BENDING OF STAPLES

SCORING OF MARGINS

FOLDING OF FLAPS

HOUSEHOLD PASTE

PINCH CLIPS

CELLOPHANE TAPE

POLAR SQUARE

EQUATORIAL SQUARES

MOST DIFFICULT

SQUARES AND TRIANGLES

SECOND POLAR ASSEMBLY

LAST TRIANGLE

—OR YOU CAN USE SEGMENTS FOR A FLAT, MOVABLE MAP (SEE PAGE 53)

Figs. 2 & 3: Fuller's Dymaxion world map assembly instructions, in *Life*, 1943 (details).

underpins the layout of naval charts and which on world maps makes Greenland appear as large as Africa. Fuller took up the cudgels against this convenient and unanimously accepted convention, which he felt introduced factors of inequality and injustice. In devising a projection which would take into account the proportions of the respective continents, avoiding implying an "up" and a "down," and be convenient for showing air routes, he imagined reducing the globe of the Earth to a quasi-sphere made of twenty triangles assembled into an icosahedron. The whole planet could then be projected onto the 20 facets of the polyhedron with minimum perspectival distortion: the icosahedron then just has to be unfolded to obtain a serviceable map—literally a *plan* of the Earth. Proposed to *Life*, the magazine long hesitated to publish the map, launching a series of expert appraisals and reappraisals by geographers and mathematicians. It finally appeared in February 1943, in the form of a very elaborate cutout that allowed the interested reader to reconstruct the quasi-sphere by folding out and sticking the bits of the map together.[8] A print run of three million copies represented record sales for the magazine.

It was from this cartographical revolution that was born Fuller's most famous architectural creation: the geodesic dome. In fact, the adjective *geodesic*, a priori unconnected with any construction technique (it designates things having to do with geodesy, that is, with the science of mapmaking) was adopted simply to attest to its singular genealogy.

In principle, the geodesic dome is, more or less, a variation of the icosahedron used to establish the Dymaxion Map: a modular construction composed of triangular elements assembled in half or three-quarter spheres and capable of enclosing a gigantic space (the larger it is the more resistant it becomes) using a minimum of materials. Even if he was not strictly its inventor—in 1922, the architect Walter Bauersfeld had employed a structure of this type as the armature in the Zeiss Planetarium at Jena—it was Fuller who made the geodesic dome the widespread building model it is today. Hundreds of thousands of them have been built in all four corners of the world (an expression Fuller would probably have balked at: the world is *not* square), in countless variations and for every conceivable purpose. If a geodesic dome housed the United States pavilion at Montreal's World Fair in 1967 (fig. 4), similar domes cover massive industrial structures and sports and commercial complexes (in Paris, the Palais des Sports at the Porte de Vincennes), as well as radar stations. Fuller failed though in one crucial respect: in developing domes for domestic architecture, something especially close to his heart.

Leading by example, he long lived in a dome built for his own use in Carbondale, Illinois. Yet, apart from hippy communes, where it was enthusiastically taken up during the 1970s, the dome was never accepted as a viable template for private housing. Its uptake was hindered not only by the symbolic inertia represented by the usual image of the house and the prevalence of traditional construction methods, but also by some very down-to-earth disadvantages (weatherproofing required millimeter tolerance in construction; greater fire risk). Nevertheless, the success of the material, concrete architectural utopia embodied by the geodesic dome consolidated—were this necessary—Fuller's belief that only a global approach (Design Science) to problems such as housing, transport, and energy acting in the service of the world government he advocated could solve the problems facing the planet.

8 "Life presents R. Buckminster Fuller's Dymaxion World," in *Life*, March 1, 1943, 41–55.

Though fundamentally altruistic in his approach, not all Fuller's statements are exempt from what might be termed self-centeredness, creating the illusion of an absolute originality of thought radically at odds with all tradition. His at the least unusual lifestyle (having, for example, decided in the 1930s that sleeping at night was a mere cultural convention, he became used to taking a nap every hour in six...), his unshakable strength of conviction (students at summer sessions in Black Mountain College, where he taught in 1948 and 1949, saw him as a kind of Zarathustra...) accentuated this veneer of uncompromising individuality (fig. 5). There can be no question of denying the originality and innovation behind Fuller's thinking; yet his illusion—for that is what it was—of total uniqueness perhaps prevented his work from gaining wider acceptance. Those components of his activity that shock rationalist sensitivities might at least be better understood, if not accepted, than when they are replaced in their original context. Fuller himself encourages us to do so. He often said how touched he was on learning of the life story of his great aunt, Margaret Fuller, who was an active participant in American literary life at the beginning of the nineteenth century. She is chiefly remembered for her work as a journalist (she was the *New York Tribune*'s first European correspondent), her early commitment to feminism, her romantic marriage to an Italian activist, and her tragic if outlandish death in a shipwreck off New York. She was also, however, editor of the newspaper *The Dial*, which published texts by the Transcendentalist school[9] (one might call it an American variant of Romanticism), a close friend of both Emerson and Thoreau, who was left distraught at her untimely death.

This ancestry would be just a footnote were it not to echo the profound affiliation between Fuller's work and the reveries of Emerson and Thoreau. Further evidence for this connection is to be found in a lengthy article of 1843 by Thoreau, "Paradise (to be) Regained,"[10] the title being a pastiche of a book by John Adolphus Etzler published ten years earlier entitled, *Paradise within Reach of All Men, without Labor, by Powers of Nature and Machinery, an Address to All Intelligent Men*.[11] In it, Thoreau comes to the defense of the strange figure of Etzler and of his vision of humanity saved by the domestication of natural energies generated by wind and water by means of a gigantic system of gears that would harness their power, for example, to work the land. Having attempted to give material form to his ideas—a sort of prototype of his universal machine, baptized The Satellite, had been erected on the Allegheny River in Pennsylvania but had collapsed under its own weight—Etzler was to live the life of a freebooter. Up to a point, the potency of Etzler's utopia survives in the praise Thoreau lavishes on it in his book review, which, however, laments the inventor's mundane pragmatism and want of moral ambition. The overlap between Etzler's book, Thoreau's commentary, and Fuller's theses is remarkable: the same eulogy of renewable energies, the same faith in salvation through the machine; like Thoreau, Fuller is fascinated by the metaphor of the lever borrowed from Archimedes ("Give me a lever long enough and a fulcrum on which to place it, and I shall move the world."). *Spaceship Earth*, like the majority of Fuller's writings, presents a very personal version of the fortuitous discovery of this principle: in prehistoric times, a hunter, clambering over a heap of tree trunks flattened and entangled during a storm, notices that, by climbing up one trunk, another he could never have moved with his bare hands lifts up. Believing the tree trunk to be magic, he takes it back to his cave. But, after realizing his error, he begins to understand the principle of leverage. ... Fuller and Thoreau also shared a mistrust of money. An American and a

9 At least at the beginning, in between 1840 and 1844. *The Dial* lasted until 1929, with interruptions and in various forms.

10 Henry David Thoreau, "Paradise (To Be) Regained," *The United States Magazine and Democratic Review* 13, no. 44 (1843): 451–63.

11 John Adolphus Etzler, *Paradise within Reach of All Men, without Labor, by Powers of Nature and Machinery, an Address to All Intelligent Men* (London, John Brooks, 1836). Of course, both the book by Etzler and the article by Thoreau bear the memory of the poem *Paradise Lost*, by Milton.

Fig. 4: R. Buckminster Fuller, Pavilion of the United States for the 1967 World Fair in Montreal, Quebec.

Fig. 5: R. Buckminster Fuller at Black Mountain College, 1948. Photograph by Hazel Larsen Archer.

patriot, a dyed-in-the-wool partisan of industrial capitalism in the vein of Henry Ford (his first large-scale geodesic dome was erected over the Ford Headquarters in 1953), Fuller vehemently rejects the path taken by financial capitalism, though, dare one say, he did not live long enough to witness its worst excesses. To lambast it in his books, he made it a kind of omnipresent despot in the shape of a certain Mr. Fincap (for *Financial Capitalism*). The economy of means evident in the domestic plywood dome in which Fuller lived at Carbondale is reminiscent of Thoreau's famous hut on the banks of Walden Pond, which, history records, cost him exactly "28$ 12½c." The founding tradition of American thought undeniably harbors a mistrust of money as a driving force that Fuller inherited and which was expressed without pulling punches in an 1880 bestseller, Henry George's *Progress and Poverty*.[12] It is moreover not out of the question that the initial idea for *Spaceship Earth* came from this work, which already compares the Earth to a ship sailing through space, and which also proposes the idea of a universal credit, a basic income, which, for Fuller, became his "fellowship income." At root, Fuller concurs with Henry George's theories, though he claims having reached similar conclusions through concrete practice, not politico-moral reasoning. "I felt," said Thoreau in his *Journal*,

> that it would be to make myself the laughing-stock of the scientific community to describe or attempt to describe to them that branch of science which specially interests me, in as much as they do not believe in a science which deals with the higher law. So I was obliged to speak to their condition and describe to them that poor part of me which alone they can understand. The fact is I am a mystic, a transcendentalist, and a natural philosopher to boot (March 5, 1853).[13]

This statement—and it can be no coincidence that it quotes notions such as *natural philosophy* and the *higher law*—Fuller might easily have made his own. Through the intermediary of the Germanist Thomas Carlyle, Emerson and Thoreau became the American heirs to the *Naturforschung*—the natural philosophy—of Schelling and Goethe, and to the transcendental aspirations of German Romanticism more generally. It would appear that the traditional Goethean quest for higher principles and original forms reached Fuller through the Transcendentalist current. The role played by the tetrahedron and its combinations for Fuller is redolent of Goethe's hypothesis concerning the matrix of every existing plant—the well-known *Urpflanze*—while his musings on the similarities between forms in nature and in technology and architecture was nourished by a similar imaginative scientific tradition that does not exclude strangeness.

Nonetheless, the "hard" sciences were to pay due tribute to the eccentric Fuller in baptizing *fullerene*, a rare carbon allotrope whose shape resembles nothing more than a geodesic dome—or else a football, since leather soccer balls actually are quasi-spheres built on the geodesic pattern.

Time Magazine was then quite right to associate Fuller with unbridled American individualism, free to do anything, including behaving weirdly and scorning money. It is a tradition represented by Thoreau and Edison—the same Thomas Edison, who, in his time off from inventing the phonograph and the cinema, was not above becoming interested in the possible therapeutic virtues of pyramidal forms. ...

12 Henry George, *Progress and Poverty* (New York: D. Appleton, 1880).

13 Henry David Thoreau, *Journal*, vol. 5, ed. John C. Broderick et al. (Princeton: Princeton University Press, 1981), 4–5.

Americans? "Overgrown children," an updated version of Flaubert's satirical *Dictionary of Received Ideas* might suggest. That is as may be, but it is also true that certain forms of wide-eyed imagination always seem to have been more acceptable in the United States than in Europe.

The great Hollywood director of *The Big Parade* and *Duel in the Sun*, King Vidor, wondered: "Must we continue to live under the old restraint that ideas cannot be photographed, only action? [...] Why must philosophical ideas continue to be confined to the written and the spoken word? [...] What might Plato or Aristotle have done with a 16mm Bolex?" In 1965, he grabbed the 16mm camera in question and shot, without budget or actors, a glorious little philosophical manifesto in moving pictures entitled *Truth and Illusion: An Introduction to Metaphysics*.[14] Vidor's film reveals a pantheistic optimism almost identical to that of the engineer architect, with the same faith in the omnipotence of thought, the same freshness of outlook. Both Fuller (born in 1895) and Vidor (born in 1894) belong to that exceptional, unjaundiced generation of Americans who heard divine voices whispering projects for peace. However alien their thought might seem to us, we should refrain from dismissing them with a positivist shrug of the shoulders. As evidence of his belief that progress takes place through imperfection, in his *Operating Manual for Spaceship Earth* Fuller cites the demonstrable fact that, in the early years of life, human children lag well behind the offspring of the other great apes, who appear to develop faster and seem adapted better to their environment. Biologists have long wondered whether this initial deficiency might not in fact be the *cause* of mankind's development—though logically it should have condemned it to falling behind in its competition with other primates. This resemblance to *adult larvae*—a characteristic humankind shares with a few bizarre creatures (such as the axolotl, the Mexican salamander celebrated by Julio Cortazar and which inspired Giorgio Agamben in his sublime "idea of infancy"[15])—is known as *neoteny*. In normal terrestrial animals, hairlessness, protuberant eyes, fragile skin, and a large braincase compared to the rest of the body are characteristic of developing fetuses or newborns, and not fully grown individuals.

We are then unfinished mammals—animals, which, against all logic, manage to reproduce and even to turn our incompleteness to our advantage. Or are we just, as a writer fascinated by the thesis of neoteny, but who resisted seeing it as the sole key to evolution, Raymond Queneau, put it, *apes gone crazy*. "Why is it that all those who have become eminent in philosophy or politics or poetry or the arts are clearly of an atrabilious temperament, and some of them to such an extent as to be affected by diseases caused by black bile, as is said to have happened to Heracles among the heroes?"[16] If Aristotle's age-old question remains unanswered, one might well also wonder why visionaries are so often suffering from eye diseases, as Fuller did. In praise of madness, of imperfection, of inadequacy: one is in the presence here at once of an extremely ancient idea and a foundation stone of modernity—that is, the era that has thrown open the gates of science to daydreamers and fantasts, and which admitted into the domain of artworks by the mentally ill, by children and "savages." The notion that limping forward is the only way to make progress; that walking is itself no more than a sequence of miraculously broken falls, and that perfection and specialization are not guarantors of life but of death. ... In Fuller's occasionally strange parlance, this is exactly what the self-educated inventor is saying.

Translated from the French by David Radzinowicz

14 This surprising short movie, forgotten for decades, can now be easily seen online : https://www.youtube.com/watch?v=fBFLFysE24Y (accessed December 17, 2019).

15 Giorgio Agamben, "Idea of Infancy," in *Idea of Prose* (Albany: State University of New York Press, 1995), 95–98.

16 Aristotle, *Problemata* XXX. (1 953a10–14). *The Complete Works of Aristotle*, vol. 2, ed. Jonathan Barnes (Princeton: Princeton University Press, 1984).

The Design Turn 2.0[1]

Wolfgang Schäffner

In 2009, after several years of research and teaching at the School of Architecture and Design at Universidad de Buenos Aires (UBA), I moved to the Department of Cultural Studies at Humboldt University of Berlin. This involved not only relocating from the Southern to the Northern hemisphere, but also returning from the world of designers and makers to the humanities, to which I belong as a historian of knowledge and media. The strange lot of the traditional humanities is that they often arrive late at the party with their admirable and much needed criticism. For the most part they study existing or historical issues: past revolutions, crises, and the exploited, failed, or missed opportunities of knowledge. It is not until the fateful events and dramatic developments are over that the humanities start to analyze them and offer their historicizing, theorizing insights. I was long caught in this humanities trap myself and (perhaps a bit naively) often wished I could work in the laboratories of the natural sciences, where researchers perform empirical experiments in order to answer questions. These experiments result not in easily refuted interpretations, but in robust "facts" for the entire research community, and they have consequences.

While still in Buenos Aires, I was able to shift from analyses of (historical) architectural and design processes to collaborations with designers and architects—that is, from research *into* the design disciplines to research *with* them. Everything that the actors thought, planned, and did was oriented toward the future, had consequences, would soon stand as buildings, or could be repeatedly produced as artifacts. On a daily basis, knowledge was transformed into a designed reality and material culture that would then be analyzed and criticized by humanities scholars like myself—often with the assessment that things should have been done differently. Through this work with designers and my integration into the design process, my role as a humanities scholar changed in fundamental ways. In addition, the School of Design in Buenos Aires—a cubic building and "processing unit" for more than 30,000 students—had a twin standing right next to it

1 This text is a fully revised and greatly expanded version of the paper "The Design Turn: Eine wissenschaftliche Revolution im Geiste der Gestaltung," in *Entwerfen—Wissen—Produzieren: Designforschung im Anwendungskontext*, ed. Claudia Mareis, Gesche Joost, and Kora Kimpel (Bielefeld: transcript, 2010), 33–45.

in which the natural sciences pursued their work. Because of this proximity, our project, which was devoted to the architecture and design of knowledge, was able to forge links not only from the humanities to the design disciplines, but also to the natural sciences. After all, it was clear that the question of future spatial revolutions in architecture and design had to include micro- and nanoarchitectures, topics that were being investigated as building blocks and spatial structures in the disciplines of physics, chemistry, biology, and mathematics right next door. This was the main reason I viewed the Walter Gropius Program at the UBA not as a framework for historical theoretical research, but as a place where I could explore the significance the Bauhaus and the Ulm School of Design could have for the hybrid cultures of Latin America, offering an agenda for a future design far from Europe.[2] It was also a place where I could ask which disciplines would be necessary to develop this program into an interdisciplinary design laboratory that incorporated the heterogeneous practices inherent in the design process.[3]

My return from Latin America to Europe and Berlin in 2009 took place at exactly the right time, as the proposal for a Laboratory of Knowledge Design had recently been accepted at Humboldt University. As a project, this lab was to take the form of an interdisciplinary cluster of excellence run in collaboration with the image researcher Horst Bredekamp.[4] An additional stroke of luck was the invitation I received from Claudia Mareis to attend the conference "Entwerfen—Wissen—Produzieren: Designforschung im Anwendungskontext,"[5] held by the Deutsche Gesellschaft für Designtheorie und -Forschung to analyze new approaches to knowledge production. There, with respect to design, "application" was identified as the actual challenge of design research, particularly on a theoretical level. The conference took place in October 2009 and afforded me the opportunity to introduce the design turn to a German and European design community I was unfamiliar with.[6] I proposed a shift from the humanities into experimental and design practices, a reorientation that stood in contrast to the other turns pervading the humanities at the time.[7] The discussion showed that the idea of making design the focus of interdisciplinary research fit in perfectly with the intention of the event, even if it was presented by a nondesigner.[8]

The design turn that was identified one decade ago as a fundamental shift in physics, chemistry, and biology and was suggested for the humanities has since caught on and gathered momentum as an interdisciplinary research strategy that has exceeded all original expectations. Of course, this shift was also indicative of a fundamental crisis that is not only a permanent condition in Latin America, but—due to ecological, colonial, and postcolonial entanglements—is also affecting all European cultures and thus becoming increasingly evident even in the more stable-seeming structures of Europe. Around 2010, though, it was impossible to foresee the degree of urgency that has since accompanied this integrative interdisciplinary approach. The increasingly evident ecological disaster that gave rise to this urgency has confirmed and emphasized the need for a fundamental shift.[9]

1. The Design Turn 2010

The "diagnosis" of a design turn was first made in the classical natural sciences, which, within the context of nanotechnology and materials science, were shifting from analyzing natural phenomena to designing the physical world. This reorien-

2 Nestor García Canglini, *Culturas híbridas: Estrategias para entrar y salir de la modernidad* (Mexico: Grijalbo, 1990).

3 Gabriela Zampini, "Usina Bauhaus 2004, una cita con el pensamiento," *ámbito* secciones especiales (August 30, 2004), https://www.ambito.com/secciones-especiales/usina-bauhaus-2004-una-cita-el-pensamiento-n3287817.

4 Horst Bredekamp, *Theorie des Bildakts: Frankfurter Adorno-Vorlesungen 2007* (Frankfurt am Main: Suhrkamp, 2010).

5 "Design—Know—Produce: Design Research in an Application Context."

6 Lecture at the 2009 conference, published as "The Design Turn: Eine wissenschaftliche Revolution im Geiste der Gestaltung," in Mareis, Joost and Kimpel, *Entwerfen—Wissen—Produzieren*, 33–46. This lecture was published in Spanish as "The Design Turn: Una revolución científica en el espíritu del diseño," *Revista Kepes 7*, no. 6 (2010): 61–78; and in Japanese in *Shiso* (February 2015).

7 Doris Bachmann-Medick, *Cultural Turns* (Berlin: Rowohlt Taschenbuch, 2016).

8 *Conference proceedings, Entwerfen, Wissen, Produzieren: Designforschung im Anwendungskontext, 6. Jahrestagung der Deutschen Gesellschaft für Designtheorie und -forschung e. V* (DGTF), http://www.dgtf.de/code/dgtf/Tagungsbericht.pdf.

9 Claudia Mareis and Nina Paim, eds., *Design Struggles* (Amsterdam: Valiz, 2020).

10 »Image Knowledge Gestaltung. An Interdisciplinary Laboratory« was a cluster of excellence integrated into Berlin's Humboldt University from 2012 to 2018 that

tation presented a special historical opportunity to establish a new convergence of different disciplines in the spirit of a new type of design. More important than the diagnosis of a design turn, though, was its explicit program and goal of transforming a unique opportunity into actual institutionalized research strategies.

Through this new focus on the design disciplines, which had been largely excluded from traditional university research, design processes moved to the fore of interdisciplinary research. Oriented toward practice, projects, and materials, this research integrated heterogeneous methods and established an exemplary work method: in close cooperation with the humanities and natural sciences, it made collaborative interdisciplinary structures possible that had previously seemed impractical due to the disciplinary specialization of research. Creative strategies such as image and information design, which in fact play a key role in all disciplines, were more closely intertwined. These efforts were cast into institutional form at the excellence cluster »Image Knowledge Gestaltung. An Interdisciplinary Laboratory« at Humboldt University.[10] As a result, the work method of design evolved from an isolated, specialized practice into an interdisciplinary collaborative process.[11] In contrast to media and engineering labs, the common interface and focus of action for all participants was not digital media, but the heterogeneous forms of knowledge and practices that could be combined in physical spaces to create a shared research process. Experimentation became essential and connected design processes more closely to the natural sciences.[12] By contrast, in the humanities, the design turn has been a difficult reorientation. After all, the traditional self-understanding of the humanities deeply contradicts the idea that "application"—previously disparaged as a merely practical field—represents the greatest challenge and perhaps the most elaborate form of theory, which has consequences in the real world. A further aim of the design turn has thus been to fundamentally expand the humanities through an experiential, intercultural, and creative epistemology, to transform them into a formative factor in the design process, to move them beyond after-the-fact analyses. This is all the more important because a transversal approach to analysis is creating an essential methodological foundation for combining and integrating heterogeneous forms of knowledge and practices. As part of this approach, the history, theory, and practice of cultural techniques, as well as images, spaces, structures, and forms, are viewed as fundamental modes of knowledge production in different cultures. As a result, the humanities have assumed a new integrative and synthetic role for the design turn, one that has become indispensable for interdisciplinary collaboration, alongside the integrative practice of design.[13]

On the basis of these developments, new opportunities have arisen for basic research in design. In many respects, the design turn has broken new ground for interdisciplinary research. The novel combination of diverse disciplines has profited from different forms of integration and convergence, which are cutting across disparate fields of research. The trend toward convergence that has accompanied the development of medical research as an integrative field is also leading to the establishment of comparable structures.[14] Materials science is bringing together areas of research that have long been separate, including engineering, materials theory, solid-state physics, chemistry, and biology, and is thus forming a hybrid, yet closely intermeshed, complex.[15] The humanities have defined this focus on materials as a "new materialism,"[16] which has created not only opportunities for a convergence with the natural sciences and design, but also the

established collaborative structures with more than forty disciplines.

11 See Wolfgang Schäffner, "Interdisziplinäre Gestaltung: Einladung in das neue Feld einer Geistes- und Materialwissenschaft," in *Haare hören—Strukturen wissen—Räume agieren: Bericht aus dem interdisziplinären Labor "Bild Wissen Gestaltung,"* ed. Horst Bredekamp and Wolfgang Schäffner (Berlin: transcript, 2015), 199–213.

12 See Séverine Marguin, Henike Rabe, Wolfgang Schäffner, and Friedrich Schmidtgall, eds., *Experimentieren: Einblicke in Praktiken und Versuchsaufbauten zwischen Wissenschaft und Gestaltung* (Berlin: transcript, 2019).

13 This was perhaps the most important methodological finding of the excellence cluster »Image Knowledge Gestaltung«. See *Image Knowledge Gestaltung: An Interdisciplinary Laboratory (2012–2018)*, final report; DOI: 10.2314/KXP:1727514998.

14 See Phillip A. Sharp, et al., "The Third Revolution: The Convergence of the Life Sciences, Physical Sciences, and Engineering," MIT White Paper, 2011.

15 See Robert Cahn, "The Science of Dirt," *Nature Materials 1* (2002): 3–4; and Bernadette Bensaude-Vincent, "The Concept of Materials in Historical Perspective," *International Journal of History & Ethics of Natural Sciences Technology & Medicine* 19, no. 1 (2011): 107–23.

16 See Rick Dolphijn and Iris van der Tuin, eds., *New Materialism: Interviews & Cartographies* (Ann Arbor: Open Humanities Press, 2012).

possibility of exchanges with other cultures. The materials that have evolved in natural processes and cultural practices over millennia are becoming the models for design, taking the place of immaterial human ideas.[17] In addition, a new structuralism, which no longer confines itself to the interpretive perspective of the humanities, but which "structures" nature, technology, and cultures in equal measure,[18] has emerged as an integrative research approach in which the symbolic, the spatial, and the material are converging.

Based on these convergences and the close ties between design, the natural sciences, and the humanities, research processes have evolved into design processes and design has evolved into an interdisciplinary research practice. Along the way, practice- and material-based design methods, experimental and historical theoretical approaches, as well as culture- and nature-based practices have formed a close interdisciplinary link that requires a corresponding new laboratory architecture.[19] Increasingly, interactive exhibition concepts are serving as open laboratories, which—as a special mode of design—enable research processes to engage in exchanges with a broader public.[20] Design theory, too, has expanded beyond its disciplinary context into a discussion space that encompasses a variety of disciplines, from philosophy to economics.[21] The necessary collaborative structures have since assumed strategic importance for research. The excellence clusters »Image Knowledge Gestaltung. An Interdisciplinary Laboratory« (2012–18) and »Matters of Activity. Image Space Material« (2019–25) were launched in Berlin,[22] and the Humboldt Lab was founded at the Humboldt Forum in Berlin to design and curate research processes that facilitate exchanges with society. In both Berlin and Buenos Aires, the international master's program "Open Design" integrates interdisciplinary and intercultural forms of knowledge in order to train participants in the new processes of project development.[23] Finally, an important axis has been established between Berlin and Paris, encompassing the SACRe doctoral program and the Chaire Arts & Sciences, held by Samuel Bianchini and Jean-Marc Chomaz,[24] as well as the Centre de Recherche en Design, directed by James Auger and Armand Behar. As part of a PhD program, ties have been forged with the University of Art and Design in Linz and the Academy of Art and Design in Basel.

2. The Diagnosis 2020

The design turn in the natural sciences is linked to two diametrically opposed strategies that are often lumped together (for example, in Richard Feynman's influential 1959 manifesto "There Is Plenty of Room at the Bottom"[25]). On the one hand, design is traditionally viewed as the conception, production, manipulation, and control of things and thus as a representation of human domination over nature. On the other hand, it can pursue the completely opposite strategy of a symbiotic and collaborative interaction with the natural environment, embedded in an adaptive process. The distinction between these two design paradigms is fundamental to the Design Turn 2.0.

Since the nineteenth century, design in the first sense has increasingly expanded as a traditional technical engineering practice. As a result, the natural physical world has become merely a passive vehicle for the production of artifacts that are created on the basis of prefabricated ideas as the teleological objective of human technology. The principle of these artifacts is governed by controllable technical

17 See Peter Fratzl, Karin Jacobs, Martin Möller, Thomas Scheibel, and Karin Sternberg, eds., *Materials Research: Inspired by Nature: Innovation Potential of Biologically Inspired Materials*, Acatec Discussion Series (Munich: Acatec Discussion, 2020); Wolfgang Schäffner, "Immateriality of Materials," in *+ultra: knowledge & gestaltung*, eds. Nikola Doll, Horst Bredekamp, and Wolfgang Schäffner, exh. cat., Martin Gropius Bau, Berlin (Leipzig: Seemann, 2017).

18 See Rivka Oxman, ed. *The New Structuralism*, special issue of *Architectural Design* (July/August 2010); Wolfgang Schäffner, "New Structuralism: A Human and Materials Science," *Graz Architecture Magazine* 12 (2016): 10–31.

19 See Charlotte Klonk, *New Laboratories: Historical and Critical Perspectives on Contemporary Developments* (Berlin: De Gruyter, 2016).

20 See Nikola Doll, Horst Bredekamp, and Wolfgang Schäffner, eds., *+ultra: knowledge & gestaltung* (2017).

21 Bruno Latour, "A Cautious Prometheus? A Few Steps toward a Philosophy of Design (with Special Attention to Peter Sloterdijk)," in *Proceedings of the 2008 Annual International Conference of the Design History Society (UK) University College Falmouth, 3–6 September*, ed. Fiona Hackne, Jonathan Glynne, and Viv Mirato (Boca Raton: Universal Publishers, 2009).

22 Excellence cluster »Image Knowledge Gestaltung«, Humboldt University of Berlin (2012–2018), and the excellence cluster »Matters of Activity«, Humboldt University of Berlin (2019–2025), see www.matters-of-activity.de.

processes that convert metals and plastics into machines, instruments, and standardized mass-produced products. The associated design processes thereby anticipate the product as an objective in the sense of a preconceived idea that is realized and produced before the process actually begins. This is the basic structure of an engineering and design logic that is responsible for the destructive effects subsumed under the concept of the Anthropocene. As long as human ideas are put into practice in physical reality as artificial foreign bodies, production will remain blind to the operations and unpredictable conditions to which the process is leading. It is extremely energy-intensive to restrict the degree of freedom of a material when creating a special functionality. For this reason, ever since the nineteenth century, artifacts have been made mainly from easily formable materials such as metals, concrete, and plastics, which can be shaped in a highly flexible, controllable way. These materials are thus an integral part of all traditional planning processes and project structures that, with their milestones and waterfall models, are oriented to the algorithmized teleological logic of operational steps. In a kind of reverse linear causality, cause is projected into the future as an end and turned into the goal of the process. Design becomes a type of reverse engineering or reverse design that always anticipates the defined goal based on a model and an ideal.

These strategies have been put into action in our physical and social environment; they form the basis of a Western culture that since the start of the modern period has spread across the globe as a system of exploitation and control.[26] They have had a massive impact on the natural world and have been a key factor in the crisis of the Anthropocene. Most of the creative nano- and material sciences, as well as computer science as the pillar of the digital age, show in fundamental ways that the destructive technical implementation of human intelligence in the environment is currently in its most radical phase. The idea of programmable matter[27] is being transferred to the entire physical world as "Industry 4.0" or as synthetic biology, extending into the strategic design of molecular life.[28]

Over the past decade, the situation has grown increasingly dramatic as the geological dimension of human culture—as described by Paul Crutzen and Eugene Stroemer as early as 2000[29]—has had increasingly clear and tangible effects not only on the physical world but also beyond. The growing awareness of the resulting global threat has even led to the emergence of a new social movement. Alarming environmental data point to the urgent need for a different organization of culture, as has been articulated by Fridays for Future since 2018.[30] The coronavirus, originating from a wild habitat in China, has shown the speed and global interconnection of human exchange processes and made clear how transmission paths can successively spread across the entire globe in just a few weeks' time. The virus can thus be seen as an indicator of the technical infrastructure and growth logic that is destroying cultural and natural stabilities. The speed at which goods, people, and viruses spread, as well as the range of their transmission, is the result of technical design and control structures whose consumption of materials and energy is causing the earth to collapse as a global system.

However, completely different design processes, which are more closely attuned to the natural world, are emerging in parallel to this destructive design strategy. These processes view biological materials mainly as a model for a technique that acts *with* nature, not *against* it. They constitute the most important pillar of the Design Turn 2.0, which is a necessary response to current exigencies. What is

23 See the Open Design program, https://www.matters-of-activity.de/en/promotion/38/master-open-design.

24 See the doctoral program SACRe (https://www.ensad.fr/en/node/334), the Chair Arts & Sciences at EnsAD/Paris (https://chaire-arts-sciences.org/?lang=en), and the Centre de Recherche en Design at ENSCI/Paris (https://www.ensci.com/recherche/le-centre-de-recherche-en-design).

25 Richard Feynman, "There Is Plenty of Room at the Bottom: Invitation into a New Field of Physics"; see also W. Schäffner, "The Design Turn," 34ff.

26 This can be described as the "Potosí principle" of colonization. See the exhibition catalog *Principio Potosí*, ed. Alice Creischer, Max Jorge Hinderer, and Andreas Sieckmann (Madrid: Museo Nacional Centro de Arte Reina Sofia, 2011).

27 Skylor Tibbits, ed., *Active Matter* (Cambridge MA: MIT Press, 2017).

28 Martin Müller, "Nach CRISPR: Zur dritten Proliferation der Biopolitik (1800/1943/2004)," in *Milieu Fragmente: Technologische und ästhetische Perspektiven*, ed. Rebekka Ladewig and Angelika Seppi, 331–44 (Leipzig: Spector Books, 2020).

29 Paul Crutzen and Eugene Stoermer, "The 'Anthropocene,'" *Global Change Newsletter* 41 (2000): 17–18.

30 See Greta Thunberg, *No One Is Too Small to Make a Difference* (London: Penguin, 2021).

crucial is a form of design that can set a process in train that is not guided by any clearly predefined objective, but is characterized by a fundamental openness, a process in which not every divergence from the imagined goal needs to be eliminated as a disturbance, but in which such disturbances become part of the design process as fundamental information that cannot be anticipated or predicted. In this case design no longer anticipates its processes and goals based on the principle of a prescriptive code, but allows unforeseeable solutions to emerge. Materials are no longer slavishly obedient and "docile," but become "active participants in the genesis of form."[31] They are not the passive vehicles of technical implementation or disruptive factors, but complex active structures whose synergetic use creates the basic conditions for an adaptive design process. This is true of both biological and virtual materials. After all, the digital world has also seen a shift from programming as a means of exerting control down to the pixel level to a code that, as self-acting material, enables unforeseeable design processes. The classical model of a programmed, controlled code is evolving into a new model of code that detaches itself from human programmers and is able to grow through biologically oriented processes. In addition, as software, this code can initiate design processes for structures with far more complex and unforeseeable behavior. This type of virtual material integrates and coordinates multiple active components. Their orientation and control exhibit the "hair-fine sensitivity" of the "unselfconscious process" in which "fitness" has traditionally been designed and produced according to natural principles.[32] In this respect, biological growth processes, which expand exponentially only in exceptional cases, are extremely sensitive and adaptive, integrating their environment as an essential inherent component.

While these forms of experience and action have become alien to Western culture, the activity of objects and materials is an essential foundation of traditional and indigenous cultures. In this sense, the Design Turn 2.0 is not an entirely new strategy; rather, as a turn, it corresponds to the fundamental shifts in perspective that also become visible when we examine the cosmologies of traditional and indigenous cultures. The ontologies of such communities, which have survived especially in Latin America, are, at their core, characterized by reversals and dissolutions of the subject-object relationship. As part of this process, animals, plants, and objects may be experienced as personified actors whose nature is based not on the manipulable passive materiality of nature, but on human beings as the actual substrate. Such perspectivism has been described by Eduardo Viveiros de Castro and Tânia Stolze Lima in studies of the Awaretê[33] and Yudjá[34] peoples in Brazil, as well as by Eduardo Kohn with respect to Ecuadorian Amazonia.[35] The Andes is yet another region in which many traditional practices have remained intact, including weaving and braiding.[36] Nevertheless, these practices, as well as their associated languages and communities, remain extremely endangered.[37] Instead of a single nature antagonistically opposed to human beings, they reveal many natures,[38] which multiply the relations with the various cultures and lend them a local specificity. What is at stake here are adaptive practices and forms of knowledge that are oriented toward interaction with the environment.[39] In this context, design represents a social and natural interactive process that encompasses the activity of materials, plants, animals, and people.

This diversity of cultures, as well as the design practices that produce and maintain them, is particularly susceptible to the normative effects of Western culture. Not only is the Anthropocene inscribing itself geologically on the planet, but it is

31 Manuel De Landa, "Philosophies of Design: The Case of Modelling Software," *Verb: Architecture Magazine* (2001): 130–43.

32 Christopher Alexander, *Notes on the Synthesis of Form* (Cambridge, MA: Harvard University Press, 1964), 55, 45ff, 15ff.

33 Eduardo Viveiros de Castro, *Métaphysiques cannibales: Lignes d'anthropologie post-structurale* (Paris: Presses universitaires de France, 2009); and *La mirada del jaguar: Introducción al perspectivismo amerindio* (Buenos Aires: Tinta Limón, 2013).

34 Tânia Stolze Lima, *Um peixe olhou para mim: o povo Yudjá e a perspectiva* (São Paulo: Editora UNESP, 2005).

35 See Eduardo Kohn, *How Forests Think: Toward an Anthropology beyond the Human* (Berkeley: University of California Press, 2013); see also Philippe Descola, "All Too Human (Still): A Comment on Eduardo Kohn's *How Forests Think*," *HAU: Journal of Ethnographic Theory* 4, no. 2 (2014): 276–73.

36 See Denise Arnold and Elvira Espejo, *El textil tridimensional: La naturaleza del tejido como objeto y como sujeto* (La Paz: ILCA, 2013).

37 See the VW Foundation's project *Documentation of Endangered Language*: https://dobes.mpi.nl. The list of endangered communities is also seemingly endless, especially in the Amazon region. See, for example, the nomadic culture of the Nukak from Colombia, Gustavo Politis, *Nukak* (Santa Fé de Bogotá: Instituto Amazónico de Investigaciones Cientificas, 1996).

38 Didier Debaise, *Nature as Event: The Lure of the Possible* (Durham: Duke University Press, 2017).

39 Philippe Descola, *Beyond Nature and Culture* (Chicago: The University of Chicago Press, 2013). The goal is to fundamentally question the concept of a single nature.

also dissolving extremely elaborate, cultural-natural adaptation structures. After all, it is not only biological species that are dying out, but languages and cultural practices that store an intelligence that has evolved over thousands of years.[40] Such traditional forms of design have arisen over extremely long periods of time as practices adapted to natural materials. These practices have integrated the intrinsic activity of natural materials into their processes and, at the same time, have been able to store this intelligence in the form of stable, handed-down operations.[41]

The loss of these traditional "unselfconscious" design practices cannot be compensated for by industrial "selfconscious processes."[42] As Christopher Alexander has pointed out, the modern mode of architectural design separates the builder from the user and thus destroys the traditional mode of perpetuating the construction process through permanent repair. Alexander's fundamental idea is related to the entire process of industrialization, which broadly eliminated the intelligence of handcraft. For this reason, the various networks of relations and interactions between people and their environment, as the components of a transcultural, transdisciplinary design process, have assumed a significance that is just as important as that of the active structures that material scientists are discovering in what they previously considered passive materials or that are emerging in the new type of code that is increasingly abandoning the control logic of traditional programming. In this regard, the shift from the colonization and domination of a passivized nature must simultaneously be seen as a shift from the colonization and scornful treatment of other "more primitive" cultures and thus a turn toward a new type of cultural interaction and diversification. After all, the point is not to establish another "better" hegemonic form of cultural design, but to enable the play of multiple activities in their spatial and cultural diversity. This requires a design turn that is fundamentally intercultural.

In other words, instead of following the path of cybernetics with its specific view of nature, and developing design as a close link between animal and machine (a link in which the idea of a *Technik der Natur*, or technic of nature, is used for a radical technological takeover of engineering implementations), these interrelations between cultural and natural adaptation processes are creating a foundation for a novel model of design for the twenty-first century. Plants have provided this model with its special guiding principle. Beyond their purely aesthetic use in gardens or the radical forms of their cultivation and exploitation as food, they represent what is perhaps the most significant blind spot in Western culture. As a result, the creative intelligence of the entire world of flora was long ignored or defined solely in terms of its special purposefulness from the perspective of an existing technic. This, in any case, was the view held by Immanuel Kant, who, with regard to organized nature, spoke of a "technic" of nature and an unintentional "technica naturalis."[43] When biologists currently analyze the mechanics of plant movement,[44] when physicists and engineers[45] study the biological materials of plants, and when ethnologists explore their social agency,[46] it becomes clear that the "homme plante" that Julien Offray de La Mettri envisioned as a further refinement of the "homme machine" in 1748 requires an additional shift in perspective. After all, in that period, La Mettrie continued to classify the "nature végétale" as the lowest form of living organism on a continuum that led to animals and humans.[47] This shift in perspective is also required (alongside other cultural ontologies) in order to illustrate the special material design processes in plants and plant tissues that are at the core of the Design Turn 2.0.

40 Laurajane Smith and Natsuko Akagawa, *Intangible Heritage* (London: Routledge, 2008).

41 These adaptive processes can be observed in the biological and cultural structures of traditional cultures that make use of plant and animal fibers. We are currently studying them in the "Weaving" project at the excellence cluster »Matters of Activity«: https://www.matters-of-activity.de/en/research/projects/55/weaving.

42 Alexander, *Notes on the Synthesis of Form*, 55ff.

43 Immanuel Kant, *Critique of Judgment*, trans. J. H. Bernard (New York: Barnes & Noble Books, 2005), 195.

44 Wolfgang Haupt, *Bewegungsphysiologie der Pflanzen* (Stuttgart: Thieme, 1977).

45 Karl J. Niklas and Hanns Christof Spatz, *Plant Physics* (Chicago: The University of Chicago Press, 2012).

46 Kohn, *How Forests Think*.

47 Julien Offray de La Mettrie, *L'homme plante: Der Mensch als Pflanze* (Weimar, 2008 [1748]), 52.

3. Program

These various elementary shifts in perspective require a new design strategy: a "program" devised for the new design turn that, in response to the extreme urgency of the current situation and the question of future action, offers not a solution, but a strategy for the processes that mark the solution's path. Here, though, "program" does not mean a prescriptive approach that anticipates the planned processes and specifies their course in the sense of the modern logic of a project. Rather, it refers to an approach that is not a program in the actual sense, but a critical act of "making" that transforms practical and epistemic experimentation into open processes adaptable to the respective conditions. This program should cover the following ideas:

1. Research is only able to respond to the urgency of current needs in the form of a design process that combines multiple disciplines in an interdisciplinary fashion, integrating the transdisciplinary expertise of different practices and procedures.
2. The central strategy of design must aim at establishing a complex design process that, when confronting problems, sets in motion an open adaptation modeled on biological growth and evolutionary processes. This implies a fundamental departure from the principle of designing preconceived solutions as projected forms and implementing them on the basis of manipulable and controllable materials.
3. Adaptive design does not operate with rigid prefabricated components, a fixed program, or a programmable objective, but with an open process, sensitive soft materials, and learning-enabled codes that adapt to conditions and develop an intrinsic activity. In this regard, the optimal form of such processes cannot be anticipated.
4. Parallel to biological and technical processes, traditional forms of design have acquired an innovative character through their special sensitivity to environmental adaptations and their use of material activity. This can be seen quite clearly in traditional and especially indigenous cultures, which is why intercultural comparisons are of vital importance for the design turn.
5. Due to the focus on natures and traditional cultures, industrially standardized forms of production are being replaced by design processes in which cultural and natural practices are increasingly converging and entering into a nondestructive relationship.
6. The growth processes of biological materials have shifted the focus to analog operations; however, they do not represent a regression within the digital age. They are being combined with a new idea about code that is no longer prescriptive but which transforms symbolic operations into automatic processes. On this level, the intrinsic analog codes of materials and the materialization of self-writing and growing digital codes merges to create a new form of active coded materials.
7. Should an adaptive process evolve on the basis of the model of biological and cultural design, it will depend on extremely long development periods. For this reason, one of the greatest challenges facing the Design Turn 2.0 will be to accelerate these developments through a combination of analog and digital processes without risking the loss of their integrative and adaptive complexity.

4. The Plant as Model

The challenge facing the Design Turn 2.0 is to respond appropriately (i.e. as quickly as possible) to the crisis of the Anthropocene, in which the technical destruction of nature has radically culminated over the last two hundred years. One of the main unquestioned factors contributing to this crisis is the use in modern industrialized technology of materials such as iron, steel, concrete, and silicon, which, being both rigid and passive, require vast amounts of energy to produce. In addition, before and after the century of petroleum, this technology has been impacted by the development of electric energy, which continues to be seen as more future-oriented than fossil fuels. This culture of mechanical and IT machinery is contrasted by that of the biological materials of plants and animals, whose active processes are governed by material principles such as adaptive growth, composite and fiber structure, as well as cellular architecture. These materials are light, elastic, and responsive to the environment. Traditional practices, which are now largely absent from production, extensively integrated these processes and thus represent a large pool of tacit knowledge about the related material activity.

Against this backdrop, it is important to provide a more detailed description of the plant model and its implications for the Design Turn 2.0. Unlike the cybernetic approach, which was based mainly on animal bionics in the sense of an anthropomorphic equivalence between animal and machine, the more recent view, driven by material science, is focused more heavily on the organic materials themselves. Interest is shifting to plants, which, in a certain way, more radically illustrate the principle of intrinsic material activity. After all, in contrast to the mechanics of movement in the animal kingdom, plants appear to be largely immobile organisms firmly tethered to the environment. It is mainly their seeds with which we associate long-distance movement. From the perspective of active inner materiality, even bones can no longer be seen as analogous to traditional machines with their rigid mechanical elements.[48] The special technicity of plant materials makes them an ideal model for a mode of future design in which natural and cultural techniques are combined. Only a few biological materials exist that can produce different functions and activities on the basis of diverse internal geometries and fiber architectures—for example, sugars as the basis of chitin and cellulose, and proteins as the basis of keratin, silk, and collagen.[49] The resulting composite materials are elastic, active, soft, and wet, and differ fundamentally from the rigid, dry, electrifiable materials of our current technology.

This means that if the soft materials of plants are used as a model, as has long been the case in traditional and indigenous cultures, design will be completely transformed. It will become a process that interacts with the active structures of materials, replacing electricity as the primary energy source with soft mechanics, water, and temperature fluctuations. The antithesis to this model is the concept of autonomous design with perfectly manipulable materials, the final painful legacy of Western idealism. The Design Turn 2.0 is thus concomitantly a material-driven turn that regards design and fitness as resulting from the adaptive evolutionary process of the material itself and its environment.

In this regard, since ancient times, wood—as ὑλή and *materies*—has been an exemplary material not only in Europe but other cultures as well.[50] Humanity has a long tradition and broad cultural history linked to the use of wood as an entirely

48 Richard Weinkamer, Philip Kollmannsberger, and Peter Fratzl, "Connectomic Description of the Osteocyte Lacunocanalicular Network in Bone," *Current Osteoporosis Reports* 17 (2019): 186–94, https://doi.org/10.1007/s11914-019-00515-z.

49 Michaela Eder, Shahrouz Amini, and Peter Fratzl, "Biological Composites: Complex Structures for Functional Diversity," *Science* 362, no. 6414 (2018): 543–47, DOI:10.1126/science.aat8297.

50 Michaela Eder, Wolfgang Schäffner, Ingo Burgert, and Peter Fratzl, "Wood and the Activity of Dead Tissue," *Advanced Materials*, August 4, 2020 ; e2001412. DOI: 10.1002/adma.202001412.

passive, rigid building material or, conversely, as a highly flexible, active one. When wood was first used to make traditional artifacts and building elements, the goal was to produce a material that was as rigid and passive as possible by neutralizing its activity and responsiveness through the particular cut or—as in the case of plywood—through a cross-layered structure. This was achieved by layering and gluing individual sheets of wood with the grain facing in alternating directions to make the material more stable and passive. However, the "working" of wood has also been functionalized in other ways. In shipbuilding, for example, the swelling of wooden planks actively seals the hull; in bow making, the layering of wood and other materials, observed in many different cultures, allows large amounts of energy to be stored and then quickly released.[51] As a composite material, wood can be incorporated into bilayer or multilayer structures such that its internal movement is further enhanced and the wooden objects bend extremely well when exposed to moisture or heat.

In other words, plant material generally consists of highly sensitive structures that produce tissue tension and elastic deformations[52] by using a small amount of energy, which is derived from the immediate environment through moisture or temperature changes. As a complexly structured fibrous material, wood is made up of specially aligned microfibrils, elastic and rigid fiber strands, as well as honeycomb structures—that is, of a total of five different layers in a material structural composition.[53] The hierarchical structure makes for a responsive dynamic material in whose intrinsic activity water plays a key role.[54] Through soft materials, the electric energy-based activation of smart materials is being replaced by activation through water and temperature.[55] The material itself is able to generate mechanical motion by combining hydrophilic and hydrophobic surfaces such that environmental moisture changes are converted into mechanical energy. In such processes, the geometry of the aligned surfaces, through their chemical reactions with water, produce the mechanical movements of the material structures. The special moisture-triggered activity of wood is not neutralized as a disruption, but acts as an essential functional component of the active material. In seed capsules and awns, the plant cellulose is more radically "mechanized": the capsules and awns resemble machines, with strong active torsion (caused by desiccation) and elongation (caused by moisture) functioning as reversible coded mechanisms.[56] In addition, they are able to release the energy stored in their structures in an explosive fashion, firing off seeds like small projectiles. The organism does not need to be alive for this activity to take place; it is present in dead material that has remained active. The material structure contains not only the code of its material functionality, but also the sensor for converting environmental moisture into signals, the motor for its activity, and the architecture or circuit board for the entire machinery. The interconnection of all these functions in the same material structure can be seen as the feature of an integrated machine that is far more advanced than all previously known machines.

The active material is not a substance that must be formed. Rather, its "consistency" must be viewed as a permanent process. This has fundamental consequences for design. After all, the dichotomy between coded activity and its inert material basis continues to be the unquestioned foundation of our modern culture. What's more, by focusing on electric energy, our modern technology has largely displaced other mechanical energy alternatives. This has had a profound impact on the reciprocal relationship between materials and energy as well as on

51 Nabih Faris and Robert Potter, eds. and trans., *Arab Archery: An Arabic manuscript of about A.D. 1500 "Book on the Excellence of the Bow and Arrow" and the Description thereof* (Princeton: Princeton University Press, 1945).

52 Haupt, *Bewegungsphysiologie der Pflanzen*, 136.

53 Peter Fratzl and Richard Weinkamer, "Nature's Hierarchical Materials," *Progress in Materials Science* 52 (2007): 1268.

54 "Wood swells anisotropically—largest size change in the direction of the annual growth rings (tangentially), less crosswise to the rings, and little in direction of the stem. In addition, different wood types swell differently." Patrick Höhne and K. Tauer, "Studies on Swelling of Wood in Water and Ionic Liquids," *Wood Science and Technology* 50, no. 2 (March 2016): 245–58, DOI:10.1007/s00226-015-0779-8.

55 The biological significance of water has long been known; see Haupt, "Wasseraufnahme und Wasserabgabe als Bewegungsmechanismus," in *Bewegungsphysiologie der Pflanzen*, 66–138. What has not been known, though, is the technical potential of water as a store of energy with its small dipole structure. See H. Lin, A. Rauf, N. Severin, I. M. Sokolov, and J. P. Rabe, "Influence of Interface Hydration on Sliding of Graphene and Molybdenum-Disulfide Single-Layers," *Journal of Colloid Interface Science* 540 (2019): 142–47.

56 Rivka Elbaum et al., "The Role of Wheat Awns in the Seed Dispersal Unit," *Science* 316, no. 5826 (May 11, 2007): 884–86.

their design options–as evidenced since the nineteenth century by industrialization, the standardized design of artifacts, as well as electrification and digitization.

Any design process that aims to use these structures and their intrinsic activity must begin deep within the material itself and perpetuate its inner logic. This makes the inner architecture of materials into the guiding principle of a mode of design that requires a diverse range of expertise, from biology to materials research, as it makes possible a new artifact-world that no longer manipulates and controls nature for human purposes, but converges with nature in an adaptive, nondestructive design process.

All of these possibilities are becoming visible today. They are not mere speculation, but a basic aspect of the Design Turn 2.0, which will take us beyond the programmable digital world and synthetic biology into a new material order of things. And because most biological materials are based on fiber structures, we can perhaps see weaving and braiding as the most elementary of cultural and natural practices. The practices linked to such active material operations are found mainly in traditional cultures, in and especially outside Western societies. For example, the Andean region is one of the largest reservoirs of traditional practices that incorporate the intrinsic activity of vegetable fibers into various processes, from spinning and weaving to patterning, while also integrating the media dimensions of process storage.[57] Even textiles have become active beings that can be equipped with features such as eyes, thus expanding the shift in perspective to include natural cultural objects.

These historical and transcultural shifts in perspective are just as important for the Design Turn 2.0 as are biomaterial expertise and the turn toward soft matter. Even within digital programming, a new type of code is emerging that will serve not as a command for humans to follow, but as a language that grows and writes itself as active symbolic matter.

If we succeed in transforming our results- and form-driven mode of design into a flexible, highly adaptable, and process-oriented practice that is able to combine technical and natural processes in a nondestructive manner, this type of design will indeed become comparable to traditional cultural practices that have evolved over longer periods—and to natural biological and evolutionary growth and development. However, the real challenge is that the urgency of our current situation makes it necessary for the Design Turn 2.0 to proceed at a faster pace for us to succeed in promptly initiating the much-needed design revolution based on the spirit of the material.

57 See Denise Arnold, Elvira Espejo, and Freddy Luis Maidana, *Tejiendo la vida: La colección textil del Museo Nacional de Etnografía y Folklore, según la cadena de producción* (La Paz: Museo Nacional de Etnografía y Folklore, 2013); and Lidia Carola Condarco Castellón de Medrano, *Fibras vivas: La colección de maderas y cestería del Museo Nacional de Etnografía y Folklore, según la cadena de producción* (La Paz: Museo Nacional de Etnografía y Folklore, 2017).

Form Given

Form Given

From the Invention of Manufacturing Processes to the Discovery of Matter

Emile De Visscher

Where do our consumer goods come from? What materials are they made of? How much energy do they consume? How far have they traveled? What waste products do they leave behind them? The contemporary ecological emergency urges us to take a closer look at the manufacturing processes of our material goods and examine their ecological impact. Instead of the environment being seen as a place made of thousands of forms and products people live among, it is worthwhile considering it as constituted of countless *formations* and *productions*. From this angle, material, long thought of as stable, isomorphic, predictable, solid, is replaced by matter—composite, evolving, perishable, malleable, and corrosive. In this way, the world gains in dynamism and matter reasserts its rights and its history.[1]

The networks of energy, transport, and waste, their extraction, transmutation, conditions of production and end in landfills, are virtually a closed book.[2] This ignorance, already pointed out by the philosopher Gilbert Simondon,[3] *disempowers* us, in the sense that Donna Haraway gives the term—that is to say, it *de-response-ibilizes* us.[4] It prevents us from seeing links between banal consumer goods and the huge global catastrophes around us (the new "plastic continent" in the ocean; the increase in Earth's average temperature; the acceleration in the melting of the icecaps, etc.), and thus from gauging the impact of our behavior on them. Every time I buy a bottle of water, I immediately initiate PET polymerization, launch a blow-molding machine, and turn on an oil pump. Production systems, essential links in the distribution channels, determine our carbon footprint, but their logics, alternatives, and limits remain out of sight.

How can knowledge of them be made more widely available? How can we coax machines out of their privately owned factories and turn them into "public things"?[5] How can they be made more comprehensible and become a subject of public debate, so they can be selected or modified by collective decision? As Carl DiSalvo shows in his interpretation of the work of John Dewey,[6] publics can only be constructed when the underlying challenges posed by a problem are understood, experienced, and shared.

1 Tim Ingold, "Toward an Ecology of Materials," *Annual Review of Anthropology*, no. 41 (2012): 427–42, here 435.

2 Sebastian Hackenschmidt, "Performance Approaches to Furniture Production," in *Keil und Kübel: Breaded Escalope*, ed. Katarina Schildgen (Vienna: DESK, 2016), 222–24, here 222.

3 Gilbert Simondon, *On the Mode of Existence of Technical Objects*, trans. Cecile Malespina and John Rogrove (Minneapolis: Univocal Publishing, 2017), 21.

4 Donna Haraway, "Sympoièse, SF, Embrouilles multispécifiques," in *Gestes spéculatifs* / Colloque de Cerisy, ed. Didier Debaise and Isabelle Stengers (Dijon: Les Presses du réel, 2015), 42–72, here 47.

5 Bruno Latour, "Composing the Political Arts: on the Modes of Being of Artworks and Their Public," interview with Samuel Bianchini and Jean-Paul Fourmentraux, in *Practicable: From Participation to Interaction in Contemporary Art*, ed. Samuel Bianchini and Erik Verhagen (Cambridge, MA: MIT Press, 2016), 771–80, here 774.

6 Carl DiSalvo, "Design and the Construction of Publics," *Design Issues* 25, no. 1 (Winter 2009): 48–63.

It is moreover in our sensory relationship to the technological that designers act—design being understood here as a discipline specializing in the articulation between humans and nonhumans.

> *For a thousand books on the benefits of objective knowledge—and the mortal risks that challenging it would entail—there are not ten on technology—and not three that signal the mortal danger we risk by not loving them.*[7]

I dare hope that herein lies a unique opportunity: that of inventing new production tools governed, not solely by efficiency and economy, but also by certain political, social, historical, aesthetic, and symbolic characteristics. Leaving the purely technical situation of the factory, machines would then take their place in environments conforming to other patterns of thinking, with other actors, linked to different sensibilities. In various ways, my work explores the discrepancies in which the invention of a new machine participates in the creation of a hybrid ontology. The aim is to find common ground between the entertainment machine—where it is governed solely by its effects—and the machine-tool, conditioned uniquely by the effectiveness of its action on matter.

The development of such objects demands a lengthy process of trial and error, both during the development process in the studio and in the transfer and collective interchange phases. The following images show the various formative stages during which the materials are shaped, implemented, placed in a setting, and, finally, treated as a subject of debate.

7 Bruno Latour, *An Inquiry into Modes of Existence* (Cambridge, MA: Harvard University Press, 2013), 209.

Fig. 1: Emile De Visscher, Biofoam experimentations, Saint-Denis, 2016.

Invention and Failure

Invention is above all the story of failure. As with writing, invention occurs on the horizon of understanding where knowledge is played off against ignorance. The game of question-and-answer, which Tim Ingold calls "transduction,"[8] often leads to a dead end. In my five-year project to produce a bio-sourced water-based foam capable of solidifying, I have tried out more than 400 different product mixtures (fig. 1). I still haven't reached my goal, however, a fact that immediately raises the question of the criteria of success: when can an experiment be considered as successful? And what if unexpected reactions of a material transform the initial hypothesis? Working with matter often entails a measure of improvisation or "poaching." It's all about tricks and dodges, about borrowing or adapting solutions from other fields, about losing oneself in one's experiments so as to discover ways of manipulating a material's behavior. Invention is profoundly "bricological"[9]: it implies accumulating, drifting, ceaselessly making new combinations.

8 Tim Ingold, *Making: Anthropology, Archeology, Art and Architecture* (London: Taylor and Francis, 2013), 102.

9 See Thomas Golsenne and Patricia Ribault, eds., *Essais de bricologie. Ethnologie de l'art et du design contemporains, Techniques et Culture* 64 (Paris: Éditions EHESS, 2015).

Scientific Research and Developing Forms

In developing my projects, I have had numerous opportunities to collaborate with scientists. For the project *Petrification*, whose aim was to transform cellulose into rock, I had the chance to work with a group of chemistry students over an entire year. Our goal was to improve and optimize both the compounds used and the material's mechanical and thermal characteristics. Initially, tests were limited to small, square samples of petrified paper. But, working independently, the students started shaping the pieces of paper. Using tweezers, they produced origami in the petrified form of birds, dragons, and boats (fig. 2). Each test was not then solely an experiment in chemistry—it also became an experience in sculpture. The *Petrification* project is intended simply to lead to a new type of ceramics based on paper and cardboard, materials known and accessible to all. In the working environment, the young chemists, although they had merely been asked to optimize the technical specifications, started undertaking formal research, thereby validating the appeal of the new process to creative appropriation.

Fig. 2: Chimie ParisTech Students, *Petrified origami*, w. Emile De Visscher, 2016.

The Advent of New Machines

In our search for stable processes, the apparatuses are constructed progressively. Some elements are bought off the shelf (below, a cylindrical ceramic kiln), before being transformed, adapted, drilled, resealed... We constantly found ourselves taking the roundabout way, employing expedients and having to return to basic principles. In the *Petrification* project, firing takes place in an atmosphere at 1400°C. To attain this temperature, I adapted a classic ceramic kiln, adding an argon injection system. To ensure the absence of oxygen during pyrolysis, however, the kiln has to work in overpressure, necessitating a variable pressure valve. In the end, the solution proved remarkably simple: a tube inserted into a jar of water. To escape, the gas needs to acquire sufficient pressure to expel the water from the tube and produce bubbles. The amount of water in the jar indicates the pressure in the tank. This is a very simple example of an improvised solution that is at once effective and controllable in the experimental environment (fig. 3).

Fig. 3: Emile De Visscher, *Petrification furnace*, La Courneuve, 2018.

The Flexible, the Fragile, the Composite

All my projects explore pliable, anisotropic,[10] and composite forms of matter: foams, suspensions, clusters of fibers (fig. 4a), sheets. I am moving further and further away from my background in materials science, which focuses mainly on metals, ceramics, and polymers (fig. 4b), all of which are thought of as noble substances: dense, solid, permanent, waiting patiently to be shaped and which can be relied upon to conserve their form. Things are quite different with foam, as Peter Sloterdijk has described: "Upsurging forces are expressed in foam that are inevitably disconcerting to friends of solid states [...]; what had seemed autonomous, homogeneous and solid is transformed into loosened structures. [...] Foam is actually existing deception—the non-entity as an entity nonetheless, or a feigner of being, a symbol of the First False, an emblem for the undermining of the solid by the untenable."[11]

Fig. 4a: Emile De Visscher, Audrey Gaulard, Nick Paget, Christophe Machet, Polyfloss closeup, La Courneuve, 2018.

Fig. 4b (overleaf): Vascularizations of PMMA by partial discharge method, LSI Lab, École Polytechnique, Palaiseau, 2020.

10 Anisotropy is the property of being direction-dependent. An anisotropic material will have different characteristics depending on its orientation, while an isotropic material will appear identical in all directions. Typically, a textile is anisotropic while a block of plastic is isotropic.

11 Peter Sloterdijk, *Spheres*, vol. 3, *Foams: Plural Spherology*, trans. Wieland Hoban (Cambridge, MA: MIT Press, 2016), 28–30.

1/2mm
0.2m
FACOM
1051
.03
INOX

8
9
10
11
12
13
14
15

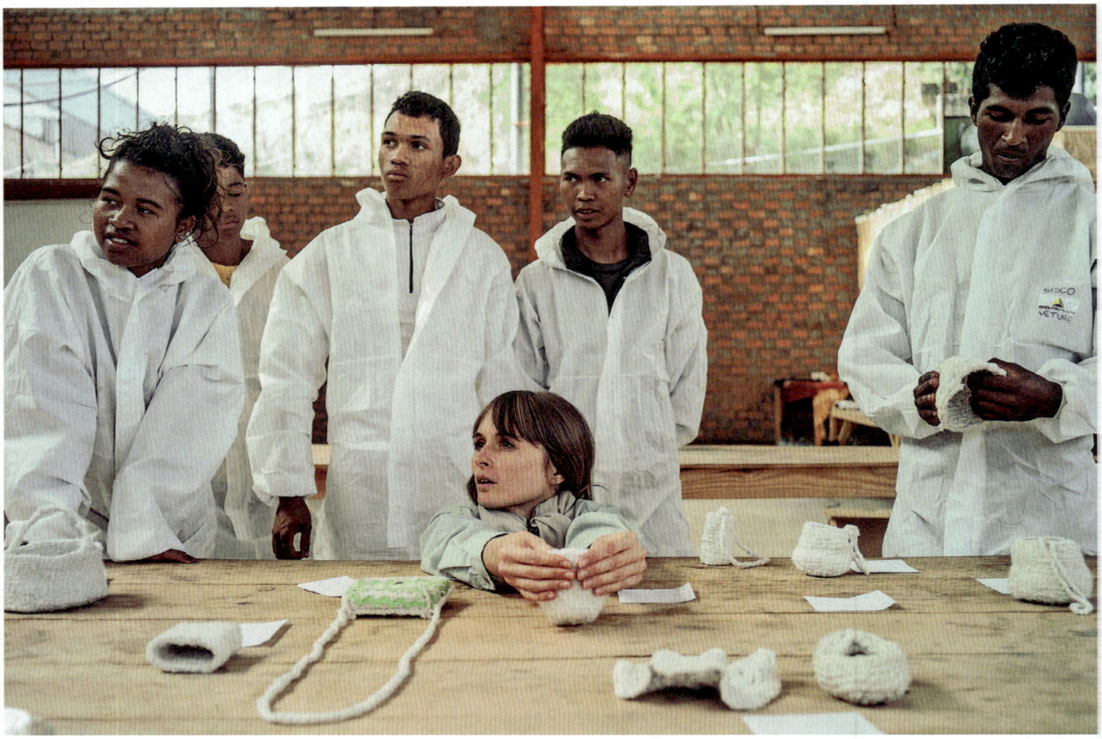

Fig. 5: N'Dao Hanavao, Polyfloss in Madagascar, lab visit by Laureline Gaillot, 2019.

Transfer and Localization

"A technical project is neither realist nor unrealistic: it takes on reality, or loses it, by degrees."[12] With respect to machines invented in a research context, the question of where they are sited and what spaces they occupy is crucial. The *Polyfloss Factory* project—centering on a new machine for recycling thermoplastic into fibers that is based on the principle of making candy floss—has ventured beyond the university setting to progressively gain in reality in accordance with the quotation from Bruno Latour above. Initially a student project (devised by A. Gaulard, N. Paget, C. Machet, and myself), before traveling on to exhibitions, workshops, and galleries, it has since been gradually applied in more concrete contexts, finally giving rise in an operational plastic recycling plant in Madagascar (fig. 5). With help from a corporate foundation and local NGOs, we picked a team of young people to train on the machine, drew up a business plan, and contacted people to collect the plastic, in the end producing "wool" and various objects using the machine. These young operators now work autonomously and sell recycled products in stores and markets in the Malagasy capital.

12 Bruno Latour, *Aramis or the Love of Technology*, trans. C. Porter (Cambridge, MA: Harvard University Press, 1992), 85.

Transitional Objects

To merely come up with a manufacturing process is rarely sufficient to convince people of its full potential in terms of economy and use. More often than not, one has first to produce a series of objects that make clear the formal and technical possibilities offered by an invention. Paradoxically, these objects (fig. 6) cannot yet be described as "products": they are often too frail, unstable, and difficult to manufacture. The design of these objects therefore presents a particularly difficult balancing act: the challenge is to come up with objects suggestive of various uses, but which, since they do not yet correspond to a practical reality, eschew rigid typologies. They are *transitory* objects in the sense that their forms go beyond the standard material sample stage and hint at other potential applications: they include structural prototypes, assemblages, micro-architectures, textural combinations—harbingers of world making. Their purpose is to firm up the link between the process and its potential for functioning materialization and to propose typologies relevant to technical operation.

Fig. 6: Emile De Visscher, *Pearling collection v1*, SACRe, EnsadLab, 2018.

The Public Unveiling of the Forms Unveiled

Making these developments public is a key aspect of my work. As well as sharing the results of our research, it also provides a platform for the evaluation of their underlying assumptions. The *Pearling* project uses a machine to produce a layer of artificial mother-of-pearl by soaking aragonite and biopolymer in a tank of water. With each dip, a few microns of the composite accrete at the base of the nacre, meaning that the process is almost as time-consuming as it is for natural pearls. The high degree of maintenance required by the machine led me to visit the site more and more often. Gradually, I became as one with my installation and discussions with the public became more and more frequent (fig. 7). Some visitors criticized the apparatus, since it mechanizes a natural process. Particularly instructive debates followed on the relationship between nature and culture, and on species ethics, slowness, and the symbolism of purity.

Translated from the French by David Radzinowicz

Fig. 7: Emile De Visscher, Pearling machine in the exhibition *ALIVE*, Fondation EDF, Paris, 2014.

Toward an Archaeology of Hanro's Design Processes of Underwear Production in the 1930s

Leonie Häsler

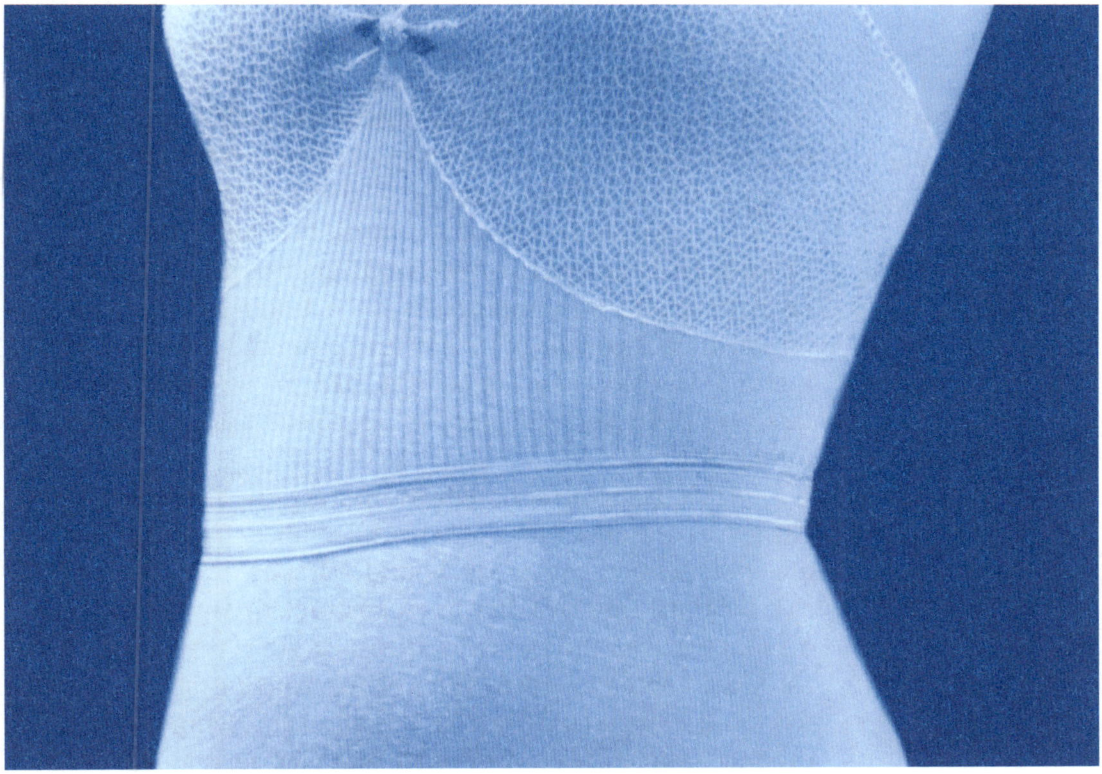

What can we possibly learn by investigating undershirts, a standard product that looks the same nearly every season?[1] If we examine the collection of fabric samples compiled by the underwear manufacturer Hanro, we find that, contrary to expectations, there is a much broader range of designs than the archetypal white double-rib undershirt might suggest.[2] Fashion and aesthetic factors are not the only reason for this diversity, as I will explain. In the twentieth century, the industrial design process for underwear was shaped by technical and economic conditions, as well as by shifts in clothing practices and concepts of body shaping. This essay uses a historical case study to illustrate the design process for women's undershirts.

A finished garment displayed in a boutique or held in a museum storeroom reveals little about the conditions governing its design and production or about the alternative designs that may have been rejected for economic reasons. Furthermore, as soon as the garment is put on, it shapes the body not only physically but socially. "Design is invisible," wrote the Swiss planning theorist Lucius Burckhardt in a deliberately paradoxical statement. By "invisible" Burckhardt meant the social dimension of design, the unseen mechanisms that objects trigger in the production process and in interactions with people. He argued that, in the design phase, these mechanisms should be considered, made conscious, questioned, and redesigned.[3] Burckhardt advanced two theses: "On design: objects owe their form to the interactions inherent to the design process. And on consumption: such objects in turn exert influence on social interaction; objects are not neutral; *Tools for Conviviality* exist (asserts Illich!), as do their opposites, objects that impede social interaction."[4]

How can we describe these interactions and conscious design processes as they apply to undershirts? Design processes are ephemeral in nature and bound to a specific place and a specific time. How can they be reconstructed? My study is based on sources from the Hanro archives. Hanro is the brand associated with the Handschin & Ronus knitting factory, founded in Liestal, Switzerland, in 1884. Initially, Handschin & Ronus produced corset covers for women and thermal undershirts for

1 I would like to thank Jörg Petruschat for his critical reading of this essay.
2 Part of the sample collection has been digitized and can be viewed under "Kulturgüterkatalog Baselland" at Kulturgüterportal Baselland, https://www.kimweb.ch/sammlungen.
3 See Lucius Burckhardt, "Design Is Invisible (1980)," in *Lucius Burckhardt Writings: Rethinking Man-Made Environments: Politics, Landscape and Design*, ed. Jesko Fezer and Martin Schmitz (Boston: De Gruyter, 2012), 153–65.
4 Burckhardt, "Design Is Invisible," 159, emphasis in the original; in the quoted passage, Burckhardt refers to Ivan Illich's work *Tools for Conviviality* (New York: Harper and Row, 1973).

men and children from fabrics made on mechanical knitting machines. Over the years, it added nightwear and underwear sets to its product range, and in the 1930s, it began offering women's knit outerwear as well. Well into the 1980s, the company was extremely successful, exporting its products around the world. However, in 1991 it fell victim to the crisis in the European textile and clothing industry and was sold to an Austrian textile manufacturer. The company archives, including advertising material, remained in Switzerland, along with design and production documents and its sample fabric collection. From its founding, Handschin & Ronus assembled a collection of every product it made. Consisting of around 20,000 objects and a document archive,[5] it is now owned by the Museum.BL, run by the Canton of Basel-Landschaft. Sources from the collection formed the starting point of my study of the design assemblage of the women's undershirts produced by Hanro in the 1930s. What factors lent the undershirts their final form and who took part in the design process?

Many of the decisions that lead to an object's final design can no longer be pieced together by outsiders, but reveal much about the object's embeddedness in the broader social, aesthetic, economic, and technical context and about the way the object is used. The following case studies aim to reconstruct the design process for undershirts, particularly for camisoles. Although the Hanro collection contains drawings of camisole models from a variety of periods, not all steps in the design process were archived, meaning that the design documentation is incomplete. I will therefore focus on the design drawings from 1939 and fashion photographs from the 1930s, which are well documented in the archive. I intend to describe the creative process from the designer's perspective in order to establish the parameters for undershirt design. Undershirts are manufactured from knit fabrics, which are elastic and afford greater comfort. Because of the fabrics' role, I will explain the significance of knitting machines in the industrial design process (figs. 1, 2, & 3). Undershirts receive their final shape from the person wearing them. What role do ideals of the human body play in the design process? In what way is the design of undergarments similar to that of outerwear? These questions are addressed in figs. 4 and 5.

5 For more information, see "Hanro-Sammlung" at https://www.museum.bl.ch/uploads/files/website/Hanro_Infoblatt.pdf.

Serial Sketching and Serial Production

Industrial production involves not the hand-crafting of individual items on the basis of a design, but the manufacture of a predefined quantity of identical, standardized products by various specialized machines and/or people—often on an assembly line. Barring technical malfunctions, machines guarantee uniform, replicable shapes and qualities. Underwear—including undershirts and underpants—is a typical mass-produced product in the clothing industry. Everyone is familiar with the simple white double-rib or single jersey styles. These are supplemented by seasonal articles whose colors and cuts are based on outerwear fashions.

My working thesis is that knitting machines and serial production are inscribed in the design of the underwear types. In other words, the series functions as a creative principle of design. This supposition is based on a binder from the Hanro collection containing undershirt drawings from 1939, some of which are presented in figs. 1a and 1b. Each drawing shows the front of an undershirt. Various strategies could be used to create variations on the front to formally and aesthetically distinguish the shirt from others in the series. This section of the undershirt required the most attention in the design process. If we assume that the binder's function was to record all the important information for the production or reproduction of the individual undershirt types, we can conclude that the back of the textile itself and the drawn undershirt was, by contrast, of minor importance. When the twenty-one undershirt types are compared to one another or across collections (fig. 1a), one feature catches the eye: there is a range of basic forms (*façons*) that apparently remained constant for years. A limited number of basic types meets the criteria of streamlined, standardized production. The elements that transformed the shirts into fashionable garments were the different colors and the use of lace in the bust area.

Generally speaking, a series is characterized by the contrasting concepts of repetition and deviation (or repetition and variation). The same applies to design drawings. Even though the female designer probably did not use stencils, there are striking formal similarities between her drawings, suggesting that the task of drawing different shirt designs was a practiced and routine activity for her. It is possible that she copied the designs onto tracing paper, which she then used to make new variations. In other words, not only were the standardized shirts mass-produced and copied, but the drawings themselves were created with efficient reproduction and duplication methods.

A characteristic feature of the designer's work is that she created not individual designs, but serial designs for the production of a series in a collection. The series has a paradoxical relationship with fashion. Fashion creations are stylized as originals but do not acquire cult status until the duplication process. The series is the opposite of the one-off piece, which it negates. In a series, there is no original. At best, there is an archetype that serves as the foundation for experimentation and variations. Through the creation of variations, the timeless archetype becomes a fashionable object—modification makes fashion. At the same time, the archetype is seen as a design ideal and stylized into a timeless classic.[6]

The designer designed series of shirts for mass production. The machinery provided the framework for her designs. In contrast to outerwear production, knitting machines handled a large part of the process. There are two types of

6 For a study of the emergence of industrial design in the early twentieth century, see Anne Sudrow, "Der Typus als Ideal der Formgebung: Zur Entstehung der professionellen Produktgestaltung von industriellen Konsumgütern (1914–1933)," *Technikgeschichte* 76, no. 3 (2009): 191–210.

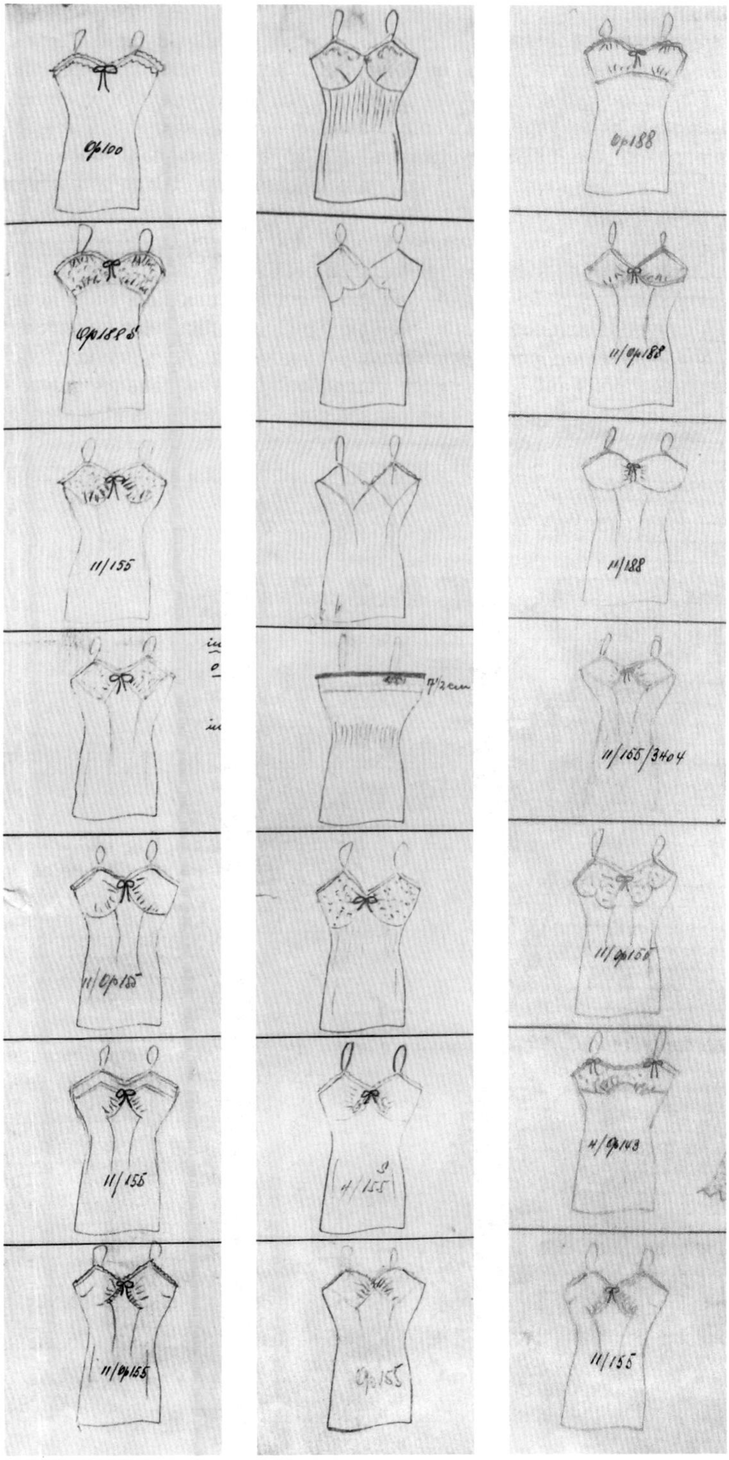

Fig. 1a (left): Design drawings for camisoles from the 1939 collection of Hanro.

Fig. 1b (bottom): A single sheet from the binder of the 1939 collection of Hanro.

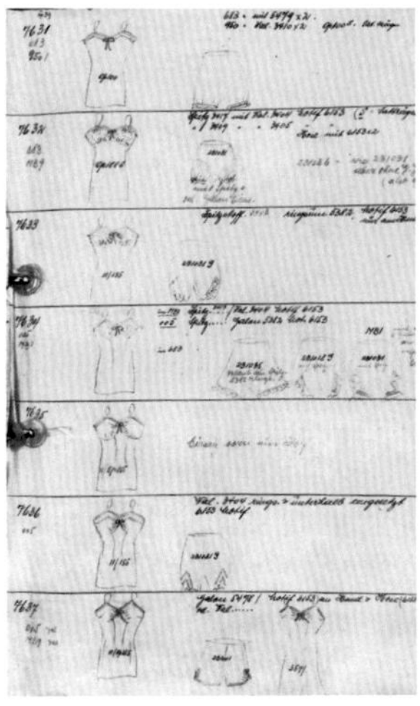

knitting machines, flat and circular, and both were and continue to be used in underwear production. For example, in the manufacture of fully fashioned goods, the number of stitches is increased or decreased to attain a specific shape. The machine knits individual sections of a pattern, which no longer need to be cut, but merely sewn together (fig. 2). In a complementary process, small circular knitting machines knit tubes in body widths that require less subsequent processing (fig. 3). Both techniques save material and time and are supported by a complex array of machines.

Knitting machines are relevant not only from a technical perspective because of their ability to knit semifinished and finished goods, but also due to the design options they make possible and the immaterial messages they incorporate and convey. These immaterial messages include promises of elasticity, snugness, shape retention, and seamlessness. In the twentieth century, knitwear shaped the perceptions and ideals of the human body that we take for granted today.[7] The "stitch" brings together humans, technology, design, and material. Figuratively speaking, technology and design meet at the knitting machine.

Fig. 2: A machine operator at Hanro checks a knitted fabric intended for a pair of ski underpants; a flat knitting machine is visible in the background. The photograph was taken in 1958.

7 See Monika Burri, *Bodywear: Geschichte der Trikotkleidung, 1850–2000* (Zurich: Chronos, 2012).

Fig. 3: Small circular knitting machines at Hanro producing seamless tubes. The photograph was taken in the 1970s.

Marketing New Styles: Fashion Silhouettes and Female Body Shaping in the 1930s

The classic undershirt we know today is an invention of the 1920s. Underpants in their current form are an even more recent phenomenon. After the First World War, the lifestyle of many European women changed fundamentally—and, with it, their fashions. The fashion silhouette for women was modernized.[8] Instead of voluminous ankle-length skirts, narrow-waisted garments, and corsets, women wore clothes in which they could move about more freely. This period saw the emergence of functional dress suits, coat dresses, and women's sweaters. Skirts became shorter, falling just above the knee, and corsets disappeared completely. Instead of forcing their bodies into unnatural shapes with the help of constricting garments such as corsets, women did physical exercise to create the body shapes they desired. The ideal figure was boyish, athletic, and slender—attributes that fashions emphasized. Women showed more skin, as evidenced by a new style of beach and swimwear called "beach pajamas" (fig. 5). This new treatment of the body and the accompanying change in women's outerwear made new undergarments necessary (fig. 4).[9] Underwear was no longer intended only to support or warm the body or to protect outerwear from perspiration or other body fluids, but to emphasize the body's natural shapes. Ideally, it was not supposed to look bulky due to excessive volume or too many seams. Light jerseys of artificial silk were popular. The shape of the upper body determined the design of the undershirt. At the same time, the elasticity of knit fabrics allowed them to adapt to individual body shapes.

Since the emergence of the ready-to-wear industry, our bodies have had to conform to predefined, globally applicable sizes and ideals of beauty, athleticism, and slenderness. In the 1930s, Hanro produced most of its women's undershirts in only three sizes: S, M, and L. With these three sizes, though, the company was able to produce clothes for a larger variety of body sizes due to the elasticity of the fabric. The smaller range of sizes needed by knitwear companies brought clear

8 Ibid., 182.
9 Cecil Willet Cunnington and Phillis Cunnington, *The History of Underclothes*, new rev. ed. (London: Faber and Faber, 1981), 149.

financial and logistical advantages over woven goods. Knitwear made it easier to serve a global market with different average body sizes. This factor contributed to the boom in the outerwear segment of the European knitwear industry in the late 1920s.

It is not known who was responsible for the design and creation of the Hanro collections in the period up to the mid-1920s. At the time, there was evidently no separate department for such activities. All of this changed in 1926, when Charles Albert Ronus joined the family-run business that had been cofounded by his father, Carl Ronus. Charles had spent a long time in the United States, where he had worked in a hosiery factory and learned modern marketing methods. Design criteria were establishing themselves as a key factor in purchase decisions, and it was becoming increasingly important for products to stand out from the competition through their design.[10] Such insights probably convinced Charles Albert Ronus to revamp Hanro's product range. He expanded the white double-rib woolen items typical of Hanro to include colored, patterned pieces. In addition, the company began knitting artificial silk into much finer fabrics in order to remain competitive domestically and abroad. The expanded product range made it necessary to purchase new Jacquard knitting machines. It was in this period that the designer in charge was mentioned by name for the first time in Hanro's records, suggesting that design had previously played a subordinate role to technology and quality. All of this changed with the undershirt designs created in the late 1920s. They were the work of the same designer responsible for the styles in fig. 1.

Translated from the German by Adam Blauhut

Fig. 4: Hanro underwear set from the 1930s. The camisole has the typical bra shape—a novelty at the time.

10 See Hartmut Berghoff, Philip Scranton, and Uwe Spiekermann, eds., *The Rise of Marketing and Market Research* (New York: Palgrave Macmillan, 2012).

Fig. 5: Knitted beachwear designed by Hanro, 1930s.

The Discreet Charm of Typography

Thomas Huct-Marchand

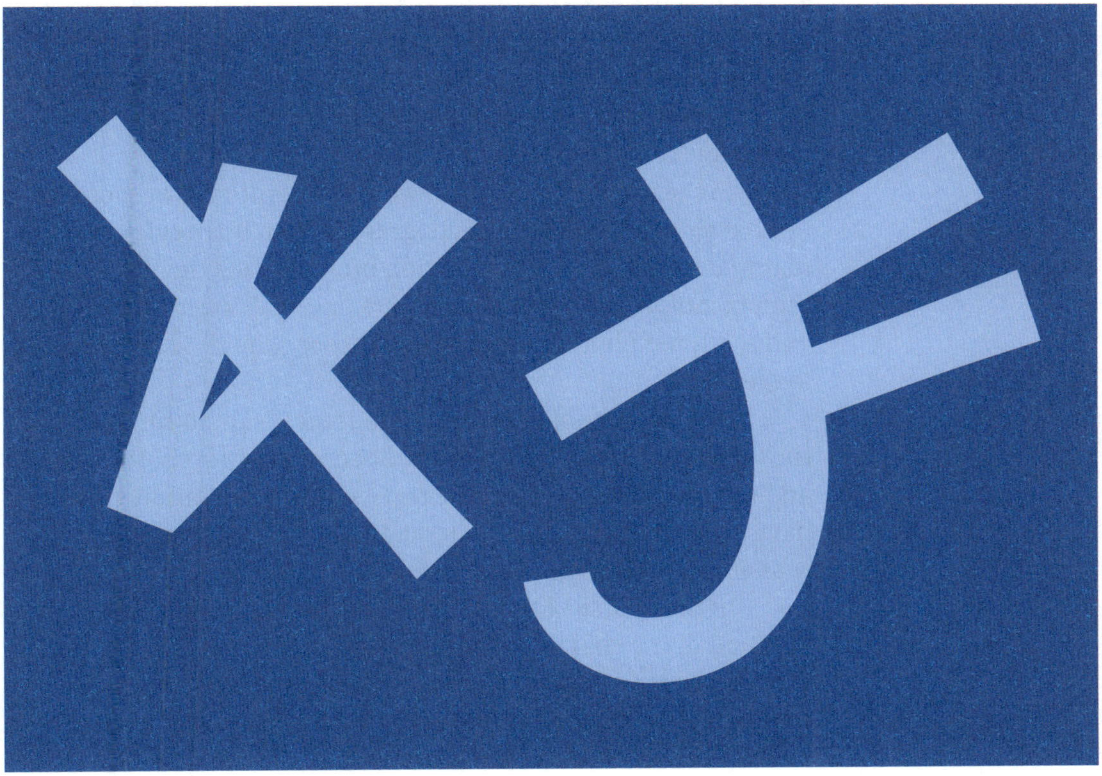

Typeface design is a conservative discipline: heir to a history longer than that of design itself, its shape bends to the uses it has been tasked with over the years. It is rarely revolutionary, for the sake of the reader and the pact of readability that binds them. To these functional limits a singular temporality is added: it is an iterative and cumulative discipline. Typefaces come and go, but never quite disappear. And if they do, they are never safe from resurrection.

In the third quarter of the fifteenth century, in a very short time, the first punchcutters accomplished a major project: that of fixing the contours of handwriting in a deferred, mechanized way, allowing texts to be multiplied. Typefaces were logically inspired by the handwritten scripts in use at the time, but also differed in many ways. The immediate and continuous gesture of the manuscript was modified by the fragmentation of the typographic composition; the thick and thin strokes produced by the calligraphic tool were replaced by the firm and definitive contours of steel punches. By 1470 the archetypal form of the typographic roman can be considered fixed, by Nicolas Jenson, in Venice. Except for a few cosmetic refinements, the technique itself remained almost unchanged until the end of the nineteenth century and the advent of hot-metal composition.

In the second half of the twentieth century, two successive upheavals gradually freed typography from its previous material limits. Photocomposition brought back the text to two dimensions: the film suppressed the physical constraints of lead and rendered photographic deformations. The transfer was no longer direct.

Digital technologies completed this disembodiment of the text: letterforms are now described in vectors, coordinates, and relative units. At the same time, editing and publishing tools have been multiplied and democratized, making typography available to everyone.

In the course of these transformations, however, the forms of typographic characters have remained surprisingly stable. Thus, fifteenth-century typefaces have bravely survived centuries, undergoing various technological adaptations, without their appearance disturbing the contemporary reader.

How does one explain such permanence? And what can justify the creation of new typefaces today, currently more intense than ever?

Let's be frank: it is rarely about solving a problem. Technologies available to compose texts are relatively stable, and reading habits are deeply established. Instead, perhaps this is due to something else.

First, type design has a very different economy and temporality than graphic design: the design of typefaces is, in a way, a deferred creation. A potential creation, which is only realized later on, by other designers, and with other texts. This discrete character ensures its plasticity and a rare ubiquity.

Typeface design is, to me, a desire for expression—I would even say narration. It is not expressed with semantic means: after all, typography is only the visible form of language. Its power is exercised on the surface of words, in the interval between visible and readable: in a "second text," linked to the materiality of its editorial enunciation.[1] A discrete charm, as in Buñuel's film or as in discrete mathematics and geometry. A world of tiny forms, in black and white, at the edge of meaning, which carries at the same time centuries of two separate but parallel histories: that of the forms of the letters of our alphabet, colored simultaneously with all of the stories told, and those we are still telling, with typefaces.

1 The editorial enunciation thus forms a "secondary text" insofar as "the signifier is not constituted by the words of the language ('primary text'), but by the materiality of the support and of the writing, the organization of the text, its formatting"; see Emmanuël Souchier, "L'image du texte. Pour une théorie de l'énonciation éditoriale," *Les Cahiers de médiologie* 6, no. 2 (1998): 137–45 (translated by the author).

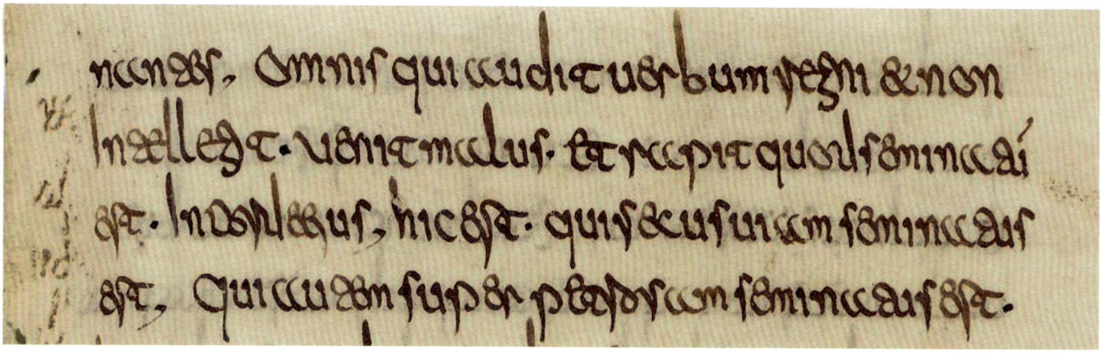

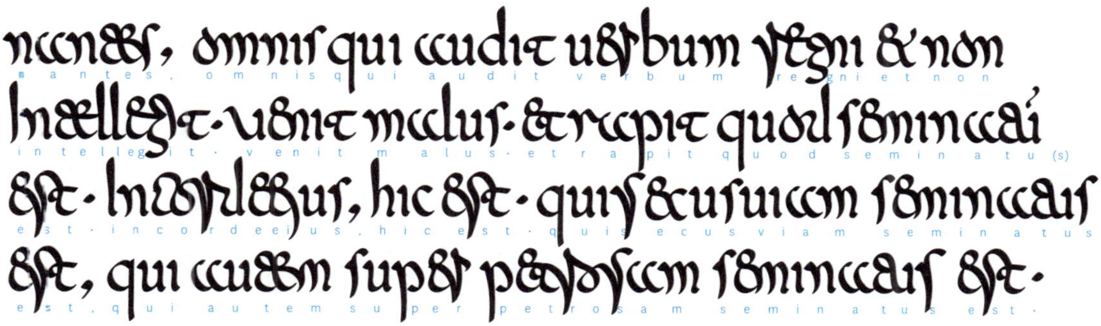

Fig. 1a (top right): *Lectionnaire de Luxeuil* (detail), early seventh century, folio 172. Paris, BnF.

Fig. 1b (bottom right): Typographic transcription. Thomas Huot-Marchand, 2015.

Fig. 1c (opposite): Typographic transcription (detail). Thomas Huot-Marchand, 2015.

Luxeuil Handwriting's Transcription

The Luxeuil handwriting is one of the rarest Latin scripts: it appears in less than forty manuscripts in the world, on fewer than 1,500 pages. More than a third of these are those of the *Lectionnaire de Luxeuil* (fig. 1a), produced by the scribes of the monastery of Luxeuil, in Eastern France. This Merovingian script from the beginning of the seventh century is derived from uncial, half-uncial, and roman cursive models: before the advent of the Carolingian Minuscule, it is considered as one of the first formal minuscule. The flow of the handwriting is noticeable, with numerous ligatures that connect 2, 3, and up to 4 letters in the same character.

Intrigued by this local unknown script, created a few kilometers from my home, I studied it with my friend Claude-Laurent François and tried to design a digital typeface out of it in 2014. I had to understand the ductus (the movement of the hand tracing the letters) and then to reproduce the gesture and stroke of the pen. Rather than drawing the outlines, I digitized the inner skeleton, and applied afterwards a virtual elliptic pen. This dynamic approach allowed me to catch the color and rhythm of the pages of the *Lectionnaire* and to create the very large number of ligatures contained in this handwriting: these ligatures are created automatically with initial, medial, or final contextual forms (figs. 1b, 1c).

Fig. 2 (opposite): Jérôme Knebusch, Almost typeface, published by Poem (2020–21).

Almost: Between Gothic and Roman

Based on in-depth research, the typeface Almost (fig. 2) was designed by Jérôme Knebusch from 2012 to 2019 in five weights and two styles, Gothic and Roman, and completed in 2021 with respective italics. Almost takes its inspiration from the fifteenth century, in the period of the 1460s and 1470s with German Gotico-Antiqua typefaces like the Durandus of Fust & Schöffer, the first type to be inspired by the handwriting of the humanists, probably based on the hand of Petrarch. A few years later, Sweynheim & Pannartz ushered in Subiaco, a type which some consider to be the first roman, although its gothic influences remain clearly visible. Roman type was finally defined in 1469–70 in Venice by the 'de Spira' brothers and Nicolas Jenson. But roman did not precipitate the death of gothic forms: mixtures of gothic and roman were tried out and the two coexisted for some time. Almost is a homage to these types, which represent a unique, transitory moment in history of typography.

Almost's fonts can be endlessly combined, starting either from roman or gothic ground, without falling in a strong, broken script nor becoming a "pure" roman design. Uncialesque and bizarre (Byzantine) letterforms and a full set of initials complete the family. They can be activated through stylistic features and offer more possibilities of gothic-roman hybridizations.

Between 2015 and 2019, Jérôme Knebusch led the Gotico-Antiqua research project at the Atelier national de recherche typographique (ANRT) in Nancy. By studying the first incunabula, fifteen fonts were created during a series of workshop sessions conducted between 2015 and 2018 in art and design schools across France, Germany, and Italy, with more than 150 students. The digital typefaces are the result of a thorough analysis and redesign of the originals, and are published under an Open Source license.[2] The exhibition catalogue and the proceedings of the two-day international symposium in Nancy (April 25–26, 2019) were published in 2021.[3]

2 See *Gotico-Antiqua*, http://gotico-antiqua.anrt-nancy.fr (accessed July 23, 2021).

3 Christelle Kirchstetter, Thomas Huot-Marchand, and Jérôme Knebusch, eds., *Gotico-Antiqua, Proto-Roman, Hybrid: 15th-Century Types between Gothic and Roman* (Nancy: Ensad-ANRT; Frankfurt am Main: Poem; Dijon: Les Presses du réel, 2021).

The Mainz Psalter
The Mainz Psalter
The Mainz Psalter
The Mainz Psalter
The Mainz Psalter
The Mainz Psalter
The Mainz Psalter
The Mainz Psalter
The Mainz Psalter

Roman
Roman
Roman
Roman
Roman

Roman Variations

Fig. 3 (opposite): Roman Text (line 1), Dual (2–3) and Skeleton (4–5), Thomas Huot-Marchand, 2019.

Fig. 4 (overleaf): Ontographs and allographs of characters A, Alpha, Alef and Aleph in PIM fonts. Elvire Volk Leonovitch, Morgane Pierson / ANRT 2014–2021.

Roman started in Rome, when I was resident fellow at the French Academy, Villa Medici, as a series of experiments on strokes and structures of the roman alphabet. I investigated the theories of Gerrit Noordzij,[4] a Dutch calligrapher and type designer, who published in the 1970s a seminal book, *The Stroke of the Pen*, in which he analyzes the typographic shapes through the scope of handwriting. Different tools and gestures create different kinds of contours.

The first "roman" typefaces, in the fifteenth century, were adapted from humanistic handwriting, then traced with a broad-nib pen. This tool creates a kind of contrast called *translation*: the internal skeleton, which corresponds to the hand gesture, is split into two parallel lines, the angle and distance of which depend on the inclination and thickness of the tool.

I experimented with the limits of this framework by applying pure translations to single-line letterforms. Roman typeface uses the OpenType variable fonts technology (1.8) jointly developed by Microsoft, Google, Apple, and Adobe, released in late 2016. It allows one to store multiple individual fonts (for example, Regular, Bold, Condensed, Extended…) within a single font file by defining variations of axes within the font.

In this case (fig. 3), Roman variation axes (stress and weight) simulate parameters of the virtual pen (angle and thickness), expressed in the font data as movements of outline nodes.

PIM: The Forms of Monetary Inscriptions

The PIM research project (Polices pour les Inscriptions Monétaires) aims to produce a suitable tool for transcribing the information contained on monetary inscriptions beyond their semantic content. The textual information and graphic features that a coin carries can provide much valuable information regarding its origin and the society in which it was minted. Since there were previously no digital fonts that could fully and accurately render the monetary inscriptions, this project was initiated in 2013 by Florence Codine in the Département Monnaies et Médailles at the Bibliothèque nationale de France (BnF); it is currently supervised by Frédérique Duyrat.

During the first phase, in 2014–15, Elvire Volk Leonovitch developed at the ANRT a Latin typeface which includes every ontograph (the reference glyph) and allograph (the stylistic variants of a given ontograph) identified in the collection of Merovingian coins (fig. 4).

In 2019 the PIM project was extended to support other collections of antique coins from Italy, Greece, Spain, North Africa, and the Middle East. Morgane Pierson has been tasked with designing typefaces for Phoenician, Cypriot, Archaic Greek, Etruscan, Umbrian, Oscan, Paleo-hispanic, Lycian, Paleo-Hebrew, Kharoshthi, and Nabatean writing systems. PIM fonts include 2440 glyphs, and this number is expected to grow even larger as the project proceeds. Digital fonts will be released in 2022 in SIL-OFL license (open source).

4 Gerrit Noordzij, *The Stroke of the Pen: Fundamental Aspects of Western Writing* (The Hague: Koninklijke Academie van Beeldende Kunsten, 1982).

PIM Latin

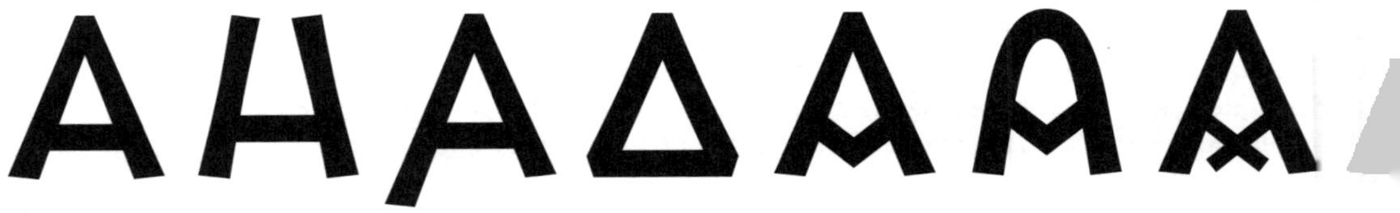

PIM Archaic Greek **PIM Hebrew** **PIM Paleo Hebrew**

PIM Oscan

PIM Nabatean

PIM Etruscan

PIM Lycian

PIM Phoenician

PIM Phoenician Punic

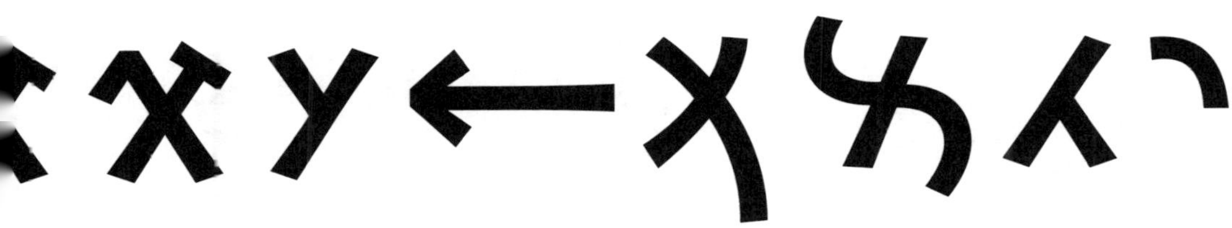

MINUSCULE SIX | 40 PT

Typo-

MINUSCULE QUATRE | 24 PT

graphies

MINUSCULE DEUX | 16 PT

Compactes:

MINUSCULE TROIS | 8 PT

Minuscule, un caractère pour les très petits corps.

MINUSCULE SIX | 6 PTS

Le projet du Minuscule est né lorsque j'ai découvert les travaux d'un ophtalmologue du XIXe siècle, Dr Louis-Émile Javal. Dans un ouvrage paru en 1905, intitulé *Physiologie de la Lecture et de l'Écriture*, il est le premier à démontrer scientifiquement le mécanisme de la lecture, en tire de précieuses conclusions pour améliorer la lisibilité des caractères typographiques, dans un chapitre intitulé *Typographie Compacte*. Ces recherches, encore très perfectibles, de son propre aveu, n'eurent jamais de suite; Louis-Émile Javal disparu deux ans plus tard, après avoir perdu la vue.

MINUSCULE CINQ | 5 PTS

Mon ambition était la suivante: dessiner un caractère de labeur qui reste lisible en-deçà du seuil de lisibilité communément admis (7 pts), et jusqu'aux tailles les plus réduites possibles. Le Minuscule a été décliné en cinq versions, optimisées pour des usages en corps 6, 5, 4, 3 & 2 points. Son développement appelait une étude préalable du mécanisme de la lecture, des critères de la lisibilité, ainsi qu'une prise en compte des phénomènes optiques et techniques conséquents d'une réduction extrême.

MINUSCULE QUATRE | 4 PT

L'enjeu majeur d'une typographie compacte est d'augmenter la quantité de texte contenue sur une page, en conservant la lisibilité. On distingue deux méthodes: *utiliser un caractère étroit*, et gagner en encombrement *horizontal* (plus de signes à la ligne); *utiliser un caractère large, et composer dans un corps inférieur*, pour gagner en encombrement *vertical* (plus de lignes à la page). Le Minuscule relève de la seconde méthode.

MINUSCULE TROIS | 3 PT

À partir des différents tests de lisibilité, plusieurs principes formels ont été retenus pour le dessin du Minuscule. Ces caractéristiques de dessin s'accentuent, à mesure que l'on descend dans l'échelle des corps:
Une structure robuste et ouverte, de manière à faire entrer un maximum de blanc à l'intérieur des signes. La graisse est assez importante, et le contraste réduit. La hauteur d'œil est augmentée au maximum, en réduisant les dépassantes, et en particulier les descendantes, qui sont moins fréquentes. Les empattements sont marqués, pour qu'ils ne disparaissent pas à de telles échelles. Des *«pièges à encre»* sont formés aux angles, pour anticiper les risques de bouchage. L'interlettrage augmente progressivement. En Deux, pour limiter les risques de confusion, un travail de simplification formelle est nécessaire, pour ne conserver de chaque signe que ce qui permettra de le distinguer d'un autre.

MINUSCULE DEUX | 2 PT

Les tailles des différents dessins du *Minuscule* sont à considérer comme des limites idéales, et non comme des valeurs absolues. Chaque version peut être utilisée à des corps supérieurs, et s'adapter aux différentes contraintes de support (type d'impression, de papier) ou de contenu.

MINUSCULE CINQ | 5 PT

Le Minuscule est aujourd'hui disponible sur:

GARAJE 0503 BLACK | 18 PT

WWW.205.TF

Typographie *compacte*
Typographie *compacte*
Typographie *compacte*
Typographie *compacte*
Typographie *compacte*
Typographie compacte

Minuscule: a Typeface for Very Small Sizes

Fig. 5a (opposite, left): Specimen bookmark of the Minuscule typeface, 50×200mm. Published in 2007 for the publication of Minuscule on 256TM, reissued in 2017 for 205TF.

Fig. 5b (opposite, right): From left to right, Minuscule 6, 5, 4, 3 and 2. Thomas Huot-Marchand, 2002–07 / 205TF.

Fig. 6 (overleaf): From left to right, Faune Display Thin, Faune Text Regular, Faune Text Bold, Faune Display Black, Faune Text Italic, Faune Display Bold Italic. Alice Savoie / Cnap, 2017.

Minuscule's design was inspired by the ophthalmologist Emile Javal's "theory of compact prints," published in *Physiologie de la lecture et de l'écriture* (Paris: Alcan, 1905). I initiated this project during the postgraduate research course at the ANRT in 2001–02 and completed it in 2006–07, during a residency in the French Academy in Rome, Villa Médici.

Minuscule comes in five versions (figs. 5a, 5b), optimized for 6, 5, 4, 3 and 2 points. The design evolves progressively as the size decreases: spacing and x-height increase, contrast decreases, ink traps appear, and the design is simplified. Minuscule 2 is the strangest weight: "At this size," said Javal, "we read most the difference between the letters." As a consequence, the particularities of each sign are exaggerated and the secondary details eliminated.

Usually narrower, the spacing of Minuscule italics is almost identical to the roman. On the other hand, the design is very different, much more angular and rhythmic.

Faune: A Mutant Typeface

The surprising ambition of Faune is to study the plurality of the animal world for the purposes of creating a new type family. Designed by Alice Savoie and commissioned by the Centre national des arts plastiques in partnership with the Imprimerie Nationale, Faune has its source in two scientific masterworks: *Histoire naturelle*, by Buffon, published between 1749 and 1788 by the Imprimerie Royale, and the monumental *Description de l'Égypte*, published by the Imprimerie Impériale (later Royale) between 1809 and 1830.

Faune draws upon the wealth and vivacity of animal forms that appear within them in order to question the notion of lineage between different typefaces, and proposes a new typographic ecosystem. The first variant takes its inspiration from a viper known as the *haje*. A second, black, variant, draws its origins from the largest mammal present in the *Description de l'Égypte*. The third style is a bold italic, which design is based on a remarkable specimen of black ibis found in the same book, chosen for the very characteristic undulation of its neck and the unique distribution of its mass between a heavy body and skinny legs. These three founding members of the type family are then rendered "genetically compatible"—a process called *interpolation* in typeface design, which consists of an operation of calculation that allows one to generate a number of intermediary variations between two different designs. This process thus results in three hybridizations, which prove to be perfectly adapted to continuous reading at text sizes.

This is Faune (fig. 6): three master variants (Thin, Italic, Black) for large sizes, and three hybrid variants (Regular, Italic, Bold) for body text. Beyond these six basic styles, it is possible to imagine a potentially infinite series of variations. While the master variants define the boundaries of the ecosystem (a.k.a. the design space), the ability to generate multiple intermediary instances is the ambition of new font formats, such as variable fonts. Faced with this ongoing upheaval, Faune is an invitation to rethink our idea of what a type family is. It is also an opportunity to envisage a dynamic relationship between the variations that comprise it, opening ourselves up to tomorrow's typography: alive, mutant, and in perpetual evolution.

fff
aaa
uuu
nnn
eee

Acting Things
Choreographing the Everyday

Judith Seng

Fig. 1: Bandltanz, May 1, 2012, Bad Kohlgrub, Germany.

The ongoing *Acting Things* project began in 2011, yet its ground has been prepared through my work experiences in the years before. I was creating material objects but aimed to also address their inherent immaterial aspects like usage and production processes or conceptual thoughts. While in other projects, I was working on new collaboration processes and wondered how to make better use of my artistic skills to actually design vs. manage such situations. It was by chance that I came across the traditional Bandltanz (fig. 1) that seemed to capture my underlying questions in one situation. Around a four-meter-tall maypole, a group of men and women danced the traditional ribbon dance, in which a structure is woven by the movement of the dancers and then loosened again. The choreography of the dancers and the shape of the weaving were directly linked and formed a moving unit of materials and people. I saw less of a folkloric fertility ritual and more of a sociomaterial production process under different conditions. And wondered: What if we see work as a social ritual and production processes as a dance or a play? And how design can learn from the performative arts to actually craft processes vs plan, organize and manage them? The intention of *Acting Things* is to examine (production) processes with theatrical and performative means to foreground dynamic social-material relations as tangible material and matter for design. Until now, the initial question has been explored and further developed through eight performative installations that are activated in theater or exhibition contexts (Cases 1–8). The black or white cube serves as a concrete, albeit abstract, space that is decoupled from the immediate constraints of everyday life but nevertheless refers to it. On a stage, we consider the interplay of bodies, objects, and interactions in space and time to be designed in order to reveal a specific narration. In that sense, the concept of stage is appropriated as a laboratory to explore and reimagine through enacting the underlying narrations that drive our ways of doing in daily life. Thus, it is less about designing material results but frameworks for situations, in which the sociomaterial interplay can emerge and evolve. For the actual work emerges only in the moment of activation and through the dynamic between people, processes, objects, and spaces. As an experience for the involved participants that can also be observed by an audience.

In *Acting Things*, materials and objects initiate production processes just as they trace them in the form of a materialized result. They are embedded in situations that try to pay attention to body, materials, space, interactions, and intentions simultaneously and equally. Thus they are in constant negotiation about who is acting, upon whom, when, and is influencing how. How can one recognize such dynamic, temporal, rhythmic and dramaturgical components in materials and objects and address them through an expanded design practice?

Over the course of the first *Acting Things* cases, more and more design elements were brought into light that together form a situation (bodies, objects, spatial setting, clothing, light, sound, atmosphere, interactions, techniques, rules, instructions, concept, narration, duration, rhythm and dramaturgy and many more). I came to realize that my approach is less to design them all but rather to choreograph how they become and shape in relation to each other. In the context of dance, today *choreography*[1] refers to the invention and study of movements. Whereas the means of action (the body) is always designed in connection with the intention of the actions (the body movements). Just as the dance action cannot be considered separately from the body in which it manifests itself, so are objects and spaces closely intertwined with situations and

1 The term *choreography* originally described the recording (*graphē*) of the circular movements of the chore (*choreia*) in Greek drama and was later extended to any form of notation of mostly dance movements. The intention was to archive to possibly reproduce the otherwise ephemeral situation/moment of the dance by emancipating the knowledge from the individual body/context/situation in which it was created. For further readings, see: Nikolaus Gansterer, Emma Cocker and Mariella Greil eds., *Choreo-graphic Figures: Deviations from the Line* (Berlin: Walter de Gruyter, 2017); Andrew Hewitt, *Social Choreography: Ideology as Performance in Dance and Everyday Movement* (Durham: Duke University Press, 2005); Gabriele Klein, *Choreografischer Baukasten: Das Buch* (Bielefeld: transcript, 2015); and Judith Seng, “Design und soziomaterielle Choreografien des Alltags,” in *Zwischenmenschliches Design: Sozialität und Soziabilität durch Dinge*, ed. Martina Fineder and Johannes Lang (Berlin: Springer, 2020), 197–208.

interactions. Thus, I do not apply the term *choreography* in a disciplinary, but in a broader sense: A choreography can shape and describe complex dynamics between various human and nonhuman actors and is viewed as a sociomaterial composition or work. A choreography not only gathers the most diverse actors, but above all deals with the specific design of such an assembly and addresses form, rhythm, and relations and thus also the power structures and agenda that underlies each assembly.

From a choreographic perspective, design can be understood as a sociopolitical yet artistic practice that addresses how we perform with things in daily life. It could develop new designerly skills that are actually able to craft (vs. manage) everyday situations as tangible, aesthetic, sociomaterial and dynamic matter.

Fig. 2: June 24, 2011, HAU 3 Hebbel Theatre Berlin, Germany.

Acting Things I – Production Theatre

The intention of the first experiment was to view objects of everyday use as embedded in sociomaterial processes and thus as dynamic unit that evolves in a space and time. *Acting Things I – Production Theatre* started like any theater evening at the Hebbel Theater HAU in Berlin. Interested guests could reserve tickets yet they did not show a purchase price but 45 minutes of working time. Guests were handed a hammer or nails along with an invitation to go onstage and build furniture in order to dine together. Both the provided material and the tools were numbered, so that random assemblies of wooden slats, nails, hammer, pliers, two people and their ideas, intentions, and social interactions emerged. The process was only guided by a few instructions and developed mainly in the interaction with the material and the respective ideas of how to dine together and what is needed to do so. In the course of the evening, a variety of sociomaterial interactions, interpreted rules and individual objectives resulted in 27 different "pieces" that were both a theater piece and a piece of furniture (fig. 2). Each participant was at the same time designer and user, director and spectator of the unique genesis of his/her "piece." The objects produced were later photographed: half furniture, half traces of actions, each referred to the dynamic processes of individual negotiations between people, materials, tools, and intentions. The ability of materiality not only to make processes visible but also to guide them led to the development of the second experiment and the question of who or what choreographs whom and in what way.

Fig. 3: June 6, 2012.

Acting Things II – Dialogue

Acting Things II – Dialogue examines the relationship between body and material. I invited the dancer Barbara Berti to improvise a dance in dialogue with a material. Through her movements she should form a modeling wax and at the same time let herself be guided by the material (fig. 3). We developed a production process between dance and handicraft: a continuous search for the same attention to body, material, space, movement, and result. Because if she concentrated on the movement in space, the object degenerated into a mere prop. When her attention was on a material result, it resembled a handicapped craft.

It took 3 hours to prepare the material from melting to slow hardening. Only for 15 minutes did the material have the right consistency for the dance: soft enough to be shaped and hard enough to resist. This required an attitude like a gardener who tries to influence the transformation process through favorable conditions. Ultimately, the wax's own processes turned out to be the real clock of the situation. The dancer also reported that the material influenced her breathing. By focusing on her body, the dancer could feel the influence of the material and report on it.

Acting Things III – Over Work

In order to acknowledge and thus learn more about the agency of the material within a production process, materials and participants were interacting within the installation over a period of 10 hours. Instead of determining themselves when to act, three participants observed the slow transformation of the material and patiently waited for the right time to intervene. The objects were both the result and the initiator of a production process. The wax objects from the previous experiment were melted down to initiate a new manufacturing process. A series of transformations that could be continued indefinitely: from liquid to malleable to solid and back—and the resulting social interactions (fig. 4). The result was a very slow, flowing dramaturgy with few highlights in the traditional sense. Instead, it opened plenty of space and time for small, otherwise easily overlooked observations. One visitor watched the melting wax for 40 minutes and left shortly before the dance started. Both the participants and the audience had to commit themselves to the speed, rhythm and dramaturgy of the material in order to experience the experiment for themselves.

Figs. 4: October 20, 2012, Graduale at Amerika Haus Berlin, Germany.

Figs. 5a & 5b:
June 10–16, 2013,
Design/Miami Basel,
CH.

Acting Things IV – Material Flow

For *Acting Things IV – Material Flow*[2] the previous process was intensified. Within the context of a collectors' fair, the very slow transformation process was repeated over 7 days, 8 hours a day. Each day 15 objects were produced and exhibited, only to melt and recolor them to produce new objects the following day (figs. 5a, 5b). The 5 participants had to commit to the slowness, simplicity, and repetition of the act of making as such that only temporarily led to a material result. The challenge was to stay focused on the moment and to reappropriate every action as if doing it for the first time, without embellishing it. This attitude proved to be a key ingredient of the production process. As when the concentration was temporarily lost, the audience immediately responded by simply moving on. Yet the stage offered spatial overlaps between participating and observing modes for both the audience (who could step into the stage area) as well as for the participants, who could sit with the audience when waiting for their next intervention to come. Now two dancers negotiated with the material—and between their individual physicality and interpretation of the shared task. It became evident that a task and score can be replicated and shared, but not how it is enacted and kept alive by each individual. Questions about enforcement or restraint were brought to the stage. Or how can one remain equally engaged while waiting, listening or supporting?

2 In the context of the collector's fair Design Miami/Basel, 2013.

Fig. 6: June 21, 2014, Kunstgewerbemuseum Dresden, Germany.

Acting Things V – Connexions

Acting Things V – Connexions[3] invited 24 random visitors of the museum into a production festivity in order to jointly produce the object to be exhibited. Working with the museum's collection, I came across bobbin laces, a complex artisan process, in which threads are rotated, crossed and knotted on the basis of a pricking, and which requires experience, dexterity and a lot of patience (fig. 6). A procedure astonishingly similar to that of the ribbon dance around the maypole. This experiment was looking into production as social ritual that interweaves materials and random people in shared procedures and situations. In a museum context, it turned visitors into makers to not only view but experience the exhibits—in this case a scaled production process of bobbin lace that connected both threads and people. Material structures and acoustic instructions acted as the score that guided 24 unskilled visitors in situ through a complex production choreography. Each participant was just a cog in the entire gear and at the same time indispensable for success.

3 At the Kunstgewerbemuseum Dresden Schloss Pillnitz, Dresden, 2014.

Figs. 7a & 7b:
July 13–August 13, 2017, Kyoto Art Center, Japan.

Acting Things VI – Spatial Canvas

Acting Things VI – Spatial Canvas[4] consisted of a three-dimensional canvas embedded in an acoustic and spatial grid in order to explore space-making as a continuous process of creation between moving bodies, social interactions and material structures. Over a period of four weeks, visitors constantly recreated the space through interacting with the material structure and each other (figs. 7a, 7b). The space was to be explored and shaped, used and created, constructed and deconstructed. Like a three-dimensional sketching process, acoustic and material traces of interactions instantly turned into spatial scores that initiated new interactions and so forth. Thus, the emerging material structures simultaneously choreographed as well as notated the social interactions of moving bodies in space and time.

Acting Things – School of Fluid Measures

Acting Things – School of Fluid Measures[5] initiates a series of embodied, silent conversations to explore how values—or meaning and understanding—are created through continuous sociomaterial negotiations. Over a period of six weeks, the installation invited visitors to negotiate the dynamics between two social values and how they relate to each other in relevant situations in everyday life. Each value was represented by one person and a pile of colored sand. A negotiation was mainly governed by two rules: (1) Not to talk, but to debate by interacting with sand and body movements in the space; (2) To create a dialogue by reacting to and building on the other's movements. The resulting sand pattern traced proportions, relations and dynamics of the two values and colors. Which were then merged into a new color and a new value to be discussed (figs. 8a, 8b).

Figs. 8a (below) & 8b (overleaf): September 20–November 4, 2018, 4th Istanbul Design Biennale, "A School of Schools," Pera Museum Istanbul, Turkey.

4 At the Kyoto Art Center/Japan, 2017.
5 At the 4th Istanbul Design Biennale at the Pera Museum, 2018, and at the LUMA Arles, 2019, Z33 – House of Contemporary Art and Architecture Hassel (2020), Tripostal Lille (2021).

In Formation & Information in Living Material

Dominique Peysson

Since Plato in Antiquity, then Hegel at the end of the eighteenth century, the history of art has focused on the ideas, the currents, the style, the schools and ideologies. In short, on form. *Formalism*, the term used by Heinrich Wölfflin in the early twentieth century to characterize his historical study of art, is the paradigm of the prevalence of form over matter. It was with modern art, and then even more strongly with contemporary art, that this reductive subjection was shattered by the artists. Nevertheless, when studied by theorists, the nature of the materials is often considered as secondary, even though some authors, such as de Mèredieu, have looked at the materiality and its relationship to the sensitive.[1]

Most of the time, it is the internal structure of the material, its inner form, that gives it its peculiar properties. For me, there is no longer a matter/form couple, since matter *is* form: it is not an homogeneous substance at all levels of size, but its internal structure—or internal *form*—can be very complex. And all the properties of matter depend on it. I am working, in my artworks, on specific materials that I call *responsive*. They can be sensitive to their surrounding environment, and capable of responding to it by modifying significantly one of their characteristics. These responsive materials answer directly, from the depths of themselves. Their behavior is not the result of a digital device, sensors, actuators, or software. It is then possible to make *responsive installations*, similar to interactive installations but without any digital system.

Luigi Pareyson establishes a clear link in his *Teoria della formatività* between "the process whereby the form emerges from the encounter with materials, but also a specific type of learning process situated within practical creativity," as Sylvia Gherardi explains.[2] For Luigi Pareyson, "meaning and matter are intrinsically entangled in formativeness."

In my work, the process of forming is very important, the forming of the matter as an organic process, or that of our thought. Because to think is to put our feelings, experiences, and reasoning in shape, to order our thoughts so that they can make sense. Like Michel Foucault says: "Order is, at one and the same time, that which is given in things as their inner law, the hidden network that determines the way they confront one another,

1 Florence de Mèredieu, *Histoire matérielle et immatérielle de l'art moderne*, 2nd ed. (Paris: Larousse, 2004), 39–40.

2 Antonio Strati and Silvia Gherardi, "La philosophie de Luigi Pareyson et la recherche esthétique des pratiques organisationnelles : un dialogue," *Le Libellio d'AEGIS* 11, no. 3 (Autumn 2015): 22, http://lelibellio.com (author's translation).

and also that which has no existence except in the grid created by a glance, an examination, a language."[3] There is then a necessary ordering of the matter of our thoughts. But this order can be a "hidden" order, which is essential to creative thinking. In his book *The Hidden Order of Art*,[4] the theorist on the psychology of art Anton Ehrenzweig explains how this hidden order is at the root of creativity, thanks to syncretic vision and unconscious scanning that make us capable to think in complexity. It is a way of thinking that children have, prior to analysis and synthesis. It is a more global perception, more flexible, more powerful. A way of thinking which allows a very rich analysis of the complexity of our world.

Back to matter, we can first notice that the notion of ordering is also what allows us to characterize living matter, compared to inert matter. Actually, it can even be one of the definitions of what is living: the living is what can organize itself by itself in a very complex way. The second point is that information can be "written" or can "flow" in living matter thanks to the order or the forming of matter. To put it another way, there is a strong relationship between forming and information. All the artworks presented here refer to active matter—or to living matter as active matter. In particular, they question the notion of information, but information which *is* matter. Information inscribed in living matter, or living matter inscribed in information.

3 Michel Foucault, *The Order of Things: An Archaeology of the Human Sciences* (London: Routledge Classics, 2002), xxi.

4 Anton Ehrenzweig, *The Hidden Order of Art: A Study in the Psychology of Artistic Imagination* (Berkeley: University of California Press, 1967).

Preparatory Drawings for *Plastic DNA*, 2017

The idea of my work *Plastic DNA* started from the comparison of two definitions. First the definition of what plastic material is: malleable and plastic only because it is constituted by particularly long molecules. Second, the living matter constituted by DNA molecules, present in all the cells of our body. The way we imagine it is the way the scientific mediators draw it, from the scientific representations used for their work: a flexible scale, shaped like a helix—a double helix—floating in the void of the page.

But what is truly DNA? We can define it as a tremendously long molecule. But all long molecules are plastic materials. So DNA is plastic! It is not a metaphor, nor an image, but reality. It leads, however, to connect two representations—that of DNA and that of plastic—that do not belong to the same categories in our thinking. Plastic is the lowest-cost material among those we use in our daily lives. On the exact opposite, DNA, whose symbolic dimension is the strongest, because it allows life and defines us in our singularity. So my question is: Can I make small plastic objects with DNA (figs. 1a & 1b)?

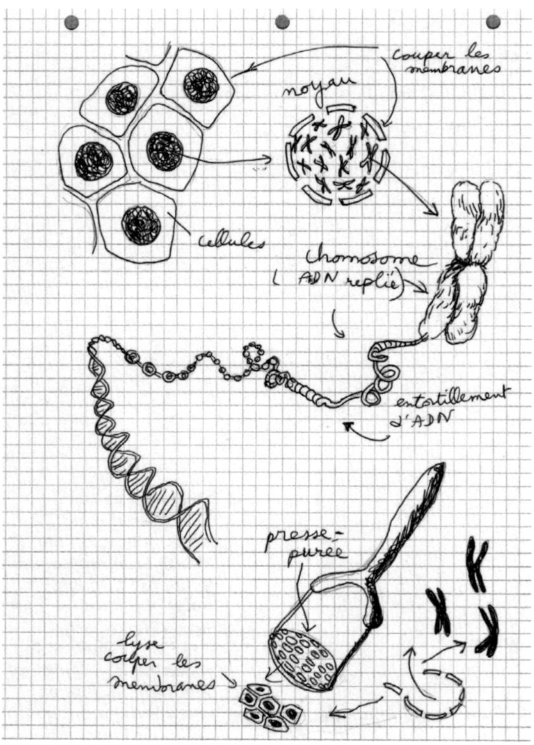

Figs. 1a & 1b: Residency at Espace J. R. Caussimon, Tremblay-en-France, in partnership with Le Lieu Multiple, the DNA school and Ebi-Carbios laboratory, Poitiers. Support: Seine-Saint-Denis Département and Région Ile-de-France.

Plastic DNA, ADN, Cement, Glass, 2017

Figs. 2a & 2b: Residency at Espace J. R. Caussimon, Tremblay-en-France, in partnership with Le Lieu Multiple, the DNA school and Ebi-Carbios laboratory, Poitiers. Support: Seine-Saint-Denis Départment and Région Ile-de-France.

In *Plastic DNA* (figs. 2a & 2b), I made objects identical to small plastic figurines that cost nothing. DNA molecules are particularly small because they are molecules. How can we move from this nanoscopic quantity to a production that allows the realization of an object of at least several grams? All researchers working on this molecule are used to manipulating it in tiny quantities.

But if DNA molecules are very small, they are in a great quantity. They constitute the largest part of the chromosomes, which are the core elements of the nucleus of our cells. And we are made up of around 37 trillion cells. Around 0.4 percent of our body weight is DNA! I extracted important quantities of DNA from vegetal cells. Since DNA refers to our own definition of identity, I followed, with a critical view, the socially predetermined codes of some little toys, say a pink princess and a green soldier, that I colored with two reagents usually used to demonstrate the presence of DNA.

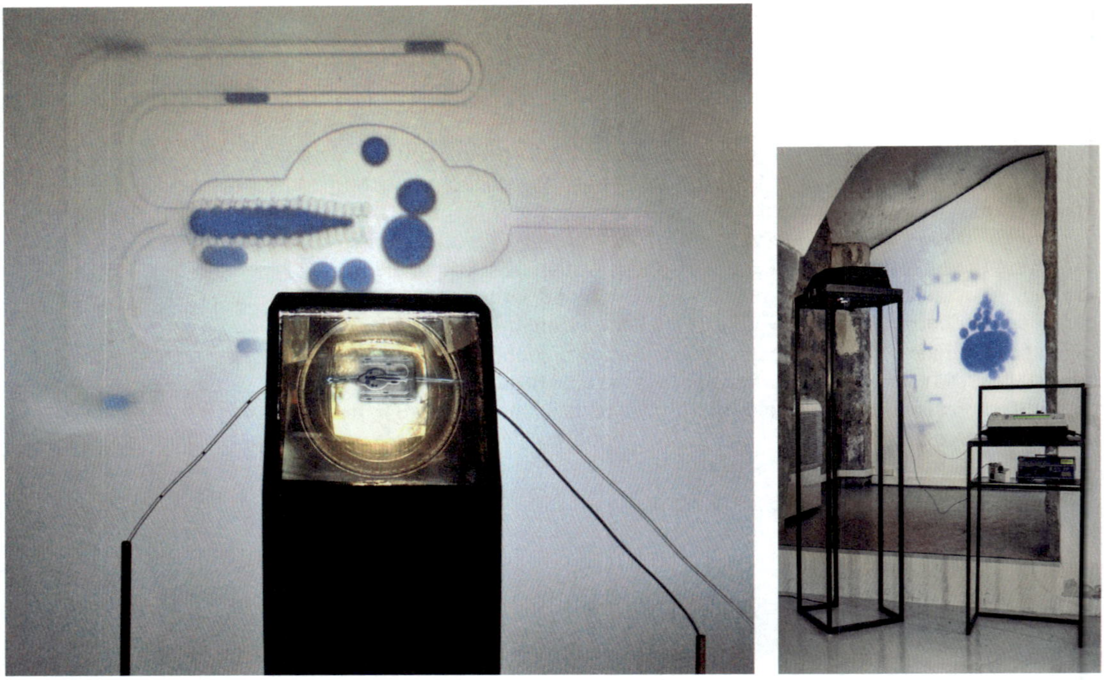

Figs. 3a & 3b: Microfluidic installation. Design with Adrien Bonnerot, Scientific Council Patrick Tabeling, Fabrice Monti, MMS laboratory, ESPCI, Reflective Interaction/ EnsadLab program, supported by EnsadLab (Laboratoire de l'École Nationale Supérieure des Arts Décoratifs), Université Paris 1 Panthéon Sorbonne and PSL.

Traffic, 2014

In *Traffic* (figs. 3a & 3b), I consider matter and information in a different way, showing droplets at the size of a cell flowing into microscopic-sized channels. I made a device with a one-way mirror to see simultaneously the small microscopic circuit and its image enlarged one hundred times projected on the wall.

My *Traffic* machines show an operativeness of the liquid matter, a quiet participation of water and oil. Multiplied by two, four, a hundred ... the droplet passes relentlessly, perfectly, then disappears and then others appear. We see a digitized fluid, drops being like many units of data in an analog continuum, recalling the visual of the first digital games that were developed. However, when it reaches a round cavity that I placed there, the drop slows down, stretches, swells; free. Then comes a new drop, which is allowed to come into the first, slowly, elastic. The drops become one. Their respective envelops deform, then they melt. Organic, they evoke images strongly related to our origins.

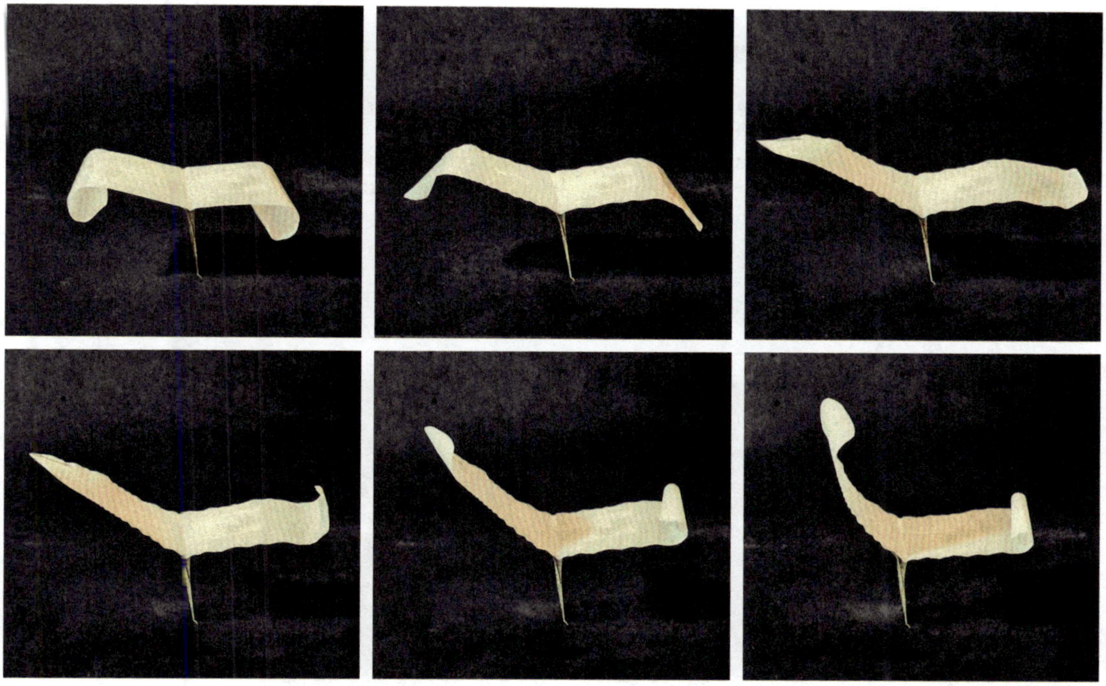

Dancing in the Rain (Danser sous la pluie), 2014

Fig. 4: Video, 5:28 min, paper, water. Etienne Reyssat Scientific Council, PMMH laboratory, ESPCI. Reflective Interaction/EnsadLab program, supported by EnsadLab, Université Paris 1 Panthéon Sorbonne and PSL.

Dancing in the Rain is a small ballet for paper (fig. 4). It is the dynamic story of little papers and raindrops, a succession of small dances executed by paper bilayers. They come alive when you moisten the air by spraying some water. It is the specific arrangement and structure of my small papers that induce the shape of their movements. No tricks, it's only the humidity that drives them. They move in a graceful and jerky manner, as plants do.

This is not surprising: the physical principle of the movement of these papers is modeled on that of some plants. Everything here is also a question of matter order. The source of moving for the system is water, coming from the humidity in the air. The mechanism is the same as that of plant tissue, which is constituted by two layers, one which swells and expands, the other one which does not. The humidity constrains the tissue bilayer, which then bends. The associated behaviors of my papers are therefore those of primitive vegetation in search of water and light. A small choreography like those of butō; slow, poetic, and minimalist.

Clouds Study (Étude de nuages), 2014

Clouds Study (figs. 5a & 5b) is a series depicting clouds, drawn with drops of water—as are the clouds. The patterns formed by the drops reproduce the skies painted by classic artists who made cloud studies or whose cloudy skies are one of the characteristics. The representation corresponds to a digital image of low resolution, 7 dots per inch—here 7 drops per inch. The water is viscosified to avoid flow or evaporation during the exhibition. However, a specific choice of viscosity makes it possible to control the speed of evaporation so that the image can take exactly the time of the exhibition to evaporate. And leave us in front of a cloudless sky.

Figs. 5a & 5b: Water, metal, 7 drops per inch. Interaction/EnsadLab program, supported by EnsadLab, Université Paris 1 Panthéon Sorbonne and PSL.

Fig. 6: Performance, 20 min. Supported by the research program "Vocality in theater and opera" of the Iris "Création, Cognition et Société", EHESS, PSL.

Life is a vapor… and then nothing (La vie est une vapeur… et puis rien), 2017

Life is a vapor… and then nothing is a performance (fig. 6) that Olivier Goulet and I conceived as a vanity. In the ancient texts, in Hebrew, the term *vanity* could be translated also as "steam." In this work it is question of life as a transition between two stages. Conceived as an experience of the limits of our corporality, this performance takes place in a totally closed space where the air is restricted. Before the performance, Olivier and I drink a cup of hot tea, and the audience can also drink with us. It is then the cycle of the water, of our life, through our body, which will be given to see… Inside the closed space, the water vapor that our bodies exhale, will, paradoxically, create a diffuse veil on the surfaces, and partially hide our bodies from the public. It is by the breath that one exhales that one shows that a human being is alive. It is also this breath that transforms us in ghostly silhouettes.

"La vie est une vapeur… et puis rien" is extracted from a verse of the poem "Celui-là était roi" by Jaime Garcia Terres.

Figs. 7a, 7b & 7c: Installation, videos. Supported by FEW: the association for the *Fête de l'Eau à Wattwiller*.

Crystal Drop (Goutte de cristal), 2019

Crystal Drop (figs. 7a, 7b & 7c) is an installation for three drops of water. As scientists know, water is diamagnetic ... Could it be that a fortune teller could read the future in a drop of water, as if it were a crystal ball? Three drops are presented on a round table, their luminous presence inviting our eyes to dive into them. Very small, but capable of containing the whole world, a microcosm, just as Leibniz monads do. A whole story, that of our world, of the beginning of life, or the future, as we can glimpse it. The water drops are very small ... but we see extremely clearly the projected video images that come to life inside! The drops are constantly renewed: a continuous water flows down through a fine pipe and makes that drop swell. Until it overflows, then the cycle continues. Magic and technology may come together here, in a small droplet of water.

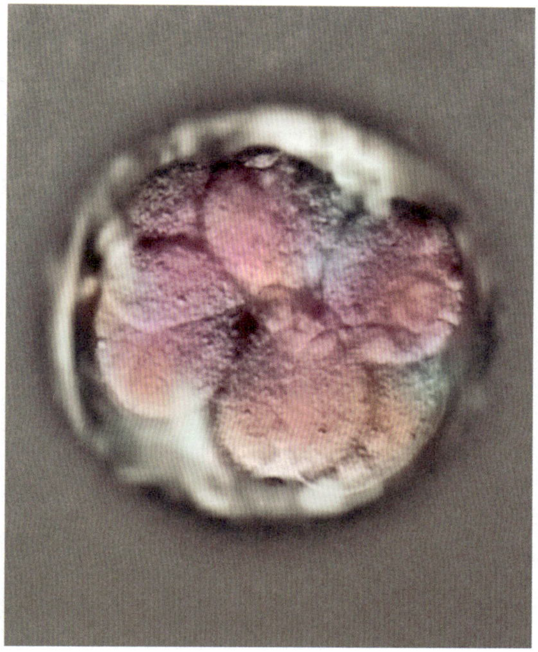

Rethinking the Materials Paradigm

Toward an Active Understanding of *Gestaltung*

Khashayar Razghandi

Imagine a biological or designed material system, say, the colorful wings of a butterfly. If someone were to ask "Why are that butterfly's wings blue?" the answer would differ depending on what was meant by the word *why*. When the *why* is intended or interpreted as "how come?" the question would be answered through a process narrative and a reductionist sense of cause and effect as in explaining the system in its physical sense—its elements, their properties, interactions and so on: "The striking blue is in fact a structural color coming from the interaction of light with the inner nano/micro structure of the wing" etc. This sense of *why* ultimately addresses the question "Why is something like this?" through "How does it do what it does?" Alternatively, *why* can also be intended or interpreted as "what for?" a response to which might be "The eye-catching blue color is used for communication and display during courting" etc. Here, it is hard to ignore a teleological sense of *why*: a sense of function, as in toward an end.

Philosopher Daniel Dennett argues that one can have different levels of description of such a system: the physical stance, the design stance, and the intentional stance.[1] *The physical stance* deals with the "how come?" of a phenomenon, treating it as a physical phenomenon with all the ontologies and causal laws of physics. *The design stance* is a level of description responding to the question of *why* as "what for?" and deals with the realms of designs, purposes, and functions. The *intentional stance* is the realms of options, will, and intent. Various works have engaged in opening the knot and interrelate and supervene these various stances, yet, one thing seems inescapable: the physical, causal descriptions of how elements and parts of a system work and bring out the activity and the phenomenon in question—as accurate or relevant as they might be—lack the "what for?" or the "ententional"[2] perspective. The "what for?" plays in the dimensions of functions and motives, which are of relevance from the perspective of the design and intentional stances respectively.

I believe that looking through and shifting between these different stances is essential for unfolding a new materials paradigm.

1 Daniel C. Dennett, *The Intentional Stance* (Cambridge, MA: MIT Press, 1989); Daniel C. Dennett, *From Bacteria to Bach and Back: The Evolution of Mind* (New York: W. W. Norton & Company, 2017).

2 Terrence W. Deacon, *Incomplete Nature: How Mind Emerged from Matter* (New York: W. W. Norton & Company, 2011).

In material science and engineering, the conventional Materials Paradigm is an integrated way of addressing the study and interrelation of different aspects of the structure, properties, processes, and performances of materials.[3] Based on this generic idea of a Materials Paradigm, and borrowing from the Stances discourse, I propose a new material paradigm for natural sciences, engineering, and design that would interrelate and expand both conceptions, by introducing intermediate stances that place activity at the core of the materials paradigm.

The proposed *active materials paradigm* encourages scientists, engineers, and designers to see matter through a range of concepts such as composition, structure, synthesis, property, operativity, performativity, function, intention, etc., as various interrelated stances situated in different historical and ecological contexts. It suggests that looking through the lens of these stances can help to cultivate a more systemic and dynamic understanding of the materiality of activity in its entangled and performative sense.[4] Acknowledging and paying attention to the proposed conceptions, as well as following a dynamic shift of perspective between these stances, can serve as a tool for engaging with these various levels of descriptions of a phenomenon, the relevant realms of ontologies and boundary conditions associated with these stances and the interrelation between them. The hope is that such an engagement helps with our thinking, questioning, explaining, or making, and nurtures a more comprehensive picture of *Gestaltung* throughout analysis and synthesis.

3 Science, National Research Council, Committee on Materials, National Research Council Solid State Sciences Committee, and National Research Council National Materials Advisory Board, eds., *Materials Science and Engineering for the 1990s: Maintaining Competitiveness in the Age of Materials: Summary* (Washington, DC: National Academy Press, 1989).

4 Karen Barad, "Posthumanist Performativity: Toward an Understanding of How Matter Comes to Matter," *Signs: Journal of Women in Culture and Society* 28, no. 3 (2003): 801–31; Jens Hauser and Lucie Strecker, "On Microperformativity," *Performance Research* 25, no. 3 (November 2020); Khashayar Razghandi and Emad Yaghmaei, "Rethinking Filter:An Interdisciplinary Inquiry into Typology and Concept of Filter, Towards an Active Filter Model," *Sustainability* 12, no. 18 (2020): 7284; Mohammad Fardin Gholami, Lorenzo Guiducci, Susanne Yani, and Khashayar Razghandi, "Rethinking Active Matter: Current Developments in Active Materials," in *Active Materials*, ed, Peter Fratzl, Michael Friedman, Karin Krauthausen, and Wolfgang Schäffner (Berlin: De Gruyter, 2022).

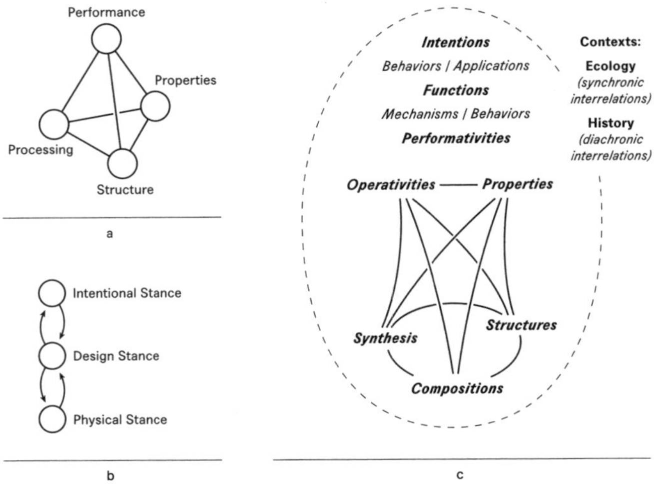

Fig. 1a: The conventional materials paradigm in material science and engineering.

Fig. 1b: Schematic conception of Daniel Dennett's three stances.

Fig. 1c: The proposed *active materials paradigm*.

Active Materials Paradigm: Expanding the Stances

(Fig. 1a) The conventional materials paradigm in material science and engineering is depicted as a tetrahedron pyramid with interrelated apices that highlight different perspectives of understanding and control of materials. The *composition* and *structure* over the range of length scale; the synthesis and *processing* of particular arrangements; the *properties* resulting from the compositions and their arrangements; and the *performance* of the material as a measure of its utility in the context.[5]

(Fig. 1b) Schematic conception of Daniel Dennett's three stances—the physical stance, the design stance, and the intentional stance—as different levels of description one can adopt to explain/predict a phenomenon.[6]

(Fig. 1c) The proposed *active materials paradigm*, broadening the engagement with matter through a range of stances dealing with the materiality of activity from different perspectives.

The walk through the diagram starts with the triad base of composition, structure, and synthesis: *Composition* refers to the elements and building blocks which we take to make. For instance, a modern smartphone contains around 70 out of the 118 chemical elements of the periodic table.

Synthesis is the variety of physical, thermodynamical, geometrical, evolutionary (etc.) laws, operations, processes (etc.) through which various elements come together to give rise to and maintain a sense of order, arrangement or organization.

Structure refers to the locally maintained relationships of this organization, and how we can talk about the architecture of a material system at various length scales.[7]

Properties and *operativities* emerge from this triad base. *Property* describes a certain state or observable tendency of a system emerging from these former stances (such as a physical or chemical property). Taking a different stance, the

5 Science, National Research Council et al., *Materials Science and Engineering*.
6 Dennett, *The Intentional Stance*.

same can be seen through the lens of *operativities*, highlighting the procedural and operative aspects, following various chains of operations through different elements and structures of a system; something operating on, through, or with something.

Placing properties and operativities as the two interrelated heads of this double-horn tetrahedron—emerging from the same triad base and in entangled relationships with one another—brings a notion of material activity to the core of the materials paradigm.

Based on this entangled dipyramid ground, the gradual walk from the physical stance to the design stance is expressed as an outward expansion from properties and operativities of various elements, structures, and processes, toward semi-demi-quasi *Teloi* of *performativities. Performativity stance* engages with the entanglements and intra-activities within the meshwork of actants and contexts.[8] Moving gradually beyond the *why* as "how come?", stance of function deals with more entangled and contextual performativities toward (and serving) an end. Function emerges as a stance relevant for understanding the *why* as in "what for?" of phenomena in the realm of biology, engineering, and design.

The same gradual walk can be imagined from functions toward intentions, passing through intermediate, more contextual, semi-demi-quasi intentionalities, such as the enigmatic concept of behavior or the more industrious notion of application. As the complexity and the spatial and temporal extent of the entangled activities expands, one starts to lurk in the blurry boundaries of motives and *intentional stance* as temporally extended care for that which matters.

These stances are situated within different ecologies and histories as synchronically and diachronically intertwined interrelations.

The diagram serves as a guiding map to remind the various stances one can take in analysis and synthesis practices of *Gestaltung*, here defined as the processes through which new ontologies and significances emerge out of the entanglements of various elements, structures, properties and operativites within a (new) whole. Playing with this dynamic multilens loupe, zooming in and out and walking through the ontologies, the interrelations and boundary conditions of each of these stances at various scales, helps one get a more comprehensive picture of the activity of material systems.

7 Mohammad Fardin Gholami et al., "Rethinking Active Matter"; Michaela Eder, Shahrouz Amini, and Peter Fratzl, "Biological Composites: Complex Structures for Functional Diversity," *Science* 362, no. 6414 (2018): 543–47.

8 Barad, "Posthumanist Performativity"; Hauser and Strecker, "On Microperformativity"; Razghandi, and Yaghmaei, "Rethinking Filter."

Fig. 2a (left): Ice plant hydro-actuation system.

Fig. 2c (right): Tracking the activity through the lens of the proposed *active materials paradigm*.

Ice Plant Hydro Actuation System: Mapping the Materials Activity

(Fig. 2a) The seed capsules of the ice plant are shown in dry (closed) and wet (open) states. The five seed-containing compartments are covered by protective valves which unfold and release the seeds upon wetting (for example, by rain) even when the plant is dead (A). The hygroscopic keels responsible for unfolding of the seed capsule are bent inward in the dry state and bend outward upon hydration (B, 1–2). Each keel consists of a network of ellipsoid-shaped cells, filled with a highly swellable cellulosic inner layer (C–E, 3–5) responsible for the reversible opening of the cells and the expansion of the honeycomb structure upon wetting and drying cycles (C, 3-4). This expansion translates into bending when the deformation of the structure is restricted at the bottom side (B, 1-2), hence the keels flex and the seed capsule opens (A-B, 1).[9]

(Fig. 2b) The ice plants in their arid habitat.

(Fig. 2c) Tracking the activity through the lens of the proposed *active materials paradigm*, the system is made up of cellulose, hemicellulose, etc. (*composition*), built into an elaborate material architecture (*structure*), while each scale of the architecture described above can be thought of as the "functional unit"[10] of the structure at the larger length scale (*function*) and serving the seed dispersal strategy of the plant as a whole (*intention*). Structures and functions at each scale are in a continuum relation to structures and functions at larger and smaller scales as well as to the environment, all of which are situated within an ecological and historical context (opening in response to rain and evolved to do so). One can zoom in on a specific scale of the system, for instance taking individual keel cells and walk through the stances lens: different sugar macromolecules making up the cell walls and the inner layers (*composition*); the way the cellulosic inner layers are formed into alternating porous and compact sheets (*structure*); enhancing the water absorption and swellability of the inner layer (*property*), and pressurizing (*operation*) the ellipsoid-shaped cells (*structure*), where the isotropic swelling of the inner layer is translated into an inflation and opening of the cells (*performativity, mechanism*), and how such cells act as the functional unit (*function*) of the larger architectural level of the system (structure) and so on.

9 Lorenzo Guiducci, Khashayar Razghandi, Luca Bertinetti, Sébastien Turcaud, Markus Rüggeberg, James C. Weaver, Peter Fratzl, Ingo Burgert, and John W. C. Dunlop, "Honeycomb Actuators Inspired by the Unfolding of Ice Plant Seed Capsules," *PloS one* 11, no. 11 (2016): e0163506.

10 Mohammad Fardin Gholami, et al., "Rethinking Active Matter."

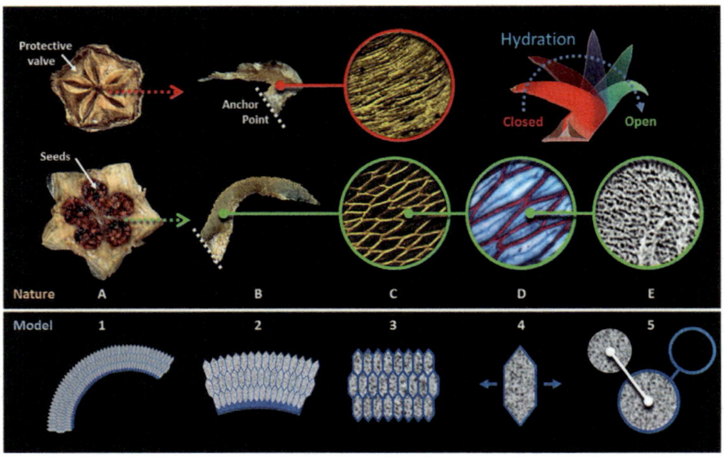

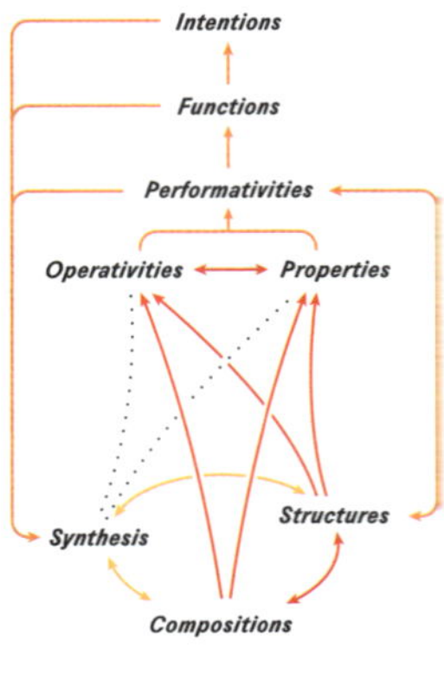

c — Active Materials Paradigm

Fig. 2b: The ice plants in their arid habitat.

Fig. 3a (top left): The Eiffel Tower.

Fig. 3b (bottom): Metal Sponge.

Fig.3c (top right): Tracking the activity through the lens of the proposed *active materials paradigm*.

The Sponge and the Eiffel Tower: Structure Matters

The sponge and the Eiffel Tower are both made from iron. Even when one accounts for the difference in the composition and processing of the iron in the two systems, they still have substantially different properties and performances as a whole. Here, the structure is the crucial defining factor of the property and function. Fibers of steel, in such entangled structure, give the elasticity and porosity associated with the performativity of a cleaning sponge. The Eiffel Tower as a whole has its famous "meshy" structure associated with lightweight structures with high elastic modules and low density, suited to build tall columns. Structure can convey and define *property* and *performativity*.

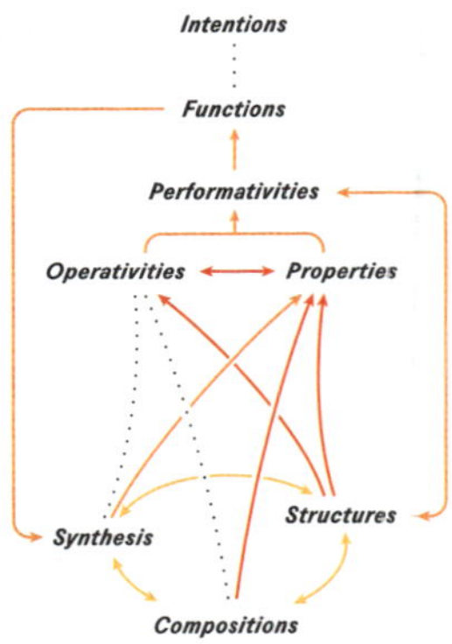

c — Active Materials Paradigm

11 Johannes T. B. Overvelde, Twan A. De Jong, Yanina Shevchenko, Sergio A. Becerra, George M. Whitesides, James C. Weaver, Chuck Hoberman, and Katia Bertoldi, "A Three-Dimensional Actuated Origami-Inspired Transformable Metamaterial with Multiple Degrees of Freedom," *Nature Communications* 7, no. 1 (March 2016): 1–8.

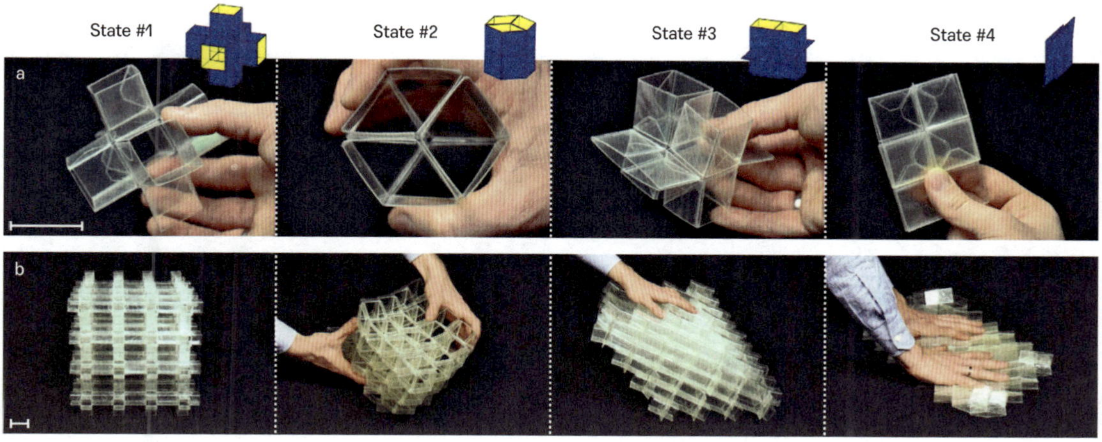

Mechanical Metamaterials; Structures and Performativities

(Fig. 4a–4c) Metamaterials are a class of materials that exhibit distinguished properties and performances mainly as a result of the arrangement of their elements and structures. Here, an extruded cube made out of polyethylene terephthalate comprises the unit cell of an exemplary reconfigurable metamaterial (fig. 4a, state #1). Such a unit cell has multiple degrees of freedom and, by applying different loads and folding the faces on specific edges, can shape-shift into different states (fig. 4a, states #2–4). By connecting the outer edges of 64 of such unit cells one gets the highly flexible mechanical metamaterial, which can undergo a collective deformation and shift shape to different configurations upon compression load (fig. 4b) or through inflation of inflatable pockets at specific edges of the unit cells (fig. 4c).[11]

(Fig. 4d) Looking at the system through the stances of the *active materials paradigm*, the composition of what the walls are made of plays a minimal role in the activity of the system, while the structure and operativity stances become the loci of attention. The snapology that defines the process of making different modules of an extruded cube is noteworthy: for instance, introducing rigid edges in a unit, or rigid connecting edges between units, or allowing the vertical transfer of the force and deformation to the neighboring units above and below while blocking the lateral transfer, enables certain operativities and folding properties. Certain performativities and deformation mechanisms are born out of these structures (and their operativities) at various length scales of the system. Function becomes relevant only when one imagines such a system in specific contexts.

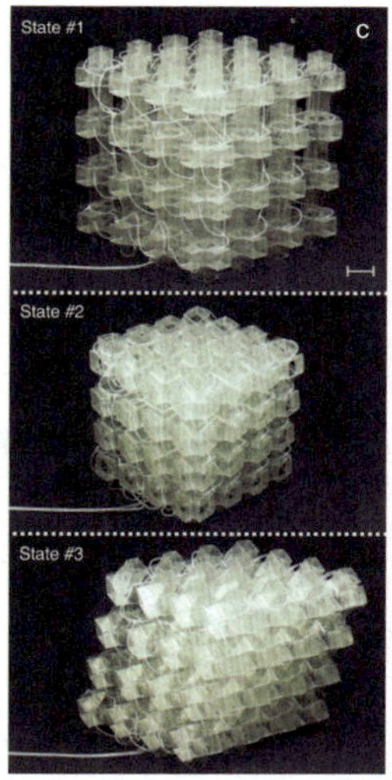

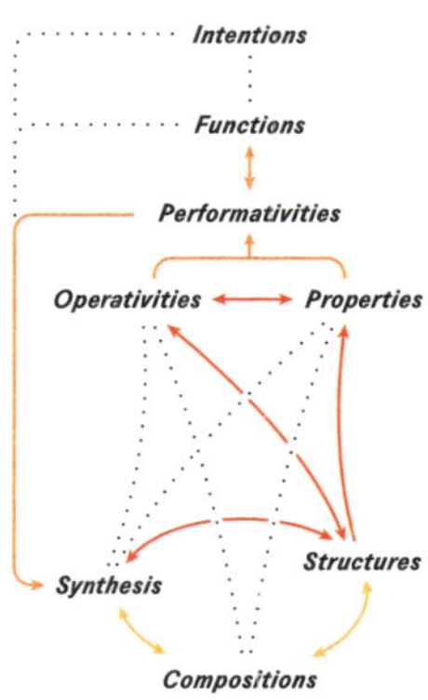

d — Active Materials Paradigm

Figs. 4a, 4b & 4c: (top): Reconfigurable metamaterial.

Fig. 4d (bottom right): Looking at the system through the stances of the active materials paradigm.

The Bark Project

Combining Science and Design to Elaborate New Models of Production for the Design Industry

Charlett Wenig

The use of wood and the evolution of human civilization are intrinsically intertwined. Trees, the "producers" of wood, are complex living organisms, and their harvest and processing does not only produce timber. The cambium, a meristematic tissue located between wood and bark synthesizes wood cells towards the inside and phloem cells to the outside. The living phloem together with older dead tissue forms the bark—the outer protective "skin" of the tree.[1] Bark makes up 10 to 20 percent of a tree[2] and is typically removed after harvest. Apart from niche applications of bark as a material, such as the use of cork from *Quercus suber* or of birch bark of *Betula* sp. for crafts, the majority of bark production is considered as waste by the wood industry. Large-scale bark use is thus mainly limited to the production of energy through incineration and mulching in horticulture. This means the potential to utilize the structure and properties of bark as a material that can be produced in large quantities is unexplored.

The motivation for the present project was to work with bark from local trees, to keep the bark as unmodified a state as possible and to make use of the inherent natural properties for different application scenarios.

The Bark Project is an example of a material-focused exploration using scientific and design methods as a possible new mode of developing more sustainable objects based on inner properties, structure and potential applications of waste materials of timber processing industries. The focus of this project is to establish and analyze the possible interactions between practice-based methods traditionally used in design and fundamental research in material science and engineering in order to develop sustainable design concepts and objects.

Selection Process of Bark Species

The broad variety of different barks (shape, thickness, development in growth) both within and between tree species makes each bark a material of its own, with unique characteristics. In a first step, nonendangered and local species in the area of Berlin and Potsdam were selected. To provide a sustainable model, another selection criterium was the economic

1 Nigel Chaffey, "Esau's Plant Anatomy, Meristems, Cells, and Tissues of the Plant Body: Their Structure, Function, and Development. 3rd ed," *Annals of Botany* 99, no. 4 (2007): 785–86.

2 Zoltán Pásztory et al., "The Utilization of Tree Bark," *BioResources* 11 (2016): 7859–88.

relevance of trees. To give an example, in 2019, 83 percent of the harvested wood in Germany was softwood such as spruce, fir, Douglas fir, pine and larch.[3] Pine and larch were the selected softwoods; and birch, oak, beech and robinia were the selected hardwoods.

How to Link Science and Design

The main idea is to create "boundary objects." A boundary object describes the different use of information by different groups. The concept was introduced by Susan Leigh Star and James R. Griesemer in 1989 and was illustrated by the example of a natural history museum in California.[4] "[Boundary objects] have different meanings in different social worlds but their structure is common enough to more than one world to make them recognizable, a means of translation. The creation and management of boundary objects is key in developing and maintaining coherence across intersecting social worlds."[5]

The flexibility to interpret any object makes the theory of boundary objects to a possible connector of design experiments and scientific research. The collection of general data about different types of bark facilitates and stimulates the discussion between science and design, with the goal to determine relevant research directions and tailor-made bark use for different species.

The process itself, which is characterized by simultaneous scientific experiments, design techniques, and crafts, generates new knowledge about the material. The results are iteratively used for the further development of design experiments, scientific experiments, and design applications.

3 "Destatis Holzeinschlag 2019: 69 Millionen Kubikmeter," Statistisches Bundesamt, https://www.destatis.de/DE/Themen/Branchen-Unternehmen/Landwirtschaft-Forstwirtschaft-Fischerei/Wald-Holz/aktuell-holzeinschlag.html (accessed June 26, 2021).

4 Susan Leigh Star and James R. Griesemer, "Institutional Ecology, 'Translations' and Boundary Objects: Amateurs and Professionals in Berkeley's Museum of Vertebrate Zoology, 1907–39," *Social Studies of Science* 19, no. 3 (1989).

5 Star and Griesemer, "Institutional Ecology, 'Translations' and Boundary Objects," 393.

Fig. 1: Peeling bark.

Peeling Bark

Tree bark was not always treated as a waste material in the past. A review of literature on material culture revealed a long and diverse tradition of bark use since the Stone Age. Bark use is documented in the European rural periphery until the first half of the twentieth century, in particular in countries with a long history of timber production like Austria[6] and Finland.[7] In these regions, tree bark was harvested by peeling as a seasonal product. Even though the technique of peeling is rarely documented, some of the reported applications, like large layers of bark that were used to build seasonal alpine huts,[8] made clear that it is possible to remove large bark pieces. The aim within the Bark Project is to study large pieces of tree bark in order to create application scenarios reaching from small-scale objects up to architectural dimensions.

The first attempts to peel trees took place in Spring 2018 and soon it became clear that some trees such as beech cannot be peeled, while for others, peeling is only possible when trees are full with water. As a result, freshly peeled bark contains a large amount of water. The drying process leads to pronounced shrinkage and warping. Warping can be avoided by fixation of the wet bark between wooden boards until dry. The harvest of large pieces of bark allows design experiments for large-scale applications; it is also possible to get an overall picture of how macroscopic as well as microscopic structure and properties change along the tree—both with design and scientific experiments (fig. 1).

6 Hiltraud Ast and Georg Winner, "Historische Holzverwendung und Waldnutzung in der Schneebergregion: Rindennutzung," Institut für Holztechnologie und Nachwachsende Rohstoffe (2011).

7 Ville Kokkonen and Florencia Colombo, *Man Matter Metamorphosis: 10000 Years of Design* (Helsinki: National Museum of Finland, 2018).

8 Hiltraud Ast and Georg Winner, "Historische Holzverwendung und Waldnutzung in der Schneebergregion."

Research on Structure and Properties

Compared to wood, bark is less well studied. This lack of knowledge is possibly a consequence of less economic interest and high variability of bark material properties. An understanding of properties requires detailed information about chemical composition, structural differences at several length scales and physical properties (thermal, mechanical, optical, ...). To get this data, materials characterization techniques such as imaging approaches (for example, light and electron microscopy, computer tomography), structural analysis (X-ray diffraction), chemical (wet chemistry) and mechanical tests (for example, tensile tests, nanoindentation) are applied. These insights allow for more targeted design experiments. By combining both scientific and design-based results, processing methods can be precisely adapted to the typical properties of different barks. In addition, fields of application are better defined, enabling more targeted and sustainable application (fig. 2).

Fig. 2: Research on structure and properties.

Fig. 3: Flat bark panel.

Densification

Standardization, such as by defined and homogenized sizes or mechanical properties, is a common method to facilitate the processing of materials. In order to transform tree bark into uniform and standardizable panels (fig. 3), various forms of compression processes were studied. The densification of two crosswise placed bark pieces with specific heat and pressure conditions led to flat bark panels with a smooth surface and mechanical stability. It is conceivable that the heat melts substances in the bark, which act as glue. In this way, a purely bio-based material without additional adhesive but reproducible appearance and mechanical properties was created.

Fig. 4: Pressed bark in 3D shapes.

Experiments with Three-Dimensional Geometries

In a second step, the potential to create three-dimensional geometries was explored as these experiments open up new possibilities for 3D elements frequently required for many industries such as transportation design or packaging industry. Metal molds with different geometries were produced and bark pieces were pressed into the predefined shapes. The experiments showed that bark can be pressed into 3D shapes (fig. 4) with the cambium facing in both directions. More critical is the fiber direction, which should follow the curvature of the mold. The method works best for oak, pine and larch. While larch and pine show a very smooth surface, oak results in a possibly high-strength material due to its large fiber content.

Fig. 5: Mirror pine bark treated with a water-glycerine solution.

Flexible Bark

Freshly harvested tree bark is full of water and at least partly flexible. The drying of bark causes not only geometric deformations but also stiffening, hardening, and increased brittleness. While numerous applications rely on stiff, hard and strong materials, others, such as textiles for different uses, require flexibility. Since we know that leaves can be preserved and protected from crumbling by treating them with glycerin,[9] a similar approach was explored for bark. Glycerin keeps water molecules in hygroscopic materials and prevents them from drying.[10]

In an experiment, mirror bark of pine (*Pinus sylvestris*) was immersed in a mixture of glycerin and water and it was possible to maintain flexibility (fig. 5).[11] In terms of applications for flexible bark, historical examples provide inspiration: Already 8,000 years ago tree bark was used for clothing in China.[12] Nowadays bark textiles are still present in Central America and Uganda.[13] While the mentioned examples are nonwoven textiles, in European peripheries, especially in Finland, birch shoes or even whole suits of birch bark were created by weaving until the 1870s.[14]

9 A. K. Babu et al., "Review of Leaf Drying: Mechanism and Influencing Parameters, Drying Methods, Nutrient Preservation, and Mathematical Models," *Renewable and Sustainable Energy Reviews* 90 (2018): 536–56.

10 Babu et al., "Review of Leaf Drying."

11 Charlett Wenig et al., "Advanced Materials Design Based on Waste Wood and Bark," *Philosophical Transactions* (2021).

12 Dawei Li et al., "The Oldest Bark Cloth Beater in Southern China (Dingmo, Bubing basin, Guangxi)," *Quaternary International* 354 (2014): 184–89.

13 Samson Rwawiire, George William Luggya, and Blanka Tomkova, "Morphology, Thermal, and Mechanical Characterization of Bark Cloth from *Ficus natalensis*," *ISRN Textiles* (2013).

14 Ville Kokkonen and Florencia Colombo, *Man Matter Metamorphosis*.

Fig. 6: Bark jacket: The first prototype (non woven). Charlett Wenig (Material), Johanna Hehemeyer Cürten (Design), Model (Friedrich Reppe).

Bark Jacket – The First Prototype

Bark is the protection of the tree stem from environmental impacts. Driven by the question whether these protective properties can be transferred into textile applications for humans, the concept of a first prototype for a jacket was developed.

The bark jacket (fig. 6) is a tailor-made nonwoven garment of flexible pine bark. This design experiment was done in cooperation with fashion designer Johanna Hehemeyer-Cürten.

This experiment revealed bark-related material characteristics, which need to be considered for future manufacturing. While it is possible to sew bark across its longitudinal fiber directions, parallel seams lead to fractures of the material. The haptic of bark appears similar to leather but bark is stiffer. The model reported that the wearing comfort is worse than leather and the jacket feels like a stiff object. To overcome this problem, another fabrication method for using flexible bark as clothing or applications requiring high flexibility had to be considered.

Weaving Experiments

To increase fracture resistance and the flexibility of bark, weaving experiments were performed on a manual weaving chair (fig. 7). The idea was to make use of the better strength properties along the fiber direction, to increase flexibility and to create a fabric with more homogeneous properties in different directions. The application of different weaving techniques and patterns expands the design space for fine tuning material properties even more. The cooperation with fashion design was a determining role in this process. In order to find suitable weaving patterns for the woven jacket, different weaving techniques have been tested and evaluated.

Bark Jacket Woven

The woven bark jacket (fig. 8) is the first application of woven flexible bark (again in collaboration with Johanna Hehemeyer-Cürten). The problems of sewing and cutting of the first bark jacket were solved and the wearing comfort was improved by an increased flexibility. A twill weave, a pattern of diagonal parallel lines by passing the weft thread over one or more warp threads and then under two or more warp threads, providing good flexibility, was used.[15] Twill is popular in denim or furniture fabrics because it is very durable, more pliable and has a better wrinkle recovery.

Conclusion and Outlook

The Bark Project is an ongoing research project. Basic research on the structure and properties of barks of different species, developmental aspects, as well as how bark changes with the age of a tree and along the stem axis are still missing. It is expected that a better understanding of the raw material will trigger further developments toward a sustainable bark use in future interdisciplinary collaborations.

15 Anni Albers et al., *On Weaving: New Expanded Edition* (Princeton: Princeton University Press, 2017).

Fig. 8 (top): Bark jacket, second prototype (woven). Charlett Wenig (Material), Johanna Hehemeyer Cürten (Design), Model (Lee Zihern).

Fig. 7 (bottom): Weaving experiments.

In the Flow
Incorporating the Formative Forces of Fluid Matter

Barbara Schmidt

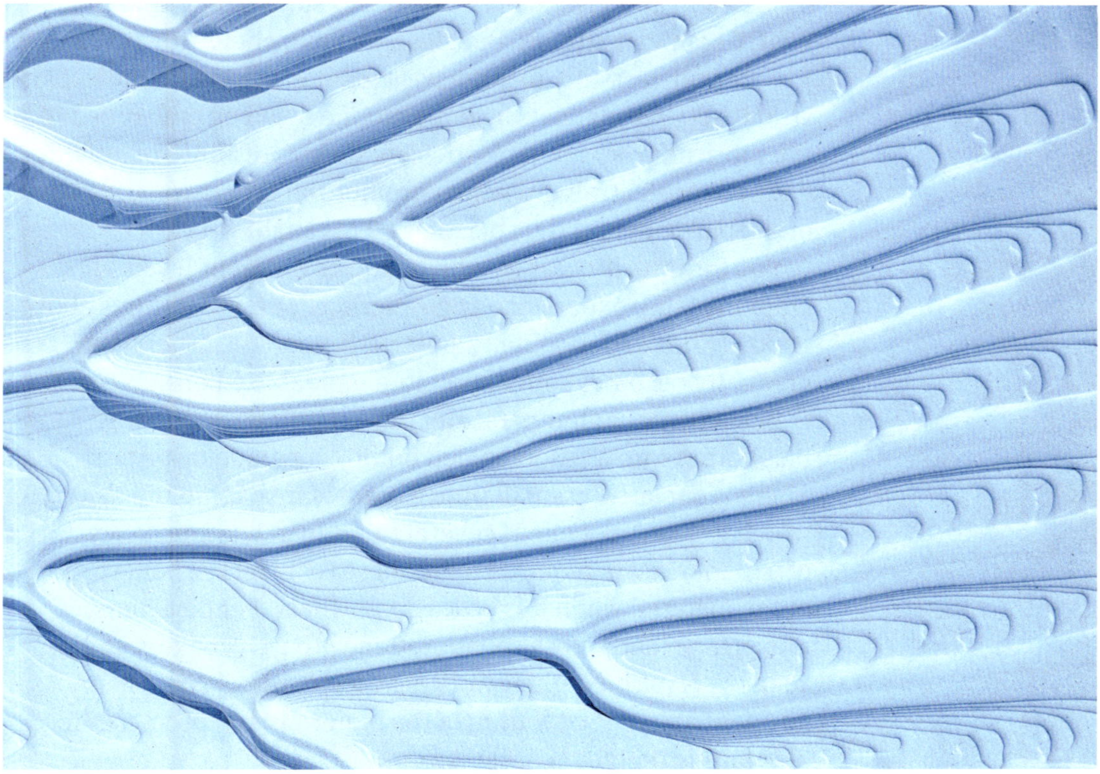

Visible signs of human workmanship on artifacts provide visual information that piques our curiosity and keeps our attention longer than smooth surfaces. But they do even more: they move us. Just like shapes and structures grown in nature, they represent aliveness and invoke the presence of an absent other. How can this be a quality also of objects that are created without—or with only indirect—involvement of a shaping human hand? Can the action of an "invisible hand" be used as a design element in the process of shaping material? How does spontaneous order arise within a material in the dynamic interface between natural phenomenon and artifact?

To be explored here is the relationship between creative intention and the inner logic of the material, between exercising control and relinquishing it, between consciously shaping and merely anticipating and steering shape-forming processes by designers. The focus is on ceramic materials and glass, made moldable by liquefaction or by plasticization with water in suspension and plastic mass, as well as softened by applying heat. Ceramic materials and glass are amorphous during the forming process and do not have a regular, organized molecular structure. Clay platelets become mobile by being embedded in the lubricant water and plasticizers such as residues of organic material or electrolytes, which promote an orderly orientation of the particles and thus plasticity. This enables a variety of "cold" forming processes, which require different levels of craftsmanship experience and expertise. At temperatures above 1000°C, the particles finally sinter. Glass, on the other hand, gradually becomes softer and more moldable when subjected to heat (at similar temperatures) and solidifies by cooling. It solidifies into a "supercooled liquid," a paradoxical state. There is a relatively small time window for shaping the material, which can be "reopened" several times by reheating. Years of experience are required to be able to control the behavior of the material when it is processed by heat. For designers, this means that a close collaboration with glassmakers and a keen observation of their work is necessary in order to gain an adequate understanding of the materials and processes for developing their own designs.

In industrial production, casting and blowing molds are used to produce copies of a form that are as identical as possible, and which do not convey any information about their production process. Still, even with these processes there are possibilities intrinsic to the technology to deviate from the given, ideal forms intended by design which can be brought to the fore as a design factor. These include sink marks or seams; surface effects such as hammer marks; irregularities in the shaping of edges, mold radii and mold details; or the formation of material thicknesses. It is also possible to cultivate the difference of rotational shapes to the ideal circle, the deformation susceptibility of geometries, and the shrinkage of ceramics in general.

Here is presented a series of projects by students and graduates of the weißensee school of art and design berlin over the course of five years. All of these process-oriented projects have in common that the shaping forces at work in the fluid state remain permanently visible in the results of the forming processes.

Through their own experience, experiments, and observations, students became familiar with the forming processes, so that they were able to develop ideas, concepts, and tools to create such possibilities under certain environmental conditions—some of those conditions were designed by themselves, some of them were found on-site. In all works, the viewer can recognize patterns and experience the behavior of the material. The specific aesthetic quality of the works lies in the partial ornamental effect of the marks left by the process, the enhancement of the form by similar, but never exactly the same repeatable "growth patterns," the actual or presumed inhomogeneity of the material used, its autonomy—visible and expressed effectively in the artifacts—or the impression conveyed by the artifacts that the material has taken shape in a collaborative creative process between the maker and the material itself.

Figs. 1a (top) & 1b (bottom): *Vågorglas*, Anton Richter, glass, found metal molds, 2018.

Vågorglas

When glass, a thermally inert material, comes into contact with materials that are better heat conductors and when there is a steep temperature drop between them, temperature gradients are created in the glass mass. Due to its viscosity, the glass mass in turn reacts by warping, especially on the surface, when it cools down quickly.

Anton Richter has explored this phenomenon from a creative perspective and recognized its potential for creating an aesthetic quality: with a minimum of forming, the glass appears to flow into the intended form by itself, developing specific design qualities in the process (fig. 1a). A "process ornament" spreads over the entire surface of the object on the side in contact with the colder material (fig. 1b). This creates an effect in the material that suggests the existence of an inner structure. He says: "Liquid glass turns solid within seconds. The flow of the glass hardens, creating a permanent shape. The possibility to freely shape cast glass can be used to create defined objects. Both pouring hot glass over negatives as well as pressing it between two forms gives the viscous material the freedom to take on a variety of shapes. Thus, the creation process of the products remains visible in their structure. The suspended flow of the glass gives the object a dynamic character, which is enhanced by the kinetic properties of some objects. The glass creates the impression of still being in motion."

Figs. 2a & 2b: *Ordre Coulant*, Christin Amann, porcelain and glass, 2019.

Ordre Coulant

The flow of the material is not restricted, but instead partially channeled by creases and edges, which remain visible as a fundamental form-shaping principle in the design of the objects. The undirected flow of the porcelain slip follows patterns and keeps forming similar shapes, for example, when the material builds up at a step and finally gushes over the obstacle. The creases and edges in the porcelain plates, which are also tools for shaping the glass, ultimately serve to position the finished glass objects and to connect the porcelain pieces and glass objects. In addition, they offer new options for arranging the created vessels on the table.

The conceptual approach of *Ordre Coulant* is based on the exploration of the strict order of the Baroque table culture. Hidden creases in the table linen help create and maintain this order. This order is adapted by establishing new rules linked to the shapes of the items that allow less structured arrangements, relationships, and compositions of the objects (figs. 2a, 2b).

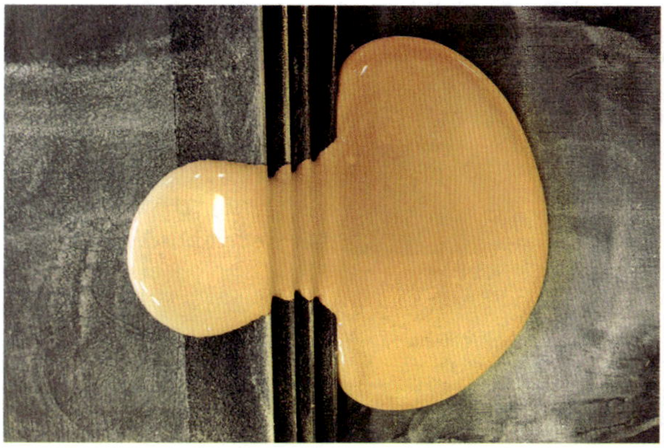

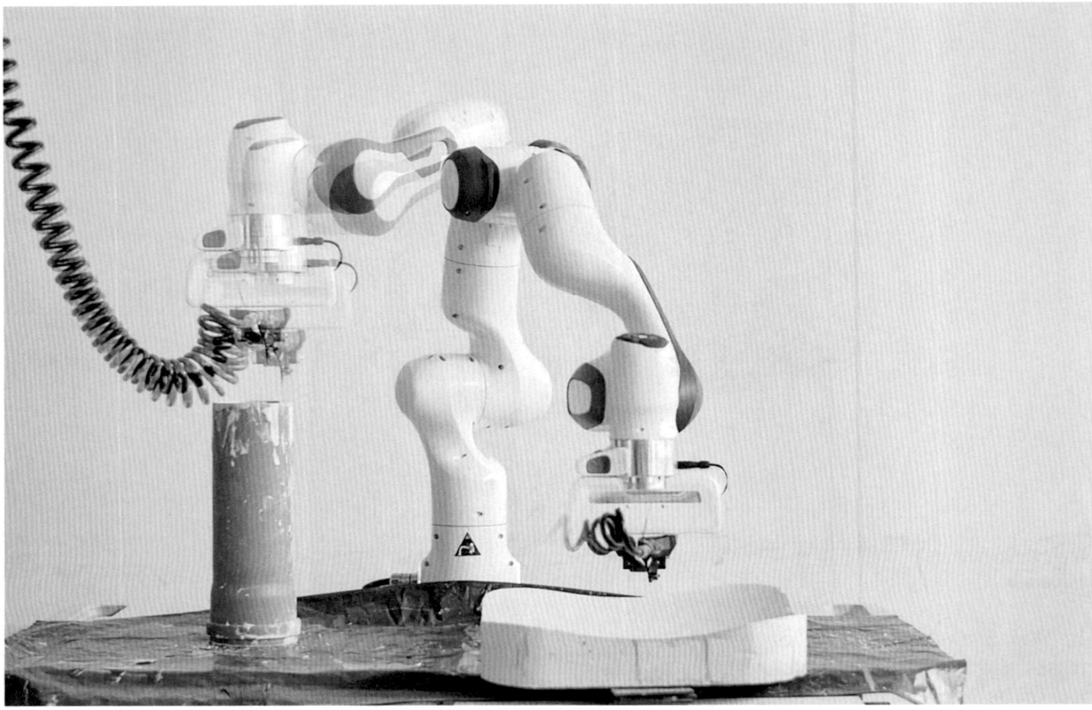

Figs. 3a (top) & 3b (opposite): *Material Driven, Digitally Produced*, Konrad Jünger, porcelain, robotics, 2019.

Material Driven, Digitally Produced

Normally, porcelain casting slip is supposed to take on a predefined shape, preferably without any internal structure of the material being visible on the surface of the object. Here, a robot arm is used as a tool that does not actually shape the material, but simply places it in the right place at the right time, whereby exposing it to the force of a few factors (fig. 3a). In addition to the geometry of the plaster mold, these factors are gravity and the inherent properties of the material, such as its composition and the resulting flowability, and finally the nature of the base material—partly plaster, partly already cast porcelain layers with a varying moisture content and corresponding absorbency.[1]

Another design factor, in addition to the digital script for the precision movements of the machine controlled by the designer, is the "fuzziness" of the material. The conditions for the added porcelain suspension layers also change in a dynamic way. This creates a complex chaotic system that still has discernible regularities. The resulting objects are built from thin, never quite identical layers that are reminiscent of naturally growing forms (fig. 3b).

1 Konrad Jünger, "Material Driven, Digitally Produced" (Master's thesis, weißensee school of art and design Berlin, 2019).

SubTiles

Figs. 4a (opposite) & 4b (below): *SubTiles*, Jonas Schneider, glazed porcelain, plaster molds, 2014.

A form initially designed with a clear geometry, a ceramic surface with relief-like depressions in the shape of spherical cuts based on the shape of the head of the CNC milling machine (fig. 4b), and whose different light-shadow effects were intended, gains a surprising element during the glazing process: depending on the depth of the negative forms, the glaze reaches across the depressions and fills them up, bulges slightly inwards to them or is drawn into them and only covers them as a thin layer. This creates the deceptive impression that the glaze was applied with intention and great effort in layers of varying thickness. These objects make it possible to experience the viscosity and surface tension of glazes in response to different structuring of ceramic carrier surfaces. Due to the behavior of the glaze during the melting process, layers of different thickness are formed, which also reveal that the glaze is not completely transparent (fig. 4a).

Digital Handmade

Pâte de verre is one of the oldest glassmaking techniques in the world. However, after a revival in the early twentieth century it is now relegated to a niche status. But in 2016, Virginia Binsch explored ways to advance the technique using digital tools.

The glass powder pressed into the mold is slowly melted in the furnace until it is sintered. During this process, the object is heated from above, that is, from the smooth side. The material in the depressions of the fine relief, which was developed with parametric software, is heated last. While the glass powder has already melted on the surface (fig. 5b), particles in the deeper layers and the branches of the relief only lightly adhere to one another and remain visible as granules (fig. 5a).

The material is chemically homogeneous. But here, different stages of sintering coexist in one object: smoothly melted with fused particles, and with particles only lightly fused together at the edges. Technical factors such as the type of glass, particle size, moisture content and firing curve, as well as the formal design and the resolution of the relief offer infinite possibilities of variations to create elaborate surfaces of great actual and visual tactility, reminiscent of sugar, pumice, sand, or concrete.[2]

2 Virginia Binsch, "Digital Handmade: Parametrisch gestaltete Oberflächen in Pâte de Verre" (Master's thesis, weißensee school of art and design Berlin, 2016).

Figs. 5a (opposite) & 5b (top): *Digital Handmade*, Virginia Binsch, pâte de verre, parametrically designed forms, 2016.

Panta Rhei

Figs. 6a (opposite) & 6b (below): *Panta Rhei*, Jihye Kang, porcelain, water, metal salt colorants, 2018.

In her work *Panta Rhei*, Jihye Kang examines the effect of water as a creative force on porcelain objects produced by slip casting, in particular its removing and deforming abilities, and its effect as a vehicle for color.[3] Water is one of the determining factors in the shape of the objects; the designer merely defines the process.

In this experiment, capillary forces distribute the water and thus the coloring metal salt. Bisque-fired porcelain cylinders stand or lie in petri dishes filled with liquid (fig. 6b). Factors such as the type of coloring salt, concentration, amount of liquid in the container, wall thickness of the object or the soaking time, but also the surrounding conditions such as the ambient temperature and humidity influence the result. In addition, the water has an effect in different states of matter when distributing the salts: cylinders are immersed in liquid vertically and horizontally.

Color is applied on porcelain objects, forming gradients and patterns that cannot be achieved with any known manual application technique. Here too, the manufacturing process itself has become part of the result (fig. 6a).

3 Jihye Kang, "Panta Rhei: Wasser formt Keramik" (Master's thesis, weißensee school of art and design Berlin, 2018).

Figs. 7a (below) & 7b (opposite): *Circular Processes and Feedback Loops in Additive Manufacturing Processes*, Babette Wiezorek, porcelain, 3D printing, 2016.

Circular Processes and Feedback Loops in Additive Manufacturing Processes

If 3D printing is done with ceramic paste instead of heated plastic filament, as is usually the case in FDM printing (Fused Deposition Modeling), it requires not only competence in developing the digital file or in programming the printer's path, but also in handling the machine's electronics and mechanics and, above all, experience with the material.[4] The printing result depends on many parameters. Exploring them and acquiring skills in a digital craft is similar to developing the manual virtuosity of an artisan.[5]

In order to explore parallels between the production of forms by computer-controlled extrusion of ceramic material and by natural growth processes, Babette Wiezorek expands and upgrades her printer both on a mechanical and an electronic level (fig. 7a). The ceramic paste is applied slightly off-center on a movable, suspended base plate, which gradually becomes more and more out of balance. A sensor detects the increasing imbalance. This is continuously reported back to the system. As a result, the tool path of the printer is recoded in real time to make adjustments. The expressive and seemingly dynamic print results show signs of the struggle to achieve balance (fig. 7b). Their shapes feedback on themselves during their creation.

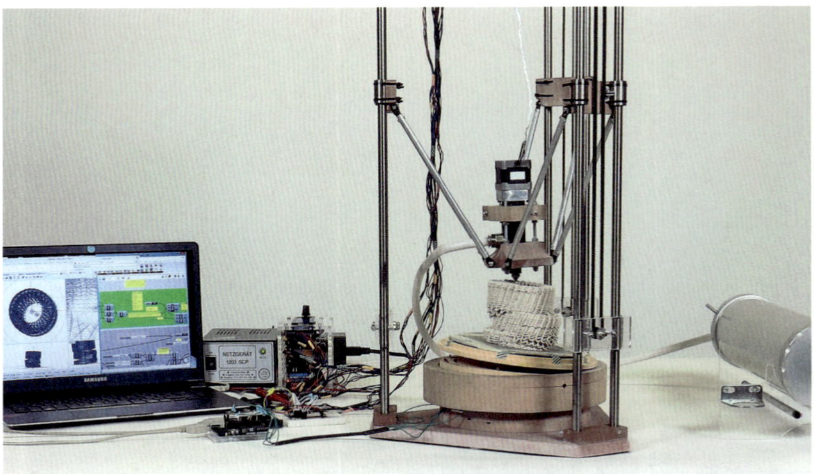

4 Jörg Petruschat, "Good Vibrations? Some Remarks on the Resonance Between Human Beings and Objects," in *Ceramics and Its Dimensions: Shaping the Future*, ed. Maarit Mäkelä (Helsinki: Aalto University, 2016), 136–54.

5 Richard Sennett, *The Craftsman* (New Haven: Yale University Press, 2008).

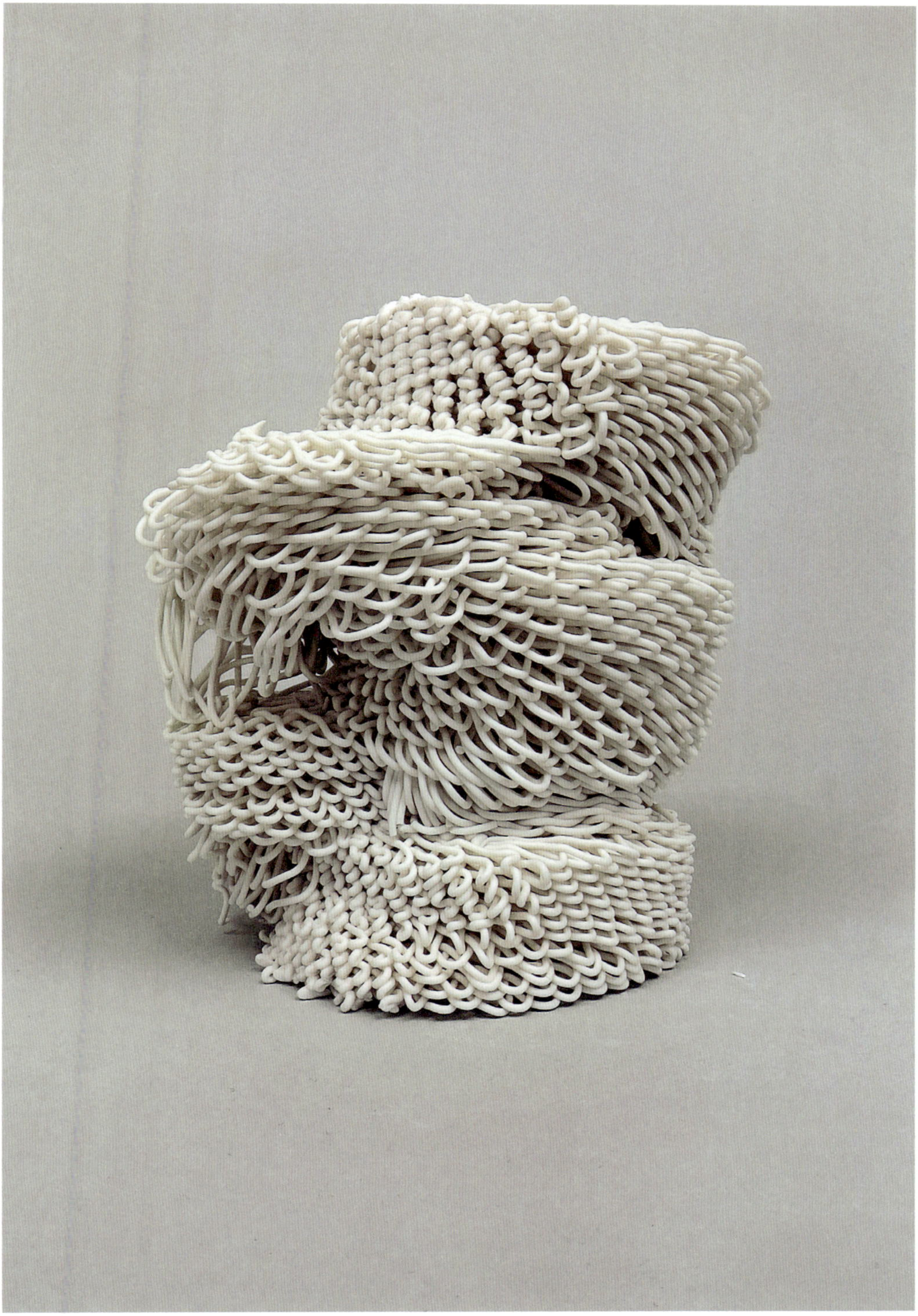

Figs. 8a (above) &
8b (opposite): *Column*,
Katharina Ruhm, glass,
flexible metal tool, 2018.

Column

To make *Column*, the glassmaking team is given a flexible tool made of loosely connected steel tubes, which is used to shape the glass during the blowing process in a controlled way (fig. 8b). The resulting glass objects have both a serial character and are unique. In addition to the pattern that the tool imprints on the objects during production, the objects also bear the individual signature of each glassmaker. The use of the same tool can produce very different results (fig. 8a). The expansion of the glass during blowing is restricted by the moveable metal tubes. The pressure exerted on certain parts of the glass from the outside when holding the mold is another critical forming factor that determines the cross-sectional shape of the objects. Thus, even without professional training in glassmaking, designers can influence the shape of the artifact during its manufacture.

Translated from the German by Sabine Voigt

Designing Openness
An Approach to Integrate Active Material Behavior into Digital Design Practice

Ianis Lallemand

The last decade has seen a rise in digital design approaches that challenge the primacy of representation over physical making. No doubt motivated by the development of the concept of active matter[1] and the strengthening of the philosophical idea of a new materialism,[2] such approaches have led designers to tap into active material behavior[3] to approach key design issues in fields ranging from architecture to product design. One could mention here, for instance, the series of architectural pavilions created by the Institute for Computational Design and Construction (ICD) and the Institute of Building Structures and Structural Design (ITKE) in Stuttgart, which combine robotic fabrication and the dynamic properties of materials such as carbon fiber or plywood.[4]

Previously, computational design research had focused mostly on digital morphogenesis, which explored the capacity of form to be generated rather than manually defined. By enabling the definition of dynamic rules and processes, programming fostered experiments in which—as in real-world systems—form did not descend over passive matter but emerged from the bottom-up interaction of a system's components. Within the last decade, the increased availability of digital fabrication tooling has extended this approach from the digital to the physical domain. Multimodal fabrication technology, such as 6-axis industrial robotic arms, enables plugging code's dynamic output into the physical properties of materials. In addition to the ICD/ITKE research pavilions mentioned above, one could cite the experiments in ceramics 3D printing of architects Ronald Rael and Virginia San Fratello,[5] designer Olivier van Herpt,[6] and designer collective Co-de-iT.[7]

Working with noncalibrated or unpredictable material dynamics within digital production frameworks, however, requires a constant adaptation of workflows so that a form of "openness" to materials can be prepared or sustained in the design phase. In my work, I address this issue by aiming to dissolve the hard conceptual and practical separation between the design and fabrication phases of a project, enabling porous digital production processes—in which geometric data does not flow only from the digital to the material, but also from the material to the digital. This objective can be achieved,

1 By this term, I refer in particular to the interdisciplinary body of research on the emergence of collective motion in living or inert systems composed of multiple interacting entities—such as a flock of birds—which has been developing within natural sciences over the past twenty years. For a general introduction to the notion of active matter within this framework, see: Gabriel Popkin, "The Physics of Life," *Nature News* 529, no. 7584 (2016): 16–18.

2 Iris Van der Tuin and Rick Dolphijn, eds., *New Materialism: Interviews and Cartographies* (London: Open Humanities Press, 2012).

3 In physics and materials science, the notion of material behavior refers to how a material performs under certain external conditions (mechanical stress, temperature...). In this text, I primarily refer to this idea, although my use of *behavior* is also informed by the rich and complex meaning acquired by the term within design and engineering practice. Of particular interest here is the connection between behavior and agency, inherited from scientific fields such as biology, psychology, cognitive science or robotics. The notion of agency, which bridges psychological behavior (real or perceived) with the physical capacity of an object to move and act on its environment, is indeed central to a range of contemporary practices at the intersection of design, art and engineering, which have engaged in designing not only the geometric form of objects but also their behavior. On this topic, see: Florent Levillain and Elisabetta Zibetti, "Behavioral Objects: The Rise of the Evocative

for instance, by preparing for the expression of material agency within the design phase (by means of designing "open notations"[8]), or by coding operative feedback mechanisms allowing physical material properties to inform digital models. Such design strategies acknowledge and seek to integrate the intrinsic form-generation capacity of materials within the design process. Envisioning a circular and networked connection between form and matter, rather than a linear and hierarchical relationship dominated by geometry, these approaches allow me to design with active material behavior, rather than trying to constrain it to predefined goals. The following case studies detail recent projects that implement such design approaches.

Machines," *Journal of Human-Robot Interaction* 6, no. 1 (2017): 4–24. For an historical perspective on the relevance of the concept of behavior within design, see also Jehanne Dautrey and Emanuele Quinz, *Strange Design: From Objects to Behaviors* (Paris: It: éditions, 2016).

4 See, for instance, Moritz Doerstelmann et al., "ICD/ITKE Research Pavilion 2014–15: Fibre Placement on a Pneumatic Body Based on a Water Spider Web," *Architectural Design* 85, no. 5 (2015): 60–65.

5 Rael Sanfratello, https://www.rael-sanfratello.com/ (accessed July 6, 2021).

6 Oliver van Herpt, https://oliviervanherpt.com/ (accessed July 6, 2021).

7 "Computational Design Italy," https://www.co-de-it.com/ (accessed July 6, 2021).

8 By this concept, which is inspired by Umberto Eco's notion of the "open work" (Umberto Eco, *The Open Work*, trans. Anna Concogni [Cambridge, MA: Harvard University Press, 1989]), I mean to qualify geometric elements that are designed to perform as "triggers" for the expression of unpredictable material effects during the production process of an object. Although composed of designed elements (such as the infill structures of the *Computational Ruins* project presented below), open notations do not seek to prescribe the final form of the object, but rather lay out the stage for the realization of form in collaboration with other agencies than the designer's (material, machines…). For more on open notations, see Ianis Lallemand, "Matière en acte : Les rapports entre conception et matérialité dans la production matérielle numérique" (PhD diss., Université Paris Sciences & Lettres, 2018), 153–87.

Fig. 1a (below): Schematic of the project's design and fabrication process, from concrete casting to demolding.

Fig. 1c (opposite): View of one of the concrete-plastic composites.

Fig. 1b (overleaf): Close-up view of a concrete casting mold with its internal variable honeycomb structure. The structure is revealed through fractures in the mold's surface created while demolding.

Computational Ruins (2015)

Computational Ruins aims at developing an experimental concrete casting process. Contrary to traditional methods, which seek precise reproduction, the project's goal is to create emergent structures resulting from the interaction of the casting process's materials—extruded plastic and concrete. To this end, 3D printing is used to fabricate dynamic and "open" plastic molds, designed to break in unpredictable ways when separated from the concrete (fig. 1a). By designing the mold's physical properties, one can thus encourage the appearance of expressive surface effects unachievable by standard machining.

This goal is achieved through the 3D printing of variable infill patterns (fig. 1b), which enable tailoring the mechanical properties of the molds at the local level. The project uses a desktop 3D printer based on fused deposition modeling technology (FDM), which usually produces parts by filling a solid outer shell with homogeneous internal structures. To obtain variable infill patterns, the printer's software is hacked to generate nonuniform honeycomb structures. Concrete molds are then printed with plastic filament (PLA). In each mold, a few low infill-density zones are prepared to "program" potentialities of failure during demolding.

As the stress caused by the demolding process causes low-density zones to break, parts of the molds remain embedded in concrete. The result is a series of concrete-plastic composites (fig. 1c). Their rich materiality—both rough and intricate, emergent and encoded—offers an opportunity to challenge traditional assumptions about 3D printing by replacing static geometric concerns with the design of dynamic material properties.

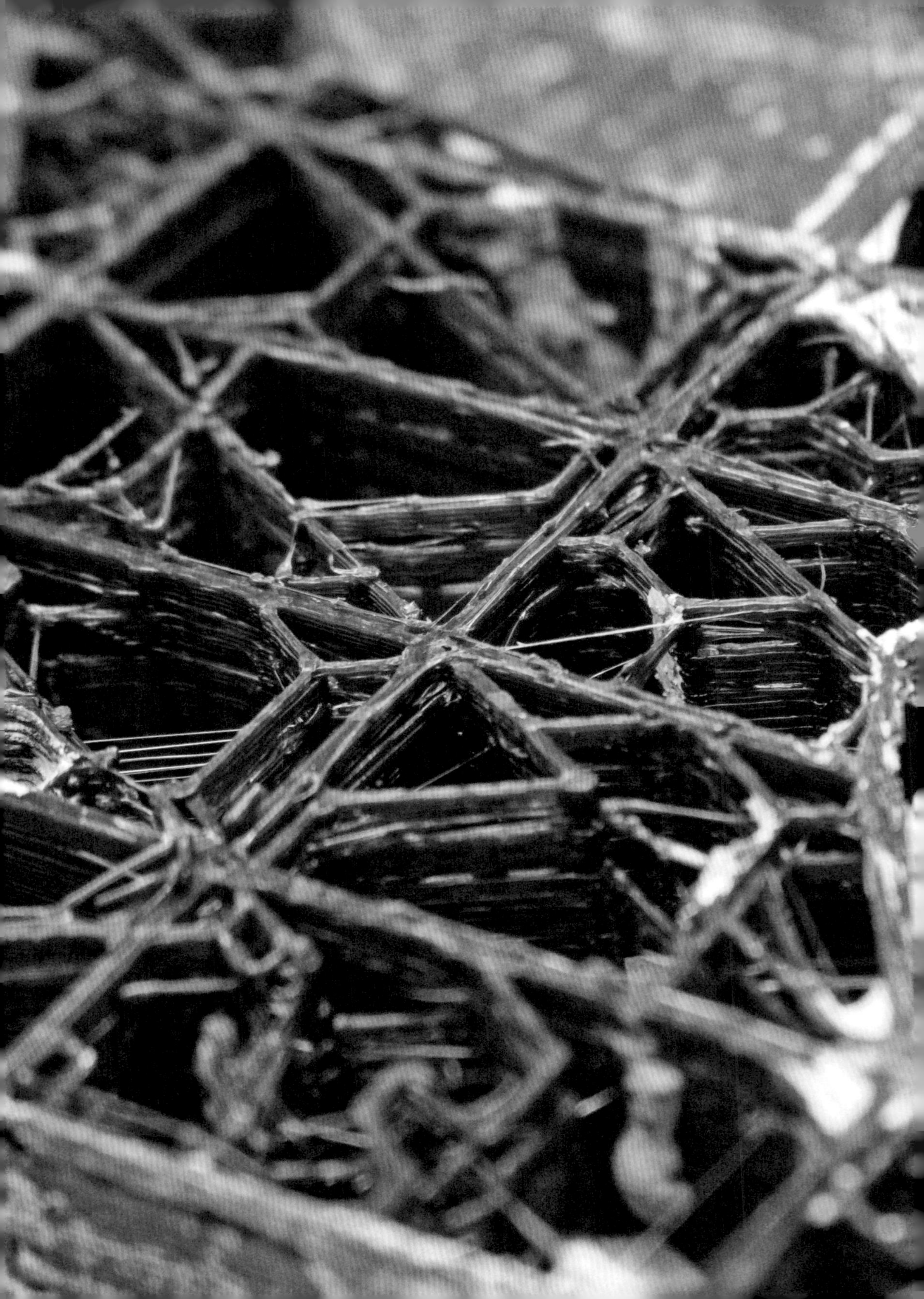

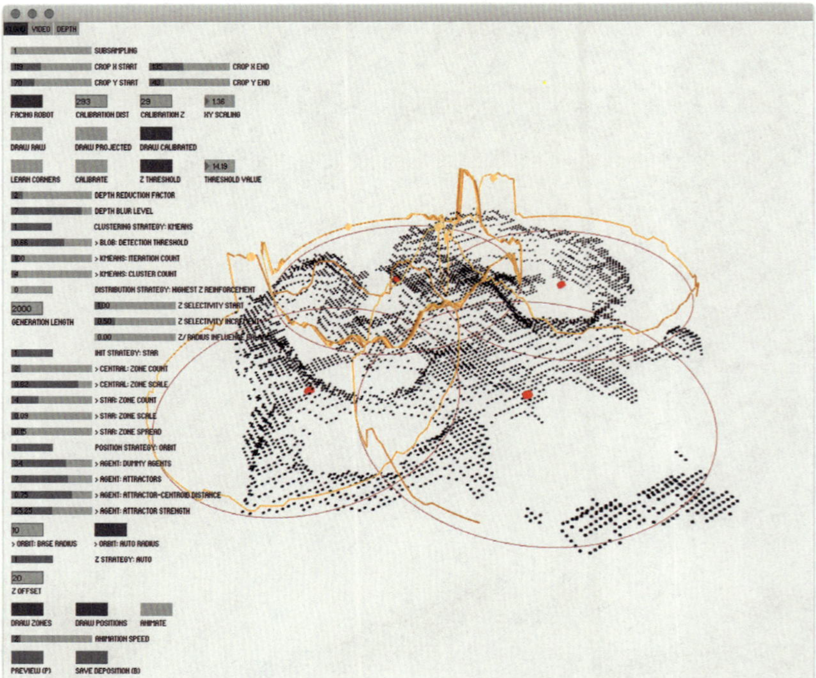
VIDEO
DEPTH
SUBSAMPLING
CROP X START
CROP X END
CROP Y START
CROP Y END
FACING ROBOT
CALIBRATION DIST
CALIBRATION Z
XY SCALING
DRAW RAW
DRAW PROJECTED
DRAW CALIBRATED
LEARN CORNERS
CALIBRATE
Z THRESHOLD
THRESHOLD VALUE
DEPTH REDUCTION FACTOR
DEPTH BLUR LEVEL
CLUSTERING STRATEGY: KMEANS
> BLOB: DETECTION THRESHOLD
> KMEANS: ITERATION COUNT
> KMEANS: CLUSTER COUNT
DISTRIBUTION STRATEGY: HIGHEST Z REINFORCEMENT
GENERATION LENGTH
INIT STRATEGY: STAR
> CENTRAL: ZONE COUNT
> CENTRAL: ZONE SCALE
> STAR: ZONE COUNT
> STAR: ZONE SCALE
> STAR: ZONE SPREAD
POSITION STRATEGY: ORBIT
> AGENT: DUMMY AGENTS
> AGENT: ATTRACTORS
> AGENT: ATTRACTOR-CENTROID DISTANCE
> AGENT: ATTRACTOR STRENGTH
> ORBIT: BASE RADIUS
> ORBIT: AUTO RADIUS
Z STRATEGY: AUTO
Z OFFSET
DRAW ZONES
DRAW POSITIONS
ANIMATE
ANIMATION SPEED
PREVIEW (P)
SAVE DEPOSITION (B)

Unspecified Clay (2016–17)

Unspecified Clay is a research project initiated in 2016 with the Italian group of designers Co-de-iT. The project takes the form of an experimental design and fabrication system making use of computational strategies and machine vision to iteratively adapt to a highly indeterminate, clay-based additive manufacturing process. Departing from conventional approaches to 3D printing and from the materialization of predefined models, *Unspecified Clay* sets up an experiment for exploring clay's morphogenetic potentialities. To this end, a retroactive production setup allows a robotic manufacturing unit to build artifacts through repeated cycles of deposition, scanning, and computation.

Based on a custom clay extruder, a 6-axis robot, a Kinect sensor, and custom software (fig. 2a), this setup enables a closed feedback loop between fabrication outcomes and generated robotic toolpaths. For each production cycle, the robot first performs the extrusion of a fixed amount of clay material, following either computed data (see later) or an initial, preprogramed pattern designed to bootstrap the fabrication process. After this step, the Kinect sensor provides the software with a point cloud representation[9] of all previously printed clay structures (fig. 5, in black). Machine learning algorithms then infer potential new deposition zones by clustering this data (fig. 2b, in red). Finally, new robotic toolpaths are computed (fig. 2b, in orange). This sequence is then repeated until exhaustion of the clay supply or intentional stop.

Within the frame of the project's interactive, playful fabrication process, the physical properties of the material are not subordinated to a geometric intent, but are free to behave as autonomous catalysts for aesthetic and structural explorations. A selected series of samples have been fired and glazed in a black gloss finish (fig. 2c). *Unspecified Clay* exemplifies one of the design strategies outlined in this chapter's introduction: by setting up a feedback mechanism that allows a digital model to be informed by physical behavior, the project is a step in the direction of eroding traditional boundaries between digital design and fabrication.

Fig. 2a (opposite, top): View of the fabrication setup (6-axis robotic arm, Kinect sensor, custom clay extruder designed by Co-de-iT).

Fig. 2b (opposite, bottom): View of the custom software used for point cloud processing and robotic toolpath generation.

Fig. 2c (below): View of one of the produced samples, processed with a black gloss finish.

9 In 3D imaging, a point cloud is a representation of a three-dimensional scene by a dense set of 3D points.

Fig. 3a (opposite, top): 3D rendering showing the vibrating plate and moving units.

Fig. 3b (opposite, bottom): View of the project's setup, exhibition at the Gaîté Lyrique, Paris, December 2–5, 2017.

Manœuvres (2016)

Manœuvres is a design research project developed with physicist Olivier Dauchot, director of the Collective Effects and Soft Matter team (EC2M) of the laboratory Gulliver UMR 7083 at the ESPCI in Paris. The project stems from one of the lab's experiments, exploring the production of large-scale collective motion by a population of self-propelled "grains." This appeared to me as closely related to the investigation of swarm behavior and flocking simulations in computational design research, with a crucial difference: EC2M's setup, which employs specially designed grains with a mechanically active structure, and a homogeneous source of energy in the form of a vibrating plate, is completely devoid of digital control or motorized elements. Collective motion thus emerges as a consequence of material properties rather than digitally programmed rules.

This realization forms the basis of *Manœuvres*—an interactive light-projection concept. The collective motion of self-propelled units is translated into a moving image, taking the form of an abstract yet human-scaled "crowd" of figures (fig. 3a). Each unit is equipped with a shadow-casting, rod-shaped structure,[10] and can be directly manipulated by the viewer as it moves (fig. 3b). This possibility of direct participation suggests a blurring of boundaries between human and nonhuman agency—an idea reflected in the production of a "human" image out of the grains' shadows. As the notion of active materials sets in within design research, *Manœuvres* offers an opportunity to reevaluate the role of design as a platform for conversation between human and nonhuman actors.

Acknowledgments

The author wishes to acknowledge Andrea Graziano, Marco Palma, Bruno Demasi, Alessio Erioli, and Olivier Dauchot for their collaboration in the projects discussed here, as well as the following institutions for their financial and material support: EnsadLab; PSL University; the SACRe doctoral program; the Chaire Arts & Sciences of the École polytechnique, EnsAD-PSL, and the Daniel & Nina Carasso foundation; digifabTURINg.

10 The moving units are fabricated with a combination of 3D-printed plastic parts and off-the-shelf components (hex nuts, rubber pad, nylon threaded rod).

To Build a Fish
Structuring Space and Material in Skeletons

Mason Dean
Júlia Chaumel
Ronald Seidel

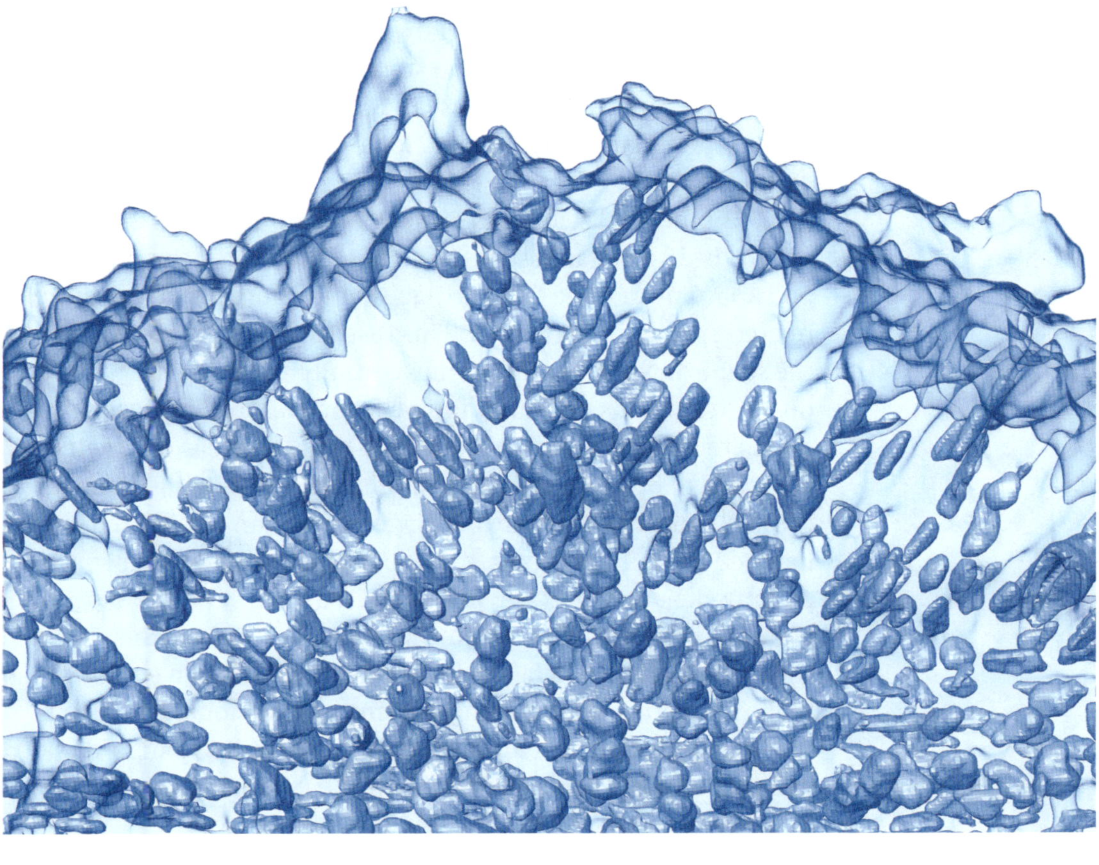

The old adage "There are many fish in the sea" is, with respect to animal diversity, quite true. Of the ~40,000 species of vertebrates (animals with backbones), more than 50 percent are fish. Fish occupy almost every body of water on the planet (from tropical to polar seas and all freshwater habitats) and are exceptionally diverse in diet, anatomy, and ecology. In our research work group, this huge variation of form and function offers a backdrop for studying how the tissues that build skeletons grow, vary, and evolve, adapting to conditions and challenges. Observing tissues outside of their biological context, only in the vials and slides of the lab, is like trying to suss out what pistons or valves do separately from the engine they belong in. We strive to fold the natural context of tissues into our work, how they are used in the animal's habitat and life history. Can they tolerate extreme temperatures or damage? Do they grow indefinitely? Do they assimilate particular elements from food? By cataloguing the natural diversity of tissue form and composition within the frames of ecology (where and how the animal lives) and evolution (species' relationships), we can start to make sense of the mosaic of animal forms and functions, and to decode the factors driving how tissues adapt—in short and long-time scales—to solve new problems.

Biomedical science is somewhat myopic with regard to the study of skeletal tissues: our understanding of the function and anatomy of bone and cartilage comes from just a few, closely related species of mammals. This restricts our perspective on the scope of what skeletal tissues actually are and what they can do. The skeletons of sharks and rays, for example, represent an opposite materials design strategy to ours: whereas our skeletons are made of bone, filled with cells charged with fixing damage, the skeletons of sharks are cartilage, which can be added to and patched up, but not repaired. Despite this, we know that shark and ray skeletons perform just as well as ours—and perhaps better, considering the extreme loads some species deal with in their lifetimes. These fascinating, alternative design solutions make fantastic fodder for engineering applications: How can a low-density material (cartilage) perform as well as a high-density one (bone)? How can a skeletal tissue be made resistant to damage so it doesn't need a cellular repair service?

Our work group combines engineering and biology approaches to study the development and mechanics of skeletons, in particular how tissue materials and architecture interact. We first characterize the geometries and tissue properties of natural systems using high-resolution engineering and materials science tools. Then to get a feel for how tissues manage and distribute forces, we build physical and digital mimics from biological data, scaling them up to sizes that make them easier to handle and test. With a multimaterial 3D printer, for instance, we manufacture biorealistic models with both rigid and flexible parts, which can be pushed, pulled, and fractured in ways that teach us about biological conditions. As in any design process, when the model raises more questions or fails to work, we return to the source—the biology—for a deeper understanding of the template.

The tools we use to look at our samples actually dictate what we see: no imaging tool is all-seeing, and so there will always be trade-offs and decisions made, building a curious subjectivity—but also creativity—into science. For example, some techniques create 3D images but are limited by how large the sample can be. Others can map chemical composition in a tissue, but only in 2D on the sample surface. In our work, the micro-CT scanning we often use won't show soft tissues unless we stain them with chemicals that add contrast, but even those agents have affinities, binding to some tissues and ignoring others. To some degree, it is a matter of choosing approaches that fit our imaging goals and limitations, the right tools for the particular job. In the following images of boxfish armor and stingray tesserae, we only wanted to visualize hard tissues and in 3D, which made micro-CT the perfect choice. Even so, targeting specific tissues doesn't preclude surprises: the many stingray spines we show pincushioning a wedgefish jaw might not have been discovered if another imaging technique had been used. To step around imaging and sampling biases, we often combine multiple tools to study the same tissue: by overlapping our hard tissue data from stingray tesserae (from micro-CT or electron microscopy) with polarized light microscopy images, we bring soft tissue architectures also into focus. We can even leverage techniques' biases to our advantage, for example, digitally filling voids in our tesserae micro-CT data (what was NOT imaged) to reveal the complex, internal cell networks. In these ways, the data we generate are reflections of our interests, but also the imaging and analysis tools we know of from experience and collaboration, those we have available, and those we choose.

There is a rich history of animal biomechanics study at organismal scales—including Stephen Wainwright's classic "To Bend a Fish," a treatise on the importance of fish skin[1] —but we push to understand form-function relationships at smaller sizes. The following pictures highlight how imaging tools can provide windows into the microscopic, hidden architectures of anatomy. By combining biology and engineering insights, we illuminate the functional roles of tissues while also pointing to generalizable features useful for building manmade composites. Given the impressive diversity, long lives, and ancient lineages of many fishes, their skeletons have much to teach us, if we are creative in how we look.

Further readings

• *Daniel Baum et al., "High-throughput Segmentation of Tiled Biological Structures Using Random Walk Distance Transforms,"* Integrative & Comparative Biology *59, no. 6 (2019): 1700–12.*
• *Júlia Chaumel et al., "Co-aligned Chondrocytes: Zonal Morphological Variation and Structured Arrangement of Cell Lacunae in Tessellated Cartilage,"* Bone *7, no. 134 (2020).*
• *Mason N. Dean et al., "Large Batoid Fishes Frequently Consume Stingrays Despite Skeletal Damage,"* Royal Society Open Science *4, no. 9 (2017): 170674.*
• *Lennart Eigen et al., "Ontogeny of a tessellated surface: carapace growth of the longhorn cowfish Lactoria cornuta,"* Journal of Anatomy *(2022). In press.*
• *Peter Fratzl et al., "The Mechanics of Tessellations: Bioinspired Strategies for Fracture Resistance,"* Chemical Society Reviews *45, no. 2 (2016): 252–67.*
• *Ronald Seidel et al., "Cartilage or Bone? Collagens in the Skeleton of 'Cartilaginous' Fishes Answer an Old Question,"* Journal of Structural Biology *200, no. 1 (2017): 54–71.*

1 Stephen A. Wainwright, "To Bend a Fish," in *Fish Biomechanics*, ed. Paul W Webb and Daniel Weihs (New York: Praeger, 1983), 68–91.

Dusty Jars and Hidden Scars

Natural history museums are libraries for Nature's works. Behind the public exhibits are countless shelves of specimens waiting to be studied and, in some cases, harboring secrets. When this jaw of a guitarfish (a large relative of stingrays) was micro-CT-scanned (fig. 1), a battery of broken stingray spines were discovered, lodged into the soft tissue of the mouth (here, colored red against the gray, translucent renderings).

Although the guitarfish was thought, due to its pebble-like teeth, to eat only small animals from the sand, this finding shows they are also voracious predators of their own relatives. This chance observation also gave unexpected insight into how shark and ray cartilage deals with tissue damage, while showing that shelved museum specimens hold clues to the habits of living animals, reminding us that we should not judge books by their covers (or jaws by their teeth).

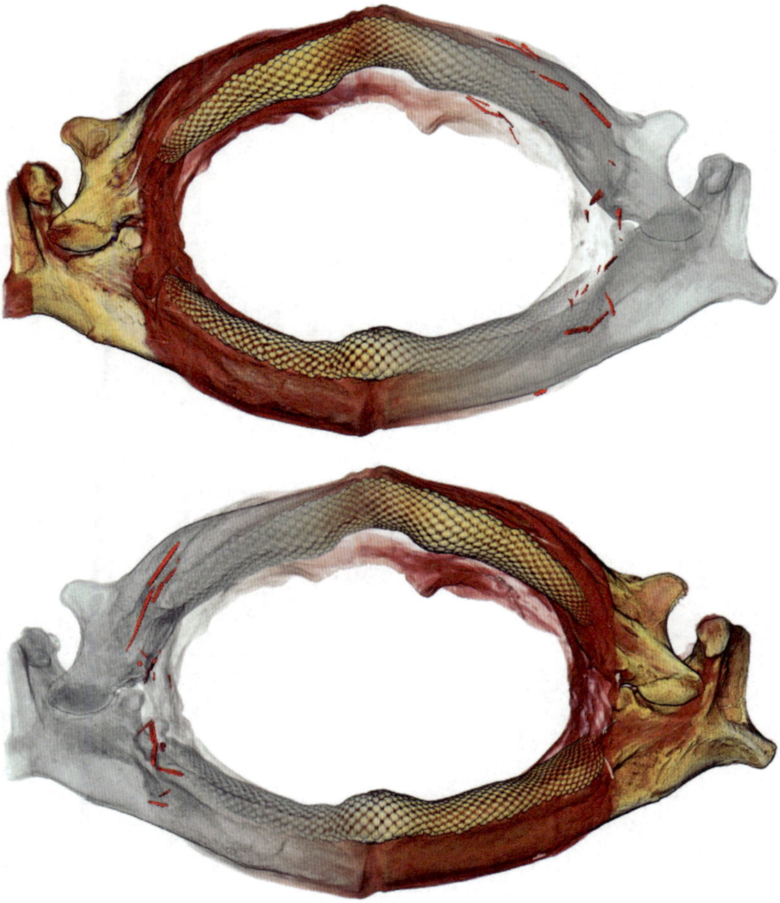

Fig. 1: Micro-CT-scanned jaw of a guitarfish, rendered half-transparent to show embedded stingray spines (red).

To Build a Stingray

To understand how Nature builds complex architectures, we can deconstruct them into their parts, but this is often easier said than done. Sharks and rays have skeletons made entirely of a curious armored cartilage, covered in an outer hull of many thousands of mineralized tiles called tesserae. This tessellated cartilage has been unique to sharks and rays for hundreds of millions of years, but has proved difficult to study and visualize due to tesserae being both numerous and small: the piece of a stingray skeleton shown here is just ~2 cm long, but it is covered by more than 3,000 tesserae of different shapes and sizes.

The image (fig. 2) is a visual record of a workflow, developed by combining materials and computer science approaches, starting from digital micro-CT data of a real specimen and, through image processing, digitally dissecting the tesserae from one another to color them according to their size. This is the first window into the architectural rules that define this skeletal design, a roadmap for the assembly of a complex biological pattern.

Fig. 2: Piece of a stingray skeleton, rendered to depict our analysis workflow, from micro-CT data, to isolated tesserae, to quantifiable networks (from left to right).

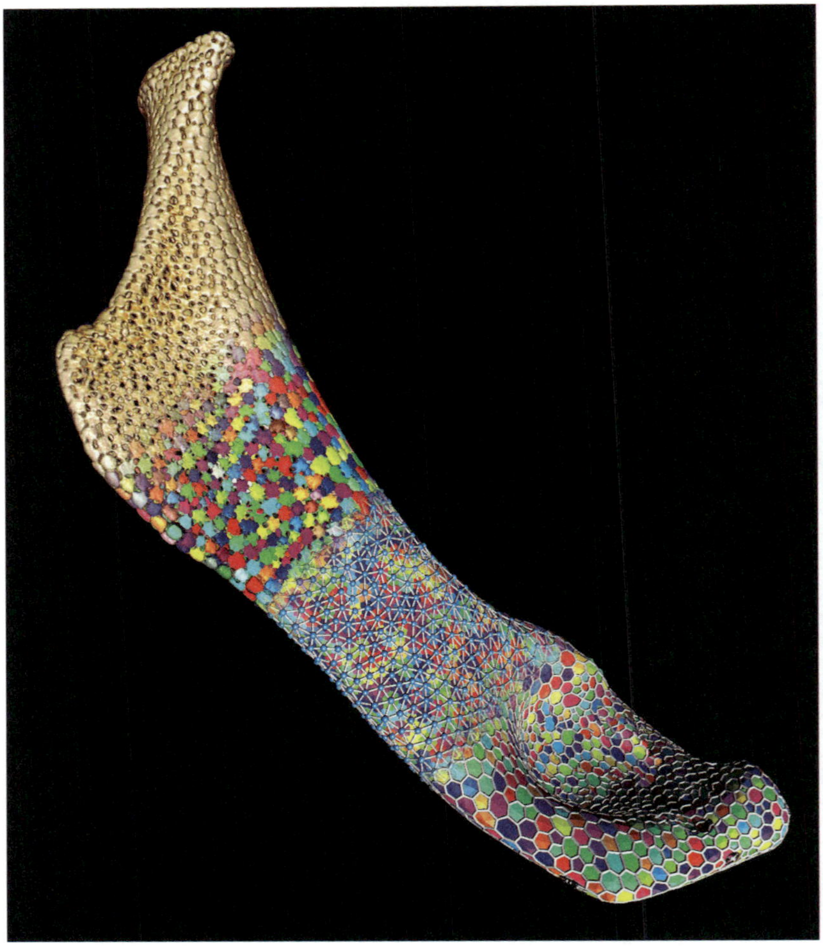

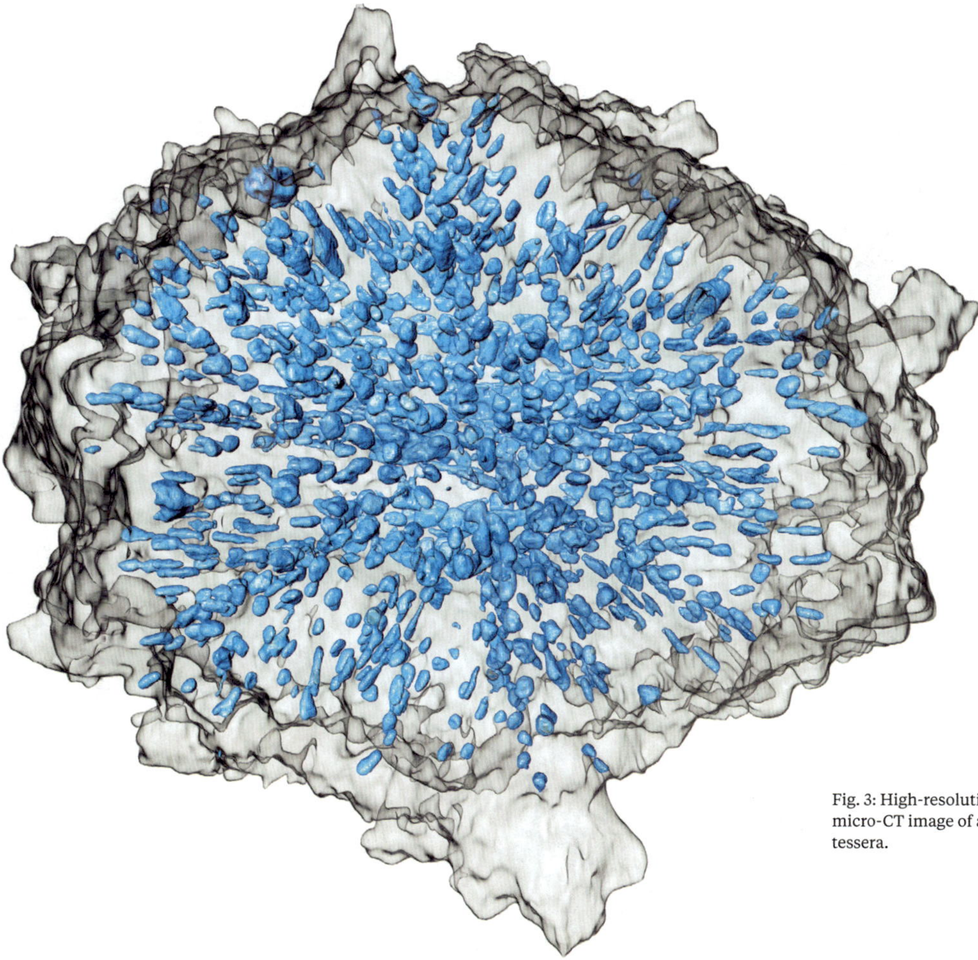

Fig. 3: High-resolution micro-CT image of a single tessera.

The Microchip of Shark and Ray Skeletons

The tesserae covering the skeletons of sharks and rays cobble together to form a hard crust (fig. 2), but are not simple blocks. The edges of each tessera are convoluted, as can be seen in this high-resolution micro-CT image of a single tessera (fig. 3), just a fraction of a millimeter wide. Moreover, each of the many thousand tesserae covering each piece of the skeleton harbor a rich population of cells that live ensconced in cavities within the hard material. By digitally filling those cavities (shown here in blue), we discovered that the cells are organized radially, connected to one another by small passages in a rich, communicating network.

The communication network is even broader than appreciated from this image: cells can interact within a tessera, but also across the gap between tesserae, like tenants in a building talking to their neighbors across the alley, perhaps allowing tesserae to connect into a broader interactive community.

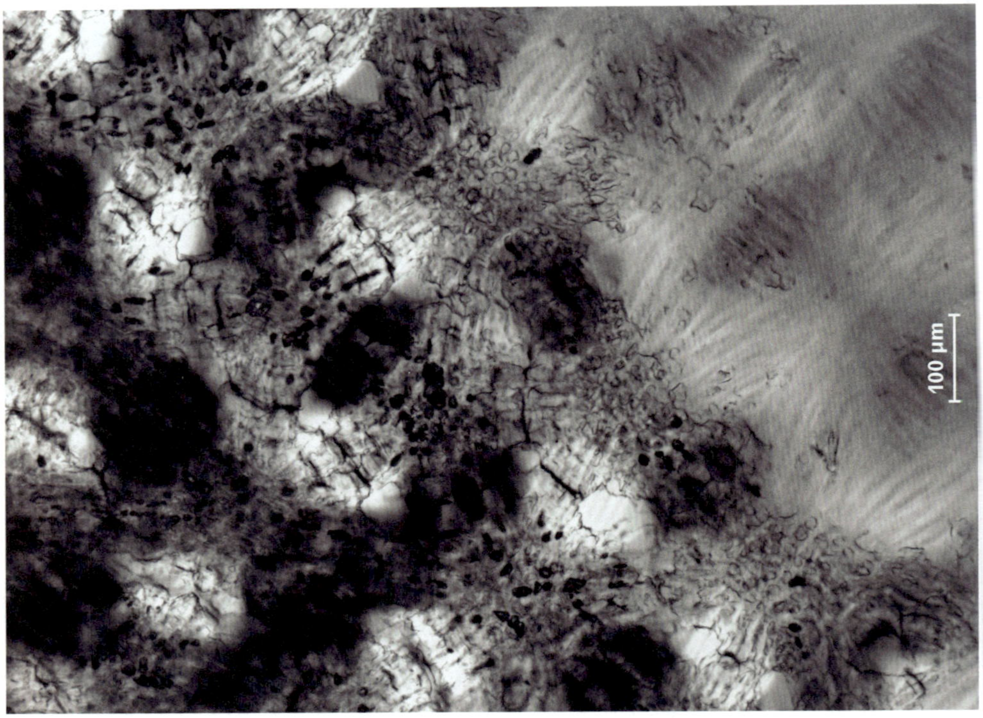
100 µm

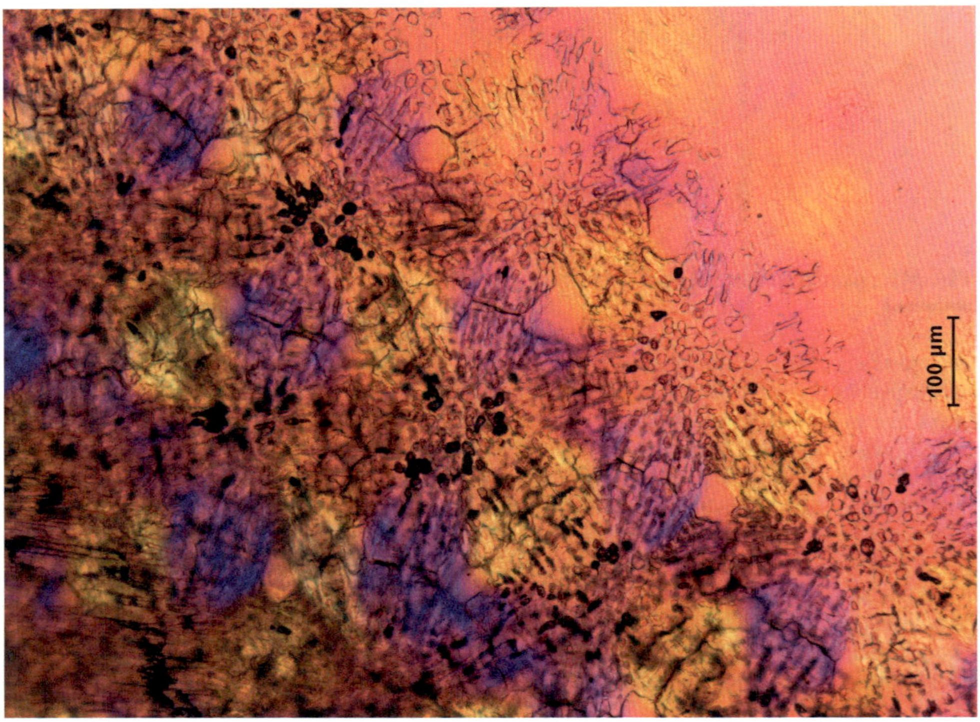
100 µm

Holding It All Together

What controls biological patterns? In growing mineralized tissues—like bone or shark and ray tesserae—collagen fibers often form scaffolds to guide where mineral crystals are tucked and packed, but the tight association of mineral and fiber can make this collagen scaffold hard to see.

The technique that produces these images, however, allows us to exploit the structure of collagen itself and to track its path through tissues. We take advantage of a tool originally developed to look at geologic crystals, but now often co-opted for visualizing fiber directions in biology: using polarizing filters (waveplates or retardation plates) in the light path of the microscope, we reveal the gross orientation of organic fibers within the tessellated layer of a stingray skeleton (fig. 4a). Both images show the same magnified region of the tessellated layer; however, in the colored image (fig. 4b), the different hues signify distinct fiber orientations, resulting from the light's being split into two perpendicular polarization directions, which pass the retardation plate at different speeds. The result is a window into the long-ranging fiber highways that act as blueprints for skeletal mineralization.

Inside Natural Building Blocks

One of the most striking aspects of biological tissues is their complexity at different length scales, which also makes them difficult to examine in their entirety, across scales. However, some microscopes can facilitate this, with a simple switch of the filter or tool used to look at the tissue. These environmental scanning electron microscope images obviously aren't identical, but actually show the same array of tesserae, the microscopic building blocks that cover all shark and ray skeletons.

The right image (fig. 5b), from a secondary electron detector, provides the topography of the sample, showing tesserae that are linked by string-like organic fibers to form flexible joints. In contrast, the left image (fig. 5a) was taken with a backscattered electron detector, revealing the distribution of heavier elements in the tissue (such as those forming mineral). The grayscale variation shows that tesserae are not uniform bricks of mineral, but rather play with how and where mineral is packed. The black regions harbor soft tissue, while the whitest regions are hypermineralized, reinforcing points where tesserae collide as the skeleton twists and turns.

Fig. 4a (opposite, top); 4b (opposite, bottom): Polarized light microscopy images of tesserae, illustrating fiber organization in the tissue, linking tesserae. The colors in the bottom image provide a visual map of fiber orientation, with similar colors indicating common fiber direction.

Figs. 5a & 5b (overleaf): Electron micrographs of a field of tesserae, a backscattered electron detector showing mineral density variation (left) and a secondary electron detector showing tissue topography (right).

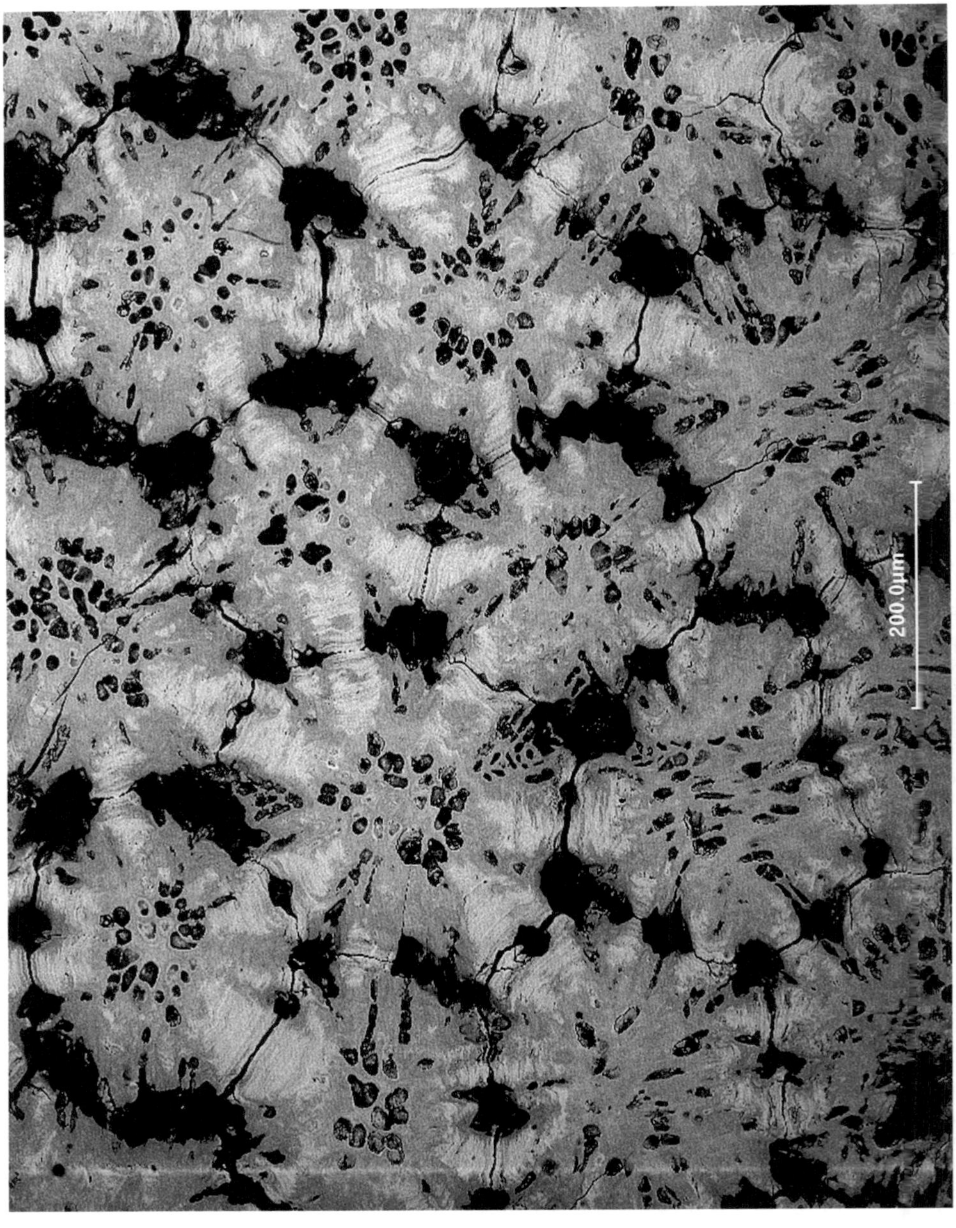
200.0µm

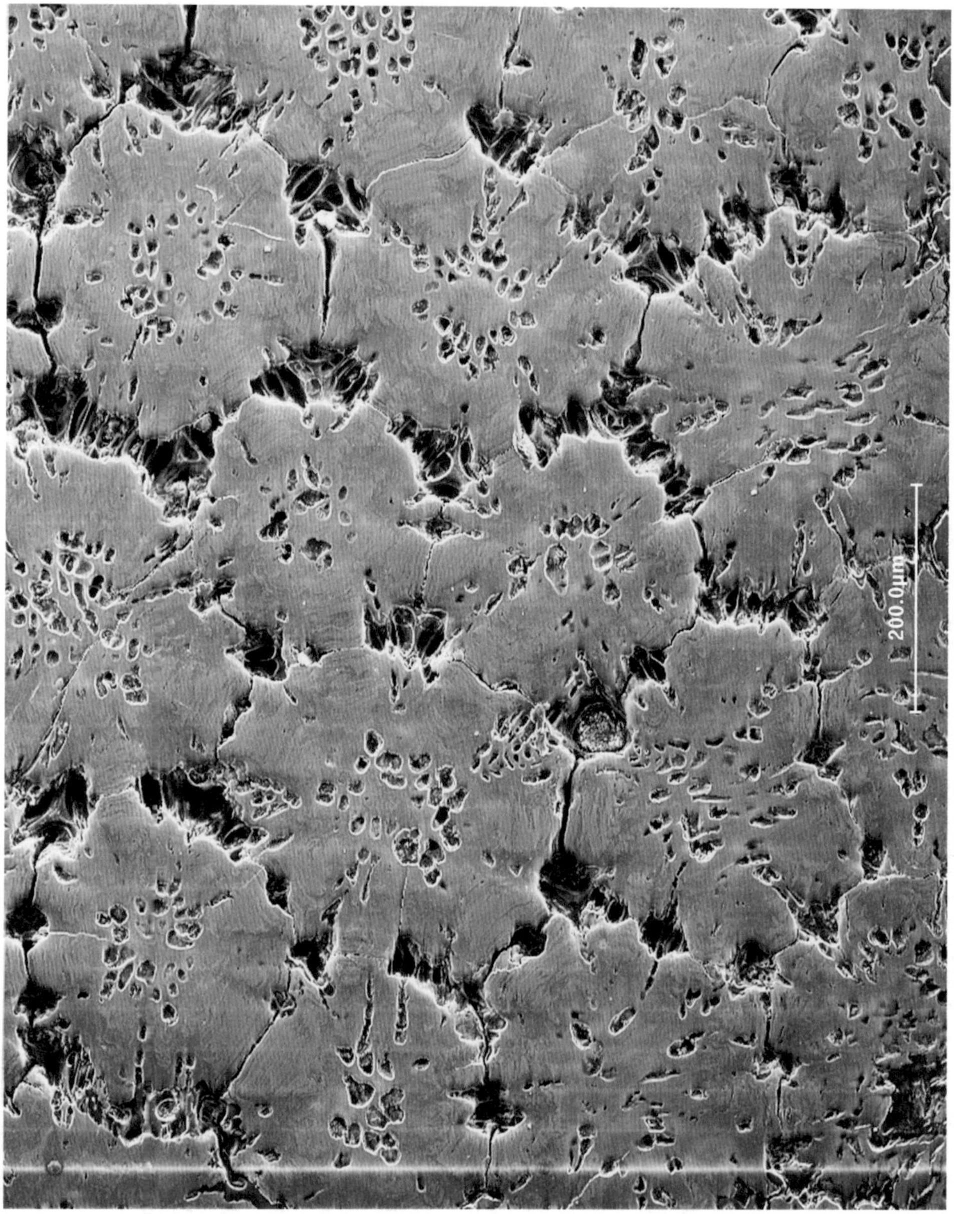
200.0µm

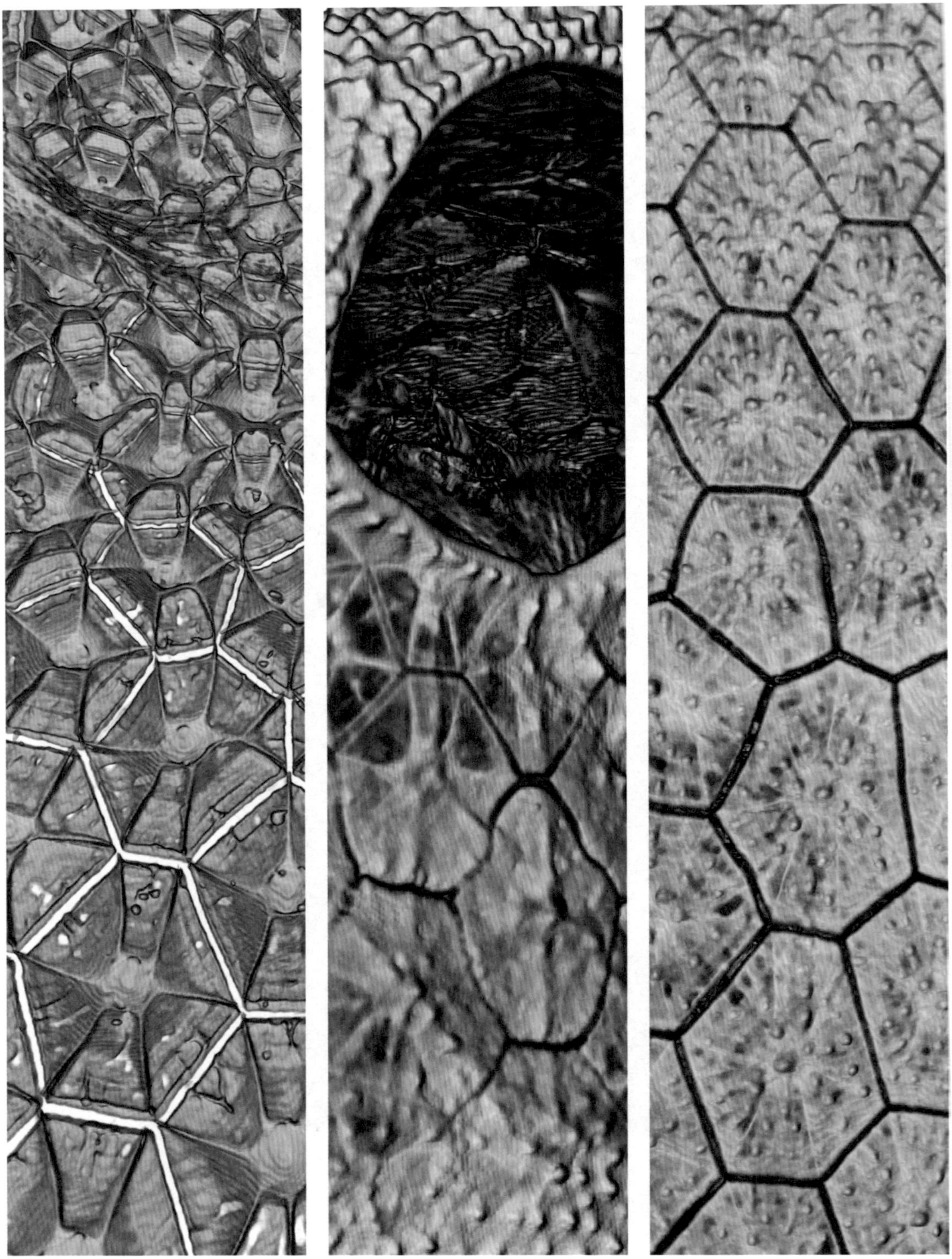

The Geometry of Armor

These micro-CT scan images (fig. 6) show the impressive plated body armor of a fish, which takes advantage of geometric principles to fortify and cover its body completely. Shark and ray cartilage is not the only biological material bearing a geometric tessellation: geometric patterning is a pervasive motif in Nature's toolkit for building tissues. This is sometimes an artifact of how the tissues grow; however, geometries like hexagons and pentagons are simply efficient shapes for covering nonplanar surfaces (as any soccer ball will attest).

These images show interior and exterior views of the body scutes of a boxfish, a small species that putters around tropical reefs. The fish's name comes from its awkward, boxy appearance, but this is a small sacrifice for protection from predators.

Fig. 6 (opposite): Micro-CT scan of boxfish armor, the digital nature of the data allowing exploration of scute structure from the interior (left) and exterior (right two images).

The Role of Mechanics in the Growth and Modeling of Biological Materials

Cécile Bidan

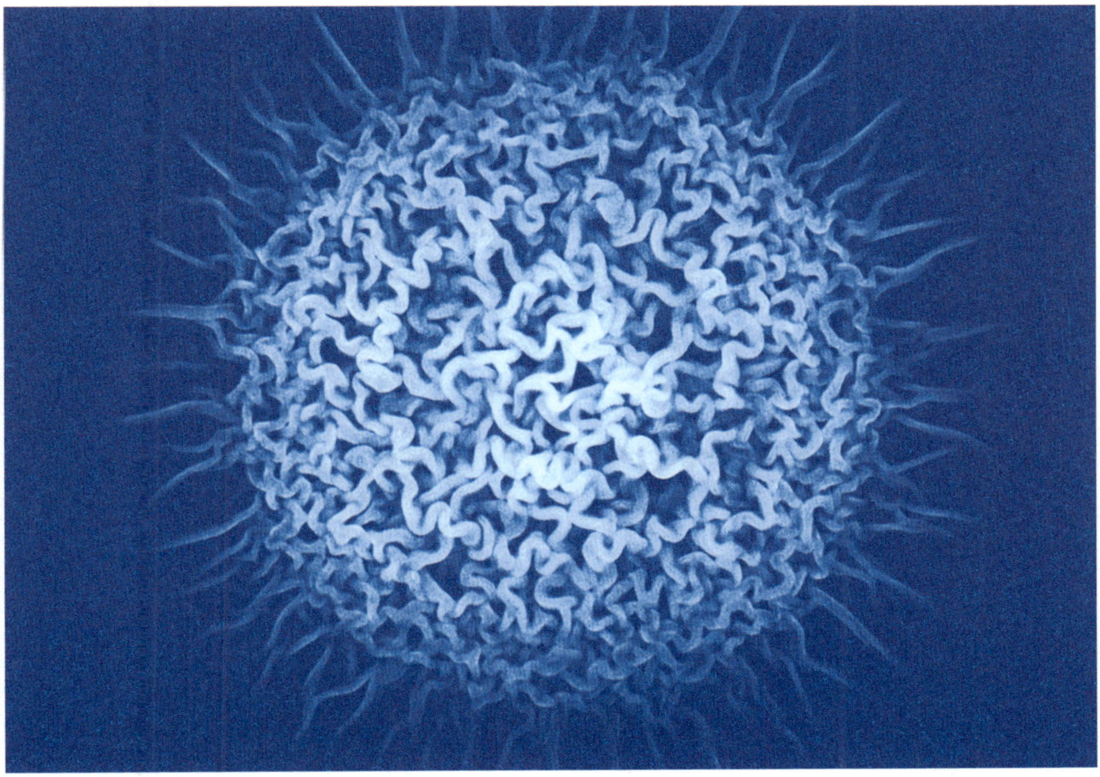

Cells give form to biological materials by multiplying themselves and producing an extracellular matrix made of fibrous proteins and sometime mineral crystals. Simultaneously, cells organize all these so-called building blocks in a coordinated choreography. They give rise to living objects called tissues or organs, which serve vital biological functions. The rigorous hierarchical organization patterns formed by the cells and the matrix components also have a structural role. For example, they ensure the integrity of the material while matching the physical constraints imposed by their surroundings. Because cells have both abilities to sense and respond to a variety of signals, they orchestrate the necessary changes in the materials structure, in order to adapt to the changes they experience in their environment.

Which physical and architectural principles determine and guide the emergence of forms in cell-produced and cell-based materials? This question tends to spontaneously arouse the curiosity of scientists who consider living tissues from the physics or materials science point of view. Indeed, researchers with a background in soft-matter physics, mechanical engineering, or structural materials would naturally question how 10µm cells manage to build centimeter- to meter-large tissues and organs, or how micron-sized bacteria build centimeter-large biofilms with one-millimeter high wrinkles. In a first intention, we hypothesize that the rules of physics also apply to living matter. However, do these microorganisms use the same strategies as two-meter-tall human beings building kilometer-large cities and skyscrapers several hundred meters tall? Many aspects of these fundamental questions remain to be solved. Luckily, the emergence of functional materials from cells inspires more and more researchers, which results in an always-growing interdisciplinary field at the border between life sciences, physical sciences, and engineering.

Typical studies on tissue morphogenesis involve feeding cells, watching them perform, appreciating their aesthetic, and characterizing their behavior. Indeed, observing cells while they are forming the biological material informs us about biological manufacturing and the intermediate steps before reaching the final product. To determine which signals are essential for the cells to design appropriate tissues, it is crucial to understand how cells read and interpret the external signals they receive from their surroundings. Therefore, such experiments are often repeated in various controlled physical environments. Thorough morphological and structural characterizations of the cell's finished product are performed to describe the architecture of biological materials. Finally, one can also learn a lot about the design of the object by watching its behavior while and after destroying it under well-defined conditions.

Observing how cells give form to materials involves entering their micro-world with the help of various pieces of equipment. Microscopes are essential in this regard: they magnify the scenery by means of lenses, thereby enabling researchers to watch the spectacle happening at the cell level. The color and the direction of the light used to illuminate the scene is also determining to expose key elements. For example, fluorescent light reveals fluorescent molecules that are located in specific components of the cells or in their matrix. In addition to their natural aesthetics, the resulting images are often rich in precious structural information, which can be perceived by the scientist as an extra layer of beauty. Microscopy is also an interactive activity. Indeed, the stage that carries the sample of interest is motorized and piloted with a joystick so that, just like in a video game, the observer wanders around in this micro-world. Sometimes looking for answers, often finding new questions. The magnified images can also be projected on a camera chip, transferred to a computer, displayed on a large screen, and saved digitally to document these explorations. Because all the organs of the microscope can be automated and controlled via the computer, one can design, program, and execute systematic image acquisition in time and space to follow, record, and quantify cell movements and tissue dynamics over several days. Analyzing the observations enables researchers to speculate on the architectural principles involved, and the resulting hypotheses can then be formulated into models, which are implemented into computational simulations predicting the key features of the morphogenesis process. Comparing the experimental and simulated results is a powerful approach to reveal principles that are relevant in the design of biological materials by the cells.

The following cases exemplify how some strategies mentioned above led us to highlight the role of mechanics on the growth and modeling of biological materials. In other words, "how cells join forces" to give forms to biological objects much larger than themselves.[1]

Watching Mammalian Cells Giving Form to Bone-Like Tissue

Bone-producing cells derived from mice are cultured in a nutritive medium and put on a silicon capillary bridge held by a thin needle. The cells adhering on this three-dimensional surface of controlled geometry proliferate and produce extracellular matrix, so as to build bone-like tissue. Imaging this process with light microscopy reveals that cells preferentially form tissue on the concave areas of the initial structure, but not on the highly convex surfaces (fig. 1). The growth pattern can be visualized by superimposing the images taken at different time points. Such behavior is reminiscent of a drop of liquid wetting a nonflat surface. Because this phenomenon can be characterized by a well-known physical law, it was possible to show that, despite being solid, bone-like tissue made by cells behaves like a fluid.[2]

Investigating How Mammalian Cells Organize Themselves within the Tissue They Formed

Mammalian cells have an internal cytoskeleton made of fibers equipped with micro-muscles, which not only are a scaffold responsible for the cells' overall shape but also provide them with the ability to contract and exert forces. To understand how cells shape and arrange themselves in the tissue they produce, the cytoskeleton fibers can be tagged with fluorescent markers, which show up when illuminated with fluorescent light. By combining this visualization technique with 3D microscopy, cells are shown to acquire elongated shapes and to coalign in a preferential direction all around the surface (fig. 2). A geometrical analysis of the underlying surface reveals that this direction follows the lines of zero curvature of the capillary bridge, with an additional angle of about 20 degrees. The elongation of the cells suggests that they are contracting in this particular direction, which in turn suggests that the curvature of the surface is an important physical cue of the environment that guides the arrangement of mammalian cells during the process of tissue formation.[3]

1 Philip Kollmannsberger, Cécile. M. Bidan, J.W.C. Dunlop and Peter Fratzl, "The Physics of Tissue Patterning and Extracellular Matrix Organisation: How Cells Join Forces," *Soft Matter* 7, no. 20 (2011): 9549–60.

2 Sebastian Ehrig, Barbara Schamberger, Cécile M. Bidan, Alan West, C. Jacobi, Kayee Lam, Philip Kollmannsberger, Ansgar Petersen, P. Tomancak, Krishna P. Kommareddy, F. D. Fischer, Peter Fratzl, John W. C. Dunlop, "Surface Tension Determines Tissue Shape and Growth Kinetics," *Science Advances* 5, no. 9 (2019): 1–8.

3 Ibid.

Fig. 1: Phase contrast images of bone-like tissue grown on a silicon capillary bridge at different culture times (pseudo-colors).

Fig. 2a (p. 334): Light-sheet microscopy of bone-forming cells with fluorescently labelled cytoskeleton (green), growing on a silicon capillary bridge.

Fig. 2b (p. 335): Directions of zero curvature on the same capillary bridge.

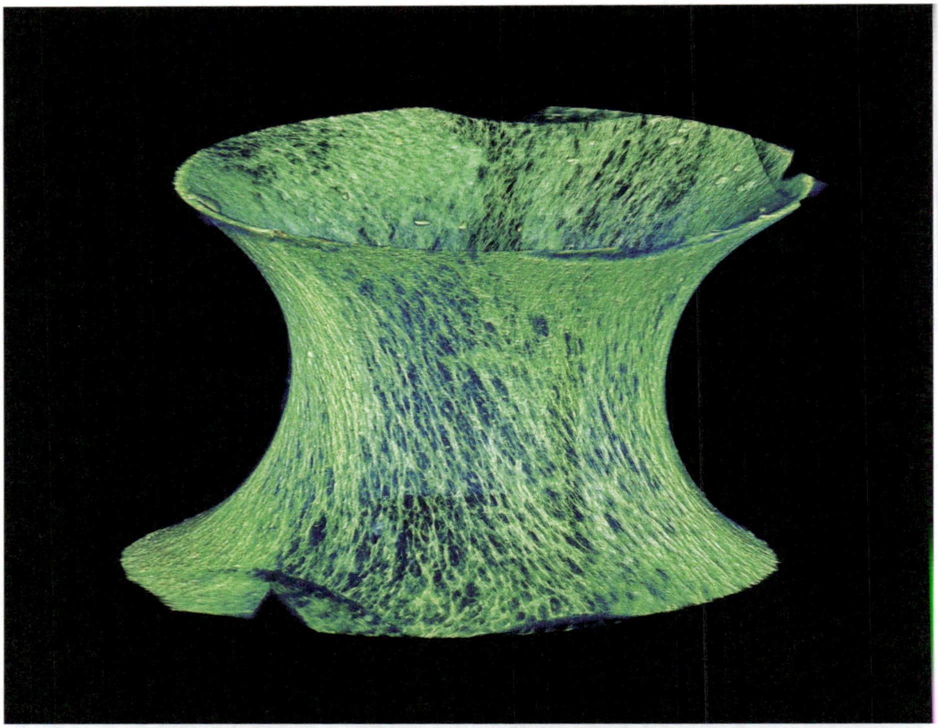

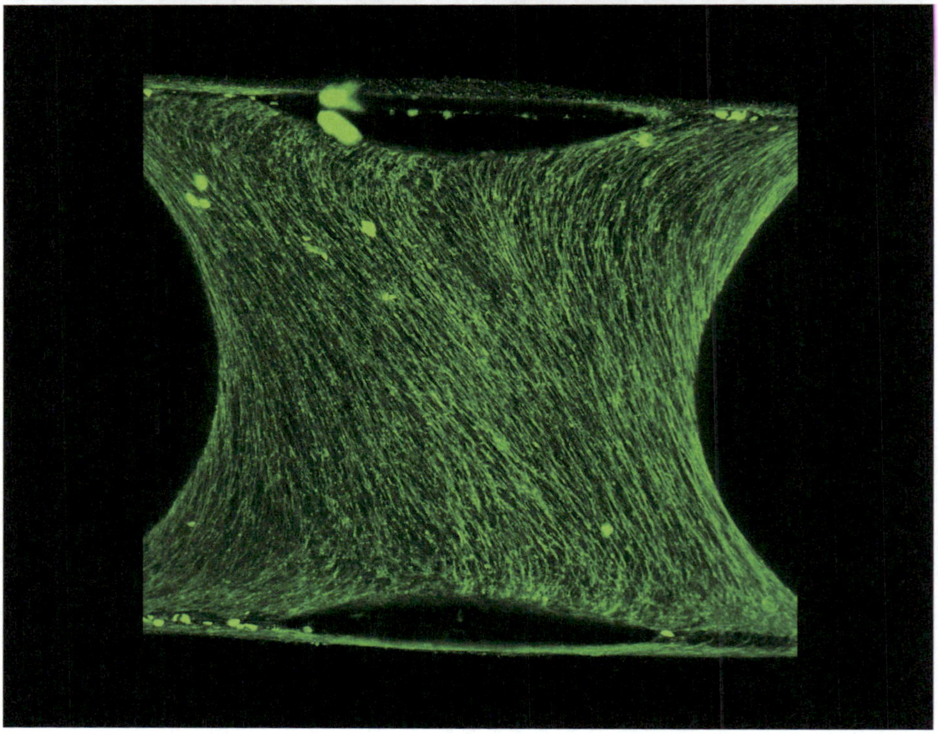

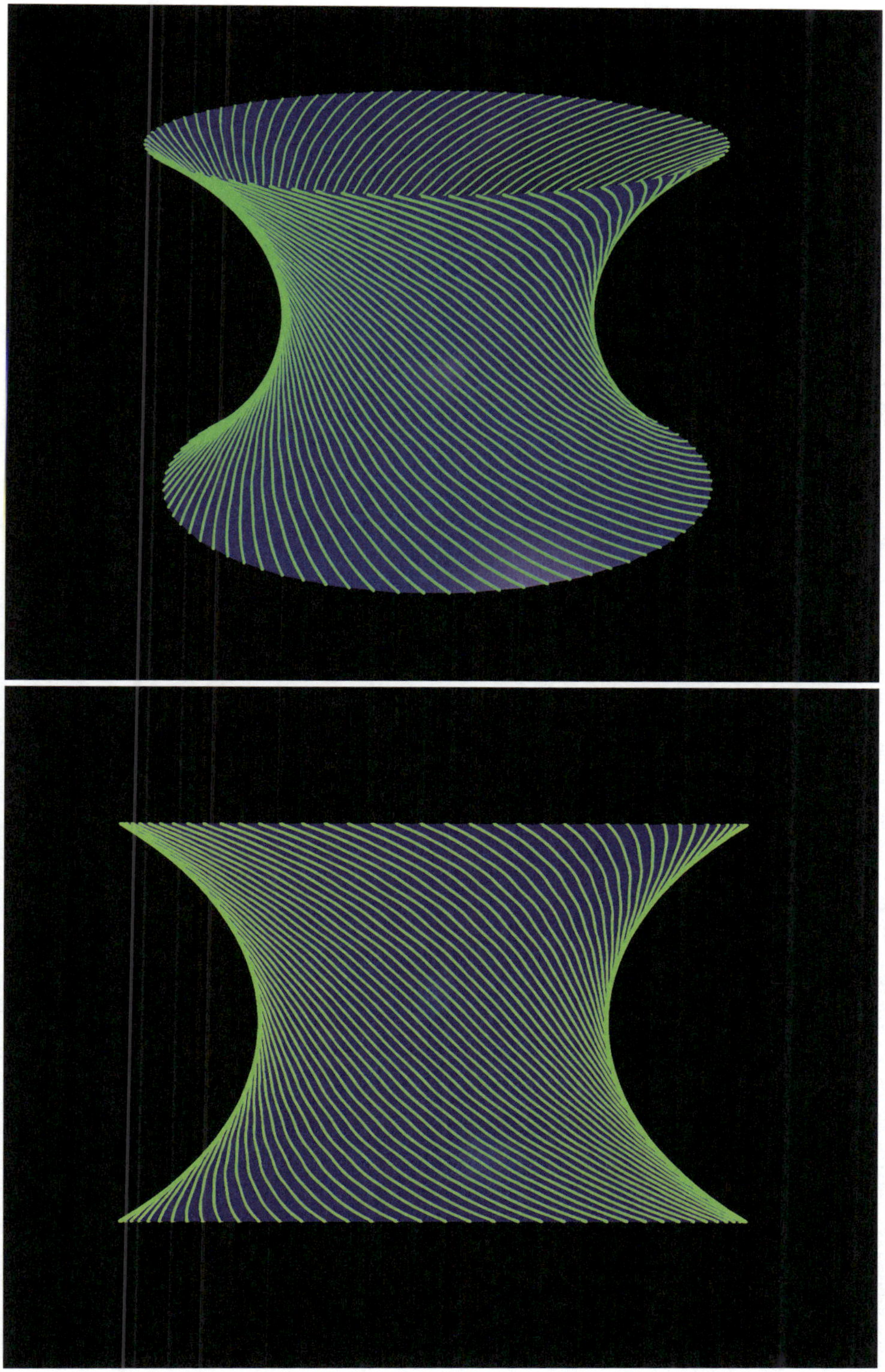

Exploring the Architecture of Bone-like Tissue Formed by Mammalian Cells

Here the cells are given a triangular pore as a substrate to deposit bone-like tissue. In a corner of the pore, cells adopt an elongated shape and assemble to smooth the surface of the tissue, as fluids would do. This particular organization of the cells is then imprinted in the structure of the fibrous extracellular matrix they assemble: first to the flexible fibronectin fibers (yellow: early deposition, red: later deposition), which cells shape like spiders would spin their webs, and then to the stiffer collagen fibers (white) meant to guarantee long-term mechanical stability to the tissue (fig. 3a).

Destroying the tissues in a controlled manner reveals that this matrix is under tension. Indeed, a thin linear cut made at the surface of the tissue induces large deformations of the tissue, much akin to the opening of a wound after accidentally cutting the skin (figs. 3b & 3c). The tension built by the cells as they acquire an elongated shape appears to be progressively transferred to the fibrous matrix of fibronectin and collagen, which have an essential mechanical role in tissue mechanical integrity.[4]

4 Cécile M. Bidan, Philip Kollmannsberger, Vanessa Gering, Sebastian Ehrig, Pascal Joly, Ansgar Petersen, Viola Vogel, Peter Fratzl, and John W. C. Dunlop, "Gradual Conversion of Cellular Stress Patterns into Pre-Stressed Matrix Architecture During In Vitro Tissue Growth," *Journal of the Royal Society Interface*, no. 13(118) (2016).

Fig. 3a (opposite, top): Projection of fluorescent confocal images of bone-like tissue grown in a triangular pore (green: actin cytoskeleton, yellow and red: early and late deposited fibronectin matrix, white: collagen matrix).

Figs. 3b (below) & 3c (opposite, bottom): phase contrast images of bone-like tissue during laser microdissection.

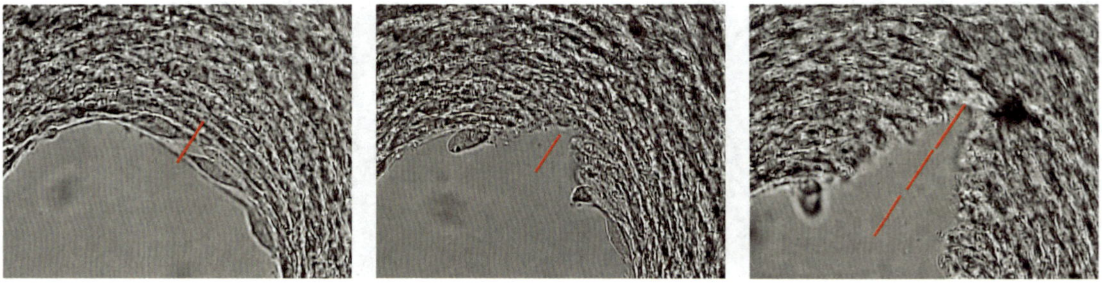

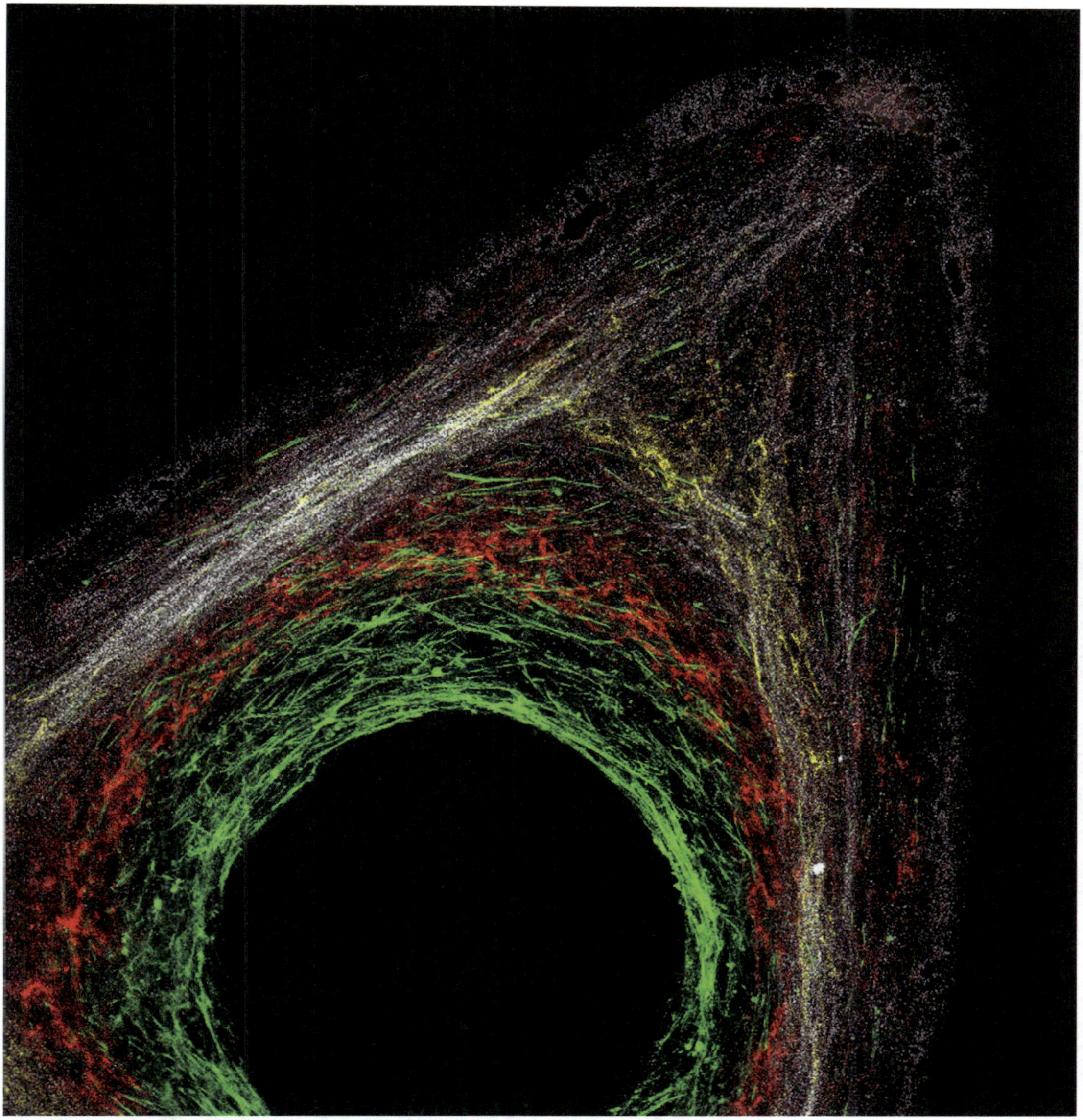

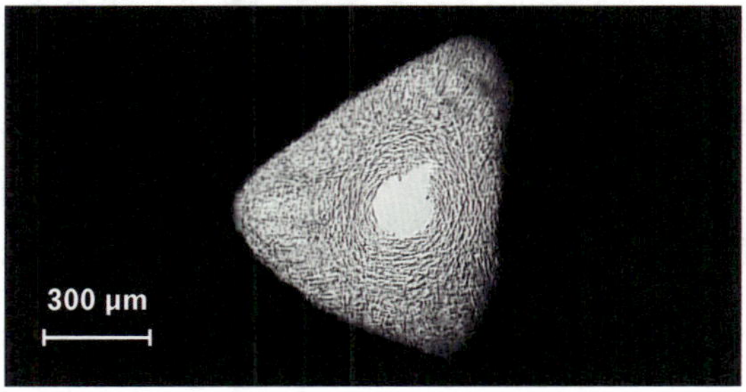
300 µm

Monitoring the Growth of Biofilms on Agar Plates

A drop of *E. coli* bacteria suspension is deposited on a flat nutritive agar gel and cultured for five days in an incubator at 28°C under an automated microscope designed for observations at low magnification (fig. 4). The microbial organisms proliferate, spread on the gel, and produce extracellular matrix components to build a protective micro-environment called a biofilm, which can extend over a few centimeters. Monitoring biofilm growth reveals the apparition of patterns about 24 hours after inoculation, and the emergence of wrinkles from these patterns a few hours later. Biofilms appear to develop in the third dimension whenever the compression forces generated by the production of biomass in the plane reach a threshold triggering buckling of the film. Quantitative analyses of such movies acquired during these experiments will help to formulate hypotheses on the mechanisms involved in biofilm formation. These hypotheses can then be tested by means of computational simulations and further experiments in different conditions.

Fig. 4: Sequence of bright field images acquired during *E. coli* biofilm growth on agar substrates (pseudo-colors).

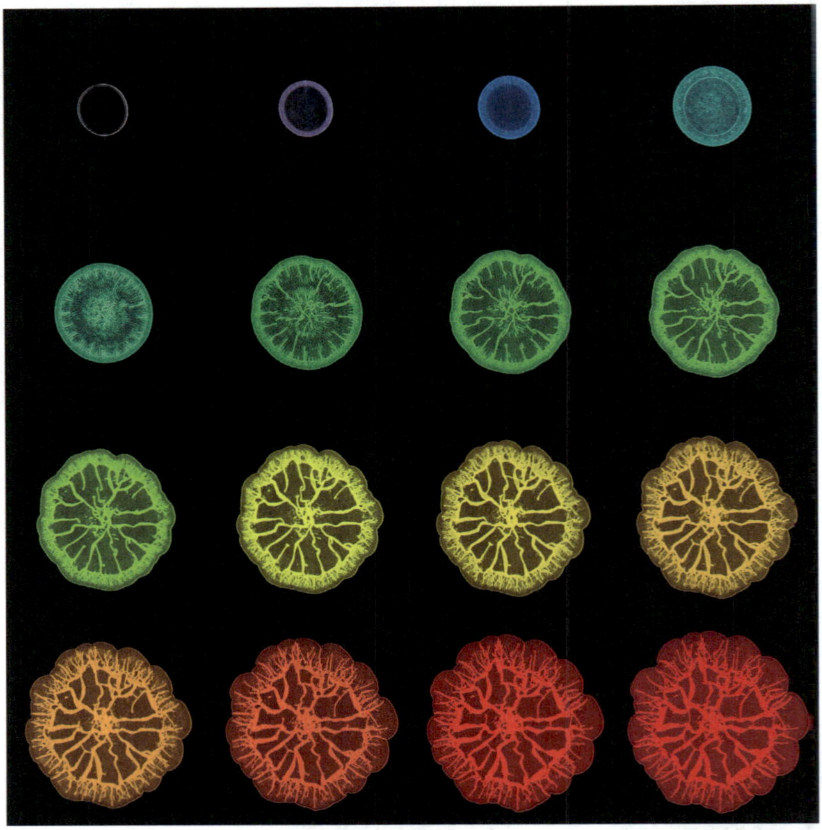

Comparing Biofilms Grown on Agar Plates: All the Same But All Different

Like in the previous case study, drops of *E. coli* bacteria were deposited on flat nutritive agar gels and cultured for five days. As they proliferate and spread on the gel, the microbial colonies form wrinkles visible here as bright lines (figs. 5a & 5b). The images show that although the wrinkles are rather disorganized in the center, they converge on an overall radial arrangement at the biofilm's outer part. Researchers in microbiology modify the bacteria genetically to identify the essential components giving rise to such morphologies, while biophysicists analyze the forces needed to shape such structures. Collaborative work involving both disciplines aim at elucidating the mechanical and biological principles involved in biofilm growth and morphing, as well as their interplay.

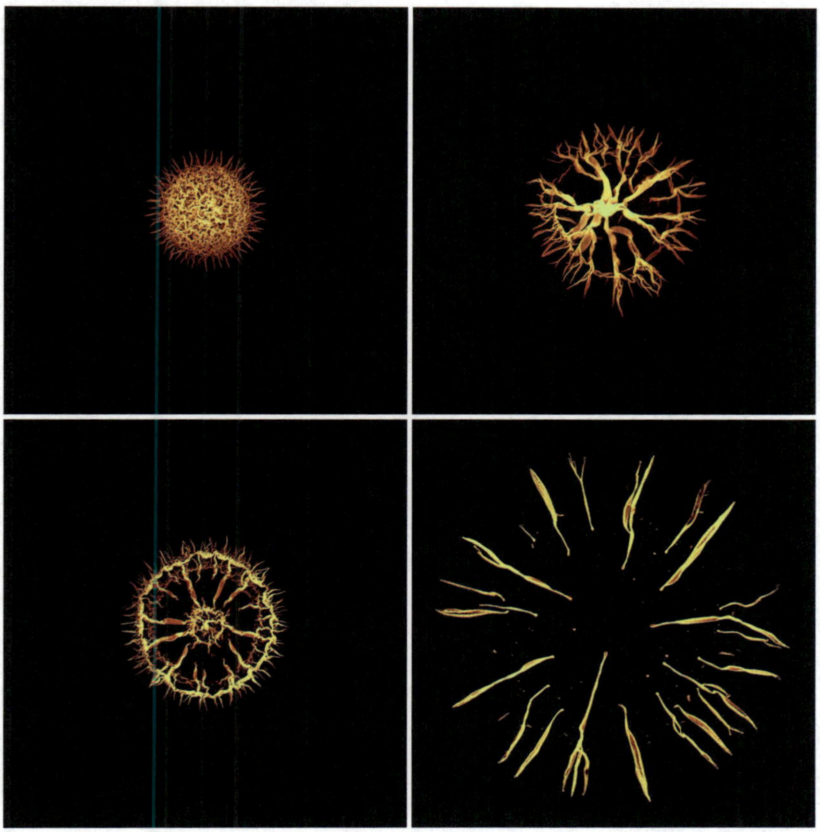

Figs. 5a & 5b (overleaf): Fluorescence images of *E. coli* biofilms grown on agar substrates supplemented with a fluorescent marker for extracellular matrix (gold).

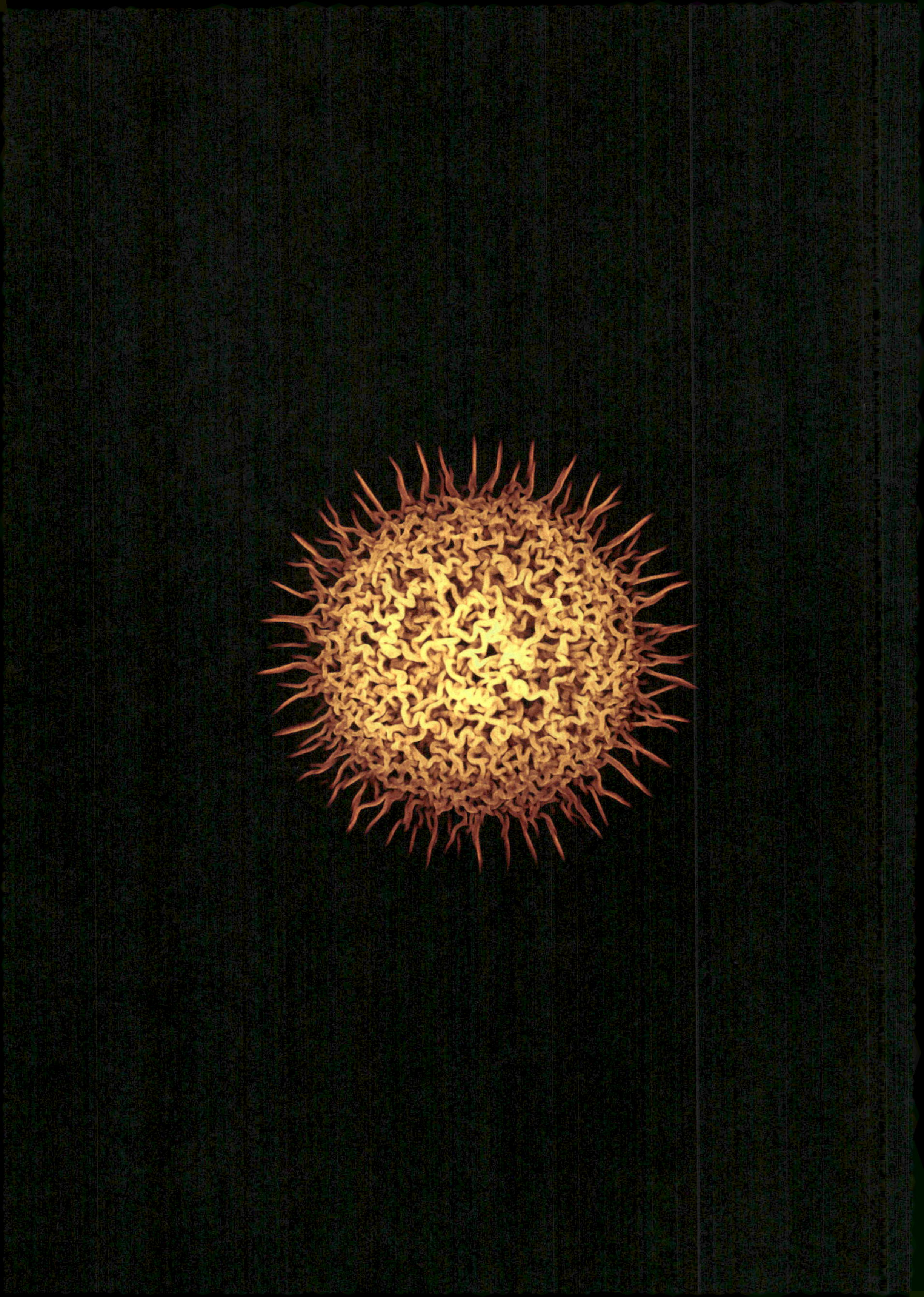

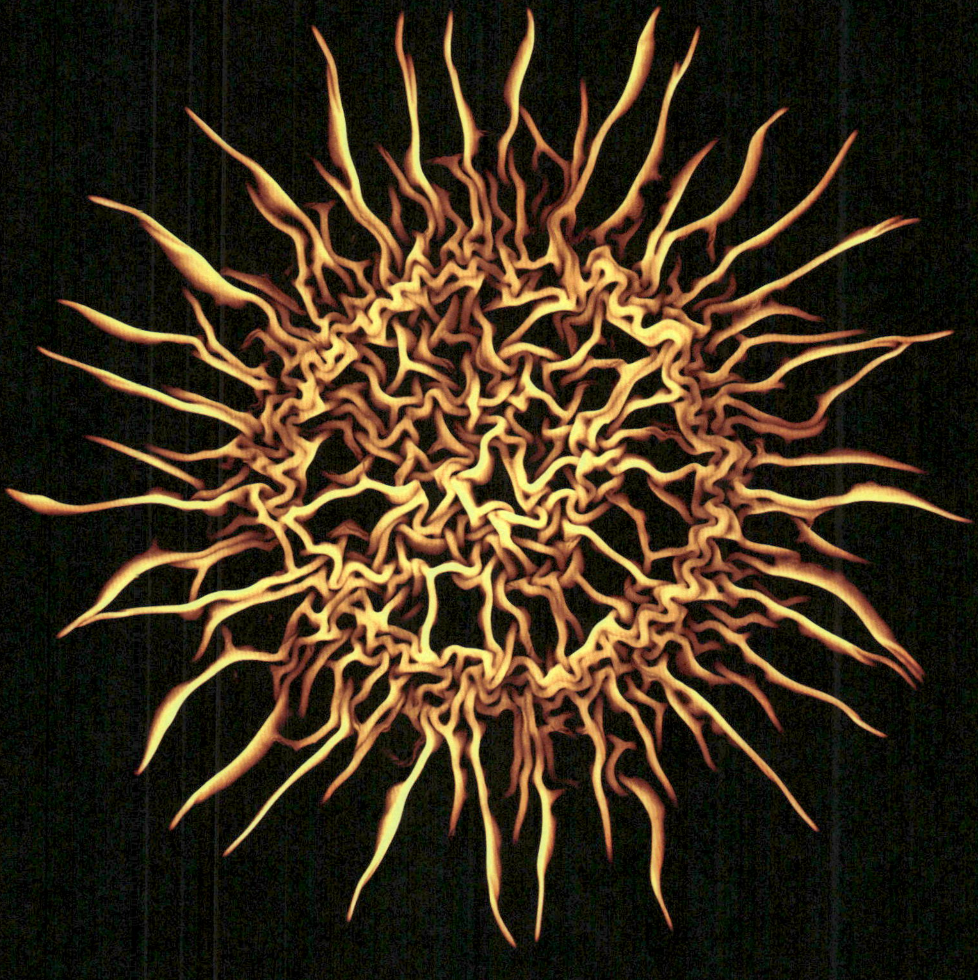

Expansions and Imperfections

Experiments on a Self-Morphing Lattice

Lorenzo Guiducci
Selma Lepart

Selma Lepart (SL) and Lorenzo Guiducci (LG): In 2018 we participated in two workshops—"Behavioral Objects/Behavioral Matter,"[1] and "Behavioral Matter,"[2] centered around the concept of behavior as applied to objects and materials. This is where our collaboration began, melding the tradition of working through practice of the artistic community with notions, methods and tools more typical of the scientific and engineering fields, thus stimulating new research questions.

LG: As a material scientist, I am interested in the mechanical actuation of biological materials which allows dead plant tissues without muscular capacity to generate forces and movements. A typical example is the spontaneous opening and closing of pine cones, caused by differential expansions upon changes in environmental humidity.[3] Inspired by such autonomous actuation, I built a morphing structure based on a flat triangular lattice assembled from plastic connectors and steel wires (fig. 1). An increase in the length of these wires creates an internal compression, which in turn forces the structure to deform from a flat to a three-dimensional shape. The starting point of this investigation was scientific: I sought to understand how the morphing behavior of the lattice depends on its geometry and on the mechanical properties of its components. Revealing this structure-function relationship would allow for the programming of complex shapes by simply acting on the wires (fig. 2) and in turn lead to applications such as tangible user interfaces or soft robotics.

Presented at the workshop "Behavioral Objects/Behavioral Matter" the lattice was well received for the wide range of movements and shape transformations that it could undergo. Small length changes of the wires resulted in quite a large variety of obtained shapes.

SL: From my artist's perspective, I am interested in the agentivity of objects. What makes us think that they are endowed with a relational capacity, a sensitive intelligence, even a consciousness? I am particularly interested in the possibility of creating "nonliving entities" that contain no organic or biological material. I started engaging with the expressive

1 "Behavioral Objects/Behavioral Matter," a workshop organized by EnsadLab, Paris, May 16–18, 2018.
2 "Behavioral Matter," a workshop organized by EnsadLab, ENSCI-Les Ateliers, (Paris) and the Cluster of Excellence »Matters of Activity« (HU-Berlin), November 21–23, 2018.
3 Dawson, Colin, Julian FV Vincent, and Anne-Marie Rocca. "How Pine Cones Open," *Nature* 390, no. 6661 (1997): 668.

capacity of the lattice, questioning to which extent life-like traits could be reproduced in a nonorganic object, and pushing us to contemplate the emotional relationship between the observer and the observed object. Acting on the wires with our hands revealed how unpredictable the morphing was: the lattice did not always follow the script. It showed small variations that seemed to be the result of its own behavior.

LG & SL: During the workshop we pursued these questions from our complementary perspectives. We connected the lattice wires to electric motors and flex sensors, making it an autonomous moving object (fig. 3). Bending the sensors would activate the motors, change the wire length and, in turn, deform the lattice: hence a responsive behavior (a reaction caused by an external stimulus) was obtained. By attaching the flex sensors on the lattice, a closed loop configuration was achieved: if perturbed from the outside, the lattice could "sense" its deformed state and the motors would respond by compensating with an opposite movement. At times, this resulted in a self-determined motion reminiscent of a "homeostatic" state—a dynamic equilibrium in which opposite reactions maintain a constant internal state variable (such as temperature in the human body) rather than an absence of reactions. These highlighted how these properties—responsiveness and homeostasis—are crucial in any living form and were indeed artificially reproduced (or at least metaphorically represented) with very little technological means.

We realized how the quality of these autonomous movements creates a strange feeling of empathy in the observer, who can interpret them as excitement, hysteria or an attempt to avoid pain (fig. 4). Either way, the objective reality of a scientific experiment (a prototype built to study morphing capacity in slender structures) met with the subjective experience of an artistic exploration. We let the observer think that this object was capable of having intentions of its own. Its regular geometric structure is far from being anthropomorphic or zoomorphic, its artificial origin is not hidden. Simply, a dynamic process occurs between the object and the observer, an atavistic instinct that makes us focus on a moving object, almost as it were demanding our attention. Our human cognition seems to fill a certain gap and enriches an artifact with a notion of interiority that it does not possess. The following report retraces the different phases of our work and raises questions from our respective disciplinary fields, which we either addressed individually or collectively.

Geometric and Manufacturing Principles of the Triangular Lattice

LG: In my research as a materials scientist, I explore different principles to design morphing structures and materials. I take inspiration from plants' seed capsules—which spontaneously deform upon swelling—and the field of mechanical metamaterials, in which structural instabilities are exploited to enrich and program the properties of a material. In this context, I built a flat triangular lattice that leverages the buckling of individual beams to obtain controllable morphing. When a slender beam (such as spaghetti) is under compression it loses its straight shape and bends. This phenomenon is called buckling, an unstable response of an elastic structure which, in order to escape a heavy load, exploits an alternative "softer" deformation mode. In the triangular lattice shown here, such buckling response is introduced by geometric construction: in the rhomboidal unit cell (fig. 1a), an expanding beam (in magenta) is under compression due to the constraint of the black beams; at low expansion (fig. 1b), the active beam is straight and the structure is still flat; at high expansion (fig. 1c), the compressive force on the active beam exceeds its critical buckling threshold: the beam bends out of the lattice plane and induces a slight out-of-plane bending of the rhombus, which will propagate to the neighboring rhombi, causing global morphing.

The lattice has a fixed rhomboidal framework made of steel wires glued to 3D-printed plastic connectors (fig. 1d). Additional wires are introduced through holes in the plastic connectors (fig. 1e): by pushing these free wires into the structure, an overall deformation of the lattice is obtained.

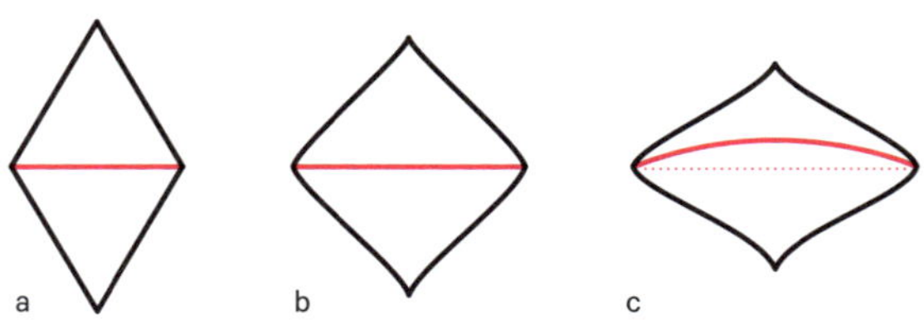

Figs. 1a, 1b, 1c: Geometric construction of the triangular lattice.

Fig. 1d (top): Fabrication of the triangular lattice (detail).

Fig. 1e (bottom): Connecting the lattice nodes with steel wire.

Morphing Capabilities: Is the Shape Predetermined or Emergent?

LG: The buckling of individual beams can be quite easily related to how much wire is fed into the lattice. Yet relating these local buckling events to the actual global deformation of the lattice proved to be more difficult. This is in part due to the many manufacturing imperfections—nonplanarity of the lattice, wires that are not perfectly straight, slight asynchronies in the activation of different wires—which, added up, lead to nonrepeatable movements (fig. 2).

SL: The lattice, held and stabilized on a table by a wooden slat and clamps, is not really thick, its shape is as minimal as possible. Our glance crosses it with ease. It does not hide anything of its composition. The plastic connectors are 3D-printed and the steel wires are chosen for their thickness, resistance, and flexibility. One recognizes the human touch in this geometrically regular arrangement of materials. Yet one cannot help but find a certain organic elegance in the changing shape of the lattice. All the manufacturing imperfections of the lattice create a choreographic richness and a sense of unpredictability. The lattice escapes our efforts of imposing certain forms while different ones emerge. Our attention is triggered by such contrast: a geometrically regular and clearly artificial object which is showing a behavior of its own, almost as a living being.

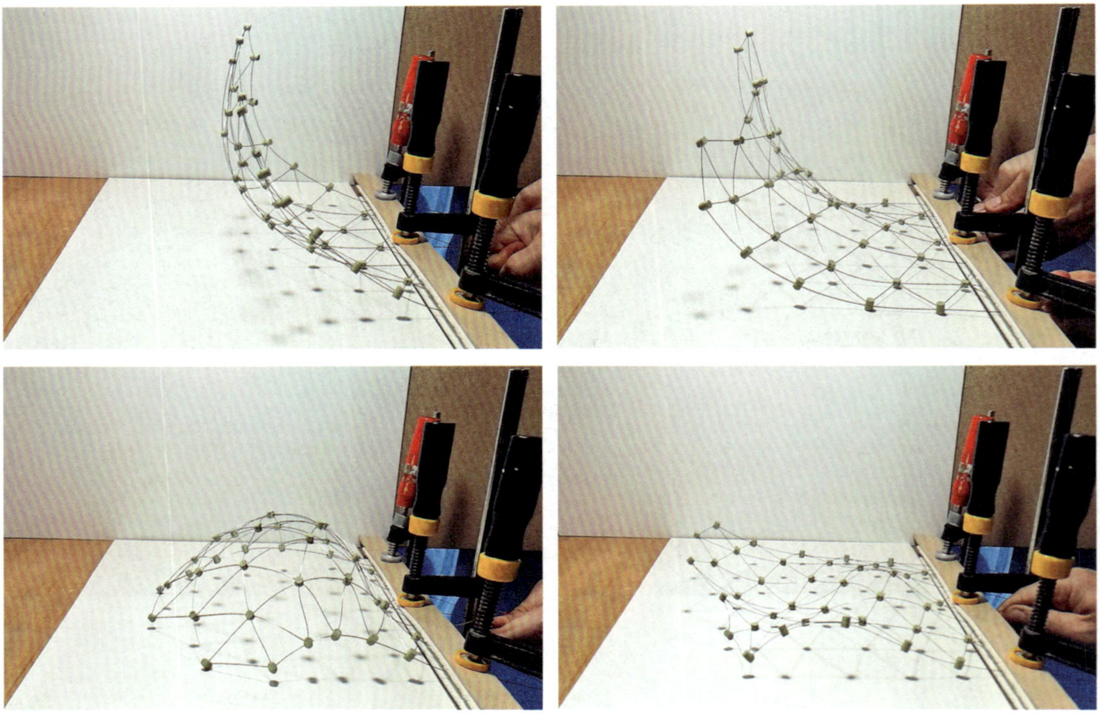

Fig. 2: Activating the lattice.

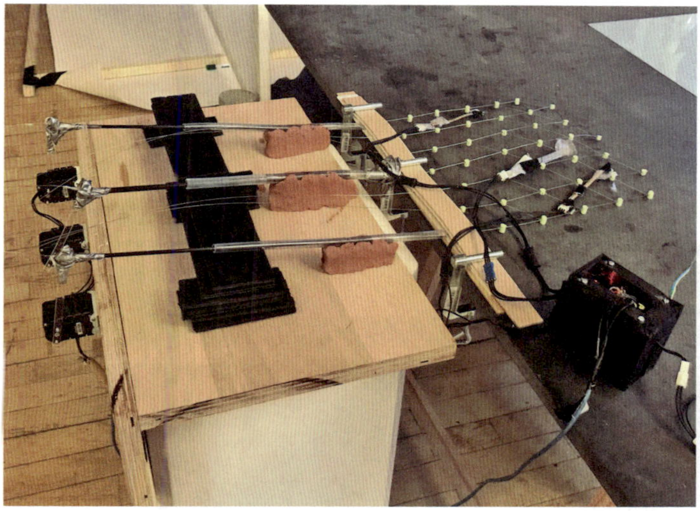

Animating the Lattice

Fig. 3a (right): Motors and flex sensors are connected to the steel wires of the lattice.

Fig. 3b (left): Controlling the movements of the structure with flex sensors.

LG: With the aim of better controlling the lattice morphing, we attached three motors to as many wires, thus replacing the human hand in this push-and-pull action. We also placed two flex sensors on the steel wires of the structure which would allow us to indicate to the motors the spatial configuration of the lattice (fig. 3a). During some initial tests we used the flex sensors as the keys of a piano to control its movements (fig. 3b).

Playing with this idea of a seemingly living yet inanimate object, we established a feedback loop between the flex sensors and the motors. The logical program (implemented in MisBKIT, courtesy of EnsadLab) simply consists of a narrow range of admissible values of the flex sensor signal: if the lattice (and hence the flex sensors) bends excessively, the motors move the wires back to reacquire the lattice reference configuration. Yet in this reaction the whole structure moves, always placing one zone or another close to the limits that have been imposed on it. As a result, the lattice is perpetually trying to rebalance itself. It is stuck in this feedback loop. We could see this attempt as an artificial reproduction of responsive behavior. Thus, we have recreated, albeit in a very rudimentary way, one of the most fundamental control mechanisms of life: homeostasis. The resulting movement is autonomous and not random. It is specific to this prototype and would not apply in any case to another, because it is in fact as if preprogrammed in the structure itself.

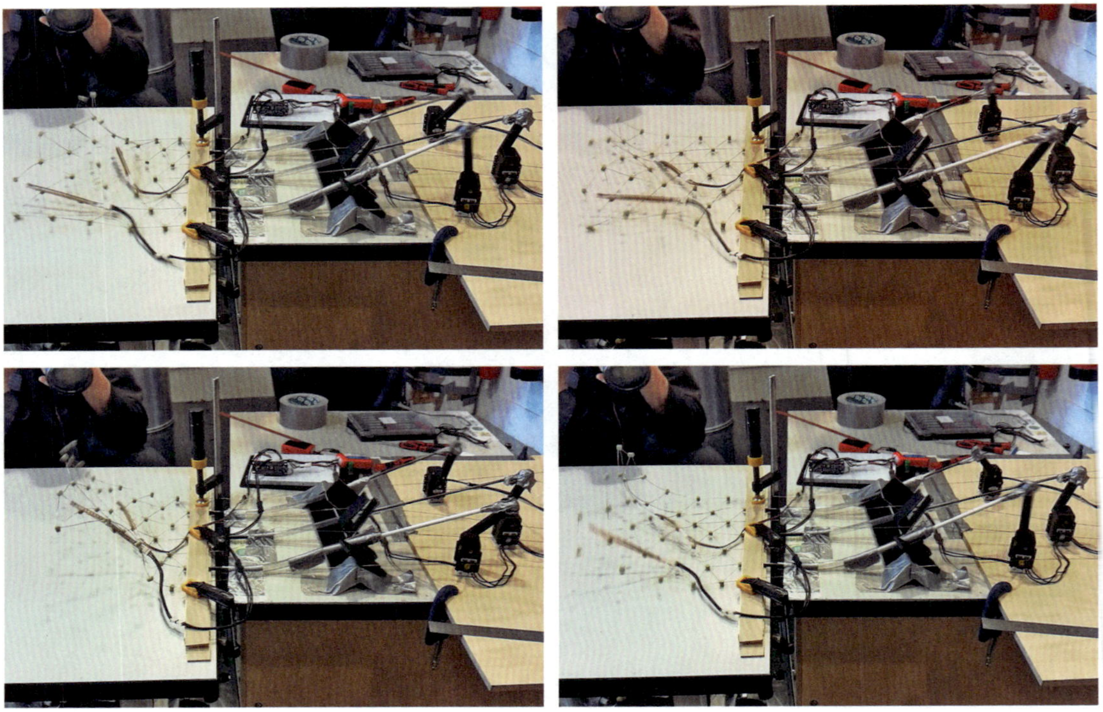

Fig. 4: Autonomous motion of the animated lattice.

Motion and Perception of the Lattice in Its Homeostatic State

SL: Equipped with motors, the lattice becomes a self-performing object. The structure and chosen materials play an active role in its capacity to move and to give the illusion of a behavior (fig. 4). A dialogue between form and movement is established and enters into resonance, revealing the behavior of the object. Shape and movement control, in a way, the course of events. These movements create a strange feeling of interiority. The lattice seems to improvise a choreographic score. The observer can almost recognize a form of primitive dance in its frenetic agitation. As if it could not bear its own condition, the lattice rises, frantically hits the ground, deforms and convulses to the limits of its physical body.

As if trapped, it is forced to the ground, firmly held by the piece of wood. It cannot escape, seemingly demanding attention and communicating a state of discomfort that can be interpreted as an attempt to avoid pain. With very little programming and outside intervention, the structural properties of the lattice (which link deformations and amplify movements) induce a strange feeling of empathy. As spectators of its struggle, we would almost like to see this thin metallic framework "escape its condition" as an object. We achieved excellent expressive results with minimal aesthetic and technical intervention.

Toward an Emotional Attachment?

SL: Our emotional attachment is focused on this lattice, which is neither anthropomorphic nor zoomorphic. This shows that it is not necessary to hide the artificial nature of an object in order to obtain "patterns" for the behavior of living beings. Perhaps this is due to a phenomenon of abstract pareidolia. As a viewer, we cannot inscribe our interpretation of the situation in a binary logic. Ours is much more complex, loaded with a referential acquired over thousands of years. In a way, we are the ones who confer this ability to be alive. We know that this object has no intentions. It is not even aware of its own presence. It does not know what it looks like. It does not know its position in space. It is not aware of the presence of a floor that it nevertheless hits frantically and with a rhythm that produces a certain musicality to our ears. It is not aware of our presence nor of the effect it produces on us.

The lattice exposes and stages itself in a dynamic process between object and public, making us believe that if an object moves, it is potentially animated by the same forces that animate us (fig. 5). The forces at work are not invisible. The three motors pulling the strings seem to be able to control it and play with it, producing the effect of a kind of mistreatment enacted upon this treatment to this object. However, the motors obey only the lattice. This relationship of domination by force that we seem to perceive is false. The motors do provide the power, but it is the lattice, in all its transparency and lightness, that controls the movements.

Fig. 5: Programming the morphing of the lattice.

Fig. 6: Selma Lepart and Lorenzo Guiducci working together. Workshop "Behavioral Matter," Paris, ENSCI-Les Ateliers, 2018.

Assessing the Collaboration: Results, Impressions and Further Questions

LG: From a scientific point of view, programming the morphing of a triangular lattice requires further experiments: we still need to understand how the local buckling of the steel wires influences the lattice's global morphing.

SL: From an artistic perspective, further experiments could allow the lattice to exhibit new "behaviors" that we haven't observed yet. How far can we go into stripping away the motors, sensors, and components and still maintain an emotional connection to it? It's hard to help but find the object slightly dysfunctional. But dysfunctional in relation to what? We don't really know. It remains an impression, since the lattice was built for the specific purpose of being an object of scientific study and not to have any other function or utility. But even if we call it an "object" for lack of a better word to designate this "autonomous nonbeing," it is not really one. Must it become useful or functional to have the right to "a form of existence"?

LG & SL: In retrospect, we understand this overall process as a dialogue, a two-way making process (fig. 6). From the scientist to the artist, from the subject to the object (and vice versa). From the design and fabrication of the lattice, in which we give, prescribe, impose form, to the stage in which we observe the same object self-generating form, through spontaneous movements.

In this process, form generation and emergence drove different research questions. Today the main paradigm of scientific research in metamaterials is to program behavior onto a material, that is, to control it. Our collaboration shows that careful (and maybe even empathic?) observation allows us to discover new behaviors and properties that were neither really expected, nor useful per se. We argue that moving away from the question of function could lead to new applications in engineering and new questions in applied artistic research.

Attempts at Explementation

Combining Material and Symbolic Operations in Art and Design Research

Samuel Bianchini

In computer science, *implementation* designates that human activity which consists in translating a set of specifications initially expressed in "natural" language into a program a computer can execute. Implementation, by enabling the shift from language to computation, can be seen as encapsulating the historical process of computer science, which consists in making forms of symbolic language operative by the production of a sequence of instructions formalized in an abstract, logical, unambiguous and, in the last analysis, computable manner. Thus converted into a program, this symbolic reality can then be transferred to a material reality (the "hardware") so as to execute various physical operations previously "ordered." Predicated on the notion that verbalization exercises control over the material world, implementation and its increasingly widespread application exemplify a form of triumphalist anthropocentrism. It reveals the domination of the performative mode first analyzed by John L. Austin and the prevalence of the speech act: when saying is doing—or, in this case, making something occur through delegation to a machine.[1]

Confronted by novel forms of materialism necessitated by the ecological crisis, this performative turn today needs to be put in perspective. Instead of viewing our relationship with the environment through the prism of how we are to control it with words, now the need is to develop novel modalities of cooperation with the material world. How can we reverse the process of implementation by listening to what matter says to us—or, rather, what it "makes us say"—and thus envisage a form of "explementation"? And how could it be seen as the action of translating into a symbolic language material operations that can take place in our presence or not, but for which humans might play the role of "spokespeople"[2]? Above and beyond interpretation, might *explementation* not remain indexed on material reality, with implementability, in return, being deployed to test its pertinence?

If this approach is often considered in the function of our increasingly computerized society, there is also reason to gauge its effects more specifically through the prism of disciplines focusing on conception, or even on the project, such as design. A substantial proportion of design, in the industrial

1 John L. Austin, *How to Do Things with Words*, ed. J. O. Urmson (Oxford: Oxford University Press, 1962).

2 See Michel Callon, "Some Elements of a Sociology of Translation: Domestication of the Scallops and the Fishermen of St Brieuc Bay," in *Power, Action, and Belief: A New Sociology of Knowledge?*, ed. John Law (London: Routledge & Kegan Paul, 1986), 196–33.

field particularly, is in fact based on approaches of conception in which precedence is taken by the word—to the point that its favorite tools are brainstorming or some other methodology intended to liberate various forms of ideation, as in the case with "design thinking." More fundamentally still, the field remains structured by the notion of the project, framed by formalization and linguistic modalities that facilitate the sharing, projecting, execution, and even replication of the object produced. Design thus conforms to the tenets of an allographic art, as posited by Nelson Goodman[3]—a form of art that passes through an "ideal" phase prior to material realization. If, in the field, such a conceptual paradigm sometimes interlocks with computer science through CAD or rapid prototyping software, the end result tends to reinforce the predominance of language over material activity, which has just to follow and conform to what is said, or, if not, to resist it—as, naturally enough, it does. The development of practice-based research in art and design fosters the reevaluation of our methods and our ways of thinking and doing. The substrate of practice obliges us to consider language not just as a precondition (thinking before doing), but also as a reflective activity during production. Coupling art with design encourages us to analyze the operations of the autographic arts (that are often traditional practices) in direct contact with their materials, in contradistinction to the hegemony of development based on the project.

3 See Nelson Goodman, *Languages of Art: An Approach to a Theory of Symbols* (Indianapolis: Hackett Publishing, 1968), rev. 1976; and, *Of Mind and Other Matters* (Cambridge, MA: Harvard University Press, 1984).

Fig. 1a: Workshop "The Misbehavior of Animated Object," in collaboration with J.-B. Labrune, H. Ishii and his team at the Tangible Media Group of the MIT Media Lab, with two teams from EnsadLab: Reflective Interaction (directed by S. Bianchini) and Sociable Media (directed by R. Bourganel), TEI 2014, Munich.

Behavioral Objects / Disabled Objects

Since 2012 in EnsadLab, we have been developing a body of research in art and design that centers on "behavioral objects" to investigate how and why nonfigurative robotic objects might be endowed with a behavioral dimension. For the practical side of this project, in setting up a workshop at the TEI conference in 2014,[4] we devised a conceptual and material structure which took the form of a modular robotics tool called MisB KIT (fig. 1a), a rapid-prototyping tool employing mechanical, motorized parts covered in Velcro. Without anticipating the projects that might be developed, such open but directed experimental conditions are tailor-made for collective practice. Thus, during one of the work sessions at EnsadLab, we started tinkering with one of these robotized objects, setting it in motion. We watched as the little agglomerate of round and rectangular plates mounted on a motorized articulated armature began to slide around. Its motion appeared somewhat inefficient. It seemed, though with scant success, to be searching for how best to move about (fig. 1b).

Encountering more and more difficulties, it eventually shuddered to a halt and fell to pieces. Observing the tension created by movements arising from such a thwarted intention gave us food for thought. The empathy it elicited encouraged us to verbalize: the object looked "disabled." Unable to go to its assistance, we endeavored instead to understand the situation, in order, perhaps, to learn from an operative interaction that is freighted with affect and meaning. Initially, we had no project in mind—no idea of what we were going to produce, no prior formalization, just experimental conditions which led us, post facto, to posit how a frustrated intention might be conveyed by motion and thus provoke empathy. By formalizing such principles anchored in practice, it became possible to reactivate them, to put them into action, and, hence, conceivably, to *implement* them.

4 See Samuel Bianchini, Remy Bourganel, Jean-Baptiste Labrune, Hiroshi Ishii, Emmanuel Mahé, and Emanuele Quinz, *The Misbehavior of Animated Object*, Studio, TEI 2014 [8th International Conference on Tangible, Embedded and Embodied Interaction], February 16–19, 2014, Munich, Germany, ACM 978-1-4503-2635-3/14/02.

Fig. 1b: Behavioral Objects, on-site workshop at EnsadLab; stills from video footage of the work, Paris, 2014.

Out of Frame – From Object to Project

A frame hangs on a wall (fig. 2). Made of untreated wood, plain and empty, without molding or other ornament, it possesses no content, no ground. But, intermittently, it moves, just a little, twisting on itself. Every now and again, these contortions become more abrupt, violent even, as if it were undergoing some involuntary motor discharge, such as those captured in nineteenth-century images of what was described at the time as hysteria. The frame appears like a body subjected to impulses beyond its control which it seems unable to "frame." Its presence is apprehended uniquely through its movements and not through a representation it might contain.

Initial experiments leading to the creation of *Out of Frame* were the outcome of a behavioral object workshop at the Théâtre Nanterre-Amandiers in 2015. Among other experiments, Didier Bouchon (in charge of research-creation engineering) constructed a square composed of articulated flexible bars that twist on the floor. I had received a request for a project for an exhibition at Ars Electronica, and, as we observed the contortions of this abstract body, the decision was made to convert the trial into a project we could exhibit. The square might be turned into a frame and its contortions become convulsions—with photographs of Charcot's patients in mind. In the end it was this motion, or rather its symbolic charge, which gave rise to a project based on experiments with an object, at once reflected on and in action. Thus, practice-based research led from the material to the conceptual—and not the other way around, as is the rule in design.

Out of Frame – Simulated yet Real Behaviors

The square frame, about a meter along each side, starts to move (fig. 3); its solid wooden structure seems to be intent on opposing a physical resistance to the impulses coursing through it. If this might already be seen as an interpretation, it is an embodied one. A struggle for power is established between the commands transmitted by the computer system and the motors in the upper corners of the frame.

"Command" might imply that it's enough to send instructions to be executed by the motors that move the frame. But it's not that simple; these commands have to respect a number of material constraints and physical possibilities. This elementary principle of robotics is though reversible: these constraints impose limits to the apparatus, and thus potentially to the program. Hardware and software equate to reciprocal conditions: they rely on one another.

In robotics too the term *embodiment* designates complex, nonlocalized, even diffuse relations between a physical thing and information, which cannot be reduced to the dichotomy "central control unit/material 'puppet' that acts to order." However elementary the form of *Out of Frame* may appear, it entails significant physical constraints: to allow the square a measure of mobility, the joints at its corners incorporate elastic bands to ensure its flexibility. Here, the robotics are of a hybrid nature—an amalgam of hard and soft materials, as in the phenomenon of tensegrity, whose geometry calls for a special approach, less deterministic than for rigid structures. Such an arrangement of materials implies a further constraint: to allow the frame to move from the corners, the force must be exerted by a lever arm of a relatively large size and this tends to overtax the motors. Didier Bouchon had already been confronted with this problem during initial experiments in the development stage of the project, during which fully functioning motors were overexerted to the point of suffering damage. It thus became necessary to come up with a programming strategy that could factor in the "strain" applied to the motors. The aim was to devise a behavioral logic for the frame able to integrate the subtle dialogue between the expression of the motors and the commands of the program, the latter responding to the calorific and energetic information relayed by the engines—that is, by what they "tell" it. Cybernetically, the system was thus able to regulate its own activity in accordance with the information provided, following a principle of homeostasis that relies on the interdependence between a physical entity and the information supplied. The behavioral dimension of the object thus became at once material, technical, aesthetic, and even psychological and social, according to the intentions that are invested in the frame.

Figs. 2 (top) & 3 (bottom): *Out of Frame*, Samuel Bianchini and Didier Bouchon, 2015. Developed and prototyped in the context of the research project "Behavioral Objects" by Reflective Interaction at EnsadLab, with the support of the Labex Arts-H2H and the Bettencourt Schueller Foundation. Hardware realization: A. Bonnerot and E. Bessis. Software realization: D. Bouchon. Photos: Filipe Pais, Ars Electronica, Campus Exhibition, Kunstuniversität Linz, Sept. 2015.

Mourners – Natural Artifice

Fig. 4a (opposite): Earliest experiments in Plexiglas for the *Mourners project*, CEA Saclay, March 2012.

Fig. 4b (top): Water flute for *Mourners*, and then *At Present (Félix Guattari)*. Here in *A Présent (Félix Guattari)*, *Curiositas* exhibition at the Château de Button, Gif-sur-Yvette, May 2017.

Starting in 2010 at Saclay, on invitation from the CEA (the French Alternative Energies and Atomic Energy Commission), we developed, in collaboration with chemistry researcher Pascal Viel, a surface treatment (fig. 4a) invisible to the naked eye that can be applied to glass so that certain zones attract water and others repel it. As the liquid runs down the surface, its flow leaves a pattern. By late 2010 these experiments had given rise to the Mourners (*Pleureuses*) project, followed by At *Present (Félix Guattari)* in 2015 (fig. 4b).

Mourners exploits the familiar sight of water droplets making their way down a pane of glass, but in this case their flow is channeled. Dripping out from a kind of "water flute" specially designed for the piece, the drops run down upright human-sized glass plates resembling steles. The drops do not seem to flow randomly: they take shortcuts, following invisible paths, accelerating and slowing down, sketching out human figures—the mourners, whose form is conditioned jointly by the process and the materials.

Mourners – Material Programming?

We started out using an innovative technology patented by the CEA, but soon abandoned it in favor of familiar chemical compounds which we adapted to each project, treating the surface of the matrix with a technique similar to screen-printing. Small areas in reserve—in this case in the form of droplets—with hydrophobic chemical properties are distributed over a hydrophilic surface. Presently endowed with a "function," the glass guides the water droplets. The conditions provided were hence sufficiently indeterminate to ensure the element of surprise, but sufficiently determinate to produce an image that maintains its major features in spite of variations. Although it would perhaps be an exaggeration to speak here of material programming, it surely harbors the promise of such an approach, since the drops can be imagined as "pixels" of water. Could such advances lead to hardware implementation processes that also allow for stochastic effects?

Mourners – Interlocking Material, Symbolic and Aesthetic Operations

Since Antiquity, subjects such as mourners have been envisaged as a mix of intense feelings with simulacra, affect with representation. Here, by playing on this tension, the sensory encounters the technological, incorporating a symbolic dimension that is intensified by artificiality, as the drops soon appear as tears (figs. 5a & 5b). As they flow downwards and inscribe figures, they are subjected to operations that could just as well be described as technical as symbolic or aesthetic—or all of them at once.

Translated from the French by David Radzinowicz

Figs. 5a (opposite) & 5b: *Mourners*, installation, 2010–16. S. Bianchini with the collaboration of P. Viel (CEA). Collaboration on the technical process: D. Desforge (CEA) | Instrumental glassware: B. Coltrinari (CEA) | Collaboration on the surface chemistry: Geoffrey Barral (CEA) | Scientific mediation: F. Bugeon (CEA) | Artistic mediation: M. Linnman (3CA). Assistance: É. Tincq and O. Porry. This project was produced with support from the Saclay research center of the CEA, Diagonale (Université Paris-Saclay), and the Department of the Essonne. Photos: S. Bianchini, La Crypte, Orsay, Nov. 2016.

Afterword

Claudia Mareis
Wolfgang Schäffner
Peter Fratzl
Horst Bredekamp

The conceptual triad of *Design, Gestaltung, Formatività* describes a variety of simultaneous and nonsimultaneous genealogies, approaches, and positions associated with processes of making, crafting, inventing, shaping, planning, and modeling. In combination with *Gestaltung* and *Formatività*, *Design* frees itself from all shortcomings which connected it traditionally—in opposition to the autonomy of the liberal arts—to technique-related services, industrial shaping of commodities, and adaptive solutions for concrete problems. It emerges similar to *Gestalt* and *Forma*, creating a body of shaped elements like notes in a melody. Design thus returns to the concept of *disegno*, embracing all human activities included in *Gestaltung* and *Formatività*. Therefore, the triad addresses both the richness of different histories and the present urgency that brings them together for a theoretical as well as practical agenda.

In relations, design unfolds. The various contributions gathered in this anthology *Design, Gestaltung, Formatività: Philosophies of Making* vividly demonstrate that design cannot be reduced to *one* history, *one* concept, or *one* definition. Rather, it lives from the multiplicity and relationality of different ways of *doing* and *thinking*. Once more it has become apparent that design in practice and theory has grown in relation with and in between the disciplines. It has emerged both outside academia as a commercial, (post-)industrial practice and within it as a reflexive tool and research methodology. Presumably, it is this state of in-betweenness that gives design such promise for cross-disciplinary collaboration and for the realization of a practical philosophy.

Design, Gestaltung, Formatività opens up a productive dialogue that explores design in its manifold facets. There exist as many different ways to practice design as there are to think, research, and speak about and with design. The present anthology at the same time documents an important moment of exchange within the more recent German-French history of design theory and practice. This postwar history obviously builds on the long tradition of the French *écoles d'art*. Design had no place in the traditional classification. In France it is to this day considered as an applied art, but not as "real" art, and, in Germany, as applied science, but not as "real" science. In this sense, the Ulm Hochschule für Gestaltung has played a significant role in establishing design as an essential field of research between art and science.[1] Important for a German-French axis of exchange represented in this book is above all the impact of the Ulm school, which served as a model not only for the Karlsruher Hochschule für Gestaltung founded by Heinrich Klotz but also for ENSCI-Les Ateliers, which was created in 1981 under the aegis of President François Mitterrand and the then French Minister of Culture, Jack Lang. The challenge of a close relationship between design and science in the industrial and postindustrial era has established the basis for the new role of design within basic interdisciplinary research as it is developed today in Berlin and Paris, e.g., at Humboldt University's Cluster of Excellence »Matters of Activity«[2] and at the Paris-based Chaire Arts & Sciences.[3]

At the same time, design has gained increasing importance in recent years, beyond its traditional contexts of application, as a management, governance and policy-making strategy, as a generalist problem-solving principle, and a practice-based research methodology. Bruno Latour, the French philosopher of science and technology, has declared that "design is applicable to ever larger assemblages of production. The range of things that can be designed is far wider now than a limited list of ordinary or even luxury goods."[4] He believes that "design," as a visual-material practice of modest, careful optimization, has even the potential to overcome both the narratives of revolution and modernization, and to shift the attention from "matters of fact" to "matters of concern."[5] One aspect that seems important to us in this regard is the question of relationality of and through design. How can design be understood as a recursive sociomaterial practice of world-making beyond traditional approaches of "human" ingenuity and promethean *hubris*? How can design critically question binary demarcations between nature and culture; how can it overcome the unsustainable chains of production and consumption; and how can the modernist design canon, which is anything but diverse, inclusive, and just, be unlearned? Design unfolds its potential, we believe, in the multiple interplays of human and nonhuman beings, nature-cultures, materials, tools, and environments. Design philosopher Donald Schön once described designing as "a conversation with the materials of a situation," in which both the designers and the situation "talk back" to one another.[6] Design accordingly implies profound involvement with social realities and infrastructures, with cultural settings and biases, with economic and political constraints and, last but not least, it constantly interacts with images, spaces, and materials.

However, this involvement is neither unilateral nor uniquely human-centered. Design is world-making in a profoundly relational and ontological sense: the worlds we design shape us and our design abilities and potential.[7] World-making by design is thus a relational practice and a situated mode of knowledge production (Haraway) in which epistemology, ontology, and ethics are constantly interwoven. In this context, the intrinsic agency of materials, images, and spaces has increasingly moved into the focus of attention in recent years. Feminist new materialist scholar Karen Barad, for example, has coined the neologism *intra-agency*

1 Tomás Maldonado and Gui Bonsiepe, "Wissenschaft und Gestaltung," *ulm: Zeitschrift der Hochschule für Gestaltung* 10, no. 11 (1964): 10–29.
2 One site that was crucial to the making of this anthology is the Cluster of Excellence »Matters of Activity. Image, Space, Material«, at Humboldt-Universität zu Berlin. »Matters of Activity« aims to create a basis for a new culture of materials. The central vision of the Cluster is to rediscover the analog in the activity of images, spaces and materials in the age of the digital. See: https://www.matters-of-activity.de/en/ (accessed August 27, 2021).
3 The Chaire Arts & Sciences was founded in 2017 by the École polytechnique, the École nationale supérieure des Arts Décoratifs-PSL and the Daniel & Nina Carasso Foundation.
4 Bruno Latour, "A Cautious Prometheus? A Few Steps Toward a Philosophy of Design (with Special Attention to Peter Sloterdijk)," in *Networks of Design Proceedings of the 2008 Annual International Conference of the Design History Society University College. Falmouth 3–6 September 2008*, ed. Fiona Hackney, Jonathan Glynne, and Viv Minton (Boca Raton: Universal-Publishers, 2009), 2–10.
5 Latour, "A Cautious Prometheus?," 2.
6 Donald A. Schön, *The Reflective Practitioner: How Professionals Think in Action* (New York: Basic Books, 1983), 78–79.
7 See Anne-Marie Willis, "Ontological Designing," *Design Philosophy Papers* 4, no. 2 (2006): 69–92.

to emphasize that agency does not belong to humans alone, but is a relational process, a web of influences and effects that arise in relation between human and nonhuman beings.[8] Accordingly, matter is not a "thing," but a "*substance in its intra-active becoming*," "*a doing, a congealing of agency*."[9]

Taking the active properties of matter seriously implies to rethink design and making, too, as suggested by the interdisciplinary research cluster »Matters of Activity. Image Space Material«: "Recognizing the inherent active structures in the creation of artifacts will completely change design processes [...]. The new strategies of engineering and *Gestaltung* no longer prescribe and anticipate intended forms, but develop active design processes that are able to react to their environment."[10] Rethinking design and making in the context of active matter also leads to novel interdisciplinary constellations between the sciences and humanities, design, architecture and engineering, and it sharpens the focus on elementary practices, such as weaving, filtering, and cutting.

Considering design as a practice beyond the dichotomy of culture and nature opens up a huge research field. A focus on the practice of weaving reveals that this technique is by no means performed solely by humans. Rather it can be a collaborative activity of "world-making" that mutually "weaves" together practitioners, fibers, cells, and bacteria. The microbiologist Regine Hengge and the literary scholar Karin Krauthausen emphasize that the weaver "is not an active subject [...] shaping a passive material into an equally passive finished product here; instead, the material and the structures that define it are involved in making decisions by simultaneously enabling and limiting possibilities to which the weaver responds creatively. In nature, too, thread-like base elements are spun into fibers, fibrils and filaments on all scales, which, in turn, are woven into three-dimensional structures. All life on our planet is based on thread-like macromolecules, which are the fundamental components of all cells, regardless of whether or not these are single bacterial cells or human cells."[11]

This insight has important consequences for the design process. This one example of fiber design operations alone—as a perspective for combining culture and nature in a nondestructive manner—shows the fundamental change in research necessary today. Beyond the hylomorphic dichotomy of matter and form, design can take the example of nature as its guiding principle. The examination of the inner architecture of biological materials shows how in nature growing is a highly adaptive and interactive process. Any process of natural design establishes a complex interplay with its environment and thus is not restricted to an isolated object. Design even in its most minimal mode is not limited to its intended place, object or scale; it invariably causes an uncontrollable impact beyond its preconceived objective or desired result. Design is always world-making, in the sense that any kind of design intervention entails an endless chain of consequences. Design approaches may also help to decipher the functionality of patterns that have appeared in the course of evolution in biological systems and thereby contribute to progress in natural science.

Considering the numerous mutually influencing manmade crises of our time, it seems indispensable to seek more sustainable ways of designing and making, to discover designs for human survival.[12] However, this implies acknowledging first that "design is immanent to crisis,"[13] as Adam Nocek and Tony Fry have stated:

8 Karen Barad, "Posthumanist Performativity: Toward an Understanding of How Matter Comes to Matter," *Signs: Journal of Women in Culture and Society* 28, no. 3 (2003): 801–31.

9 Barad, "Posthumanist Performativity," 822 (italics in the original).

10 Wolfgang Schäffner, "Full Proposal »Matters of Activity: Image Space Material«" (Berlin: Humboldt-Universität zu Berlin, 2018), 15.

11 Regine Hengge and Karin Krauthausen, "The Event of a Fibre," *Gropius Bau Journal* (blog), 2021, https://www.berlinerfestspiele.de/en/gropiusbau/programm/journal/2021/regine-hengge-karin-krauthausen-the-event-of-a-fibre.html.

12 See Friedrich von Borries, *Weltentwerfen: Eine politische Designtheorie*, 2nd ed. (Berlin: Suhrkamp, 2017), 119–37.

13 Tony Fry and Adam Nocek, "Design in Crisis, Introducing a Problematic," in *Design in Crisis: New Worlds, Philosophies and Practices*, ed. Tony Fry and Adam Nocek (London: Routledge, 2021), 4.

"modern design is at the ontological root of the universalisms responsible for the asymmetrical forms of violence that human and non-human life are facing today and in the future. What has yet to be determined is what it means to conceptualise design as this ontological negating force, and how to go about mitigating the ontological horizon of this practice without resorting to worn-out theoretical paradigms and meaningless slogans."[14] Following this idea, it is all about un- and re-learning design: "Design must un-design its own designing, but in so doing, it cannot make this a design project. In short: design must become unrecognisable to itself."[15]

It is high time to replace the image of the Promethean subject, exploiting the "web of life"[16] by means of design, with postheroic notions of distributive agency and pluriversal design politics.[17] To explore and acknowledge multiple and diversified approaches toward transitional, transformative, resilient, just, and posthumanist designs.[18] Finally, design needs and has already started to interlock with scientific and engineering efforts to ensure that the transformation of matter to materials and back again becomes more sustainable. In this sense the present anthology with all its contributions offers the possibility for a comparative analysis of design strategies that will allow their future shape to develop. In short: for a design that unfolds in relations.

14 Ibid., 2.
15 Ibid., 10; Madina Tlostanova, "Unlearning and Relearning Design," in Fry and Nocek, *Design in Crisis*, 163–80.
16 Jason W. Moore, *Capitalism in the Web of Life: Ecology and the Accumulation of Capital* (London: Verso, 2015).
17 Arturo Escobar, *Designs for the Pluriverse: Radical Interdependence, Autonomy, and the Making of Worlds* (Durham: Duke University Press, 2018).
18 Suggestions in this regard come, for example, from: Terry Irwin, "Transition Design: A Proposal for a New Area of Design Practice, Study, and Research," *Design and Culture 7*, no. 2 (2015): 229–46; Wolfgang Jonas, Sarah Zerwas, and Kristof von Anshelm, eds., *Transformation Design: Perspectives on a New Design Attitude* (Basel: Birkhäuser, 2015); Alexandra Lee, *Resilience by Design* (Cham: Springer, 2018); Laura Forlano, "Posthumanism and Design," *She Ji: The Journal of Design, Economics, and Innovation* 3, no. 1 (2017): 16–29; and Sasha Costanza-Chock, *Design Justice: Community-Led Practices to Build the World We Need* (Cambridge, MA: MIT Press, 2020).

Biographies

Samuel Bianchini is an artist and lecturer-researcher at the École nationale supérieure des Arts Décoratifs (EnsAD) / Université Paris Sciences et Lettres (PSL). He is the head of the Reflective Interaction Research Group and cohead of the Chaire Arts & Sciences (of École Polytechnique, EnsAD-PSL and Fondation Daniel & Nina Carasso). He is also an associate member of Hexagram and of the Cluster of Excellence »Matters of Activity«. He coedited with Erik Verhagen *Practicable: From Participation to Interaction in Contemporary Art* (Cambridge, MA: MIT Press, 2016). https://reflectiveinteraction.ensadlab.fr and www.dispotheque.org.

Cécile Bidan is a materials scientist. After her engineering studies in Grenoble, she pursued a PhD on the geometric control of tissue growth at the MPI of Colloids & Interfaces in Potsdam. She then investigated airway mechanics at the universities of Groningen and Harvard, before developing substrates for cell mechanotransduction at the Laboratory for Interdisciplinary Physics in Grenoble. In 2017 she started a group on biofilms in the Biomaterials department of the MPI-CI and joined the Cluster of Excellence »Matters of Activity.«

Horst Bredekamp is an art & image historian and professor at Humboldt-Universität zu Berlin. As senior deputy director, he leads the Cluster of Excellence »Matters of Activity« together with Peter Fratzl, Claudia Mareis, and Wolfgang Schäffner. Before, he was director of the Cluster of Excellence »Image Knowledge Gestaltung« together with Wolfgang Schäffner. In 2000 he founded the project "The Technical Image" at the Hermann von Helmholtz Center for Cultural Techniques, and from 2015 to 2018, he was one of the three founding directors of the Humboldt Forum.

Júlia Chaumel is a marine scientist specialist in diversity and evolution. Her research interests are based on how animals have adapted to survive in different habitats, from how corals are adapted to live in dark waters to how flies can distinguish colors. She received her PhD at the Max Planck Institute in 2021, studying the composition and growth of shark and ray skeletons from the cellular point of view. To visualize cells and tissue she uses different laser and X-ray techniques, to reconstruct the images in 3D.

Tiago da Costa e Silva holds a BA in industrial design, an MA in communication and semiotics and a PhD in history and theory of design from the Universität der Künste – Berlin. He worked at the Cluster of Excellence »Image Knowledge Gestaltung« of the Humboldt Universität zu Berlin. In 2017 he received the Charles S. Peirce Young Scholar Award. His research interests are design, engineering, art and philosophy. Recent publication: *The Logic of Design Process: Invention and Discovery in Light of the Semiotics of Charles S. Peirce* (Bielefeld: transcript, 2018).

Mason Dean is a marine biologist and zoologist, formerly in the Department of Biomaterials, Max Planck Institute of Colloids and Interfaces, now based at the City University of Hong Kong. He is also an associate investigator in the Humboldt-Universität zu Berlin's Excellence Cluster »Matters of Activity,« collaborating with designers, engineers, and architects to study tessellated materials systems in nature. His work on form-function relationships in animal skeletons allows him to combine his background in zoology and comparative anatomy with his interest in illustration and 3D digital visualization.

Emile De Visscher is a mechanical engineer (UTC, 2009), designer (RCA, 2012) and holds a PhD in design (SACRe, PSL and EnsAD program, 2018). His work focuses on the invention of new production processes, combining material science, engineering, design, performance and fieldwork. He is currently a research associate in the Cluster of Excellence »Matters of Activity« (HU Berlin), in the interdisciplinary group "Material Form Function."

Peter Fratzl is director at the Max Planck Institute of Colloids and Interfaces in Potsdam, Germany. He holds an engineering degree from the École Polytechnique Paris, France, and a doctorate in physics from the University of Vienna, Austria. He is an honorary professor at Humboldt University Berlin and at Potsdam University. He has published more than 500 papers (see www.mpikg.mpg.de/bm) in the area of interdisciplinary materials sciences and has received the Leibniz Prize for his work on biological materials. He is a member of several Academies of Science and of both the German and the US National Academy of Engineering.

Thomas Golsenne is a senior lecturer in modern art history and visual studies at the Université de Lille. He works on ornamentality in the Renaissance or in contemporary art, on the anthropology of images, technique in contemporary art, and published the monograph *Carlo Crivelli et le matérialisme mystique du Quattrocento* (2017). He cocurated (with B. Blümlein and S. Tritz) the exhibition *Bricologie: La souris et le perroquet* (2015) and coedited *Essais de bricologie* (with P. Ribault, 2015). He also coedited *Par-delà art et artisanat* (with F. Cozzolino, 2019).

Lorenzo Guiducci is a biomedical engineer with a PhD in physics, science of biomaterials. He is coleader of the "Material Form Function" project in the Cluster of Excellence »Matters of Activity.« Research topics include computational mechanics, bio-inspired engineering, mechanical actuation of plant tissues, active architected solids, self-shaping textiles. Publications include: "An Introduction into the Physics of Self-folding Thin Structures," in *On Folding*, ed. Wolfgang Schäffner and Michael Friedmann (Berlin: transcript Verlag), 175–210.

Leonie Häsler is a media and cultural theorist and a research associate at the Museum.BL in Liestal (Switzerland), and previously at the Department of Cultural History and Theory at Humboldt-Universität zu Berlin (2019–21). Her research interests are textile culture, design theory, and fashion studies. In 2020, she received her doctorate in cultural anthropology from the University of Basel. Recent publication: *Textiles Entwerfen in Serie. Nahtlosigkeit als Gestaltungsprinzip bei der Hanro AG 1884–1991* (Berlin: Reimer Verlag 2022).

Thomas Huot-Marchand is a graphic designer and typographer. He has been the director of the Atelier national de recherche typographique in Nancy since 2012. He taught graphic and typographic design in Besançon and Amiens (2002–12) and was a resident fellow at the Académie de France à Rome – Villa Medici in 2006–07. He published the catalogue *ANRT Archives, 1985–2006* (2016), and designed *Minuscule* (2007), *Minérale* (2018), *Garaje* (2020) and *Album* (2021), distributed by 205TF. In 2019, he was a typographer in residence at the Hoffmitz Milken Center for Typography in Pasadena.

Pierre-Damien Huyghe is a philosopher and professor emeritus at the Université Panthéon-Sorbonne. A thinker of modernity, he situates his analyses in a philosophical framework that extends from Aristotle (*Le différent esthétique*, ed. Circé, 2004), to Bruno Latour (*Modernes sans modernité*, Lignes, 2009), via Walter Benjamin (*Du commun*, Circé, 2002). Defining art as a technical conduct, Huyghe develops a theory of apparatuses in works such as *Art et industrie* (repr. Circé, 2015), *Le cinéma avant, après* (De l'incidence, 2012) or the series *À quoi tient le design*, currently being republished.

Ianis Lallemand is a Paris-based designer, researcher, and educator whose work is situated at the intersection of computation, generative design, and digital manufacturing. He is an assistant professor at the École supérieure d'Arts et de Design TALM in Le Mans, an associated researcher in the Reflective Interaction group at EnsAD Paris and a Co-de-iT member. He received a PhD in design from PSL University / EnsAD Paris in 2018.

Gaëlle Le Page is a doctor in psychology, as well as a clinical psychologist, and she teaches at the faculty of Human and Social Science of the Catholic University in Angers. She also works in the field of professional training. She is a psychoanalyst and a teacher at the Loire Clinical College of psychoanalysis of Forums du Champ lacanien. Her latest publication is "Forme, présence et objet virtuel" in *Nouvelles technologies, nouvelles psychologies ? Éducation, santé, lien social : usages et mésusages* (Paris, Éditions L'Harmattan, 2019).

Selma Lepart is a visual artist and researcher in the anthropology of life team of the Laboratoire d'anthropologie sociale (LAS) of the Collège de France. She is also a member of the IDH laboratory of the LIRMM (Laboratory of Computer Science, Robotics and Microelectronics of Montpellier). Her work is built on a multidisciplinary convergence between arts, anthropology, and robotics. It explores the human/object/matter relational issues, as well as the notion of sensitive intelligence.

Claudia Mareis is a graphic designer, design researcher, and cultural historian. Since 2021 she has been a professor of design and the history of knowledge at the Department of Cultural History and Theory at the Humboldt-Universität zu Berlin and the codirector of the Cluster of Excellence »Matters of Activity« (since 2019). Her research interests include history, theory and methodology of design, experimental design and media practices, cultural history of creativity, design and material politics.

Martin Müller is a postdoctoral researcher at the Cluster of Excellence »Matters of Activity« and at the Department of Cultural History and Theory at Humboldt-Universität zu Berlin, where he also teaches since 2015. He is a co-director of the experimental laboratory for science communication and speculative design "CollActive Materials", funded by the Berlin University Alliance. His former affiliations include: Visiting scholar at Waseda University in Tokyo (2019), Universidad de Buenos Aires (2017), Université Paris-1 Panthéon-Sorbonne (2013), Columbia University in New York City (2012). Research interests: History of bio- and zoëpolitics, critical theory of synthetic biology and genome editing, urgencies of making and design research, theory of the postmetabolic.

Luigi Pareyson (1918–1991) was one of the major figures of Italian philosophy in the second half of the twentieth century. He was professor of aesthetics at the University of Turin from 1945 to 1964, before taking up the chair of theoretical philosophy. His work first focused on existentialism and later on the notion of interpretation. He challenged the positivist and idealist aesthetics of Benedetto Croce in his 1954 monograph, *Estetica: Teoria della formatività*. He had many famous students, including Mario Perniola, Gianni Vattimo, and Umberto Eco. Published in English are: *Truth and Interpretation* (SUNY Press, 2013), *Existence, Interpretation, Freedom: Selected Writings* (The Davies Group Publishers, 2009).

Jörg Petruschat is a philosopher, editor (*form+zweck: Zeitschrift für Gestaltung*) and a professor for theory and history of design at weißensee kunsthochschule berlin. Research topics include design and growth, design as cognition, and *Gestaltung* as the basis of knowledge. Recent publications include: *Ungehorsam der Probleme* (Berlin: form+zweck, 2017), and "Von Grund auf: Einige Bemerkungen zum *Experimentieren im Design*," *in Experimentieren: Einblicke in Praktiken und Versuchsaufbauten zwischen Wissenschaft und Gestaltung*, ed. S. Marguin, H. Rabe, W. Schäffner, and F. Schmidgall (Bielefeld: transcript, 2019), 227–46.

Dominique Peysson is a visual artist and researcher in Paris. She holds a PhD in arts (2014), and a PhD in material physics (1994). Peysson works in association with exact science laboratories. Closely combining practice and theory, she regularly exhibits her visual art. Research topics include research by contemporary art on the advances of high technologies concerning high-performance materials, living matter, artificial living and their hybridizations. Recent publication: *The Image-Matter: Emerging Materials and Imaginary Metamorphosis*, trans. Vanessa Place (Paris: Dis Voir Ed., 2016).

Emanuele Quinz is an art and design historian and curator, and an associate professor at Paris 8 University and at the École nationale supérieure des Arts Décoratifs, Paris. His research focuses on contemporary art theories and practices crossing disciplines, like visual, media and performing arts, music and design. Since 2012 he has been coordinating the Behaviors research project with Samuel Bianchini. Among his publications are *Strange Design* (ed., it: éditions, 2014), *Le cercle invisible* (Les presses du réel, 2017), *Uchronia* (ed., Sternberg Press, 2018), and *Le Comportement des choses* (ed., Les presses du réel, 2021).

Khashayar Razghandi is a material scientist (Dr.-Ing.) working at the intersection of the natural sciences, humanities, and design, between the Max Planck institute of Colloids and Interfaces, Biomaterials, and the Cluster of Excellence »Matters of Activity« (HU Berlin). Research topics include science-design practices, materials activity, and materials sustainability. Recent publications include F. Gholami, L. Guiducci, S. Yani, and K. Razghandi, "Rethinking Active Matter: Current Developments in Active Materials," in *Active Materials*, ed. P. Fratzl et al. (Berlin: De Gruyter, 2022).

Patricia Ribault holds the professorship for performative design research at weißensee kunsthochschule berlin since 2020 and she is a principal investigator for the Cluster of Excellence »Matters of Activity« (HU Berlin). She is also a lecturer at Beaux-Arts de Paris. She started her career as a glass blower and developed her research around the notions of gesture, techniques, design, and craft. Her interest in form-giving processes led her to coedit a book on the notion of bricology: *Essais de bricologie. Ethnologie de l'art et du design contemporains*, ed. Thomas Golsenne, Patricia Ribault (Paris: Ed. EHESS, 2015).

Wolfgang Schäffner is a historian of science and media technologies, professor for cultural history of knowledge at the Department of History and Theory of Culture at Humboldt-Universität zu Berlin, former director of the Hermann von Helmholtz Center for Cultural Techniques (HU Berlin), and director of the Cluster of Excellence »Matters of Activity« (HU Berlin), together with Horst Bredekamp, Peter Fratzl, and Claudia Mareis. He has also been permanent guest full professor and director of the Walter Gropius Program at the Faculty of Architecture, Design and Urbanism at the Universidad de Buenos Aires since 2005.

Barbara Schmidt is a product designer with focus on porcelain, ceramics, and glass and also works in the field of exhibition design. Since 2014 she is professor for product design with the perspective Design and Experiment at weißensee school of art and design berlin. Since 1991 she has been working for KAHLA/ Thüringen Porzellan GmbH, where she took on an important role in the redirection of the company. Recent monographic exhibitions include: 2013 *Barbara Schmidt, Poesie & Industrie* (Berlin: Bauhaus Archiv, 2013), and 2018 *Von A nach O*, Kunststiftung Sachsen-Anhalt, Halle, Germany. In 2020, she initiated the international project *glass – hand formed matter*.

Ronald Seidel is a marine zoologist and media designer who is passionate about the variety of complex skeletal systems animals have evolved over the course of time. He devotes his research to design principles in skeletal architectures and material composition to reveal structure-function relationships. As a former research associate at the Museum of Natural History Berlin and the Max Planck Institute of Colloids and Interfaces, Potsdam-Golm, his interdisciplinary research, together with paleontologists, chemists, and engineers, focuses on noninvasive imaging and material characterization techniques.

Didier Semin is an art historian, a conservator (Musée des Sables d'Olonne, Musée national d'art moderne [Centre Pompidou], Paris) and a professor emeritus at the École nationale supérieure des beaux-arts de Paris. Recent publications include *Duchamp: The Paradigm of the Cartoon*, The Forestay Museum of Art 17 (Vienna: Verlag für moderne Kunst, 2105); *Barry Flanagan, Solutions imaginaires*, exh. cat. (Paris: Galerie Lelong & Co., 2019); and *Duchamp contre Picasso: L'Applaudimètre étalon* (Paris: L'Échoppe, 2019).

Judith Seng is a Berlin-based designer who explores the possibility of expanded design practice, taking a choreographic approach to address the sociomaterial dynamic. She codeveloped the transdisciplinary, practice-based research project design reaktor berlin at the University of the Arts Berlin. As a Fellow of the Graduate School of Arts and Science at UdK Berlin, she initiated the experimental production series *Acting Things*. Besides running her studio practice, Seng is also a guest professor in design at HDK Valand – Academy of Art and Design at the University of Gothenburg, Sweden.

Gilles A. Tiberghien is a philosopher and associate professor for aesthetics at the Université Paris I Panthéon-Sorbonne. He edited numerous books and is a member of the editorial board of *Les Cahiers du Musée d'art Moderne* and *Les Carnets du paysage*. He has translated Carlo Michelstaedter, Benedetto Croce, Luigi Pareyson, John Dewey, and Giorgio Agamben. Latest publications include: *Récits du monde : Explorer, décrire, imaginer* (IMEC éditions, 2018), *De la nécessité des cabanes* (Bayard, 2019), and *Le paysage est une traversée* (Parenthèses, 2020).

Charlett Wenig is a product and material designer with a main research focus on biological materials. She is cofounder of the design studio Atelier3punkt for experimental design. In the research group »Adaptive Fibrous Materials« at the Max Planck Institute of Colloids and Interfaces she creates design scenarios for bark use while taking into account her research findings on structure, properties and functions. Research topics include boundary objects in science and design, material design, design and crafts. Her most recent work includes *bark sphere* (2020), *bark fashion collection* (2019), *bone crowns* (2015), and *bone kneepads* (2016).

Image Credits

Bianchini
Figs. 1a, 1b: © Samuel Bianchini - EnsAD
Figs. 2, 3: © Filipe Pais - EnsAD
Figs. 4a, 4b, 5a, 5b: © Samuel Bianchini

Bidan
Fig. 1: © Sebastian Ehrig and Cécile Bidan
Fig. 2: © Sebastian Ehrig
Fig. 3: © Cécile Bidan
Figs. 4, 5: © Berit Schulze and Cécile Bidan

Bredekamp
Fig. 1: © Bildarchiv Foto Marburg
Fig. 2: © bpk/ Zentralarchiv, SMB
Fig. 3: © Bundesregierung / Guido Bergmann
Figs. 4, 5, 6, 7: © Olaf Avenati
Fig. 8: © Ministry of Culture—National Archaeological Museum of Naples, photo by Giorgio Albano
Fig. 9: © Antikenmuseum Basel und Sammlung Ludwig
Fig. 10: © Attilio Maranzano/Courtesy Fondazione Prada
Fig. 11: © H. Patzelt/Ambach
Fig. 12: © Florence, Biblioteca Medicea Laurenziana, Ms. Ashb. 361, f. 5r, by permission of the MiC
Fig. 13: © Venice, Galleria dell' Accademia
Fig. 14: From: Albrecht Dürer, *Von Menschlicher Proportion*, facsimile reprint of the original Nürnberg 1528, Nördlingen 1980. P. J iiii
Fig. 15: © ALBERTINA, Wien
Figs. 16, 18, 19, 20: © Photo Scala, Florence
Fig. 17: © Aurelio Armendola, in Frank Zöllner, Christof Thoenes, and Thomas Pöpper, eds., *Michelangelo 1475–1564, Das Vollständige Werk*, Cologne, 2007, 47
Fig. 21: From: Jean-Nicolas-Louis Durand: *Précis des leçons d'architecture données à l'École polytechnique*, 1802, table 20
Fig. 22: © Staatliche Graphische Sammlung München
Figs. 23, 24: © Barnett Newman Foundation/ VG Bild-Kunst, Bonn 2021
Fig. 25: © Kate Rothko-Prizel & Christopher Rothko/ VG Bild-Kunst, Bonn 2021
Fig. 26: © Gottfried Wilhelm Leibniz Bibliothek—Niedersächsische Landesbibliothek
Figs. 27, 28: © Hans-Georg Preissel
Fig. 29: © ESA and the Planck Collaboration

Dean
Figs. 1, 2, 6: © Mason Dean
Fig. 3: © Júlia Chaumel
Figs. 4a, 4b, 5a, 5b: © Ronald Seidel

De Visscher
Fig. 1: © Boris De Visscher
Figs. 2, 3, 4a, 4b, 7: © Palta Studio
Fig. 6: © Henitsoa Rafalia
Figs. 5, 8: © Emile De Visscher

Golsenne
Fig. 1: © Rheinisches Bildarchiv Köln, Fotograf, rba_d031385
Fig. 2: © John Baldessari, courtesy: Ringier Collection, Switzerland

Guiducci, Lepart
All images: © Lorenzo Guiducci and Selma Lepart

Häsler
All images: Hanro Collection, Archäologie und Museum Baselland, Liestal (Switzerland) ©HANRO International GmbH, Götzis (Austria)

Huot-Marchand
Figs. 1a, 1b, 1c, 3, 5: © Thomas-Huot Marchand
Fig. 2: © Jérôme Knebusch
Fig. 4: © Elvire Volk Leonovitch, Morgane Pierson / ANRT 2014-2021
Fig. 6: © Alice Savoie / Cnap 2017

Lallemand
All images: © Ianis Lallemand

Mareis
Figs. 1, 2: © Picture-alliance / dpa/ Uwe Anspach
Fig. 3: © Christos Vittoratos, 26 April 2014, 16:42:27, Wikipedia, Creative Commons Attribution-Share Alike 3.0 Unported license (CC BY-SA 3.0) https://commons.wikimedia.org/wiki/File:Ulmer-hocker-hfg-ulm-max-bill.jpg
Fig. 4: From: Gui Bonsiepe, *Interface. Design neu begreifen*, Mannheim, 1996, 20
Fig. 5: © Ludwig Zeller

Peysson
All images: © Dominique Peysson

Quinz
Figs. 1a, 1b, 2, 3, 4, 6, 9: © Courtesy Archivio Gianni Colombo, Milan
Fig. 5: Photo: © Patrick Christe, GFF GmbH, Biel. Courtesy Giovanni Anceschi, Milan
Figs. 7a, 7b, 7c: Photo: © Valerio Anceschi, Courtesy Archivio Giovanni Anceschi, Milan
Figs. 8a, 8b: Photo: © Antonio Ria. Courtesy Archivio Giovanni Anceschi, Milan

Razghandi
Fig. 1a: © National Research Council, 1989
Figs. 1b, 1c, 2c, 3c, 4d: © Khashayar Razghandi + graphic design Olaf Avenati
Fig. 2a: © Guiducci & Razghandi et al. (2016, under Creative Commons Attribution 4.0 International License)
Fig. 2b: © Michaela Eder
Fig. 3a: © Pegah Redjai Sani
Fig. 3b: © Anna Schäffner
Figs. 4a, 4b, 4c: © Overvelde et al., 2016, under Creative Commons Attribution 4.0 International License

Schmidt
Fig. 1b: © Anton Richter
Figs. 1a, 8b: © Barbara Schmidt
Figs. 2a, 2b: © Christin Amann
Figs. 3a, 3b: © Konrad Jünger
Figs. 4a, 4b: © Jonas Schneider
Figs. 5a 5b: © Virginia Binsch
Figs. 6a, 6b: © Jihye Kang
Figs. 7a, 7b: © Babette Wiezorek
Figs. 8a, 8b: © Katharina Ruhm

Semin
Fig. 1: © R. Buckminster Fuller, National Portrait Gallery, Smithsonian Institution; gift of *Time* magazine
Figs. 2, 3, 4, 5: © R. Buckminster Fuller Estate

Seng
Figs. 1, 4a, 4b, 4c, 4d, 5a, 5b, 6: © Rudi Schröder
Figs. 2, 3, 8a, 8b: © Studio Judith Seng
Figs. 7a, 7b: © Kim Song Gi

Wenig
Figs. 1, 3, 5, 7: © Charlett Wenig
Figs. 2, 4: © Florian Weisz
Figs. 6, 8: © Studio Patrick Walter

Acknowledgments

I wish to thank all the people who either inspired me or contributed to the realization of the present volume:

All the participants at the symposium *Design, Gestaltung, Formatività*, organized in 2018 with the support of the Cluster of Excellence »Image Knowledge Gestaltung. An Interdisciplinary Laboratory« of the Humboldt-Universität zu Berlin: Cécile Bidan, Tiago da Costa e Silva, Mason Dean, Peter Fratzl, Guillian Graves, Christian Kassung, Ianis Lallemand, Gaëlle Le Page, Dominique Peysson, Wolfgang Schäffner, Gilles Tiberghien, Jeanne Vicérial, Richard Weinkamer, and Charlett Wenig. They are the true pioneers of this book.

The French partners who initiated this collaboration: Armand Behar at the École Nationale Supérieure de Création Industrielle (ENSCI-Les Ateliers); and Samuel Bianchini and Emanuele Quinz at the École nationale supérieure des Arts Décoratifs (EnsAD-PSL), who have continued developing and expanding this cooperation to this day.

My research associates Tiago da Costa e Silva, who co-organized the symposium *Design, Gestaltung, Formatività* and initiated the book project with me, and Leonie Häsler, who helped produce the book, reading through it and taking it to completion. All the student assistants involved in organizing the symposium and realizing this book: Matthieu Praun, Alexander Soytek, Jasmine Wenzel, Franziska Blume, Yannick Schütte, Anna Schäffner and Alexandra Ruppert, for their invaluable help all along the way.

Members of the administrative team of the Cluster »Matters of Activity« who helped me in so many different ways: Kathrin Bauer, Sandra Bauer, Deborah Zender and particularly Kerstin Germer, who provided experienced and wise advice all along the way.

The director of the Centro Studi Filosofia Luigi Pareyson, Claudio Ciancio, and Davide Pareyson, for their kind support to the translation of Luigi Pareyson's text and the book project.

The translators of the book, and particularly David Radzinowicz, who translated all the texts from the French to English (including my own) with kindness, dedication and patience.

The graphic designer of the book, Olaf Avenati, who constantly discussed *la forme et le fond* with me and other authors, something which, given the topic of the book, was immensely fortunate.

Ben Lignel and Didier Semin, who were the first careful readers of my introduction. Their constructive and knowledgeable critique improved it immeasurably. Lucy Conticello, who helped me resolve some thorny translation issues.

The board members of the institutions who made the symposium and this book possible, with either logistical and/or financial support: The Clusters of Excellence »Image Knowledge Gestaltung. An Interdisciplinary Laboratory« and »Matters of Activity. Image Space Material« of the Humboldt-Universität zu Berlin, the Chaire Arts & Sciences of the École polytechnique, the École nationale supérieure des Arts Décoratifs (EnsAD)—Université Paris Sciences et Lettres (PSL), the Fondation Daniel et Nina Carasso, the Max Planck Institute of Colloids and Interfaces, and the weißensee kunsthochschule berlin.

Baharak Tajbakhsh and Katharina Kulke at Birkhäuser, for the constructive discussions around the publication project.

All the contributors, who collectively have put together such an original vision of the processes of giving form.

Editor
Patricia Ribault

Translators
Bennett Bazalgette, Adam Blauhut, Allison Brown, Benjamin Carter, Karen Margolis, Uli Nickel, David Radzinowicz, Marlene Schoofs, Sarah Voigt

Image rights coordination
Patricia Ribault, Alexandra Ruppert, Anna Schäffner, Yannick Schütte

Project management
Baharak Tajbakhsh, Katharina Kulke

Production
Heike Strempel-Bevacqua

Graphic Design
Olaf Avenati

Image Editing
LVD Gesellschaft für Datenverarbeitung mbH

Paper
100 g/m² Munken Lynx

Printing and binding
Gutenberg Beuys Feindruckerei GmbH

This publication was made possible thanks to the support from the Clusters of Excellence »Image Knowledge Gestaltung. An Interdisciplinary Laboratory« and »Matters of Activity. Image Space Material« at the Humboldt-Universität zu Berlin, funded by the Deutsche Forschungsgemeinschaft (DFG, German Research Foundation) under Germany's Excellence Strategy – EXC 2025 – 390648296, the Chaire Arts & Sciences of the École polytechnique, the École nationale supérieure des Arts Décoratifs (EnsAD)—Université Paris Sciences et Lettres (PSL), the Fondation Daniel et Nina Carasso, and the Max Planck Institute of Colloids and Interfaces.

Library of Congress Control Number
2022939363

Bibliographic information published by the German National Library
The German National Library lists this publication in the Deutsche Nationalbibliografie; detailed bibliographic data are available on the Internet at http://dnb.dnb.de.

P.O. Box 44, 4009 Basel, Switzerland
Part of Walter de Gruyter GmbH, Berlin/Boston

ISBN
978-3-0356-2243-0

e-ISBN (PDF)
978-3-0356-2244-7

9 8 7 6 5 4 3 2 1
www.birkhauser.com

Cluster of Excellence Matters of Activity Image Space Material

Funded by DFG

Image Knowledge Gestaltung
Interdisciplinary Laboratory in the Hermann von Helmholtz Center for Cultural Techniques

Sponsored by DFG

école nationale supérieure des arts décoratifs

PSL Université Paris

La chaire arts & sciences

MAX PLANCK INSTITUTE OF COLLOIDS AND INTERFACES